Global Warming

Global Warming

Economic Policy Responses

edited by Rudiger Dornbusch
and James M. Poterba

The MIT Press
Cambridge, Massachusetts
London, England

This book was set in Palatino by Achorn Graphics Services and was printed and bound in the United States of America.

Library of Congress Cataloging-in-Publication Data

Global warming: economic policy responses / edited by Rudiger Dornbusch,
    James M. Poterba.
        p.   cm.
    Includes bibliographical references and indexes.
    ISBN 0-262-04126-X
    1. Air—Pollution—Economic aspects—Congresses.   2. Air—
Pollution—Government policy—Congresses.   3. Environmental impact
charges—Congresses.   4. Global warming—Congresses.   5. Greenhouse
effect, Atmospheric—Congresses.   I. Dornbusch, Rudiger.
II. Poterba, James.
HC79.A4G56   1991
338.9—dc20
                                                          91–4717
                                                            CIP

Contents

Conference Participants

Edward B. Barbier, London Environmental Economics Center

Lars Bergman, Stockholm School of Economics

Joanne C. Burgess, London Environmental Economics Center

William R. Cline, Institute for International Economics

Peter Diamond, Massachusetts Institute of Technology

Emilio Gerelli, Universite de Pavia

Lester B. Lave, GSIA, Carnegie Mellon University

Alan Manne, Stanford University

Sérgio Margulis, IPEA/INPES, Rio de Janeiro, Brazil

John P. Martin, Growth Studies Division, Economics and Statistics Department, OECD

Thorvald Moe, Norwegian Ministry of Finance

David M. Newbery, University of Cambridge

William D. Nordhaus, Cowles Foundation, Yale University

James M. Poterba, Massachusetts Institute of Technology

Eustáquio Reis, IPEA/INPES, Rio de Janeiro, Brazil

Norman J. Rosenberg, Resources for the Future

T. C. Schelling, University of Maryland

Andrew R. Solow, Woods Hole Oceanographic Institute

Hirofumi Uzawa, University of Tokyo

John Whalley, University of Western Ontario

Lutz Wicke, Technical University of Berlin, Federal Environmental Agency

Gerrit Zalm, Netherlands Central Planning Bureau

Preface

This volume contains the proceedings of a conference that brought together economic experts from Europe, the United States, Latin America, and Japan to evaluate key issues in the policy debate in global warming. The conference was held in Rome in October 1990, with the gracious support of the Fondazione San Paolo di Torino under the patronage of Italy's President of the Council of Ministers.

The conference benefited from the active participation of European legislators and officials with a responsibility in the environmental area. We would like to take this opportunity to acknowledge the great interest brought to our project, especially from the Italian policy community. Because of space limitations it was impossible to include a record of the discussion and interventions made at the conference. This represents a genuine loss, best appreciated by the participants.

We owe a special debt to Professor Gianni Zandano, Chairman of the Istituto Bancario San Paolo di Torino, for his enthusiastic personal support of the conference. We are also grateful to Giovanni Fossati, Director of the Fondazione, and James Ruscoe, the Scientific Advisor, for their support and constructive input in planning the conference. We also appreciate the tireless efforts of the other Fondazione staff who handled conference logistics.

We are very grateful to the staff at the MIT Press, particularly Melissa Vaughn, for helping to improve the quality of our conference proceedings and for producing the conference volume with extraordinary speed.

Finally, we wish to thank our administrative assistants at the MIT Economics Department, Theresa Benevento and Shirley Sartori, for their expert handling of the myriad administrative details that arise in organizing a conference with participants from four continents.

Global Warming

Introduction

Three issues are at the core of debates on alternative policies to address global warming:

• What is the scientific evidence on the magnitude of global warming and the extent to which it is due to human activities?

• What economic tools are available to control the anthropogenic emissions of greenhouse gases, and how vigorously should they be applied?

• What political economy considerations influence the design of an international program for controlling greenhouse gases?

The research papers in this volume offer many perspectives on these issues. They include reports on the approaches to remedying environmental problems that are currently being pursued in Europe and the Pacific Rim, a discussion of deforestation in Amazonia and ways to slow it, and public finance assessments of both the domestic and international policy issues raised by plans to levy a "carbon tax" on the carbon emissions from various fossil fuels. The balance of this introduction presents a brief summary of the research in each of the subsequent chapters.

The Scientific Issue

The scientific debate on global warming centers on two questions: Is global warming occurring? And do greenhouse gases play a critical role in contributing to any such warming?

Accumulation of carbon dioxide and other trace gases affects the process by which solar radiation heats the earth. The larger the buildup of trace gases in the atmosphere, the higher the mean global surface temperature. Without greenhouse gases, some estimates suggest that mean global temperature would be 33° C cooler. Historical evidence on global climate clearly indicates an increase in global temperatures of 0.3–0.5° C during the last century.

The chapter by Andrew Solow reviews the scientific evidence on global warming. Solow describes the difficulties in establishing a firm scientific basis for judging what has happened and in assessing the role of greenhouse gases in the change in global temperature. He particularly emphasizes the role of emerging research, writing that "available evidence changes very rapidly under the pressure of research: three years ago the estimate of the mean rise in sea levels over the next century was 3 meters, today it is believed to be only 1 meter."

Solow also draws attention to the problem of rapidly correcting the rising atmospheric concentration of greenhouse gases. To stabilize atmospheric CO_2 at current levels, for example, the flow of new emissions would need to fall by 75 percent.

The Remedies

There are many different policy proposals designed to reduce greenhouse gas emissions. Regardless of the specifics, however, each proposal confronts a basic question: How quickly should greenhouse policies proceed, given the economic costs of containing environmental damage on one hand and the risks and uncertainties about the timing and buildup of environmental damage on the other? Economic analysis is central to resolving these aspects of the policy debate, since it can be used to assess alternative emissions-reduction strategies such as controls or taxes, and to perform cost-benefit analyses of alternative programs.

Current proposals differ along a variety of dimensions. Emissions-reduction programs might be limited to the initiative of individual governments, or they might be global. These programs might involve a comprehensive attack on all emissions, or they might be targeted to specific activities that are well suited to control or that offer other side benefits. Emissions-reduction targets might be implemented through programs of quantitative controls and standards, or they might involve adopting new taxes on activities that generate greenhouse gases.

Two conclusions emerge from the economic analysis. First, special attention should be focused on activities that are intensive producers of greenhouse gases. Encouraging the development and use of alternatives to these activities is a high priority. Second, some further taxation of gasoline should probably be pursued on a world level. Higher taxes would encourage conservation and the development of alternative transport modes. There is disagreement on the vigor with which higher taxes should be pursued. This reflects disparate beliefs about the extent and timing of global warming, as well as differences in optimism about the future role of research. If the next decades bring cleaner technology, then we do not need to worry about future pollution as much, can afford to pollute more today, and have less need for higher gasoline tax burdens. If technological alternatives to high-emission technologies are currently available at small extra cost, taxation offers an easy and convenient means to remedy externalities.

Several papers in this volume address issues at the core of policy debate. The study by Barbier, Burgess, and Pearce reports on the availability of substitutes for many current sources of greenhouse gases. The authors describe both the technological options currently available and those that seem likely to emerge in the near future, and provide some evidence of the reduction in greenhouse gas emissions from each technology.

The treatment of uncertainty in cost-benefit analysis is a critical issue for analyzing policies toward global warming. The paper by Nordhaus deals with this issue, which has been the subject of substantial amounts of recent research.[1] Nordhaus argues that the risks of global warming lie so far in the future, with vast opportunities for technology to offer dramatic change in the meantime, that it would be inappropriate to levy large "greenhouse taxes" at this time. Flexibility is an important attribute of the policies that Nordhaus suggests.

Nordhaus calls for "no-regret" policies, those which will not have large costs even in the event that global warming does not prove to be an important problem. Some other conference participants are far more absolutist on this issue. The comments indicate, for example, that some would rather risk a major unnecessary control program than a dramatic change in world climate.

The single most common policy that is suggested to reduce greenhouse gas emissions is a "carbon tax," a tax on fossil fuels in proportion to the amount of carbon they emit when burned. The studies by Poterba and by Whalley and Wigle address a range of issues concerning the design and incidence of these taxes. These authors consider the level of carbon taxes that would be needed to achieve particular reductions in CO_2 emissions, the costs that higher taxes will impose on households and firms as they adjust their fuel use, and the distribution of tax burdens both across households within each nation and across countries. The international distribution of tax burdens is quite sensitive to the way the carbon tax is designed. If it is collected as a tax on users of fossil fuels, for example, revenues will accrue to largely developed nations. If the tax is collected at the place of extraction, however, a substantial share of the tax revenue will accrue to less-developed oil-exporting nations.

Prospects for Global Action

The greenhouse problem is a global problem. While the regional effects of global warming differ, all nations will be affected by global warming. The costs (or benefits) of greenhouse gas emissions in a given nation are independent of whether that nation is currently contributing to the greenhouse gases. But countries are contributing to the greenhouse problem, particularly with respect to CO_2 emissions, on a very unequal basis. The United States and the other developed nations are the principal sources of CO_2, while less-developed nations may bear the principal burdens of global warming. Nations also differ widely in their prospective ability to defray the costs of slowing global warming. Less-developed nations, for example, could not be expected to make a dramatic contribution.

Three chapters in the volume address issues of international cooperation with respect to global warming. The chapter by Schelling addresses the issue of international burden sharing. He develops a very concrete evaluation of the agenda for action. At the center of his proposal is a negotiation among OECD countries to arrive at national emission quotas and marginal carbon taxes. The chief means for enforcing these policies would be publicity and persuasion rather than sanctions. Developing countries would have to be enticed, with transfers, to join the cause. A key conclusion of Schelling's analysis is that substantial international revenue transfers are extremely unlikely to occur. Such transfers would occur, for example, with a global carbon tax imposed by an international agency.

Two other chapters focus on policy actions in specific regions. The chapter by Gerelli discusses current European policy initiatives. It provides some insight on the economic merits of various plans and also tries to explain why European policy makers appear much more aggressive in environmental policy than their U.S. counterparts. Uzawa's chapter is concerned with the Pacific Rim. He notes that a central problem in multilateral action in this region will be achieving equitable solutions, particularly given the large disparities in per capita income across Asian nations. Uzawa shows rigorously that if transfers across nations are not possible, then it will be optimal to levy carbon taxes at different rates in different countries. Under a variety of assumptions, he shows that these taxes will be proportional to per capita income. More-developed nations, therefore, should impose higher carbon taxes and achieve greater proportionate reductions in carbon dioxide emissions.

Much of the policy debate on global warming proceeds as though policy makers must do something now, and must do it dramatically. Careful economic analysis of policy responses to global warming, however, suggests that neither of these premises is necessarily correct. The tremendous uncertainties associated with global warming, as well as the contrast between the long horizon over which warming will take place and the short horizon over which costs of precipitous action will accrue, suggest that gradual action may be more appropriate. Investing in research—to reduce the uncertainties associated with the costs, benefits, and level of global warming—is appropriate to some extent. The chapters in this volume recognize that policies to combat global warming are not categorically distinct from a large set of other policies in environmental and other areas. These policies have costs and benefits, and these must be carefully weighed in designing appropriate actions.

Note

1. A review of the various policies available—further research, conservation, and imposed reductions in emission levels—may be found in Manne and Richels (1990).

Reference

Manne, Alan S., and Richels, Richard G. 1990. Buying greenhouse insurance. Working paper, Stanford University, Stanford, CA. [To appear in *Global 2100: The Economic Costs of CO_2 Limits* (Electric Power Research Institute, forthcoming).]

1   Is There a Global Warming Problem?

Andrew R. Solow

The greenhouse effect refers to the process by which trace gases such as carbon dioxide (CO_2) trap reflected long-wave solar radiation and warm the atmosphere. This effect was identified by Arrhenius more than a century ago, and there is no question about its existence—without it, the Earth would have the same climate as the Moon. More than fifty years ago, Callendar recognized that the consumption of fossil fuels contributes substantial quantities of CO_2 to the atmosphere and that this could lead to global warming through an enhancement of the greenhouse effect. In response to Callendar's work, a number of scientists pointed out that, although the basic argument was sound, complex and poorly understood interactions in the climate system precluded predictions about a climatic response to changes in atmospheric composition from simple theory. It was also pointed out that climate exhibits considerable natural variability and that the attribution of any particular climatic variation to a specific cause was fraught with uncertainty.

Although the global warming issue has been raised periodically over the past fifty years, it has now caught the public's eye and promises to be the premier environmental issue of the 1990s and beyond. To those who follow this issue, it seems that there is some debate within the scientific community over whether it is a serious one. In many ways the broad outline of this debate has remained unchanged over the past fifty years. Atmospheric science and climatology have advanced quite a lot over that period, however, and the details of the debate are somewhat clearer. The purpose of this chapter is to outline current scientific understanding of the global warming issue as a means of providing background to the debate.

The global warming issue involves a large number of scientific questions, and, not surprisingly, there is a vast literature on this subject. The most comprehensive treatment of this issue is contained in the report of the Scientific Working Group of the Intergovernmental Panel on Climate Change (Houghton, Jenkins, and Ephraums 1990).

The Greenhouse Effect

The Earth's climate is driven by solar radiation. Solar radiation reaches the Earth's atmosphere in the amount of 1370 $W \cdot m^{-2}$ (watts per square meter) of energy. Approximately 30 percent of this energy is immediately reflected back into space, primarily by clouds. The remaining energy reaching the Earth's surface (whose area is four times its cross section) amounts to 240 $W \cdot m^{-2}$ and is absorbed and reemitted. In the long term, the energy absorbed from solar radiation must be balanced by outgoing radiation from the Earth and atmosphere. Since the amount of energy emitted by a body depends on the temperature of the body, this temperature will adjust until the radiation budget is in balance.

The energy emitted by the Earth and atmosphere takes the form of long-wave infrared radiation. While short-wave radiation can pass through a clear atmosphere relatively unimpeded, long-wave radiation is partially absorbed and reemitted in the atmosphere by certain trace gases (called greenhouse gases). Since the atmosphere is cooler than the Earth's surface, the emission of energy to space is reduced. Both the atmosphere and the Earth's surface warm until the net outgoing energy balances the incoming energy. This is the greenhouse effect. If the atmosphere contained no greenhouse gases, the mean global surface temperature would be 33° C cooler.

The main greenhouse gases are water vapor (H_2O), carbon dioxide, methane (CH_4), nitrous oxide (N_2O), and chlorofluorocarbons (CFC-11 and CFC-12). Of these, H_2O is by far the most important, with an atmospheric concentration of around 1 percent. With the exception of H_2O, all of these gases have significant anthropogenic sources (table 1.1).

The most important anthropogenic greenhouse gas is CO_2, with an atmospheric concentration of around 0.04 percent. Approximately 3 percent of the annual flux of carbon to the atmosphere is due to human activities; the rest is due to natural exchange with the oceans, soils, and plants. Historically, anthropogenic sources of greenhouse gases have been closely related to population growth and economic

Table 1.1
Sources of greenhouse gases

Gas	Sources
CO_2	Fossil fuels, deforestation
CH_4	Rice cultivation, ruminants, biomass burning, coal mining, natural gas venting
N_2O	Fossil fuels, biomass burning, agricultural practices
CFC-11, CFC-12	Refrigerants, propellants, solvents

Table 1.2
Atmospheric concentrations of greenhouse gases

	CO_2 (ppm)	CH_4 (ppm)	N_2O (ppb)	CFC-11 (ppt)	CFC-12 (ppt)
Preindustrial	280	0.8	288	0	0
Current	350	1.7	310	280	484
Current annual rate of change	1.6	0.02	0.8	10	17
Lifetime (years)	50–200	10	150	65	130

Table 1.3
Carbon emission balance (gigatons carbon per year)

Fossil fuel emissions	5.4
Land use emissions	1.6
Atmospheric uptake	3.4
Ocean uptake	2.0
Net imbalance	1.6

development—primarily the consumption of fossil fuels and the development of agriculture. As these activities have expanded, so have the levels of greenhouse gases. Table 1.2 summarizes the growth of these greenhouse gases over time.

Although these changes in the atmospheric concentrations are fairly well established, with the exception of the CFCs there are major gaps in the understanding of the sources and sinks of the greenhouse gases. For example, table 1.3 gives current estimates of the components of the global carbon cycle. This unexplained imbalance has led to an as yet unsuccessful search for a terrestrial carbon sink comparable to the oceanic. Similarly, the sources of CH_4 and N_2O are not

Table 1.4
Greenhouse effects of gases

Gas	Relative change in forcing	Global warming potential (time horizon, years)		
		20	100	200
CO_2	1	1	1	1
CH_4	58	63	21	9
N_2O	206	270	290	190
CFC-11	3,970	4,500	3,500	1,500
CFC-12	5,750	7,100	7,300	4,500

entirely understood. There is, for example, some evidence that increases in CH_4 are due to changes in atmospheric chemistry rather than to changes in anthropogenic input.

In considering policy options for controlling greenhouse gases, it is necessary to have a measure of the relative abilities of each gas to change the radiative properties of the atmosphere. The relative radiative impacts of the greenhouse gases over time depend on a number of factors, including their radiative properties and their lifetimes. The instantaneous contribution of a particular greenhouse gas to the greenhouse effect depends on how strongly and at what wavelength it absorbs infrared radiation. Table 1.4 summarizes the change in radiative forcing per unit mass relative to CO_2 for current concentrations of the main anthropogenic greenhouse gases.

This information can be combined with information about the atmospheric lifetime of the gas to give a measure of the time-integrated radiative effect of the gas. One such measure, called the global warming potential (GWP), is defined as the radiative effect over a fixed period of an emission of a unit mass of gas relative to that of CO_2. Specifically,

$$GWP(t) = \int_0^t \alpha\, c(u)\, du \, / \int_0^t \alpha_0 c_0(u)\, du,$$

where α denotes radiative forcing per unit mass, $c(u)$ denotes concentration at time u after release, and the subscript 0 denotes the values for CO_2. The values of GWP for the common greenhouse gases are summarized in table 1.4. Although CO_2 is the least effective greenhouse gas per unit emission, the overall radiative effect depends on both the GWP and the level of emissions. For example, although the GWP of CO_2 is only around 0.00015 that of CFC-12, current emissions of CO_2 are 52,000 times as large, so that the current effect of CO_2 is nearly ten times that of CFC-12.

These calculations refer to radiative effect and not directly to warming effect. While it is *relatively* easy to predict how the radiative properties of the atmosphere will change in response to a given change in atmospheric composition (to within an overall error of perhaps 25 percent), it is much more difficult to translate a given change in the radiative properties of the atmosphere into a change in temperature.

Climate Processes

The climate system is driven by incoming short-wave solar radiation and outgoing long-wave radiation. The climate system itself consists of five components: the atmosphere, the ocean, the cryosphere (ice and snow), the biosphere, and the geosphere. Each component plays an important role in determining the Earth's climate.

Most incoming solar radiation is absorbed at the surface. Heat is transferred to the atmosphere, which transports the heat meridionally. The behavior of the atmosphere is governed by a number of factors, including turbulent transfer of heat, moisture, and momentum at the surface; surface albedo; latent heating associated with the condensation of H_2O; the reflective and radiative properties of clouds; the greenhouse effect; and a variety of miscellaneous factors, including atmospheric dust and aerosols, orbital parameters, and surface topography.

The ocean plays a central role in the climate system. Nearly 50 percent of CO_2 emissions are taken up by the ocean. A number of chemical and biological mechanisms control the ocean's storage of CO_2. Carbon dioxide is transferred from the atmosphere to the ocean by a physical pump driven by a partial pressure differential. Plankton then convert dissolved CO_2 to particulate carbon, which sinks. In addition to sequestering CO_2, the ocean absorbs more than 50 percent of incoming solar radiation, which is stored in the ocean and redistributed by currents before being released to the atmosphere as latent heat of evaporation. The currents are driven by the exchange of heat, H_2O, and momentum between the ocean and the atmosphere. Key oceanic processes include transient eddies that transport chemicals and heat horizontally; small-scale patches of deep-water convection that transport chemicals and heat from shallow water to deep water; thermohaline ventilation that transports chemicals and heat from deep water to shallow water; large-scale circulation patterns that influence sea-ice formation and regional climate; and the biological pump that sequesters dissolved CO_2 in the deep ocean.

The main components of the cryosphere are seasonal snow cover, which contributes to global albedo; sea ice, which also contributes to global albedo and tends to decouple the ocean-atmosphere system by inhibiting the exchange of H_2O and momentum; the Greenland and Antarctic ice sheets, which contain 80 percent of the existing fresh water; and minor components including mountain glaciers and permafrost.

The main climatic role of the biosphere is to influence fluxes of CO_2 and CH_4 and also to contribute to global albedo.

The geosphere influences climate primarily through the exchange of gases and moisture with the atmosphere.

In addition to their roles in equilibrium climate, each of the five components of the climate system responds to changes in radiative forcing and temperature. These responses are called feedback, and they may be positive (in the sense that they operate on temperature in the same direction as the initial forcing) or negative (in the sense that they operate in the opposite direction as the initial forcing). In the absence of feedback mechanisms, it would be relatively easy to predict the climatic effects of a given change in radiative forcing. In fact, understanding feedback is the key to understanding the actual climatic response to greenhouse forcing.

A simple approach to feedback is the following. Let ΔQ be a fixed change in radiative forcing. The corresponding change in surface temperature is given by $\Delta T = L \Delta Q$, where L is the climate sensitivity:

$$L = (\Delta F/\Delta T - \Delta S/\Delta T)^{-1},$$

where ΔF and ΔS are changes in emitted infrared and downward solar flux, respectively.

To have an idea of the calculations involved, consider an instantaneous doubling of atmospheric CO_2. The corresponding change in radiative forcing is around 4 $W \cdot m^{-2}$. In the absence of feedback, $\Delta F/\Delta T = 3.3$ $W \cdot m^{-2} \cdot {}^{\circ}C^{-1}$ and $\Delta S/\Delta T = 0$, so that $L = 0.3^{\circ}$ $C \cdot m^2 \cdot W^{-1}$. It follows that $\Delta T = 1.2^{\circ}$ C. This figure will be modified by feedbacks.

The best understood feedback mechanism is a result of increases in atmospheric H_2O that are due to an intensification of the hydrologic cycle. The effect of increased H_2O is to reduce $\Delta F/\Delta T$ to 2.3

$W \cdot m^{-2} \cdot {}^{\circ}C^{-1}$ through the greenhouse effect. This increases L to 0.43° $C \cdot m^2 \cdot W^{-1}$, which implies that $\Delta T = 1.7^{\circ}$ C. There is a further amplification due to the H_2O feedback through an enhanced absorption of solar radiation. This amounts to increasing $\Delta S/\Delta T$ to 0.2 $W \cdot m^{-2} \cdot {}^{\circ}C^{-1}$ and to an increase in ΔT to 1.9° C. There are a number of other important feedback mechanisms.

The Snow-Ice Albedo Feedback

This feedback occurs because of changes in the reflectivity of the Earth's surface due to changes in the extent of snow and ice cover. This may have been the most important feedback mechanism in ice age cooling, for which the trigger was a change in the Earth's orbital characteristics. It has long been assumed that under greenhouse warming this feedback will be positive, due to the polar amplification of greenhouse warming which will act to reduce polar ice and snow cover. More recent model results indicate a reduced polar amplification due to changes in ocean circulation, with a consequent reduction in the strength of this feedback mechanism. In addition, the amount of snow and ice does not depend only on temperature. Increased precipitation at high latitudes due to global warming may actually increase snow and ice and act to reduce this feedback further.

Cloud Feedback

Global warming will cause increased evaporation, leading to increases in atmospheric H_2O and changes in clouds. Cloud feedbacks are large in magnitude, extremely complex, and poorly understood. In the current climate, the greenhouse forcing due to clouds is 31 $W \cdot m^{-2}$. This is offset by the cloud albedo effect of 44 $W \cdot m^{-2}$. The overall impact of clouds is a net cooling effect of 13 $W \cdot m^{-2}$. The relative magnitude of these influences depends on cloud amount, cloud altitude, and cloud water content. Unfortunately, the details of these relationships and the way in which these factors will change in response to warming are not known. The great sensitivity of L to cloud feedback is illustrated by the reduction in L from around 1.3 to 0.5 in the British Meteorological Office climate model due to a change in the way in which clouds were handled. This amounts to a reduction in δT from around 5.5° C to around 2° C.

Ocean Feedback

The capacity of the ocean to store CO_2 and the rate at which it will be released to the atmosphere depend on the thermal structure of the oceans. This process controls the development of global warming on the scale of hundreds of years. Because the solubility of CO_2 in seawater is temperature dependent, global warming will tend to accelerate the release of CO_2 to the atmosphere. This process (and its reverse under global cooling) plays an important role in the succession of glacial and interglacial periods. The absorption, storage, and transport of heat by the ocean controls the development of global warming on the decadal scale. The timing and geographic distribution of greenhouse warming will depend to a large extent on the way in which the ocean responds to changes in temperature. Although the processes involved are reasonably well understood, it is difficult to simulate the small-scale transient motions that are particularly critical. Climate models that assume a passive ocean typically exhibit more rapid warming and greater polar amplification than models that assume some oceanic response.

The discussion so far has focused on global climate change. In fact, the impact of climate on human society depends very much on regional climate. Regional climate is determined by a number of processes, including atmospheric circulation, ocean currents, and topography. The regional distribution of temperature, which has a large scale of variability, is relatively insensitive to small-scale features. For precipitation, which exhibits substantial variability over relatively short spatial scales, small-scale processes are very important. To assess the regional response of climate to changes in atmospheric composition, it is necessary to move away from simple calculations based on theoretical considerations and toward the use of detailed numerical climate models.

Climate Models

Climate models seek to represent current understanding of the climate system through a system of coupled partial differential equations. These equations must be solved numerically. Even if it were possible to incorporate perfectly current understanding of the climate system into a climate model, the significant uncertainties in current understanding would remain in the model. Unfortunately, limitations on computing power preclude climate models from making full use of current understanding. The two most serious generic simplifications in climate models are the external parameterization of processes with spatial scales smaller than the resolution of the model and the unrealistic coupling of the ocean-atmosphere system.

External parameterization refers to the exogenous treatment of endogenous climate processes. The most important parameterization in any climate model is the radiation component, since this is what transfers the effect of greenhouse gases to the general circulation. The most sensitive part of the radiation parameterization is the calculation of the radiative effects of clouds. As noted, the response of this effect to changes in radiative forcing is unknown. Early models did not allow any cloud feedback. Later models did allow the amount of clouds to respond to changes in relative humidity. Only the most sophisticated models take water content into account.

In order to model climate realistically, it is necessary to couple the ocean and atmosphere into an overall model. The main difficulty in doing so arises from the great disparity between atmospheric time scales (on the order of one day) and oceanic time scales (on the order of one year to one millennium). So-called synchronously coupled ocean-atmosphere models are prohibitively time-consuming to run except with an unrealistic static ocean model. Various tricks have been employed to use asynchronous coupling as a way of accelerating convergence, but the problem remains unsolved. A second problem with coupled models—and one that illustrates a basic weakness in the climate models—is that of model drift. An uncoupled model can be forced to be more or less realistic by constraining energy fluxes at the ocean-atmosphere interface at their observed levels. In a coupled model, this kind of calibration is not possible, and the model is driven solely by solar radiation. As a consequence, coupled models typically drift into an unrealistic state. To avoid this drift, flux correction terms are introduced. The key point is that, without careful calibration, the climate models do not behave like the real climate system.

Greenhouse experiments with climate models are carried out in the following way. A control run is performed with current forcing conditions to establish a baseline climate. The experiment is repeated with an altered forcing. The difference between the outputs of the two runs is identified as the climatic response to the change in forcing.

It is important to distinguish between two types of experiments. In an equilibrium response experiment, forcing is changed by instantaneously doubling CO_2 concentration and allowing the model to reach equilibrium. Since ocean feedbacks primarily affect the timing of greenhouse warming, equilibrium experiments can be run with simple ocean models. For such models, the time to equilibrium is on the order of several decades. For a fully coupled ocean-atmosphere model, the time to equilibrium would be much longer, and such simulations are not computationally feasible.

Equilibrium results for a doubling of CO_2 concentration for a number of models have been produced. The corresponding global warming ranges from around 1.5° C to 5° C. Increases in global precipitation range from 3 to 15 percent. More detailed work suggests that the models are in good agreement over clear-sky sensitivity but that the radiative effects due to changes in cloud climate vary by a factor of three. The models generally agree in qualitative terms over the regional distribution of warming. There are gross disagreements, however, over the regional distribution of changes in precipitation.

Since CO_2 concentration will not double instantaneously and since the uptake of heat by the ocean will delay atmospheric warming by several decades, equilibrium experiments are misleading if they are taken as forecasts of actual climatic change. Time-dependent or transient experiments seek to avoid these problems by increasing CO_2 at a realistic rate and by using a fully coupled dynamic ocean-atmosphere model. However, because of their great cost, only a handful of such experiments have been performed. Given the great uncertainties over the dynamic response of the ocean to greenhouse warming, no such experiment can be taken as particularly reliable. In general, transient simulations indicate the following:

• Land areas warm faster than oceans.

• The warming is generally greater at high latitudes in the Northern Hemisphere.

• The inclusion of ocean dynamics reduces warming around Antarctica and in the North Atlantic.

• Global mean temperature rise in the near term can be approximated by a fixed fraction of the equilibrium value lagged by around 10 years. (The fractions are approximately 0.8, 0.70, and 0.6 for equilibrium warming of 1.5° C, 2.5° C, and 4.5° C, respectively.)

Finally, it is worth noting that the use of transient model simulations as forecasts requires forecasts of future concentrations of greenhouse gases.

Historic Temperature Data and the Detection of
Greenhouse Warming

There is much room for improvement of climate models. Unfortunately, significant improvement is unlikely in the short term, and in the meantime such models provide the only way to forecast future climate. It is, therefore, important to have some idea of the precision of forecasts from these models. Perhaps the only way to assess forecast precision is to use the model to reconstruct recent climate and to compare the model reconstruction to what is actually known about climate over the same period. Broadly speaking, validation exercises of this type have been carried out for three time periods: around ten years, around 100 years, and around 18,000 years. This section will focus mainly on 100-year validation experiments. Because climate models suggest that there already should have been a temperature response to changes in atmospheric composition over the past century, 100-year validation experiments also address the so-called detection question: Is it possible to detect the onset of greenhouse warming in existing data?

Ten-year validation studies are performed to assess the ability of a climate model to reproduce current climate. Unlike long-term validation studies, which follow the temporal evolution of climate over long periods, ten-year studies look only at seasonal and spatial climate patterns *averaged over the ten-year period*. It is important to bear in mind that climate models are tuned in many ways to current climate, so that success in ten-year validation should not be overemphasized. In general terms, the models perform well at reproducing seasonal surface climate at large spatial scales (on the order of 5,000–10,000 km). On regional scales (on the order of 1,000–2,000 km), however, there are significant errors. Mean surface temperature errors of 3° C occur, as do errors of 50 percent in mean rainfall. The models also exhibit substantial sensitivity to resolution and external parameterizations.

Validation studies have also been performed over the last 18,000 years to test the ability of the models to simulate very large-scale climatic changes. This period covers the last major glaciation and the interglacial period that followed. A rich variety of indirect climate measurements is available for this period. While this provides a reasonably good basis for qualitative comparison, it is not possible to make detailed comparisons of the magnitude and spatial and temporal patterns of climate change. In general, these studies have found reasonably good qualitative agreement between model simulations and observations on continental scales, with systematic errors again occurring at smaller spatial and temporal scales.

Before turning to 100-year validation experiments, it is useful to consider briefly some very long-term data that have received wide attention. Ice cores have been drilled at a number of locations, the best known being Vostok in the Soviet Union. It is possible to extract from these cores records of CO_2 concentration and temperature based on isotopic measurements going back 160,000 years (see figure 1.1). These records show a clear correlation between CO_2 and temperature. It is erroneous to conclude from this that changes in CO_2 concentration were responsible for the large temperature changes (on the order of 5°–10° C) during this period. The trigger for these large climate changes was relatively small changes in the Earth's orbital characteristics, which changed the seasonal and latitudinal distribution of incoming solar radiation. The direct temperature effects of this change were relatively modest—a mean global cooling of perhaps 1° C. This cooling was amplified by positive feedback mechanisms. The most important of these was a year-round increase in ice extent, which increased albedo. The second most important feedback was a change in the carbon cycle—increased uptake of CO_2 by a cooler ocean and decreased production of CO_2 by plants. Another possible positive feedback mechanism was an increase in atmospheric dust. In summary, while the causality in the relationship between temperature and CO_2 in the ice-core data clearly runs both ways, the large magnitude of the temperature changes cannot be explained by changes in CO_2 alone.

Instrumental temperature records are available for a large number of locations since the middle of the nineteenth century. From these, it is possible to construct records of mean global and hemispheric surface temperature. Typically, these records show an irregular global warming amounting to around 0.5° C since 1880 (see figure 1.2).

There are several problems with these records. For example, although the number of recording stations may be large, their geographical distribution is not truly global. The majority of stations lie in the Northern Hemisphere, particularly in Europe and North America. There are relatively few marine stations in either hemisphere. Also, errors arise from changes in instrumentation, recording protocol, and so on. Another problem is that some stations have

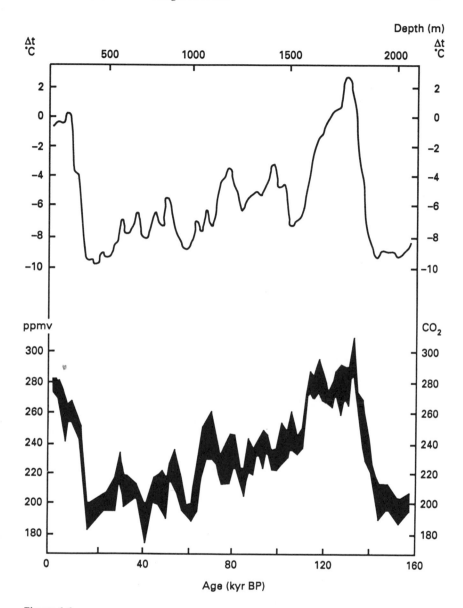

Figure 1.1
Carbon dioxide concentration and temperature during the past 160,000 years as estimated from the Vostok ice core

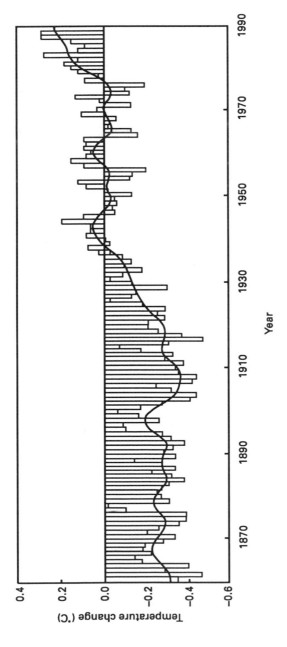

Figure 1.2
Estimated mean global surface temperature, 1860–1985

experienced substantial local warming due to changes in land-use and population density. This is commonly referred to as the urban heat island effect, although it is not restricted to large cities. Attempts have been made to correct temperature records for this effect, which may account for up to a third of the warming in the records.

Despite these problems, there appears to have been a mean global warming of 0.3°–0.5° C over the past century. It is sometimes claimed that this warming is "broadly consistent" with an enhancement of the greenhouse effect in response to changes in atmospheric composition over this period. For a number of reasons, this claim cannot be supported. First, the bulk of the historic warming occurred between 1880 and 1940. This was a period of relatively slow growth in atmospheric concentrations of greenhouse gases. Since 1940, the growth of greenhouse gases has been relatively rapid. However, there has been no net warming during this period (although the 1980s were rather warm).

Second, the geographic distribution of the historic warming is not consistent with current understanding of greenhouse warming. The bulk of the historic warming occurred in the Southern Hemisphere and was concentrated in the tropics. This is particularly true of the 1980s when much of the warmth was associated with El Niño events in the equatorial Pacific.

There is no evidence of warming at either pole (although this situation is complicated by the cooling effect due to ozone depletion). For the continental United States, which is expected to experience significant greenhouse warming, there has been no warming (and no change in precipitation) since 1895.

Third, there is an alternative explanation for the historic warming. The most significant global climatic event of the past 1,000 years was the Little Ice Age. Beginning around A.D. 1300, the Little Ice Age was characterized by pulses of cooling of up to 1° C. In some places, glacial advance during the Little Ice Age surpassed that during the last major glaciation. There is substantial indirect evidence of this cool event in records of harvests, tree rings, lacustrine deposits, and the like. The terminal pulse of the Little Ice Age occurred in the late eighteenth and early nineteenth centuries. Although the cause of the Little Ice Age is unknown (one possible explanation being reduced solar irradiance during the Maunder Minimum in sunspot activity), it was almost certainly natural. The historic warming is consistent with a natural recovery from the Little Ice Age.

This discussion illustrates two critical points in the analysis of climate data. First, by obscuring temporal and spatial detail, the consideration of annual global averages can be misleading. There is important information in the seasonal and geographic pattern of climate change. Second, greenhouse warming, when it occurs, will be superimposed on a climate that is highly variable. This point has been brought home forcefully by control runs of climate models (i.e., runs in which external forcing is held constant). Such runs exhibit periods of cooling and warming of up to 0.5° C over periods of fifty years and more. When natural variability is so great, it is dangerous to attribute any particular change to any particular cause.

It is also instructive to consider in gross terms how well model reconstructions of global temperature over the past century compare with the observational record. The net forcing due to changes in atmospheric composition over the past 100 years has been around 2 $W \cdot m^{-2}$. Of this, more than half has occurred over the last thirty years. Using the approximate result that in the short term transient warming is a fixed proportion of equilibrium warming lagged ten years, then under the assumption that there has been 0.5° C transient greenhouse warming over the past 100 years, the implied climate sensitivity is around 2° C. The same general result can be found by more sophisticated modeling exercises. This semiempirical estimate of climate sensitivity is at the low end of the range cited by the Intergovernmental Panel on Climate Change.

Broadly speaking, in modeling the response to historic changes in radiative forcing with simple coupled ocean-atmosphere models (figure 1.3), it is possible to vary two key parameters: overall temperature sensitivity and time to equilibrium. If time to equilibrium is fixed at around 100 years, then the temperature sensitivity giving the best fit to the data (under the assumption that all historic warming is attributable to an enhancement of the greenhouse effect) is around 2° C (figure 1.4). On the other hand, if temperature sensitivity is fixed at 3°–4° C, then the time to equilibrium giving the best fit to the data (under the same assumption) is on the order of 300–400 years. In other words, the historic temperature record is inconsistent with a combination of high sensitivity and short delay. Moreover, if some part of the historic warming represents a natural recovery from the Little Ice Age, then the implied temperature sensitivity is lower and the implied delay time is longer.

This kind of result has led to two lines of investigation: one aimed

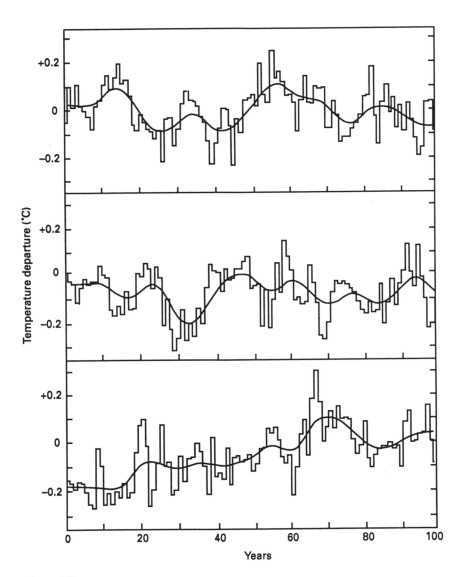

Figure 1.3
Examples of 100-year control runs from coupled ocean-atmosphere models

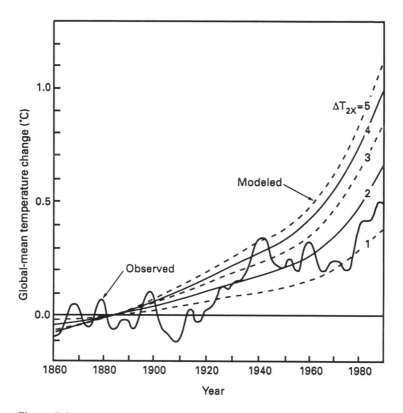

Figure 1.4
Observed and modeled mean global surface temperature, 1860–1989, for selected
values of climate sensitivity

at identifying the sources of oversensitivity in the models and the
other aimed at identifying historic cooling effects that have sup-
pressed an otherwise more rapid warming. The discussion of the
previous section suggests that the source of model oversensitivity
may lie in the treatment of clouds and the ocean. One possible source
of cooling may be stratospheric aerosols from volcanic eruptions and
tropospheric aerosols from the combustion of fossil fuels. To some
extent, however, these are speculations, and the true sources of the
discrepancies between the models and the data are not yet known.

Attention has recently focused on changes in forcing due to solar
variability. Solar irradiance, which has only been measured accurately since 1978, fluctuates with the eleven-year sunspot cycle.
Changes in solar forcing over the sunspot cycle are on the order of 0.1
percent or 0.25 W·m^{-2}. While this value is comparable to greenhouse

forcing over the same period, the periodic nature of these fluctuations rules out the possibility of long-term effects. A number of longer term solar effects have been proposed. While some of these are intriguing, current scientific understanding places an upper limit on changes in solar forcing of around 1 W·m^{-2} on the time scale of 100 years.

Many types of climate data other than surface temperature have been measured through time. These include precipitation, relative sea level, and tropical storm counts, among others. In some cases (e.g., precipitation), these measurements can be used for model validation. In other cases (e.g., storm counts), these measurements are useful for constructing empirical relationships between temperature and other climate processes not directly represented in models. This point is important because the climatic changes with the greatest impacts on human society need not be directly related to changes in temperature. There are, however, even more serious problems with these data than with temperature data. In the foreseeable future, attempts to detect the onset of greenhouse warming will probably continue to be based on a model-data comparison of the temporal and spatial behavior of temperature. It is worth pointing out that concern over greenhouse warming should not rest on its detection in existing data. On the other hand, the difficulty of detecting greenhouse warming *predicted by climate models* in existing data does cast doubt on the ability of these models to predict future climate.

Is There a Global Warming Problem?

Based on a balanced reading of the scientific literature, it is virtually certain that global warming will occur in response to ongoing changes in atmospheric composition. While the timing and magnitude of this warming are uncertain, there is some convergence of opinion away from a rapid, large-scale warming. From the point of view of human society, the direct effects of warming will probably be smaller than the indirect effects such as changes in precipitation and soil moisture, sea level, and storm climate. For the most part, predicting these indirect effects is more difficult than predicting changes in temperature. Here, too, however, there seems to be some movement away from the more apocalyptic scenarios. For example, the current best estimate of sea level rise over the next century or so is somewhat less than 1 meter. This is in contrast to estimates of 3 meters or more just a few years ago. Of course, as science progresses, the predicted scenarios may deteriorate as quickly as they have apparently improved.

It is certainly possible that mean global temperature will be as high in the next century as it has been in the last 10,000 years. This possibility, in itself, does not constitute a problem. In fact, there is some irony in the description of global warming as problematic, since it is not unreasonable to view human history as a struggle to stay warm. Callendar regarded the possibility of global warming as an unalloyed benefit, even suggesting that it would postpone the next ice age. Even now, human populations tend to migrate toward warmer areas. It is difficult to believe that warming would not benefit countries like Canada and the Soviet Union. Certain regions and economic sectors in Europe and the United States are also likely to benefit. In any case, whether or not there is a global warming problem hinges not so much on whether or not there will be global warming as on the impacts of that warming.

While it is not yet clear how large a problem global warming will be, it is certain that an attempt to stabilize atmospheric composition by restricting emissions of greenhouse gases will be a problem. It has been estimated that CO_2 emissions would have to be reduced immediately by around 75 percent to stabilize CO_2 concentrations at their present level. It is inconceivable that a rapid reduction of that magnitude could be achieved without massive economic dislocation. It is most clearly in this sense that there is a global warming problem.

Reference was made at the beginning of this paper to a debate within the scientific community over the seriousness of the global warming problem. In fact, there is relatively little debate over the science of global warming. The debate is really over how, given all the uncertainties, we should respond to the possibility of climate change. Beyond establishing the facts and assessing the uncertainties, science can contribute relatively little to this debate.

Bibliographic Notes

Ramanathan (1988) contains a good review of the greenhouse effect. Historic and projected future trends in greenhouse gases are discussed in Wigley (1987). The global carbon cycle is discussed in the volume edited by Bolin (1981). Tans, Fung, and Takahashi (1990) describe the observational constraints on the global carbon budget. Alternative measures of global warming potential are discussed in

Derwent (1990). Wetherald and Manabe (1988) discuss cloud feedback, ocean feedback is discussed in Bryan and Spelman (1985), and
Ingram, Wilson, and Mitchell (1989) discuss albedo feedbacks. Washington and Parkinson (1986) provide background on climate modeling. Cess and Potter (1988) give a general approach to studying
feedback in climate models. Schlesinger and Mitchell (1987) describe
some equilibrium model experiments, while Manabe, Bryan, and
Spelman (in press) describe transient experiments involving coupled
models. A comparison of model reconstructions with climate data
over the past 18,000 years is given in COHMAP (1988). Grotch (1988)
considers short-term model-data comparisons. Wigley and Raper
(1990) discuss model-data comparisons on the century time scale.
Karl et al. (1989) review the evidence of greenhouse warming in climate data. The Little Ice Age is discussed in the monograph by Grove
(1988). The volcanic and solar influences on climate are discussed in
Hansen and Lacis (1990).

References

Bolin, B. 1981. *Carbon Cycle Modeling*. Scientific Committee on Problems of
the Environment 16. New York: Wiley.

Bryan, K., and Spelman, M. J. 1985. The ocean's response to a CO_2-induced
warming. *Journal of Geophysical Research* 90:11679–11688.

Cess, R. D., and Potter, G. L. 1988. A methodology for understanding and
intercomparing atmospheric climate feedback processes in general circulation
models. *Journal of Geophysical Research* 93:8305–8314.

COHMAP. 1988. Climatic changes of the last 18,000 years: Observations and
model simulations. *Science* 241:1043–1052.

Derwent, R. G. 1990. Trace gases and their relative contributions to the greenhouse effect. AERE–R13716. Harwell, Oxon.: Atomic Energy Research Establishment.

Grotch, S. L. 1988. Regional intercomparisons of general circulation model
predictions and historical climate data. DOE/NBB–0084 (TR041). Washington, DC: U.S. Department of Energy.

Grove, J. M. 1988. *The Little Ice Age*. London: Methuen.

Hansen, J. E., and Lacis, A. A. 1990. Sun and dust versus greenhouse gases:
An assessment of their relative roles in global climate change. *Nature*
346:713–719.

Houghton, J. T., Jenkins, G. J., and Ephraums, J. J., eds. 1990. *Climate Change:
The IPCC Scientific Assessment*. Cambridge: Cambridge University Press.

Ingram, W. J., Wilson, C. A., and Mitchell, J.F.B. 1989. Modeling climate change: An assessment of sea-ice and surface albedo feedbacks. *Journal of Geophysical Research* 94:8609–8622.

Karl, T. R., Tarpley, R. G., Quayle, H. F., Diaz, H. F., Robinson, D. A., and Bradley, R. S. 1989. The recent climate record: What it can and cannot tell us. *Review of Geophysics* 27:405–430.

Manabe, S., Bryan, K., and Spelman, M. In press. Transient response of a global ocean-atmosphere model to a doubling of atmospheric carbon dioxide. *Journal of Geophysical Research.*

Ramanathan, V. 1988. The greenhouse theory of climate change: A test by inadvertent global experiment. *Science* 240:293–299.

Schlesinger, M. E., and Mitchell, J.F.B. 1987. Climate model simulations of the equilibrium climatic response to increased carbon dioxide. *Review of Geophysics* 25:760–798.

Tans, P. P., Fung, I. Y., and Takahashi, T. 1990. Observational constraints on the global atmospheric carbon dioxide budget. *Science* 247:1431–1438.

Washington, W. M., and Parkinson, C. L. 1986. *An Introduction to Three Dimensional Climate Modeling.* Mill Valley, CA: University Science Books.

Wetherald, R. T., and Manabe, S. 1988. Cloud feedback processes in a general circulation model. *Journal of Atmospheric Science* 45:1397–1415.

Wigley, T.M.L. 1987. Relative contributions of different trace gases to the greenhouse effect. *Climate Monitor* 16:14–29.

Wigley, T.M.L., and Raper, S. C. 1990. Natural variability of the climate system and the detection of global warming. *Nature* 344:324–327.

Comments

Alan Manne

The participants in this conference are much indebted to Andrew Solow for summarizing the geophysical evidence on global warming. In one sense, there is no problem. Ever since the scorching summer of 1988 and the end of the cold war in 1989, the greenhouse phenomenon has become an article of faith among journalists, political leaders, and the public at large. It is no longer a scientific hypothesis but an ethical proposition. "We don't inherit the earth from our ancestors; we borrow it from our children." With this perspective, it is exceedingly difficult to find common ground between economics and other disciplines.

To an economist, it is reassuring to learn that the geophysical sciences employ methods of reasoning much like ours. The strongest empirical evidence comes from a *geographical cross section*. That is, the greenhouse effect "explains the very hot temperatures on Venus (whose thick atmosphere is mostly carbon dioxide) as well as the frigid conditions on Mars (whose largely carbon dioxide atmosphere is very thin)" (Schneider and Rosenberg 1988, 7).

Time series evidence is abundant for our own planet, but its interpretation can be a bit puzzling. According to the Vostok ice core record, there is a strong positive correlation between CO_2 concentrations and the temperature at different points of time during the past 160,000 years. In his April 1990 *New York Times* op-ed piece addressed to skeptics on global warming, Senator Albert Gore cited these records as "compelling evidence." And yet Solow is far more cautious. He points out:

It is erroneous to conclude from this [correlation] that changes in CO_2 concentration were responsible for the large temperature changes (on the order of 5°–10° C) during this period. The trigger for these large climate changes was relatively small changes in the Earth's orbital characteristics, which changed the seasonal and latitudinal distribution of incoming solar radiation. The direct temperature effects of this change were relatively modest—a mean global cooling of perhaps 1° C. This cooling was amplified by positive feedback mechanisms. The most important of these was a year-round increase in ice extent, which increased albedo. The second most important feedback was a change in the carbon cycle—increased uptake of CO_2 by a cooler ocean and decreased production of CO_2 by plants. . . . In summary, while the causality in the relationship between temperature and CO_2 in the ice-core data clearly runs both ways, the large magnitude of the temperature changes cannot be explained by changes in CO_2 alone.

Solow is careful to point out that there are serious difficulties in interpreting the short- as well as the long-term time series records:

There appears to have been a mean global warming of 0.3°–0.5° C over the past century. It is sometimes claimed that this warming is "broadly consistent" with an enhancement of the greenhouse effect in response to changes in atmospheric composition over this period. For a number of reasons, this claim cannot be supported. First, the bulk of the historic warming occurred between 1880 and 1940. This was a period of relatively slow growth in atmospheric concentrations of greenhouse gases. Since 1940, the growth of greenhouse gases has been relatively rapid. However, there has been no net warming during this period (although the 1980s were rather warm).

When the empirical evidence gets shaky, what do geophysicists and economists have in common? We turn to dynamic computer simulation models—sometimes large and sometimes small. Among the critics of such models, it is common to describe the small ones as "simplistic" and the large ones as "inscrutable." Empirical validation is the holy grail, but can seldom be established to the satisfaction of all parties to the debate. Both the positive and negative feedback effects are exceedingly difficult to specify—whether we are dealing with global climate or with macroeconomic issues. (For a readable introduction to global climate models, see Post et al. 1990.)

It is easy for the geophysicists to agree that there is a lot of guesswork in all this, that our knowledge will be vastly improved in a decade or two, and that it would be helpful to provide hundreds of millions of additional dollars in the form of government funding for further research. These are among the "principal findings" in the Marshall Institute's 1989 report. Solow's concluding sentence has a similar tone, and I wish that he would change it: "Beyond establishing the facts and assessing the uncertainties, science can contribute relatively little to this debate."

It seems to me that the geophysicists can indeed contribute a great deal to the public debate. Solow points out that "the current best estimate of sea level rise over the next century or so is somewhat less than 1 meter. This is in contrast to estimates of 3 meters or more just a few years ago." Instead of a global catastrophe, this bit of geophysical research suggests that we may be facing a manageable problem—one that is of limited interest to headline makers.

True, the greenhouse problem has special characteristics. It has a time horizon of at least a century, and the problem will be defined away if we employ commercial real discount rates of 10 percent or more. The problem is global in nature, and we must somehow deal with the "free rider" question. There are North-South equity issues, and we haven't done well in reaching agreement on these—despite the Brandt Commission and countless UN deliberations. Today's global greenhouse gas emission decisions must be made under uncertainty, and it is unlikely that these uncertainties will be resolved for decades. Uncertainty does *not* provide an excuse for inaction, but it does require that we analyze the value of different types of information and the extent to which today's decisions lock us in to one or another future outcome.

Political leaders are likely to opt for "no regrets" formulae—do those things which reduce greenhouse gas emissions, and which are also costless (or perhaps negative in cost). The advocates of nuclear power and the advocates of mandatory energy conservation have one thing in common. Both groups claim that the life-cycle costs of their specific program will be zero or negative *and* that it will save the global environment. If they are right, there is no need to hurry to spend large amounts of money on geophysical research, and there is no need to undertake careful benefit-cost analyses. If these advocates are wrong, we will have to take a closer look at both the benefits and the costs of curtailing greenhouse emissions. My suspicion is that there is plenty of work left for the benefit-cost analysts.

References

G. C. Marshall Institute. 1989. *Scientific Perspectives on the Greenhouse Problem.* Washington, DC.

Post, W., et al. 1990. The global carbon cycle. *American Scientist,* July–August.

Schneider, S., and Rosenberg, N. 1988. The greenhouse effect: Its causes, possible impacts, and associated uncertainties, ch. 2 in N. Rosenberg et al. (eds.), *Greenhouse Warming: Abatement and Adaptation.* Washington, DC: Resources for the Future.

2   Economic Approaches to Greenhouse Warming

William D. Nordhaus

There is growing international concern about "greenhouse warming," which is a scientific theory that predicts that increases in CO_2 and other atmospheric gases may produce significant climatic changes over the next century.[1] This concern is only one of a number of areas where population and economic growth have threatened to have significant impacts upon the global environment. Other concerns include increasing evidence of widespread damage from acid rain; the appearance of the antarctic "ozone hole," interpreted by some as the harbinger of global ozone depletion that threatens to remove the shield that protects organisms from harmful ultraviolet radiation; deforestation, especially in the tropical rain forests, which may upset global and local ecological balance; and a depletion of genetic resources that arises from urbanization and other impacts upon major ecosystems.

Global environmental problems raise a host of major policy questions. They are all scientifically complex and controversial, and no scientific consensus is likely to emerge until irreversible decisions have been made. The costs and benefits of these changes transcend national boundaries, and nations, which cannot appropriate the global costs and benefits of such changes, are unlikely to be able or willing to make efficient decisions on how to combat these global externalities. In addition, these concerns sometimes have impacts over hundreds of years and thereby strain political decision making, which often functions effectively only when the crisis is at hand.

This chapter considers some of the economic issues involved in deciding how to react to the threat of global warming. I first review the theory and evidence on the greenhouse effect. I then present evidence on the impacts of greenhouse warming, the costs of stabilizing climate, and the kinds of adaptations that might be available. In the final section, I review the policy initiatives that nations might follow in the near term.

Scientific Issues

The Greenhouse Effect and Greenhouse Gases

For almost two centuries, scientists have suspected that changing the chemical composition of the atmosphere would alter our planet's climate. In the first careful numerical calculations, S. A. Arrhenius estimated in 1896 that a doubling of the atmospheric concentrations of carbon dioxide (CO_2) would increase global mean temperature by 4° to 6° C.[2]

What causes the greenhouse effect? The atmosphere consists of several "radiatively active" gases that absorb radiation at different points of the spectrum. The "greenhouse gases" are transparent to incoming solar radiation but absorb significant amounts of outgoing radiation. The net absorption of radiation produces a happy result, raising the earth's temperature about 33° C (59° F). The greenhouse effect helps explain the hot temperatures on Venus along with the frigid conditions of Mars.

The concern about the greenhouse effect arises because human activities are currently raising atmospheric concentrations of greenhouse gases and threatening a significant and undesirable climate change. The major greenhouse gases (GHGs) are carbon dioxide, methane, nitrous oxides, and chlorofluorocarbons (CFCs). Scientific monitoring has firmly established the buildup of the major GHGs. Table 2.1 shows the important GHGs, recent and projected concentrations, and the past and estimated future growth rates of major GHGs.

Greenhouse gases differ greatly in their quantitative impact on climate because they have different radiative properties and different lifetimes. Table 2.2 shows the important greenhouse gases, their "instantaneous" and "total" contribution to global warming,[3] and the industries in which the emissions originate. Carbon dioxide is the major contributor to global warming, with most CO_2 emissions coming from the combustion of fossil fuels. Of the fossil fuels, natural gas has 60 percent as much CO_2 emissions per unit energy as coal, and petroleum has 80 percent as much CO_2 per unit energy as coal. The second most important source of GHG emissions is the CFCs,

Table 2.1
Estimated concentrations of important greenhouse gases

Greenhouse gas	Concentration (parts per billion)			Growth (percent per year)	
	1850	1986	2100[a]	1850–1986	1986–2100
Carbon dioxide (000)	290	348	630	0.16	0.52
Methane	880	1,675	3,100	0.56	0.54
Nitrogen oxides	285	340	380	0.15	0.10
Chlorofluorocarbons[b]	0	0.62	2.90	—	1.37

SOURCES: Wuebbels and Edmunds 1988 and EPA 1989b.
a. Projected are from EPA 1989b.
b. Includes only major sources, CFC-11 and CFC-12.

which are small in volume but have a warming potential almost
20,000 times as powerful as CO_2 per unit of volume.

In analyzing policies, it is important to find a common unit of
measurement for different gases. In this paper, I will translate all
impacts and costs into a common unit, the "CO_2 equivalent" of GHG
emissions, measured in terms of the *carbon* content of CO_2. By working in this metric, we can attempt to ensure cost effectiveness of
policies in different sectors.

Climate Models and Forecasted Climate Change

There is no dispute about the buildup of greenhouse gases in the
atmosphere. To project climate changes many years into the future,
however, requires use of climate models that trace out the effect of
a changing radiative balance upon major climatic variables. Because
we are heading into uncharted waters, the models cannot rely
upon historical experience but must extrapolate beyond current
observations.

Climate models are mathematical representations of important
variables such as temperature, humidity, winds, soil moisture, and
sea ice. Large "general-circulation models," or GCMs, simulate
changes in weather, in steps of a few minutes, over a century or
more. The largest models use 500-kilometer-square grids through
several layers of the atmosphere. Such models are unfortunately extremely expensive to run, and a single CO_2 scenario might take the
largest supercomputer nearly a year to calculate.

Table 2.2
Estimated contribution of greenhouse gases to global warming for
concentration changes, 1985–2100

A. Sources by chemical compound

| Greenhouse gas | Relative contribution (%) | | Source of emission |
	Instan-taneous[a]	Total[b]	
CO_2	76.1	94.7	Largely from combustion of fossil fuels
Methane	9.6	0.8	Unknown; from a wide variety of biological and agricultural activities
CFCs	11.6	3.3	Wholly industrial, from both aerosols and nonaerosols
Nitrous oxides	2.7	1.2	From fertilizers and energy use

SOURCE: Nordhaus 1990a.
a. Instantaneous contribution measures the impact of concentration change at the instant of release.
b. Total impact estimates the relative contribution to global warming over indefinite future.

B. Sources by economic activity

| Greenhouse gas | Relative contribution (%) | | Source of emission |
	Instan-taneous	Total	
Energy	62.8	76.2	CO_2 emissions, nitrous oxides, methane
Agriculture	20.6	19.8	CO_2, methane, nitrous oxides
Industry	0.7	0.1	Methane
Natural	4.3	0.7	Methane, nitrous oxides
Other	11.6	3.3	CFCs

SOURCE: Nordhaus 1990b. Estimates of emission sources are from EPA 1989b, vol. 1, ch. 2.
Note that sources are highly uncertain for methane and nitrous oxides.

Three important features of the results emerge from existing studies. First, the central estimates of the *equilibrium* impact of a CO_2-equivalent doubling have changed little since the earliest calculations. The last thorough review by the National Academy of Sciences concluded, "When it is assumed that the CO_2 content of the atmosphere is doubled and statistical thermal equilibrium is achieved, all models predict a global surface warming. [GCMs] indicate global warming [from CO_2 doubling] to be in the range between about 1.5 and 4.5° C" (National Research Council 1983, 28).

Second, though short-run weather forecasting has improved dramatically in recent years, model estimates of the impact of CO_2 doubling are not converging. A recent survey of eighteen GCM simulations from seven different modeling groups found a median equilibrium increase from CO_2 doubling of 4° C, with a range of estimates from 1.9° to 5.2° C. While all current models find a positive impact of elevated GHG concentrations on global temperature, the range is uncomfortably wide and is not narrowing.

Third, while the climate modelers have concentrated upon the equilibrium climate change, the more important question for economic policy concerns the rate of realized or actual warming. Because of the heat capacity of the oceans, the actual warming is likely to lag behind the equilibrium by several decades. To illustrate, note that estimates are that GHG concentrations have already increased by an amount that will in equilibrium produce about one-half of a CO_2 doubling (say, 0.95° to 2.6° C, according to the just-cited range). Yet the actual warming over the last century is clearly far less than the estimated equilibrium amount (being, say, 0.3° to 0.6° C). Considerable scientific work is required to narrow down the time lags of the climate behind the GHG emissions.

General-circulation models produce a vast output of interesting numerical results on predicted future climates. Table 2.3 reports an attempt to characterize the results and uncertainties about future climate change. Most experts believe that mean temperature will rise and that the warmer climate will increase precipitation and runoff. Some models foresee hotter and drier climates in midcontinental regions, such as the U.S. Midwest. Forecasting climate changes at particular locations (such as in California or Cortina) has proven intractable, and many climate modelers do not expect to be able to forecast regional climates accurately in the foreseeable future.

Table 2.3
Range of estimates from climate models about equilibrium impact on major
variables of doubling of CO_2

Variable	Projection of probable global average change	Distribution of regional change	Confidence in prediction[c]	
			Global average	Regional average
Temperature	+2° to +5° C	−3° to +10° C	High	Medium
Sea level[a]	+10 to +100 cm		High	
Precipitation	+7 to +15%	−20 to +20%	High	Low
Soil moisture	?[b]	−50 to +50%	?[b]	Medium
Runoff	Increase	−50 to +50%	Medium	Low
Severe storms	?[c]	?[c]	?[c]	?[c]

SOURCE: Adopted from L. Mearns, P. H. Gleich, and S. H. Schneider, "Prospect for Climate Change," in Paul Waggoner, ed., *Climate Change and U.S. Water Resources* (New York: Wiley, forthcoming).
a. Increases in sea level are the average of the global rate. Sea-level rise in particular locations will be higher or lower than this figure depending upon local geological conditions.
b. No basis for forecast of this variable.
c. The "confidence in prediction" is a subjective estimate of experts of the confidence that the range of estimates provided is accurate. These estimates are based upon formal models, historical analogy, and other experience.

Consistency with the Historical Temperature Record

One of the major problems with GCMs is the challenge of validating predictions. There are several possible ways to test the models, but the proof of the pudding will ultimately occur when and if global temperatures actually begin to rise.

Historical records indicate that global mean temperature has increased by 0.3° to 0.6° C since the 1880s. Whether the observed temperature record is consistent with the predictions of climate models is a hotly debated question. Some authors have used statistical techniques to test for the presence of a "greenhouse signal" in the upward trend of temperature over the last century. The hypothesis that the climate is a trendless process can be rejected at a high level of confidence. Still, a great deal of evidence suggests that climatic variables fluctuate over periods of a century or more.

Unfortunately, we do not know enough about the background

trends and cycles to know whether the warming in recent years is normal climatic fluctuation or something new and different.[4] To date, statistical analysis of the historical record has lagged far behind construction of new and more refined GCMs. But the historical record is an important, independent source of evidence about the pace of global warming, and the signal-to-noise ratio is likely to increase over the coming years, allowing a firmer test of the temperature-CO_2 sensitivity.

Impacts of Climate Change

Although a great deal of effort has gone into constructing scenarios about climate change, studies of the impact of climate change on society are in their infancy. Even though we may not be able to predict the future climate change, it may, ironically, be possible to say a great deal about the economic impact of future climate changes. This section first describes the effects of greenhouse warming upon the economy, then presents some estimates of what measures to slow greenhouse warming would cost, and finally addresses the issue of potential adaptations to greenhouse warming.

Impacts of Greenhouse Warming

It will be useful to begin with some general remarks about the relationship of climate to human societies. To begin with, it must be recognized that human societies thrive in a wide variety of climatic zones. People today live in virtually every climatic zone from the tropics to the arctic, with the zone of tolerance ranging from $-60°$ to $55°$ C. Climate variables like temperature or humidity have little effect upon the net value of economic activity in advanced countries. Indeed, owing in part to technological changes like air conditioning, migration patterns in the United States have favored warmer regions. Today, for the bulk of economic activity, variables like wages, unionization, labor-force skills, and political factors swamp climatic considerations. When a manufacturing firm decides between investing in Hong Kong and Warsaw, climate will probably not even be on the list of factors considered.

At the same time, although most analyses focus primarily upon globally averaged surface temperature, this variable is not the most important for impacts. Variables like precipitation or water levels and extremes of droughts or freezes are likely to be more important. Mean temperature is chosen because it is a useful *index* of climate change that tends to be associated with most other important changes.

A related point involves the size of projected climate changes in comparison to the day-to-day changes we normally experience. The variations in weather that we experience in our daily lives will swamp the likely changes over the next century. The change in temperature while this paper is being read is likely to be greater than the expected change from 1990 to 2090. Few people are likely to notice the CO_2 signal amidst the noisy pandemonium of their daily lives.

Economic Effects of Climate Change: United States

I next consider detailed studies of the impact of climate change on economic activity, beginning with studies of advanced countries and then turning to developing countries.

Climate change is likely to have different effects on different sectors.[5] In general, sectors of the economy that have a significant interaction with unmanaged ecosystems—that is, those that are heavily dependent upon naturally occurring rainfall, runoff, or temperatures—may be significantly affected by climate change. Agriculture, forestry, and coastal activities fall in this category. Most of the U.S. economy has little *direct* interaction with climate, and the impacts of climate change are likely to be very small in these sectors. For example, cardiovascular surgery and microprocessor fabrication are undertaken in carefully controlled environments and are unlikely to be directly affected by climate change.

Table 2.4 presents a breakdown of U.S. national income, organized by the sensitivity of the sector to greenhouse warming.[6] Approximately 3 percent of U.S. national output originates in climate-sensitive sectors and another 10 percent in sectors modestly sensitive to climatic change. About 87 percent of national output comes from sectors that are negligibly affected by climate change. These measures of output may understate the impact of climate change on well-being because they omit important nonmarket activities or noneconomic value that may be more sensitive to climatic change than measured output, an important qualification that I will return to shortly.

What are the likely effects of climate change on individual sectors?

Table 2.4
Breakdown of economic activity by vulnerability to climatic change, 1981

Sector	National income		
	Value (billions)	Percent of total	
Total national income	2,415.1	100.0	100.0
Potentially severely impacted			3.1
Farms	67.1	2.8	
Forestry, fisheries, other	7.7	0.3	
Moderate potential impact			10.1
Construction	109.1	4.5	
Water transportation	6.3	0.3	
Energy and utilities[a]			
Energy (electric, gas, oil)	45.9	1.9	
Water and sanitary	5.7	0.2	
Real estate[b]			
Land-rent component	51.2	2.1	
Hotels, lodging, recreation	25.4	1.1	
Neglibible effect			86.8
Mining	45.1	1.9	
Manufacturing	581.3	24.1	
Other transportation and communication	132.6	5.5	
Finance, insurance, and balance real estate	274.8	11.4	
Trade	349.4	14.5	
Other services	325.2	13.5	
Government services	337.0	14.0	
Rest of world	50.3	2.1	

SOURCE: Data are based on the U.S. National Accounts, Survey of Current Business, July 1984.

a. National income in electric, gas, sanitary industry is subdivided on the basis of consumption of major components.

b. Estimate of land-rent component is drawn from two sources: national balance sheet data on values of land and structures and from surveys of housing prices. Estimate assumes that 25 percent of nonlabor income in real estate industry is from land rents.

Table 2.5
Impact estimates for different sectors, for doubling of CO_2

Sectors	Cost (billions of dollars, 1981)
Severely impacted sectors	
Farms	
Impact of greenhouse warming	
and CO_2 fertilization	10.6 to -9.7
Forestry, fisheries, other	small
Moderately impacted sectors	
Construction	negative
Water transportation	?
Energy and utilities	
Energy (electric, gas, oil)	
Electricity demand	1.65
Nonelectric space heat	-1.16
Water and sanitary	positive?
Real estate	
Land-rent component	
Estimate of damage from	
sea-level rise	
Loss of land	1.5
Protection of sheltered areas	0.9
Protection of open coasts	2.8
Hotels, lodging, recreation	?
Total central estimate	
National income	6.2
Percent of national income	0.26

The following is a synopsis of recent studies, and the quantified impacts are summarized in table 2.5.

Agriculture

Agriculture is the most climate-sensitive of the major sectors. Studies suggest that greenhouse warming will reduce yields in many crops. On the other hand, the associated fertilization effect of higher levels of CO_2 will tend to raise yields, particularly in C3 species (which included most major crops except corn). After a careful review, a recent National Academy of Sciences report stated, "Thus, we do not regard the hypothesized CO_2-induced climate changes as a major direct threat to American agriculture over the next few decades" (National Research Council 1983, 45). The Environmental Protection Agency found that the value of U.S. agricultural output is likely to rise or fall by as much as $10 billion annually depending on the magnitude of the climate change (EPA 1989a).

A recent study of Kane, Reilly, and Tobey (1990) goes beyond yield estimates to estimate the general-equilibrium impacts of climate change in a world agricultural model. Their estimates range from an optimistic finding that world real income would increase *over a half century or more* by 0.1 percent to a pessimistic scenario in which world output decreases by 0.3 percent. In the pessimistic scenario, the major loser is China, with a 5 percent decrease in GDP. To put these figures in perspective, measured per capita income in China grew at a rate of 5.2 percent over the period 1965–1987. Say the rate of growth was only half as high over the next half century. Then the pessimistic scenario of Tobey et al. suggests that climate change would lower the average growth rate from 2.6 to 2.5 percent per annum.

Sea-Level Rise
Most studies indicate a gradual rise in average sea level over the next century. The Intergovernmental Panel on Climate Change (IPCC) estimates that sea-level rise over the next eighty years will be 44 cm, although this figure has a large range of uncertainty. By comparison, over the past eighty years the sea level has risen 8 to 12 cm.

For a sea-level rise of 50 cm, EPA projects the costs to be land loss of around 6,000 square miles, protection costs (by levees and dikes) of high-value property, and miscellaneous protection of open coasts. The total capital outlay is on the order of $100 billion (EPA 1989a), which is approximately 0.1 percent of cumulative gross private domestic investment over the period 1985–2050.

Energy
Greenhouse warming will increase the demand for space cooling and decrease the demand for space heating. The net impact of CO_2 doubling is estimated to be less than $1 billion at 1981 levels of national income.

Other Marketed Goods and Services
Many other sectors are likely to be affected, although numerical estimates of the effects are not available. The forest products industry may benefit from CO_2 fertilization (Binkley 1988). Water systems (such as runoff in rivers or the length of ice-free periods) may be significantly affected, but the costs are likely to be determined more

by the rate of climate change than the new equilibrium climate. Construction in temperate climates will be favorably affected because of a longer period of warm weather. The impact upon recreation and water transportation is mixed depending upon the initial climate. Cold regions may gain, and hot regions may lose; investments in waterskiing will appreciate, while those in snow skiing will depreciate.[7] But for the bulk of the economy—manufacturing, mining, utilities, finance, trade, and most service industries—it is difficult to find major direct impacts of the projected climate changes over the next fifty to seventy-five years.

Nonmarketed Goods and Services
Many valuable goods and services escape the net of the national income accounts and might affect the calculations. Among the areas of importance are human health, biological diversity, amenity values of everyday life and leisure, and environmental quality. Some people will place a high moral, aesthetic, or environmental value on preventing climate change, but I know of no serious estimates of what people are willing to pay to stop greenhouse warming. One study projects important gains for the United States from modest increases in average temperature (see National Research Council 1978). I am aware of no studies that point to major nonmarket costs, but further analysis will be required to decide whether these omitted sectors will affect the overall assessment of the cost of greenhouse warming.

In sum, the economic impact upon the U.S. economy of the climatic changes induced by a doubling of CO_2 concentrations is likely to be small. The point estimate today is that the impact, in terms of variables that have been quantified, is likely to be around one-fourth of 1 percent of national income. However, current studies omit many potentially important effects, so this estimate has a large margin of error.

Economic Effects of Climate Change: Outside the United States[8]

To date, studies for other countries are fragmentary, and no general conclusions are possible at this time. Existing evidence suggests that other advanced industrial countries are likely to experience modest impacts similar to those of the United States. On average, high-income countries have less than 5 percent of their GDP originating in agriculture. Detailed studies for the Netherlands, as well as a less comprehensive study for six large regions (the United States, Europe, Brazil, China, Australia, and the USSR) found that the overall impact of a CO_2-equivalent doubling will be small and probably difficult to detect over a half century or more (see Coolfont Workshop 1989).

On the other hand, small countries that are heavily dependent on coastal activities or suffer major climate change may be severely affected. Studies suggest that significant parts of Bangladesh and the Maldives may be inundated. Particular concerns arise where activities cannot easily migrate in response to climate change. Such situations include natural reserves (like Bharatpur) or populations limited to small areas (like South Sea Islanders).

Developing countries are probably more vulnerable to greenhouse warming than are advanced countries, particularly those poor countries living on the ragged edge of subsistence with few resources to divert to dealing with climate change. However, most poor countries are heavily dependent upon agriculture, so the benefits of CO_2 fertilization might offset the damages from climate change. Countries classified by the World Bank as "low-income economies" had 31 percent of GDP produced in the agricultural sector in 1987; these countries hold 2.8 billion people. Figure 2.1 shows the share of output in agriculture for nine major countries in 1965 and 1987, with a mechanical projection of past trends to 2050. This illustration suggests that cli-

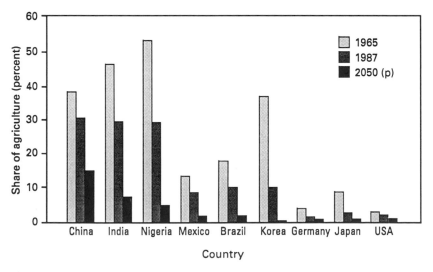

Figure 2.1
Vulnerability to climate change, measured by share of agriculture in GDP

mate vulnerability of most countries has decreased over time and will further decrease as the climate changes.

These reflections lead to a surprising conclusion: Our best guess is that CO_2-induced climate change will produce a combination of gains and losses with no strong presumption of substantial net economic damages. However, these changes are likely to take place over a period of a half century or more and may get lost in the background noise of social, economic, and political change. This conclusion should not be interpreted as a brief *in favor of* climate change. Rather, it suggests that those who paint a bleak picture of desert Earth devoid of fruitful economic activity may be exaggerating the injuries and neglecting the benefits of climate change.

Policies to Cope with the Threat of Global Warming

In response to the threat of global warming, a wide variety of responses is available. A first option, taking steps to slow or prevent greenhouse warming, has received the greatest public attention. Most policy discussion has focused on reducing energy consumption or switching to nonfossil fuels, while some have suggested reforestation to remove CO_2 from the atmosphere. One important goal of policy should be cost-effectiveness—structuring policies to get the maximal reduction in harmful climatic change for a given level of expenditure.

A second option is to offset greenhouse warming through climatic engineering. Measures in this category include changing the albedo (reflectivity) of the earth, increasing the rate of removal of greenhouse gases, or changing water flows to cool the earth.

A final option is to adapt to the warmer climate. Adaptation could take place gradually on a decentralized basis through the automatic response of people and institutions or through markets as the climate warms and the oceans rise. In addition, governments could prevent harmful climatic impacts by land-use regulations or investments in research on living in a warmer climate.

Preventive Policies

The major policy question surrounding the greenhouse effect is whether steps should be taken in the near term to prevent global warming. Whether preventive action should be taken depends on the costs of preventing GHG emissions relative to the damages that the GHGs would cause if they continue unchecked.

Knowledge of the costs of slowing climate change is rudimentary. This section will review the costs of slowing greenhouse warming through reduction of emissions and atmospheric concentrations of greenhouse gases. These examples—reducing CFC emissions, reducing CO_2 emissions, and reforestation—are not the only options, but they have been studied most intensively.

In calculating the cost of preventive measures, we measure costs in terms of tons of CO_2 equivalent. Measures that cost up to $5 per ton of CO_2 equivalent are inexpensive; at this cost, global warming could be stopped dead in its tracks at a total cost of less than $40 billion per year (about 0.2 percent of global income). Costs near $10 to $50 per ton CO_2 equivalent are expensive but manageable (costing 0.5 to 2.5 percent of global income). Measures in excess of $100 per ton of CO_2 are extremely expensive.

Reducing CFC Emissions
A first strategy involves reducing emissions of chlorofluorocarbons (CFCs) into the atmosphere. This step is particularly important because CFCs are extremely powerful greenhouse gases. It is currently believed that new chemical substitutes for the two most important CFCs can be found that will significantly reduce greenhouse warming. A rough estimate is that these substitutes can reduce warming at a cost less than $5 per ton of CO_2 equivalent. This policy is extremely cost-effective, bringing a significant reduction of warming at modest cost.

Reducing CO_2 Emissions
Any major reduction in GHGs will require a significant reduction in CO_2 emissions, of which more than 95 percent come from the energy sector and deforestation. Carbon dioxide emissions can be reduced through increases in energy efficiency, decreases in final energy services, substitution of less GHG-intensive fossil fuels for more GHG-intensive fossil fuels, substitution of nonfossil fuels for fossil fuels, and technological change that allows new techniques of production along with new products and services.

Because energy interacts with the economy in so many ways, good estimates of the costs of reducing CO_2 emissions require complex models of the energy system. Such models must incorporate the be-

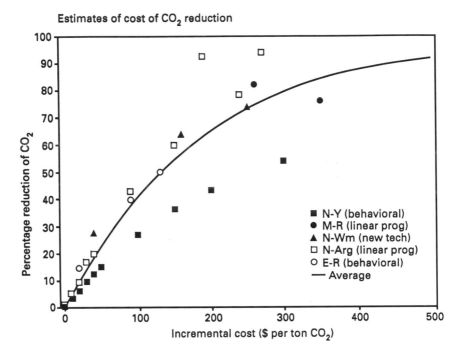

Figure 2.2
Estimates of cost of CO_2 reduction

havior of both producers and consumers along with consideration of each of the possible methods for reducing emissions. I have reviewed a number of studies,[9] and I will discuss the current estimates of the long-run costs of reducing CO_2 emissions.[10] Figure 2.2 shows a compilation of the estimates of the marginal cost of reducing CO_2 emissions as a function of the percentage reduction from a baseline projection.

(Note that in this figure as elsewhere in this paper, the estimates of the cost of reduction are relative to a trajectory in which there is no greenhouse policy. That is, when we discuss "the cost of a *y* percent reduction in greenhouse gas *x*," this calculates the cost of a *y* percent reduction from a baseline path in which no taxes, regulations, or other greenhouse policies are exercised. The baseline path is *not* a constant emissions or concentrations path, but a path in which emissions would be growing at the rate determined by fundamental factors such as GNP growth, energy prices, and technological factors.)

The studies of the *long-run* costs of CO_2 reduction that I have reviewed lead to two major conclusions. First, the cost of reducing CO_2 emissions is low for small curbs. Reductions of up to 10 percent of CO_2 emissions from the energy sector can be attained at an average cost of around $10 per ton of CO_2 reduced. With current global annual emissions of around 6 billion tons of CO_2, a 10 percent reduction would cost around $6 billion annually.[11]

The second conclusion is that the cost of reducing CO_2 emissions grows rapidly and becomes extreme for substantial reductions. I estimate that, in the long run but with today's energy technologies, the marginal cost of a 50 percent reduction in CO_2 emissions is approximately $130 per ton of CO_2. In other words, inducing producers and consumers to reduce their CO_2 emissions by one-half would require a carbon tax (or the regulatory equivalent thereof) of $130 per ton of CO_2, which would generate annual taxes of around $400 billion. The *total* resource cost of a 50 percent reduction in CO_2 emissions is about $180 billion annually, slightly less than 1 percent of world output at current price and output levels.[12]

The incremental costs of reducing CO_2 emissions rise rapidly because no substitutes currently exist for many uses of fossil fuels. For example, a major reduction in CO_2 emissions from transportation would require either that people travel less or that fewer goods be transported, both of which would be quite costly.

Forests
Several studies have proposed using trees as a method of removing carbon from the atmosphere. Among the major proposals are slowing the deforestation of tropical forests; reforesting open land, thereby increasing the amount of carbon locked into the biosphere; a "tree bounty," which subsidizes the sequestration of wood in durable products; and a "tree pickling" program, in which trees are stored indefinitely.

No detailed study of the economics of tropical forests has been undertaken here. However, deforestation may be adding 500 million to 3 billion tons of carbon per year to CO_2 emissions (amounting to between 5 and 30 percent of total GHG emissions). Much deforestation is uneconomic in tropical regions even without invoking greenhouse considerations. If so, the cessation of uneconomical deforestation can significantly and inexpensively slow greenhouse warming.

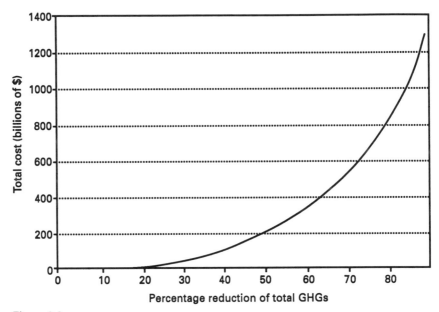

Figure 2.3
Total cost of GHG reduction (global costs, 1989 U.S. dollars)

NOTE: Figure shows the estimated total long-run cost of different levels of GHG reductions. The calculations assume 1989 levels of world output and prices and 1989 levels of GHG emissions per unit output. Details of the calculations are provided in Nordhaus 1990b.

I estimate that the three other reforestation options can remove carbon from the atmosphere at modest costs; however, they can contribute only marginally to reducing atmospheric concentrations.

Summary on Costs of Prevention
As shown in Figure 2.3, it appears that a significant fraction of GHG emissions—perhaps one-sixth—can be eliminated at relatively low cost. The most cost-effective policies to slow greenhouse warming include curbs on CFC production and preventing uneconomic deforestation. Putting all the low-cost options together, I estimate that around one-sixth of CO_2-equivalent emissions can be reduced at an average cost of $4 per ton of CO_2 equivalent, for a total cost of about $6 billion annually.

After the low-cost options have been exhausted, further reductions in GHG emissions will require curbing CO_2 emissions—say, through taxes or regulations on the carbon content of fuels. But curbing GHG

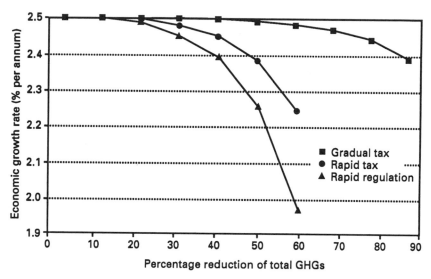

Figure 2.4
Growth versus climate change: Speed of phase-in and policy efficiency

emissions rapidly hits diminishing returns: a 50 percent reduction in
GHG emissions in the long run will cost about $200 billion annually,
which is about 1 percent of global output. Attempts to restrict GHG
emissions severely in a short period would be even more costly.

Figure 2.4 shows the trade-off between economic growth and slowing emissions. The upper path shows the trade-off if policies are
efficient (say through a uniform global carbon tax) and introduced
gradually over a period of time. The middle path shows the trade-off
with an efficient policy and a rapid phase-in (phasing out existing
capital over a twenty-year period). The bottom curve shows the
trade-off with a rapid phase-in and inefficient policies (such as
sector-by-sector regulations) that double the cost of controls. These
curves show the importance of a gradual phase-in and efficient design of policies.

Climatic Engineering

In approaching a task, my grandfather always advised me, "Use
brains, not brawn." The preventive strategies of planting hundreds
of billions of trees or reducing fossil-fuel use through trillions of dollars of investments represent the brawn philosophy. A promising

new approach to the threat of greenhouse warming is to use our brains to find a way to offset greenhouse warming through climatic engineering; this is the global equivalent of turning on an air conditioner. Potential approaches are changing the albedo (reflectivity) of the earth, increasing the rate of removal of greenhouse gases, or changing the circulation of water to cool the earth.

Careful analysis of these proposals is just beginning, but a number have already been identified that appear much more cost-effective than plugging the oil wells and shutting down the coal mines. One approach would be to create a sunscreen by sending tiny particulates into the stratosphere to cool the earth. These particles could be shot up with 16-inch naval rifles, lifted by hydrogen balloons, or deposited by tuning the engines of aircraft to burn somewhat richer than normal. One estimate finds that 100,000 kilograms of carbon can be offset with 1 kilogram of particles. That's real leverage!

A further intriguing possibility raised by Martin and his associates is placing trace quantities of iron in the North Pacific and Antarctic ocean regions. Studies suggest that this procedure would increase the limiting nutrients, foster much greater photosynthesis, and increase the rate of carbon precipitation to the ocean floor. Preliminary estimates indicate that this option might well annually remove from the atmosphere a quantity equal to current CO_2 emissions.[13]

Preliminary estimates suggest that the cost of the geoengineering options is in the order of $0.10 to $10 per ton carbon equivalent, which is far less than many perennial favorites like reforestation, fuel switching, or energy conservation. These proposals surely sound like panaceas. At the same time, they pose unknown risks by perturbing a complex system that is already being perturbed. They deserve careful study.

Adaptation Policies

Faced with the prospect of changing climate, societies may decide to adapt. The most important adaptations are those taken by *private* agents—consumers and businesses, for example. Decentralized adaptations—population migration, relocation of capital, land reclamation, and technological change—will occur more or less automatically in response to changing relative incomes, prices, and environmental conditions.

Governments also play an important role by ensuring that the legal and economic structure is conducive to adaptation, particularly by making sure that the environmental or climatic changes get reliably translated into the price and income signals that will induce private adaptation. Fulfilling this role may prove difficult because so many of the impacts of climate change are not properly priced. For example, greenhouse warming may alter runoff patterns of major rivers (see Ravelle and Waggoner 1983; Waggoner 1990). Because water is allocated in such an archaic way, there is no guarantee that it will be efficiently allocated when water availability changes. Governments can improve adaptation by introducing general allocational devices (such as water auctions) that will channel water resources to their highest-value uses. Use of land near seacoasts and in floodplains poses similar issues.

Speeds of Adjustment in Prevention and Adaptation
Adaptation and prevention are often treated as symmetrical policies. They differ in one crucial respect, however: While preventive policies must generally precede global warming, adaptation policies can occur simultaneously. This distinction is crucial here, for cause precedes effect by a half century or more. To stabilize climate, immediate action is necessary; adaptations can wait for many years. This point of contrast underscores one of the major obstacles to responding intelligently to threatening climate change—the long time scale involved in climate change.[14]

A common mistake in thinking about this issue is to impose a slowly changing climate upon today's world and to ignore the inevitable evolution that will take place over the coming decades. If it takes eighty years or more for CO_2 doubling, as suggested earlier, adaptations will be spread over a similar period. Yet social and economic structures change enormously over such a time. Recall how much the world has changed since 1910. That was the age of empires, when the Ottoman, Austrian, and czarist regimes ruled much of Eurasia. The map of Europe has been redrawn three times since 1910 and is being restructured again today. The power density of the United States was about 1.5 horsepower per capita as opposed to 130 horsepower per capita today; one-sixth of horsepower was horses, and the 21 million horses were the major polluters. Air conditioning, nuclear power, and electronics were unheard of.

This catalog makes clear how foolish it would be to prescribe adaptive steps *now* to smooth the transition to climate changes over the next century. The time scale of most adaptations is much shorter than the time scale of climate change. Carbon dioxide doubling will take place over the next century. By contrast, financial markets adjust in minutes, product prices in weeks, labor markets in a few years, and the economic "long run" is usually reckoned at no more than two decades. To adapt now would be akin to building the Maginot Line in 1935 to cope with military threats of the 1990s, which would be little use for the petroleum wars of today.

These considerations suggest that it would be unwise to undertake costly adaptive policies unless they satisfy one of three criteria: (1) they have such long lead times that they must be undertaken now to be effective; (2) they have a clear presumption of being economical even in the absence of climate change; or (3) the penalty for delay is extremely high. By these criteria, it is difficult to enumerate any adaptive measures other than the general maxim to promote a healthy economy, to strive to internalize most external effects to ensure an appropriate response to changing climatic signals, to broaden the scope of markets so that individuals, firms, and nations receive the appropriate signals of scarcity, and to ensure a high saving rate to provide the investments needed for changing infrastructure.

Approaches to Policies on Global Warming

Research to date suggests that the costs of climate change are likely to be small for most advanced economies over the next fifty to seventy-five years. At the same time, the prospect that the climate may change in a catastrophic fashion might justify steps to slow climate change. How should nations respond today to the threat of global warming over the next century?

In related work, I have attempted to estimate the costs and benefits of policies to slow global warming (see especially Nordhaus 1990a). In studies of policy, it is useful to define government actions as carbon taxes that penalize emissions of greenhouse gases in proportion to their global warming potential. These "taxes" are a metaphor for explicit government steps to reduce GHG emissions through energy or gasoline taxes, CFC bans or regulatory limits, prohibitions on tree cutting, taxes on carbon emissions, or energy-efficiency standards.

Using the estimates of damages outlined previously and assuming a low discount rate on future damages from climate change, I calculate that an efficient policy would impose a penalty on GHG emissions of around \$5 per ton CO_2 equivalent (carbon weight).[15] This level of penalty would produce a total reduction of about 12 percent of GHG emissions, including a large reduction in CFCs and a small reduction in CO_2 emissions. As table 2.6 shows, such a tax amounts to \$3.50 per ton tax on coal, 58 cents per barrel on oil, and 1.4 cents per gallon on gasoline. Annually, U.S. revenues from a \$5 per ton carbon tax would amount to about \$10 billion. Table 2.6 also shows the impact of a severe restraint—\$100 per ton CO_2—which would be close to the tax required to reduce CO_2 emissions by one-half. The "high-tax" strategy would have a significant impact upon the U.S. and other economies.

It will be useful to compare these costs with historical events or regulatory programs. A low-cost program for slowing global warming (say one associated with the low-tax proposal in table 2.6) would impose a burden equivalent to a major U.S. regulation, such as those on drinking water, noise, or surface mining (see Litan and Nordhaus 1983, ch. 2).

The more stringent program to cut GHG emissions by half (associated with the high-tax scenario in table 2.6) would impose annual costs (or, more technically, dead-weight losses) of around 1 percent of world output. This figure can be compared to the costs of *all* environmental, health, and safety regulations in the United States, which were estimated to cost 1 to 3 percent of GNP (ibid.). Another parallel is with the impact of the energy price increases of the 1970s. Jorgenson and Wilcoxen (1990) estimate that the energy-price increase lowered U.S. output growth by 0.2 percent per year, or a total of about 3 percent, since 1973.

Discounting, Nonlinearities, and Learning

Cost-benefit analyses are a useful starting point for considering government policies, but they raise several issues that must be addressed before making policy recommendations. To begin with, many values cannot be incorporated in a quantitative cost-benefit analysis. For example, climate change may threaten a society's cultural heritage in ways that are not possible to evaluate in an economic framework but which are nonetheless unacceptable. While being unable to put a price tag on Venice, we might decide that it is unacceptable to take actions that threaten Venice's existence. There is not much economic science can say about this issue except to identify such trade-offs.

Table 2.6
Illustrative measures of impact of different carbon taxes

Sector of impact	Level of stringency of GHG reductions	
	Low tax	High tax
Tax effect		
Tax on CO_2 equivalent (per ton carbon)	$5.00	$100
Impact on fossil fuels prices (1989 prices)		
Coal price		
Per metric ton	$3.50	$70
Percentage increase	10%	205%
Oil price		
Per barrel	$0.58	$11.65
Percentage increase	2.8%	55%
Gasoline price		
Per gallon	1.4 cents	28 cents
Percentage increase	1.2%	23.3%
Overall impacts		
Estimated reduction of GHG emissions (CO_2 equivalent)	10%	43%
Total tax revenues, U.S. (billions of dollars)	$10	$125
Estimated global net economic benefits (+) or costs (−), billion of dollars per year, 1989 global economy[a]	$4	−$114

NOTE: Figures do not take into account the reduction in GHG emission in response to carbon tax; that is, they are "without feedback." These estimates are drawn from Nordhaus 1990a.

a. Assumes a discount rate equal to 1 percent in excess of the growth of output and damages from a CO_2 doubling equal to 1 percent of global output.

In addition, greenhouse warming poses particularly difficult issues because of the importance of the discount rate and the presence of nonlinearities and learning over time. On these issues, economics has a great deal to say.

The Discount Rate and Future Climate Damages
How should the costs of future climate change be discounted in making current decisions? This issue is particularly thorny because of the long lags in the carbon cycle. Carbon dioxide emissions have an extremely long atmospheric residence time, in the range of 200 to 500 years, so actions today can affect economic welfare in the distant future. How should we balance CO_2-reduction costs in 1990 against benefits in lower costs of climate change in 2040 or 2090?

In part, the issue of discounting is an ethical question, reflecting the relative valuation of well-being of current and future generations. But the revealed social discount rate is embedded in numerous public and private decisions, such as government fiscal and monetary policy and the rate of public investment, so the discount rate on climate change should not be chosen arbitrarily and without regard to other decisions. A real discount rate on goods and services close to the return on capital in most countries—say 8 percent per year or more—would imply that we should invest little today to slow the projected climate changes and concentrate instead on more immediate problems.

On the other hand, a low discount rate—say 4 percent per year or less—would give considerable weight today to climate changes in the late twenty-first century. But such a low discount rate would also imply that all investment opportunities with yields above 4 percent are exhausted—an assumption that is inconsistent with knowledge about rates of return on business and human capital in most advanced countries.

We might also ask whether a major commitment to slowing climate change is a worthwhile investment for developing countries who are likely to be the regions most vulnerable to climate change. Surveys of developing countries suggest that social rates of return well in excess of 10 percent per year are abundantly available in poor countries. For example, the social rate of return to investments in education in poor countries is estimated to be around 26 percent for primary education, 16 percent for secondary education, and 13 percent for higher education (see Psacharopoulos 1985). To devote many billions of dollars of resources to slowing climate change at the expense of equivalent investments in education, energy conservation, or tangible capital in developing countries would probably hurt poor countries and give little return in high-income countries.

A low discount rate on climate change along with a high return on capital is simply inconsistent. Faced with the dilemma of a low social discount rate and a high return on capital, the efficient policy would be to invest heavily in high-return capital now and then use the fruits of those investments to slow climate change in the future.

Uncertainty
Clearly, global warming is rife with uncertainty—about future emissions paths, about the GHG-climate linkage, about the timing of climate change, about the impacts of climate upon flora and fauna, about the costs of slowing climate change, and even about the speed with which we can reduce the uncertainties. How should we proceed in the face of uncertainty?

One approach would be to take a "certainty equivalent" or "best guess" analysis, which would ignore uncertainty and the costs of decision making and charge ahead. The cost-benefit analysis performed above embodies this approach. It is appropriate as long as the risks are symmetrical and as long as the uncertainties are unlikely to be resolved in the foreseeable future. Unfortunately, neither of these conditions is likely to be satisfied for the greenhouse effect.

Virtually all observers agree that the uncertainties of climate change are asymmetrical; we are likely to be increasingly averse to climate change as the change becomes larger. To go from a 2° to a 4° warming is much more alarming than to move from a 0° to a 2° warming. The greater the warming, the further we move from our current climate and the greater the potential for unforeseen events. Moreover, it is the extreme events—droughts and hurricanes, heat waves and freezes, river flooding and lake freezing—that produce major economic losses. As probability distributions shift, the frequency of extreme events increases (or decreases) proportionately more than the change in the mean. Whether the increases in unpleasant extremes (like droughts in the corn belt) will be greater or less than the increases in pleasant extremes (like frost-free winters in the citrus belt) is, like most questions about climate change, unanswered.

In addition, climatologists generally think that the chance of unpleasant surprises rises as the magnitude and pace of climate change increases. We must go back 5 million to 15 million years to find a climate equivalent to what we are likely to produce over the next 100 years; the concentrations of GHGs in the next century will exceed levels previously observed.

Moreover, climate systems are complex systems, and some models have shown two or more locally stable equilibria (see Manabe and Stouffer 1988). There is historical evidence that climates have changed sharply (in or out of ice ages) in as little as a century, as occurred in the Younger Dryas period.

Among the kinds of responses that have been suggested and cannot be ruled out are major shifts of glaciers, leading to a rise in sea level of 20 feet or more in a few centuries; drastic changes in ocean currents, such as displacement of the North Atlantic deep currents that would lead to a major shift in climates of Atlantic coastal communities; large-scale desertification of the grain belts of the world; and the possibility that climate changes will upset the delicate balance of bugs, viruses, and humans as the tropical climates that are so hospitable to spawning and spreading new diseases move poleward. No one has demonstrated that these impacts *will* occur. Rather, it seems likely that unexpected and unwelcome phenomena, like the antarctic ozone hole, will occur more frequently under conditions of more rapid climatic change.

The threat of an unforeseen calamity argues for more aggressive action than a plain-vanilla cost-benefit analysis would suggest. However, the possibility of resolving uncertainties about climate change argues for postponing action until our knowledge is more secure. Most scientists believe that research can improve our understanding about the timing, extent, and impacts of climate change. Improved understanding could sharpen our calculations about appropriate policies. The best investment today may be in *learning* about climate change rather than in *preventing* it.

Putting this propostion concretely, we could easily make serious mistakes in attempting to prevent climate change. Imagine that the United States had mandated a massive nuclear-power program twenty years ago, only to find that the technology was expensive and unacceptable. Learning to cope with the threat of climate change includes not only improving our estimates of the consequences of climate change but performing R&D on inexpensive and reliable ways of slowing climate change.

A Framework for Policies to Slow Greenhouse Warming

I conclude by suggesting the direction that policy should follow in slowing greenhouse warming. In designing policies to slow global warming, we must first take into account that this is a *global* issue. Efficient policies will involve steps by all countries to restrict GHG emissions. In order to induce international cooperation, the United States and other rich nations may need to subsidize actions by poor nations (say to slow tropical deforestation or to phase out CFC use). While unilateral action may be better than nothing, concerted action is better still.

Given the identified costs of global warming, it would be sensible to take three modest steps to slow global warming while avoiding precipitous and ill-designed actions that may later be regretted.

1. Improve Knowledge A first set of measures should aim to improve our understanding of greenhouse warming. Such steps would include augmented monitoring of the global environment; analyses of past climatic records, as well as intensive analysis of the environmental and economic impacts of climate change, past and future; and analyses of potential steps to slow climate change. Understanding of climate change has improved enormously over the last two decades, and further research will help to sharpen our pencils for the tough decisions to be made in the future.

2. Develop New Technologies Countries should support research and development on new technologies that will slow climate change—particularly on energy technologies that have low GHG emissions per unit of output. Too little is invested in these technologies because of a "double externality": Private returns are less than social returns both because the fruits of R&D are available to those who spent nothing on research and because the benefits of GHG reductions are currently worth nothing in the marketplace.

Energy technologies that replace fossil-fuel use require greater government support than they currently receive. Inherently safe nuclear power, solar energy, and especially energy conservation are particularly promising targets for government R&D support.

In addition, a number of technical fixes should be investigated to determine whether they might provide low-cost relief to future climate change. In particular, measures to sequester carbon and proposals for climate engineering should be carefully studied and field-tested to evaluate their merits. It is possible that these new approaches would be far more cost-effective than severe measures to curb fossil-fuel consumption.

3. "No-Regret" Policies   A third approach is to identify and accelerate the myriad otherwise-sensible measures that would tend to slow global warming. Many steps could contribute to slowing global warming at little or no economic cost. These steps include efforts to strengthen international agreements to restrict CFCs, moves to slow or curb uneconomic deforestation, and steps to slow the growth of uneconomic use of fossil fuels, say through higher taxes on gasoline, on hydrocarbons, or on all fossil fuels. If nations were to take such actions and climate change were to disappear, there would be few regrets about such policies.

Should we go further than these three steps? I believe not. The agenda of unsolved problems is long; resources and political will are scarce; and I believe it is premature to take costly steps to slow climate change at this time. But others might disagree and find the risks of climate change more frightening, or we might tomorrow uncover new information that would increase the likely future costs of climate change. In these cases, if we desire to press further in reducing long-term risks, I would turn to carbon taxes as a way of further reducing GHG emissions.

4. Carbon Taxes   A final measure to slow climate change would be a set of global environmental taxes levied on the CO_2-equivalent emissions of greenhouse gases, particularly on CO_2 emissions from the combustion of fossil fuels. The analysis in this study suggests that a GHG tax in the order of $5 per ton of CO_2 equivalent would be a reasonable response to the future costs of climate change.[16]

The design of the carbon taxes goes beyond the scope of this paper, but a few remarks are in order.[17] To be effective, carbon taxes should be imposed in all countries. Consider first the issue of fossil fuel combustion as the source of CO_2. If the tax rate were harmonized among nations, then taxes on fossil fuel production would suffice as long as the production received no offsetting government subsidy. Since most carbon in fuels ends up in the atmosphere, no complicated chemical analysis is required.

For other sources of greenhouse gases, several complications arise. First, it would be necessary to convert the global warming potential of each gas into its CO_2 equivalent. The translation will depend on the discount rate because different GHGs have different lifetimes. The translation is relatively straightforward for the CFCs, but the sources and chemical transformations for methane are extremely complicated. Second, some sources are not immediately emitted into the atmosphere, but gradually decay, as is the case for CFCs, which requires a complicated economic analysis of the shadow price of emissions at different periods. Third, there might be a "bounty" on sequestering activities, such as reforestation, which raises complicated problems of monitoring and keeping carbon inventories; tax specialists are generally wary of tax credits, and the possibility for abuse is significant.

Another set of issues concerns the international application of carbon taxes. The most significant question concerns whether they are production or consumption taxes, and who should receive the revenues. I believe that it is not politically practical to have much of the revenues accruing to those outside the nations that levy them. Moreover, production-based taxes are much simpler to administer, but the distribution of consumption-based taxes will be more appealing to industrial countries.

The design of consumption-based taxes is complicated by the need to calculate the carbon content of international trade flows on the basis of their CO_2-equivalent content. These adjustments might be significant for coal-based and petrochemical feedstocks, but to pursue carbon content far into the input-output table would mainly create employment for tax specialists and matrix inverters. With differential international standards or taxes, another set of issues concerns whether firms could employ "emissions offsets," whereby they would get credit in the high-tax regions for emissions reductions or carbon sequestration in other regions. Already, some utilities are assuaging environmental consciences bothered by the combustion of fossil fuels by planting trees in tropical regions.

Clearly, carbon taxation is a complicated issue of tax design; it would be useful to have a team of specialists design such a tax to see whether it is administrable. However, a carbon tax would be far preferable to regulatory interventions because taxes provide incentives to minimize the costs of attaining a given level of GHG reduction while regulations often do not. None of the dilemmas facing carbon taxation would be avoided by adopting emissions limitations or quotas; rather, the monetary flows and redistributions simply become murkier because the impact on prices and incomes of quantitative limitations is less visible.

While these arguments for a carbon tax are persuasive, I do not recommend it today. Negotiating a global carbon tax would be a daunting task even for a president who likes taxes and is not occupied in the Saudi desert with making the world safe for gas guzzlers. Reducing the risks of climate change is a worthwhile objective, but humanity faces many other risks and has many other worthy potential investments, such as oil conservation, factories, equipment, training, education, health, hospitals, transportation, communications, research, development, housing, environmental protection, population control, and curing drug dependency.

In conclusion, the United States and other major countries would be well served by continuing to take steps in the three areas outlined above—improving knowledge, investing in R&D in new technologies, and adopting "no-regret" policies that tilt away from greenhouse gases. Pursuing this approach, we will be prepared for whatever developments unfold in the future—for a tightening of the screws if the threat of global warming accelerates or for a relaxation of policy if science or technology were to alleviate our concerns. The struggle with the threat of greenhouse warming is likely to be a long one, and flexibility is the key to sensible policies.

Notes

1. This chapter draws on a number of earlier articles by the author, and helpful comments were provided along the way by Henry Aaron, Jesse Ausubel, Thomas Schelling, Charles Schultze, Paul Waggoner, and Gary Yohe.

2. A short history of scientific concerns about the greenhouse effect is provided in Ausubel 1983.

3. The traditional estimate of the relative importance of different greenhouse gases uses the *instantaneous* contribution of a gas to global warming (in °C). The traditional estimate has the defect that GHGs differ in their lifetimes and chemical transformations. In order to calculate the *total* contribution of each GHG, which is sometimes called "total warming potential," the table shows the sum of the instantaneous contributions over the indefinite future (in °C-years).

4. One eminent climatologist stated that he had "99 percent" confidence that the warming of the 1980s was associated with the greenhouse effect (see

Hansen 1988). By contrast, four other respected scientists wrote that "no conclusion about the magnitude of the greenhouse effect in the next century can be drawn from the 0.5° C warming that has occurred in the last 100 years" (Marshall Institute 1989, 8).

5. The most careful studies of the impact of greenhouse warming have been conducted for the United States, and this review will therefore concentrate here. The most comprehensive is a recent study by the U.S. EPA (1989a). Although the studies reviewed here use different assumptions, we should envisage the estimated impacts as occurring late in the second half of the next century.

6. "National income" is total national output measured at factor costs. It equals GNP less indirect business taxes and depreciation.

7. A recent study of the impact of climate change in the Canadian Great Lakes region illustrates the substitution of different activities. According to the projected impact, global warming would shorten the length of the ski season by one-third, causing a $50 million loss in revenues. However, the camping season is expected to lengthen by forty days, offsetting the revenue losses.

8. I reiterate that the studies reviewed here represent "best-guess" scenarios of climate change. They omit uncertainties and possible nonlinearities, a topic that I shall examine in the last section.

9. These studies include estimates from specific technologies (such as CO_2 scrubbing and substitution of methane for oil and coal); econometric or elasticity studies (often using highly aggregated models); and mathematical programming or optimization approaches (which often use activity-analysis specifications of energy technologies). For all three of these approaches, one can estimate the cost of reducing CO_2 emissions as a function of the *penalty* or *tax* imposed upon those who emit CO_2. See Nordhaus 1990c.

10. Note that these estimates are of the long-run cost—that is, the cost after the capital stock has fully adjusted. Attempts to reduce CO_2 emissions in the short run would be much more expensive. Also, these costs do not include any adjustments for unmeasured or external environmental, health, or economic effects.

11. Indeed, some studies suggest that CO_2 emissions can be reduced at "negative" costs. That is, there are opportunities to reduce GHGs whose costs are less than the benefits when these opportunities are evaluated at the appropriate social shadow prices. One set of examples concerns activities that emit greenhouse gases and have other environmental externalities. For example, use of CFCs is contributing to ozone depletion. Steps to protect the ozone layer by phasing out CFCs would have the additional benefit of slowing the buildup of greenhouse gases. Other areas are murkier from an economic point of view but might also qualify as negative-cost actions. For example, subsidies to energy prices in many countries lead to much higher levels of energy consumption than would be the case were prices to reflect realistic market prices or world prices. Market imperfections or informational

deficiencies in capital markets, electric utilities, or capital-goods purchases are also alleged examples. The extent of negative-cost opportunities is controversial, but from a policy perspective the real issue may not concern the existence of negative-cost opportunities but the difficulty of finding tools to exploit them.

12. The chapter by John Whalley in this volume provides an estimate that is higher than this consensus estimate.

13. These estimates are derived from a recent unpublished study by Robert Frosch, to whom I am grateful for clarifying several issues.

14. Many of the issues in this section are developed at length in a superb essay by Schelling (1983).

15. The analysis draws upon Nordhaus 1990a. More precisely, it assumes that the discount rate on goods and services exceeds the growth rate of the economy by 1 percent per year. If the damage from a doubling of CO_2 is 0.25 percent of total output, then the efficient CO_2 tax is $3.2 per ton CO_2 equivalent; if the damage is 1 percent of output, the efficient tax is $12.7 per ton. I have chosen $5 as an illustrative intermediate figure.

16. Some would argue that carbon taxes fall in category 3 as sensible economic policy. Consumption of fossil fuels has many negative spillovers beside the greenhouse effect, such as local pollution, traffic congestion, wear and tear on roads, accidents, and so forth. In addition to slowing global warming, carbon taxes would restrain consumption of fossil fuels, encourage R&D on nonfossil fuels, favor fuel switching to low-GHG fuels like methane, lower oil imports, reduce the trade and budget deficits, and raise the national saving rate. Indeed, in the tax kingdom, carbon taxes are the rara avis that increases rather than reduces economic efficiency.

17. The chapters in this volume by James Poterba and John Whalley go into the design of carbon taxes in greater detail.

Bibliography

Ausubel, Jesse H. 1983. Historical note. In National Research Council 1983, 488–491.

Binkley, Clark S. 1988. A case study of the effects of CO_2-induced climatic warming on forest growth and the forest sector: B. Economic effects on the world's forest sector. In M. L. Parry, T. R. Carter, and N. T. Konijn, eds. *The Impacts of Climatic Variations on Agriculture*, 197–218. Dordrecht, Netherlands: Kluwer Academic Publishers.

Coolfont Workshop. 1989. *Climate Impact Response Functions: Report of a Workshop Held at Coolfont, West Virginia*, September 11–14, 1989. Washington, DC: National Climate Program Office.

EPA. 1989a. U.S. Environmental Protection Agency. *The Potential Effects of Global Climate Change on the United States: Report to Congress*, EPA-230-05-89-050, December 1989.

EPA. 1989b. U.S. Environmental Protection Agency. *Policy Options for Stabilizing Global Climate*, Draft Report to Congress, February 1989.

Hansen, James. 1988. Testimony before the Senate Energy Committee, June 23, 1988.

Jorgenson, Dale W., and Wilcoxen, Peter J. 1990. The cost of controlling U.S. carbon dioxide emissions. Processed, Harvard University.

Kane, Sally, Reilly, John, and Tobey, James. 1990. An empirical study of the economic effects of climate change on U.S. agriculture. Processed, July 1990.

Litan, Robert E., and Nordhaus, William D. 1983. *Reforming Federal Regulation*. New Haven, CT: Yale University Press.

Manabe, S., and Stouffer, R. J. 1988. Two stable equilibria of a coupled ocean-atmosphere model. *Journal of Climate* 1:841–866.

Marshall Institute. 1989. Frederick Seitz, Karl Bendelsen, Robert Jastrow, and William A. Nierenberg, *Scientific Perspectives on the Greenhouse Problem: Executive Summary*. Washington, DC: George C. Marshall Institute.

Martin, J. H., Gordon, R. M., and Fitzwater, S. E. 1990. Iron in Antarctic waters. *Nature* 345:156–159.

National Research Council. 1978. *International Perspectives on the Study of Climate and Society*. Washington, DC: National Academy Press.

National Research Council. 1983. *Changing Climate*. Washington, DC: National Academy Press.

Nordhaus, William D. 1990a. To curb or not to curb: The economics of the greenhouse effect. Paper presented to the annual meetings of the American Association for the Advancement of Science, New Orleans, February.

Nordhaus, William D. 1990b. Contribution of different greenhouse gases to global warming: A new technique for measuring impact. Processed, February.

Nordhaus, William D. 1990c. A survey of the costs of reduction of greenhouse gases. *Energy Journal*, Fall.

Psacharopoulos, George. 1985. "Returns to Education: A Further International Update and Implications," *Journal of Human Resources* 20 (Fall):583–604.

Ravelle, Roger R., and Waggoner, Paul E. 1983. Effects of a carbon dioxide–induced climatic change on water supplies in the western United States. In National Research Council 1983, 419–432.

Schelling, Thomas C. 1983. Climatic change: Implications for welfare and policy. In National Research Council 1983, 449–482.

Wagonner, Paul E., ed. 1990. *Climate Change and U.S. Water Resources*. New York: Wiley.

Wuebbles, Donald J., and Jae Edmonds. 1988. *A Primer on Greenhouse Gases*, prepared for the Department of Energy, DOE/NBB-0083, March.

Comments

Peter Diamond

Bill Nordhaus has given us a wonderful introduction to the likely magnitude of the economic effects of global warming and the magnitudes of the costs of trying to address this problem. Summarizing his chapter crudely, I would describe it as having three messages: the aggregate (global) problem is not as costly as you might have thought[1] (although locally, for some nations or regions, the problem is likely to be severe); some proposed solutions are very costly, so do only the cheap ones; and corrective taxes, not regulations, are the way to go. I want to ask a few questions about the cost measurements and then pursue one dimension of the problems that he has raised— the need for policies to address the issue of adaptation.

The chapter surveys many cost studies and identifies several ways in which the studies are limited. It would be very good to have some sense of the sensitivity of the cost estimates to these dimensions. For example, Nordhaus writes: "Forecasting climate changes at particular locations (such as in California or Cortina) has proven intractable." It would be useful to know the responsiveness of cost estimates to different distributions of temperature and precipitation changes, holding constant the average level of either temperature or precipitation.[2]

The cost estimates are focused on a typical point in the distant future (note 5). Yet the costs of adaptation may be large, depending on the speed with which the changes occur. And the lags are not well understood. Again it would be good to have an estimate of the sensitivity of costs (both short-run and present discounted value costs) to speed of change.

Nordhaus could not go into detail on the estimation methods in the many studies he cited. I suspect that competitive markets and no other externalities are implicit assumptions in many of these studies. Particularly with agriculture as the major source of both the costs and the benefits of changes and with agriculture as one of the most highly regulated sectors worldwide, the problem of estimating costs needs to reflect both current regulation and likely scenarios of future regulation. An essentially similar issue arises with estimating the costs of different policies to slow global warming (as Nordhaus recognizes in singling out some policies that are cheap—for example, slowing or curbing uneconomic deforestation). In considering such policies, one also needs to recognize the noncompetitive nature of the market for oil.

After proposing an extension of the set of cost estimates far beyond what can reasonably be done in the near future, I want to turn next to the issue of policies for adaptation. Nordhaus writes:

> The most important adaptations are those taken by *private* agents. . . . *Governments* also play an important role by ensuring that the legal and economic structure is conducive to adaptation, particularly by making sure that the environmental or climatic changes get reliably translated into the price and income signals that will induce private adaptation. Fulfilling this role may prove difficult because so many of the impacts of climate change are not properly priced.

He goes on to cite water as an example of an improperly priced resource. While he is right that the efficiency of the adaptation to a changed environment will be enhanced by allowing price signals to suitably encourage adaptation, I think it would be good to consider the policy environment that is likely to occur in more detail. In particular, it is worth thinking about this policy environment in advance if the legislation of general adaptation policies can decrease the extent of poor policy choice in the face of pressures arising from the impacts of climate changes.

While existing evidence suggests that it is very likely that climatic change will come slowly, it is possible that this view is wrong. Possibly more important is the likelihood that public awareness of the effects of global warming will come in bursts. If it is the arrival of a major destructive storm that leads people to conclude that rising sea levels should alter the location of economic activity in a major way, then there will be large and rapid changes in property values (from revised expectations) accompanying a high level of storm damage. Similarly, if it is a prolonged drought in some region that leads to the generally held conclusion that agricultural practices in some region have a limited future (or a need for massive changes), then again forward-looking property value revisions will coincide with large financial shocks. In such an environment, the political pressures for a rapid policy response make the design of good policies difficult. In both cases, there will be large pressures on the government to protect the incomes and wealth of the people involved from the effects of climate change. These pressures may have even larger political impact if the inactivity of the government is blamed for global warming.

It is right for governments to be concerned about the income-distribution impacts of differences in the future from what has been anticipated. The issue is to select redistributive policies that are efficient responses to both the outcomes realized and the risks faced. This process involves two dimensions. One is that the policies should be related to adapting to change rather than encouraging nonadaptation. The second is that the presence or likelihood of such policies should not result in too much lack of anticipatory self-protection. Let me consider two current parallels. Large impacts of imports on domestic industries are a widespread phenomenon. Protective policies preserve the costly industry in the face of changed circumstances. Policies to subsidize movement out of the industry can often be a more efficient response to a genuine income-distribution problem. Second, disaster relief is a common governmental response to earthquake and flood damage. Yet this encourages investment in vulnerable areas. The U.S. government has not done well in trying to limit such relief in a way that will discourage excessively risky investments.

Research to bring together the lessons of past responses to changed circumstances with the likely scenarios for future shocks would be very useful. In doing this, it would be good to recognize that some shocks will be financial rather than physical. Thus weather changes that raise agricultural outputs in some regions while lowering them in others are likely to imply changes in relative prices. Agricultural policies are already a major source of inefficiency and political tension. Examining how alternative agricultural policies would work in changing physical and political environments would be useful. Designing adaptation policies in advance (when political pressures are less), as well as designing them to withstand rising political pressures, has the potential to hold down the costs of responding to whatever events unfold and falls under Nordhaus's category of "all-weather" policies.

Notes

1. "These reflections lead to a surprising conclusion . . . a combination of gains and losses with no strong presumption of substantial net economic damages."

2. In table 2.3 the distribution of regional temperature change is given as −3° to +10° C; of precipitation, −20 to +20%.

3

Tax Policy to Combat Global Warming: On Designing a Carbon Tax

James Poterba

Mounting scientific evidence suggests that carbon dioxide emitted in fossil-fuel combustion contributes to global warming. This possibility has prompted discussion of carbon taxes, taxes levied in proportion to the carbon emissions that result from burning different fuels, in virtually all developed nations. Because each individual nation's contribution to global CO_2 emissions is relatively small, most advocates of the carbon tax call for coordinated multinational action. The long-run prospects for coordinated action appear dim, however. A tax large enough to significantly slow carbon dioxide emissions would collect revenues equal to several percent of world GDP, and it seems unlikely that national governments would cede control over such a pool of resources to any international body.

Most countries cannot noticeably slow the rate of global greenhouse gas emissions. Nevertheless, Finland, Sweden, and the Netherlands have taken unilateral action in adopting carbon taxes. Other nations may follow their lead, with revenues accruing to the domestic treasury. Most previous discussions of the carbon tax, however, have been concerned only with plans for multilateral action. This paper addresses a number of tax design issues that are likely to emerge if the current trend toward unilateral carbon tax adoption continues.

This chapter is divided into five sections. The first describes the basic structure of the carbon tax, focusing on the policies already in place in Europe as well as proposed taxes for the United States. The second section considers the distributional burden of carbon taxes across income groups. Household data for the United States suggest that the carbon tax falls most heavily on low-income groups. This regressivity could be ameliorated, however, in various ways. The third section examines the production and consumption distortions from a carbon tax, using a simple partial-equilibrium model of the energy market. These estimates do not correspond to the net efficiency cost of carbon taxes because they neglect the reduction in negative externalities associated with these taxes, but they indicate the cost that must be balanced against potential efficiency gains from the externality channel. The fourth section discusses the short- and long-run macroeconomic effects of adopting a carbon tax, drawing on previous empirical studies of the relationship between tax rates and real output growth. A central issue in this regard is the disposition of carbon tax revenues. If the tax proceeds are used to reduce other taxes, the adverse output effects of the tax would be significantly smaller than if they are used to finance higher government outlays for climate research or other programs. The macroeconomic effects of a carbon tax are also likely to depend on the way monetary authorities respond to the new levy. The fifth section considers several design issues relating to carbon taxes, such as harmonization with other greenhouse taxes and the difficulty of taxing fossil-fuel use in imported intermediate goods. There is a brief concluding section that discusses broader issues of policy design.

The Carbon Tax: Existing Legislation and Proposals

The carbon tax is a tax on carbon emissions generated by the combustion of fossil fuels. Of the three major fossil fuels, coal produces the most carbon per unit of energy, followed by oil and then natural gas. The carbon tax is a *specific* tax—that is, a fixed absolute amount per ton of coal or barrel of oil. The tax is designed to internalize the externalities associated with fuel consumption, so it should not vary with shocks to fuel prices as an ad valorem tax would.

To provide a perspective on the potential of a carbon tax to affect greenhouse warming, table 3.1 reports current gas emissions by nation. The entries are presented in terms of "equivalent tons of CO_2" using conversion factors developed by the World Resources Institute.[1] The table illustrates the importance of carbon dioxide in contributing to the global greenhouse. Carbon dioxide from fossil-fuel combustion currently accounts for 42 percent of net greenhouse emissions, and for 56 percent of the non-CFC emissions. This fraction is significant for long-range policy because current regulations in developed nations promise to reduce emissions of CFCs sharply during the coming decades. Because carbon dioxide emissions are also ex-

Table 3.1
Regional and national contributions to greenhouse warming

Country	CO$_2$ emissions	Methane emissions	CFC emissions	Total
Europe	0.520	0.085	0.480	1.085
United States	0.556[a]	0.130	0.350	1.036
USSR	0.450	0.060	0.180	0.690
Brazil	0.563[b]	0.028	0.016	0.607
China	0.260	0.090	0.032	0.382
Other	1.351	0.407	0.342	2.100
World	3.700	0.800	1.400	5.900

SOURCE: World Resources Institute, *World Resources, 1990–91*, Table 24.2. Each entry reports CO$_2$ equivalent emissions from different sources. Note that the fossil-fuel column includes CO$_2$ emissions from cement production.
a. 0.026 of this total due to land use.
b. 0.540 of this total due to land use.

pected to grow rapidly in the coming half century, CO$_2$ is even more important than the table suggests.

Table 3.1 also illustrates, however, that no single nation or group of nations is sufficiently important to affect the rate of global carbon emissions significantly. The United States, the largest carbon emitter, accounts for just over 20 percent of world CO$_2$ emissions from fossil-fuel consumption.[2] All of Europe accounts for an emission level comparable to that from the United States. Projected growth in energy utilization during the next century suggests that China will become an increasingly important source of carbon emissions as it uses its large coal deposits to spur industrialization.

Current Carbon Taxes

Despite the limited effect of any single nation's carbon tax on global warming, Sweden, Finland, and the Netherlands have already adopted such taxes. Flavin (1990) discusses a number of other proposals for action in Europe as well as particular states of the United States. Part of the argument for unilateral action is presumably to provide a role model for other nations. Table 3.2 shows the tax rates on coal, petroleum derivatives, and natural gas in each nation. The Swedish tax is levied at a rate of approximately $62 per ton of carbon, compared with approximately $6.50 per ton in Finland and $1.50 per ton in the Netherlands. The taxes in both Sweden and Finland are

Table 3.2
Carbon tax rates (U.S. dollars), Sweden, the Netherlands, and Finland, 1990

	Sweden	Netherlands	Finland
Gasoline and diesel fuel	$16.03/bbl	$2.73/bbl	$11.51/bbl[a]
Coal	97.69/ton	1.49/ton	3.89/ton
LPG	118.17/ton	1.94/ton	?
Natural gas	$2.63/10^3$ cu ft	$0.029/10^3$ cu ft	$0.08/10^3$ cu ft
Effective date	1/1991	2/1990	1/1990

NOTES: Calculations for Sweden assume an exchange rate of 5.75 SEK per dollar; those for the Netherlands assume 1.75 guilders to one dollar; and those for Finland assume a rate of 3.73 Finnish marks to one dollar.
a. The Finnish gasoline rate is uncertain because there are many levies beside the carbon tax that affect retail prices.

set at rates that reflect the marginal carbon emissions from each fuel. There are some divergences from this principle in the Dutch scheme, which places a higher relative tax on petroleum derivatives than the carbon criterion alone would suggest.

Carbon taxes are not the only excises on fossil fuels in any of the nations that have adopted them. In Finland, for example, the tax rate on gasoline and diesel fuel is higher than that required for "carbon parity" with the coal tax as a result of the traffic-fuels tax. In Sweden, a preexisting tax on all energy was cut in half when the carbon tax was enacted, but the total tax rates on different energy sources still reflect the sum of the general energy tax and the carbon levy. The net taxes on different fuels are thus not dictated by their carbon contents alone; the analysis later in this chapter suggests that they should not be.

Although the United States does not have a carbon tax, several proposals for such a tax are before Congress. For example, H.R. 4805, a bill introduced by Representative Pete Stark, calls for a tax of $15.00 a ton on coal, $3.25 per barrel on oil, and $0.40 per MCF on natural gas. These tax rates are well below those which a recent study by the Congressional Budget Office (1990) suggests would stabilize carbon dioxide emissions at their 1988 level by the year 2000.

Table 3.3 provides descriptive information on the policy analyzed by the Congressional Budget Office, a $100 a ton carbon tax, as well as a more modest tax of $5 a ton that would be roughly equivalent to the tax per unit of greenhouse gas activity embodied in U.S. taxes on chlorofluorocarbons. The table reports the specific tax rates on coal, oil, and natural gas, and also shows the percentage change in

Table 3.3
Proposed CO_2 stabilization and reduction taxes, United States

	Coal (ton)	Oil (barrel)	Natural gas (10^3 cu ft)
Tons of carbon/unit of fuel	0.605	0.130	0.016
Carbon emissions/billion BTUs	0.025	0.020	0.015
Average mine-mouth or wellhead price, 1989	$23.02	$17.70	$1.78
CO_2 stabilization tax ($100/ton)			
Absolute tax	$60.50	$12.99	$1.63
Percentage of price	263%	73%	92%
Slower CO_2 growth tax ($5/ton)			
Absolute tax	$3.17	$0.65	$0.08
Percentage of price	13%	4%	5%

NOTES: Data for row 3 are drawn from Manne and Richels (1989), for row 4 from the U.S. Department of Energy (1990), and for rows 2 and 5 from the Congressional Budget Office (1990). Rows 6 and 7 are based on author's calculations.

fossil-fuel prices as a share of the wellhead or mine-mouth price. The CO_2 stabilization tax would raise coal prices to roughly four times their current level. Natural gas prices would nearly double, and oil prices would increase more than 60 percent. The price changes are proportionately smaller under the more modest carbon tax plan.

The carbon tax applies only to fossil fuels. In this way it differs from an across-the-board energy tax, for example a BTU tax, since it encourages both energy conservation and substitution toward energy sources like hydro power or nuclear power that do not emit carbon dioxide. It also differs from targeted excises such as a gasoline tax in taxing all combustion of fossil fuels, rather than those in particular industries or applications. Levying higher taxes on only some segments of fossil-fuel use requires higher tax rates on the taxed sectors to achieve a given reduction in emissions, and also introduces distortions across uses. There is little reason to introduce these distortions if the ultimate aim of policy is reducing the level of greenhouse emissions at least cost.

The Revenue Potential of Carbon Taxes

Carbon taxes have the potential to generate substantial revenues for most developed countries. Table 3.4 illustrates this point, showing

Table 3.4
Fossil-fuel consumption and revenues from $100/ton carbon tax

Country	Fossil-fuel consumption			Carbon tax revenues	
	Coal (million tons)	Petroleum (million bbl)	Natural gas (billion cu ft)	Level[a]	Percent of GNP
OECD Europe	609	4,511	8,812	109.8	1.99
France	32	656	1,007	12.1	1.28
West Germany	211	884	2,075	27.7	2.30
Italy	25	660	1,283	12.1	1.47
United Kingdom	124	613	1,990	18.8	2.31
Canada	60	584	2,353	15.1	3.12
United States	883	6,308	17,933	164.6	3.42
Japan	125	1,727	1,586	32.6	1.15
OECD total	1,776	13,482	31,332	333.7	2.40

SOURCE: U.S. Department of Energy, *International Energy Annual, 1988* (Washington, DC: Government Printing Office).
a. Billions of 1988 U.S. dollars.

total consumption of each of the three fossil fuels as well as carbon tax revenues from a $100/ton carbon tax. The ratio of revenues to GNP is highest in the United States, the most fossil-fuel-intensive nation. A $100/ton carbon tax would raise revenues of more than 3 percent of GNP. By comparison, the same tax would raise only 1.2 percent of GNP if instituted in Japan. This difference reflects the greater energy efficiency of the Japanese economy.

A central issue in carbon tax design involves who receives the revenue. As Schelling aptly observes in Chapter 6 of this book, no industrialized nation is likely to surrender control over revenues equal to one-thirtieth (or even one-hundredth) of GNP to an international organization. Proposals for a global carbon tax therefore face a dilemma. If the tax rate is high enough to reduce emissions significantly, few if any countries will allow an international agency to collect the taxes. If the tax rate is low enough to make an international agency operational, however, it is unlikely to discourage significant amounts of fossil-fuel combustion. The next several sections therefore concentrate on unilateral domestic carbon taxes.

Distributional Incidence of Carbon Taxes

One of the central objections to adopting carbon taxes in developed nations is the perceived regressivity of excise taxes, of which carbon taxes are an example. Claims of excise tax regressivity typically rely on annual surveys of consumer income and expenditures which show that energy expenditures are a larger fraction of income for very-low-income households than for middle- or high-income households. A household's annual income may be an unreliable indicator of its actual well-being, however. The essence of the life-cycle and permanent-income theories of consumption is that household income may vary from year to year, for both predictable and stochastic reasons, but that consumption is set on the basis of long-run income. These theories imply that a household's total expenditures may be a more reliable indicator of economic well-being than the same household's annual income.[3]

This section uses data from the United States' Consumer Expenditure Survey to assess the claim that carbon taxes are regressive, measuring household well-being on the basis of both annual income and consumption outlays. The results support the view that a carbon tax is regressive, but the findings based on the expenditure measure of incidence are less dramatic than those based on income rankings. They nevertheless suggest that if a carbon tax were adopted without any offsetting changes in other tax or transfer programs, the burden would fall more heavily on low-income than well-off households.

Energy Expenditure Patterns

The 1985 Consumer Expenditure Survey is a stratified national sample of approximately 2,000 households.[4] To illustrate patterns of energy expenditures across the distribution of household well-being, households are grouped into deciles based either on their income in the previous quarter or their total expenditures in the current quarter. Table 3.5 shows the average expenditure patterns for households in each of these categories, focusing on outlays for heating oil, gasoline, electricity, and natural gas. There are some omitted energy outlays, such as direct household outlays for coal and wood, but these are a small fraction of the outlays shown in the table.

Since energy is a necessity, it is not surprising that the share of income that low-income households devote to heating fuel, electricity, and gasoline is significantly higher than that of better-off households. The upper panel in table 3.5 classifies households by income and reports energy expenditures as a share of income. For the lowest income decile, which spends substantially more than its income, both gasoline and electricity outlays exceed 10 percent of income. Because many households in the bottom income strata may be experiencing transitory income reductions, however, a more reliable picture of the distribution of energy outlays emerges from focusing on the second and third income deciles versus the top deciles. These data suggest a clear pattern of larger outlays as a share of income at lower rather than higher income levels. Total energy outlays for households at the 25th percentile of the income distribution are approximately 16 percent of income, compared with only 7 percent for households at the 75th percentile of the distribution.

The lower panel in table 3.5 presents comparable data with households grouped into deciles according to total expenditures. The results are significantly different from those based on the income ranking, and indicate the potential importance of choosing among the alternative approaches to measuring distributional incidence. The disparity between the shares of income devoted to various energy sources at low and high incomes is much larger than the variation in

Table 3.5
Distribution of energy expenditures, United States, 1986

Income decile	Expenditures as a percentage of income			
	Natural gas	Fuel oil	Gasoline	Electricity
1 (lowest)	4.6	2.0	14.7	12.6
2	3.9	0.6	6.1	6.3
3	3.1	0.6	6.7	5.2
4	2.7	0.6	6.3	4.6
5	2.1	0.5	5.6	4.0
6	1.5	0.5	5.2	3.1
7	1.3	0.4	4.5	2.8
8	1.0	0.3	4.2	2.4
9	0.9	0.3	3.8	2.1
10	0.7	0.1	2.5	1.6

Expenditure decile	Expenditures as a percentage of total outlays			
	Natural gas	Fuel oil	Gasoline	Electricity
1 (lowest)	2.4	0.4	5.2	4.8
2	2.8	0.3	4.1	4.5
3	2.3	0.5	5.6	4.3
4	2.3	0.5	5.3	3.8
5	2.1	0.4	5.5	3.6
6	1.7	0.4	5.8	3.5
7	1.6	0.4	5.6	3.6
8	1.3	0.4	5.6	3.1
9	1.2	0.4	5.2	2.9
10	1.1	0.2	4.2	2.7

SOURCE: Author's tabulations based on 1985–1986 Consumer Expenditure Survey.

expenditure shares between low- and high-expenditure households. For example, a household in the second expenditure decile devotes approximately 12 percent of total outlays to energy items, compared with just under 10 percent for a household in the ninth expenditure decile. The ratio of income shares devoted to energy for households in the second and ninth income deciles, by comparison, is more than two to one.

The expenditure ranking is likely to provide a better perspective on the distributional burden of energy outlays and associated taxes for two reasons. First, some households experience transitory shocks to income—unemployment or illness, for example—and their expenditures will reflect long-run economic circumstances rather than transitory conditions. Second, life-cycle variation in the outlay-income ratio—for example, periods of low income relative to expenditure during retirement—can make current income a misleading guide to economic well-being. The data in table 3.5 thus suggest that energy outlays are higher among less well-off households, but not by as much as typical incidence measures might suggest.

Carbon Tax Burdens

The energy expenditure patterns in table 3.5 are a critical input in analyzing the distributional burden of the carbon tax. The analysis that follows considers a specific proposal: a $100/ton carbon tax instituted in 1990.[5] This avoids the problem of forecasting energy producer prices in future years, and it also corresponds better to the available data on expenditure patterns. The analysis also assumes that the United States imposes a unilateral carbon tax, so that producer prices of each fossil fuel are unaffected; there is complete forward-shifting of the tax.

These assumptions translate into substantial increases in the retail prices of fossil fuels. Based on projected retail energy prices in the year 2000, as reported by the U.S. Energy Department (1990), the retail prices of fuel oil and gasoline would rise by 27 percent and 25 percent, respectively, the retail price of natural gas by 23 percent, and the retail price of coal by 114 percent. The other important component of the incidence calculation is the change in electricity prices. Although coal accounts for 57 percent of the electrical generating capacity in the United States, compared with 5.5 percent for oil and 9.4 percent for natural gas, coal costs are only 17.1 percent of the total for U.S. electrical generation.[6] Petroleum accounts for 4.4 percent of total costs, and natural gas for another 8.7 percent. These fractions have shifted significantly during the last fifteen years as U.S. electric utilities have converted from oil to coal to reduce the nation's oil imports. Following the *Annual Energy Outlook* (1990) assumptions regarding the difference between the retail prices of fossil fuels and those faced by utilities, the retail price of electricity is estimated to rise by 36 percent as a result of a $100/ton carbon tax.

Estimated changes in retail prices can be combined with the data on energy expenditure patterns in table 3.5 to estimate the distributional burden of the carbon tax. Results of this exercise are shown in table

Table 3.6
Distributional incidence of $100/ton carbon tax, United States, 1986

Income decile	Distribution across income classes	
	Total burden	Percent of income
1 (lowest)	$451.9	10.1
2	374.6	5.0
3	484.6	4.6
4	521.0	4.1
5	563.7	3.6
6	608.6	3.0
7	689.6	2.7
8	762.6	2.3
9	875.3	2.1
10	889.7	1.5

Expenditure decile	Distribution across expenditure classes	
	Total burden	Percent of outlays
1 (lowest)	$252.5	3.7
2	349.8	3.7
3	465.6	3.8
4	527.5	3.7
5	588.6	3.4
6	681.3	3.4
7	772.3	3.2
8	804.2	2.8
9	944.2	2.7
10	871.4	2.3

SOURCE: Author's tabulations based on 1985–1986 Consumer Expenditure Survey.

3.6, which reports both the absolute dollar cost and the extra outlays as a share of income and expenditures for various income and outlay deciles. The tabulations suggest that carbon taxes are regressive, regardless of whether income or expenditures are used as the basis for ranking households. For households in the bottom three income deciles, for example, a $100/ton carbon tax would pose an average burden of more than 5 percent of annual income. For households in the top two income deciles, the estimated burden is less than 2 percent. The disparities in the estimated burdens are smaller when expenditure rather than income is used to rank households, but these differences are still substantial. Households in the bottom three expenditure deciles would face burdens which averaged 3.7 percent of their total expenditures, while the burdens for those in the top three deciles would average 2.6 percent of total outlays. The relative burden declines smoothly as one moves up the expenditure distribution.[7] Although these calculations relate to the $100/ton carbon tax, the general distributional pattern would apply to any carbon tax. A $5/ton tax, for example, would impose costs of roughly one-twentieth those reported in table 3.6.

These findings do not completely describe the distributional incidence of carbon taxes. First, they ignore the general equilibrium effects of higher fossil-fuel prices. The prices of steel, aluminum, autos, and other energy-intensive commodities would rise in response to a carbon tax. While the magnitude of these price changes will be smaller than the first-order effects analyzed here, they should be addressed in future work. Second, the analysis ignores asset market effects. Even if the world price of fossil fuels stays fixed, the returns to intermediaries, such as oil refiners and distributors, would fall. If this reduced the value of equities in oil companies, it would appear as an additional burden falling primarily on those in the higher income and expenditure categories. Finally, the analysis neglects the macroeconomic effects that might follow from enactment of a carbon tax. If households at different points in the income or expenditure distribution face different exposures to unemployment, then slower growth would burden households differentially.

Policies to Offset Regressivity

The carbon tax would be regressive if it were instituted as a standalone policy. However, this is not an especially plausible scenario. The recent history of tax policy in most industrial nations suggests strong political resistance to imposing higher taxes that particularly burden the poor. A central issue is therefore likely to involve designing schemes to neutralize the distributional effects of the carbon tax.

Several policies would reduce the burdens on low-income and low-expenditure households. First, many transfer programs are already indexed for price changes. Since the carbon tax will be paid by consumers in the form of higher retail prices, indexed components of income will partly adjust to offset the tax burdens. In the United States, for example, two-thirds of the income received by households in the lowest expenditure decile is indexed, reflecting the importance of elderly families who receive Social Security as well as other transfer recipients in this group.[8]

Indexed income is not a complete antidote to carbon tax regressivity. Not all low-income households are transfer recipients, and even for those who are, the data in table 3.5 show that their expenditure patterns place more weight than average on energy outlays. Thus transfer adjustments based on average budgets will undercompensate low-income or low-expenditure households for their higher energy prices.

A second approach to ameliorating the distributional burdens of the carbon tax is increased use of redistributive income taxes. In the United States, for example, the earned income tax credit (EITC) provides a natural device for reducing the tax burdens on those low-income households who receive labor income rather than transfers. Changing the level of personal allowances in the tax code would provide another way to redistribute toward low-income and low-expenditure households, although with different incentive effects.

Still a third approach to reducing regressivity would be an explicit policy of tax credits for energy expenditures. Allowing each household a tax credit equal to the first 1 or 2 percent of income devoted to purchasing energy would enable the tax authorities to alter the *average* price of energy, hence blunting the carbon tax's redistributive effects, while preserving the marginal price effects of the tax.

None of these redistributive schemes will completely offset the distributional impact of a carbon tax. If transfers are increased, households who do not receive transfers will still be worse off. If tax credits are used, households with incomes below the tax-filing threshold will not be compensated. Yet the distributional effects of the carbon tax do not appear insuperable. A combination of income tax and transfer policies could be used to neutralize the tax reform for most households.

Production and Consumption Distortions from a Carbon Tax

A carbon tax would affect the behavior of firms and consumers. By raising the price of fossil fuels relative to other energy sources, and by changing the relative prices of different fossil fuels, the tax would induce both interfuel substitution and lower energy consumption. Although these changes may on balance be beneficial because of their long-run effects on global climate, they nevertheless represent production and consumption distortions relative to the no-tax scenario. The costs associated with these distortions must be balanced against the benefits from reduced "bad" externalities, i.e., the lower risk of global warming. This section presents simple estimates of these costs.

Partial Equilibrium Tax Analysis

The standard approximation for the deadweight loss from a commodity tax *when there are no external effects associated with consumption of the good* is $DWL = dQ \cdot dq/2$, where Q is the quantity and q is the consumer price of the good. The derivatives represent the effects of a small tax imposed with no preexisting taxes, and the analysis takes prices in all other markets as given and fixes producer prices in the market being analyzed. When only one price is affected by a specific tax, a convenient expression for this efficiency cost is

$$DWL = \eta_D \cdot (\tau/p)^2 \cdot (pQ)/2. \tag{1}$$

In this expression, η_D is the compensated elasticity of product demand, τ is the specific tax rate, and p is the (fixed) producer price.

When several prices change, as when a carbon tax alters the prices of coal, oil, and natural gas, the analysis must recognize both own- and cross-price effects. This consideration is particularly important in the current context, where changes in the prices of all three fossil fuels will lead to smaller changes in the demand for each fuel than would changes in each market in isolation. In this case, the cost of production and consumption distortions is given by

$$DWL_i' = \left[\sum_{j=1}^{j} \epsilon_{ij}(\tau_{j/pj}) \right] \cdot Q_i p_i \cdot (\tau_i/p_i)/2. \tag{2}$$

The bracketed expression represents the proportional change in the quantity of good i demanded as a result of tax changes in each of the j markets.[9]

These results involve a first-order approximation that applies to small taxes introduced around the no-tax equilibrium. Coordinated international action with respect to carbon taxes would inevitably alter producer prices for fossil fuels. For unilateral policies, however, it is more natural to treat the world fossil-fuel price as fixed. The partial equilibrium framework may be suitable for this problem, even though for larger taxes it is necessary to use computable general-equilibrium models.[10]

Table 3.7
Production and consumption distortions for carbon taxes, United States

	Coal	Oil	Natural gas
Domestic use[a]	20	304	33
Demand elasticities			
Coal	-0.56	0.22	0.16
Oil	0.10	-0.70	0.10
Natural gas	0.12	0.13	-0.52
Slower CO_2 growth tax ($5/ton)			
Percentage of price	13	4	5
Deadweight loss[a]	0.09	0.17	0.02

SOURCE: Row 1 is drawn from table 3.4, row 2 from the *Annual Energy Outlook, 1990*, rows 2–4 from Anderson, Hoffman, and Rusin (1990), and rows 5 and 6 are the author's calculations.
a. Billions of 1989 U.S. dollars.

Demand elasticities are the central parameters needed to estimate the deadweight burden of carbon taxes. There is a voluminous previous literature devoted to the estimation of energy demand; Bohi (1981) surveys this field. Energy demand elasticities are very sensitive to the horizon being analyzed; short-run elasticities are far smaller than long-run values. With respect to gasoline, for example, Pindyck (1979) reports a first-year demand elasticity of −0.11, rising to −0.49 at a five-year horizon and −0.82 at ten years. The dramatic differences are due to the variety of margins on which consumers can optimize. In the first year after a price shock, most of the response takes the form of reduced driving, but over longer runs there is a change in fuel efficiency of the auto fleet that exerts much more important effects on gasoline demand. Similarly, in industry, the short-run response to energy price changes will involve changes in the scale of operations; in the longer run, capital equipment may be modified or replaced to optimally adapt to the new price regime.

Table 3.7 presents benchmark own-price demand elasticities for coal, oil, and natural gas for use in deadweight loss calculations. These reflect consensus estimates as reported by Anderson, Hofmann, and Rusin (1990). They are within the range of long-run elasticities reported by Bohi (1981), although they are lower than some of the final-demand energy elasticities he reports. For evaluating the carbon tax, however, the elasticities of interest are those for coal, crude oil, or natural gas demand with respect to the mine-mouth or wellhead price. The comparison of these values with retail gasoline price elasticities, for example, is therefore inappropriate. Nevertheless, it is important to understand that low elasticity estimates imply small deadweight losses; the efficiency cost is proportional to the elasticity. Thus it is straightforward to evaluate the sensitivity of the results to, for example, a doubling of each own-price elasticity.[11] The table also shows significant cross-price elasticities for the various fossil fuels.

Estimating Production and Consumption Distortions

The local approximation approach described in the preceding section is unsuitable for analyzing the effects of large tax changes such as the $100/ton CO_2 stabilization tax for the United States discussed previously. This tax would raise coal prices by 263 percent, and oil and gas prices by between 70 and 100 percent. This approach can, however, be used to analyze smaller tax changes, such as the $5/ton carbon tax that has been suggested by Nordhaus (1990b).[12]

The results of this calculation, which are presented in table 3.7, suggest that distortionary costs are not a critical consideration in evaluating low-rate carbon taxes. The total production and consumption distortion in the three markets is less than $300 million, measured in 1989 dollars, or less than 0.01 percent of GNP. At least for policies like the "precautionary" carbon tax, the efficiency loss from the tax would be small.[13] This analysis awaits further confirmation using general equilibrium modeling tools.

Macroeconomic Effects of Carbon Taxes

The efficiency costs isolated in this chapter correspond to the distortions in firm and household behavior in an economy with otherwise perfect markets. In such a setting, these would be the only effects of enacting a carbon tax. Prices of many goods would adjust to the tax, but such adjustments would not generate any macroeconomic effects. In practice, both nominal wages and nominal prices are costly to adjust, and excise tax shocks can have real effects. A number of recent studies[14] indicate that adopting the sort of carbon tax considered here would reduce U.S. real GNP by between 1 and 3 percent.

There are two channels through which a carbon tax could have such effects. First, a $100/ton carbon tax adopted without any offsetting policies would substantially reduce the federal deficit. Estimates for the United States suggest that such a tax would collect revenues of more than 3 percent of GNP. This would represent a radical shift toward contractionary fiscal policy. While deficit reduction might convey long-run benefits, in the short run there might be adverse macroeconomic effects. These might result from the higher overall tax rates, direct and indirect, associated with such a policy; this could discourage labor supply, for example.

A carbon tax need not raise revenue, however. It could be combined with other fiscal reforms to ensure revenue neutrality. In European countries that rely on indirect taxes for significant revenue shares, a natural policy would involve reducing the VAT or other excise tax rates when the carbon tax is introduced. For the United States, it would be possible to reduce income taxes to offset carbon tax revenues. The critical simulation is thus a *revenue neutral* increase in carbon taxes, and this has not usually been reported in the prior literature.

The second channel through which a carbon tax could affect real output involves the sluggish adjustment of wages and prices in response to higher taxes. The importance of these effects depends critically on how monetary policy responds to the tax policy shock. To illustrate this effect, consider enactment of a carbon tax with an offsetting reduction in labor income taxes.[15] The household's after-tax real wage is given by $w(1 - \beta)/p(1 + \theta)$, where β is the labor income tax rate and θ is the total indirect tax rate. The real wage facing firms is w/p, where w is the nominal wage paid by the firm and p is the producer price level. The revenue neutrality of the tax policy should keep $(1 - \beta)/(1 + \theta)$ approximately constant, so the producer real wage that was an equilibrium before the tax shock will also be an equilibrium after it.

In the money market, the real supply of money $M/[p(1 + \theta)]$ equals the demand, which in turn depends on real output. If output were unaffected by the tax change *and the money supply were also fixed,* then an increase in θ would require a reduction in producer prices p. If prices were fully flexible, higher indirect taxes would lead to an immediate and equiproportionate fall in producer prices and wages, and there would be no effects on real activity. If nominal wages are slow to adjust, however, then the fall in producer prices following the tax change will raise the real wage facing firms. This wage increase will reduce labor demand and lower real output.

This scenario need not occur, however. If the monetary authority increases the supply of money to accommodate the tax increase, then the initial level of w and p will continue to be an equilibrium; the only difference is that the price *level* will be higher after the indirect tax increase than before. The extent to which a revenue-neutral shift to indirect taxes such as the carbon tax raises prices, and the extent to which it reduces output, therefore depends on the monetary response to the fiscal change.

The importance of price rigidities, and hence the magnitude of the forgone output associated with adoption of a carbon tax, is controversial. The empirical evidence presented in Poterba, Rotemberg, and Summers (1986) suggests that a shift of 3 percent of GNP from direct to indirect taxation would reduce real GNP by 0.6 percent in the quarter when the tax change took effect. The lost output in the first three years after the tax policy takes effect is nearly 3 percent of one year's GNP.

One important feature of this analysis, which relies on price rigidities, is that in the long run a revenue-neutral shift to higher energy taxes would not affect real activity. This view is inconsistent with the finding of some recent studies that suggest that higher energy prices would adversely affect long-run productivity growth rates and therefore have progressively larger adverse effects on economic performance. If the growth slowdown coincident with, and following, the 1973 oil price shock is attributed to higher energy prices, taxes that raised energy prices would be predicted to have similar effects in the future. Whether the productivity slowdown of the 1970s was caused by the oil price shock or actually began well before the price increase is an open issue with obvious implications for policy analysts concerned with global warming.

Implementing Carbon Taxes

This section addresses four issues which arise in implementing carbon taxes: the choice of carbon taxes in the presence of other externalities, the control of cross-border energy flows, the subsidization of processes which withdraw carbon from the atmosphere, and the harmonization of the carbon tax and other taxes which affect greenhouse emissions. Each of these issues is considered in turn.

The Greenhouse and Other Externalities

While excise tax rates on fossil fuels that are proportional to their CO_2 output may be appropriate to correct greenhouse externalities, they are not necessarily the *optimal* tax rates on the different fossil fuels. Standard results on optimal taxation in the presence of externalities—for example, Sandmo (1975)—recognize that optimal tax rates depend on three factors: (1) the net externalities associated with a good's consumption; (2) the distribution of a good's consumption across households with different marginal social welfare weights; and (3) (if there is a positive revenue requirement) the compensated elasticities of demand for the taxed good, as well as other goods, with respect to the price of the taxed commodity.

A detailed calculation of "the" optimal tax rates on various fossil fuels is beyond this paper, but it is possible to sketch how other considerations might affect optimal taxes. First, with respect to other externalities, coal is a more substantial contributor to other types of air pollution (sulfur dioxides and particulates, for example) than either oil or natural gas. Estimates of the externality costs of these emissions vary. In the case of sulfur emissions, however, Bernow and Marron (1990) suggest a value of $1,500/ton of SO_x. For the United States, average SO_x emissions per ton of coal burned by electric utilities are approximately 42.2 pounds,[16] suggesting an externality cost of $32. Similar calculations could be performed for other pollutants and other fuel sources to find the total externality-correcting taxes that are needed.

Second, distributional considerations do not yield particularly strong guidance in setting the relative tax rates on the different fossil fuels. Table 3.5 suggested that electricity outlays are skewed more toward low-income households than are expenditures for other types of fossil fuels. Since coal is important for electricity generation but not for direct energy purchases, this observation would suggest *ceteris paribus* that tax rates on coal should be lower. One issue that might warrant attention concerns the burden of reduced coal output. Coal miners bear the brunt of such changes, and previous policy debates have explicitly considered compensation plans to avoid these effects (see Congressional Budget Office 1986).

Carbon Taxes and Border Controls

One of the major administrative concerns with a unilateral carbon tax concerns imports. The appropriate taxes on domestic fossil fuel production are relatively straightforward to enforce, as are the taxes on imports of coal, natural gas, and petroleum derivates. More difficult assessment problems arise with respect to imports of intermedi-

Table 3.8
Fossil fuel embodied in U.S. imports, 1985

	Direct U.S. consumption	Energy imports	Energy embodied in nonenergy imports
Coal (million tons)	773.6	2.9	106.3
Refined petroleum (million bbls)	5,632.2	69.2	340.8
Natural gas (billion cu ft)	16,372.3	920.9	1,910.9

SOURCE: Author's calculations based on U.S. Congress, Office of Technology Assessment (1990).

NOTE: If row 2 focused on crude oil, the entries would be 4603, 1189, and 278.2, respectively.

ate or final goods that have been produced using fossil fuels. Unilateral carbon tax policies that do not effectively tax such commodities could be unattractive both because they create production inefficiencies, distorting production of these intermediate goods away from domestic locations, and because the opportunities for offshore production reduce the revenue potential of the tax.

Table 3.8 presents evidence directed at the potential importance of this problem. The table synthesizes information from the 1985 input-output table of the U.S. economy developed by the U.S. Congress, Office of Technology Assessment (1990). The first column shows direct U.S. consumption of oil, coal, and natural gas.[17] This is the total of fossil-fuel use in either production or household activities for the year in question. Column 2 shows energy imports. This component of imported fossil fuel would be relatively easy to tax. The third column shows the amount of fossil fuel embodied in non-fossil-fuel U.S. imports. These estimates were made using the 1985 input-output table, which shows the total inputs of coal, oil, and natural gas to each of eighty-five categories of goods. Combining these data with information on the value of imports in each category and assuming that the energy use coefficients for foreign production are the same as those in the United States yields estimates of the amount of each fossil fuel that was used in producing imported goods.

Two conclusions emerge from this table. First, the embodied energy imports are not trivial. The estimate in the third column equals approximately one-eighth of total coal consumption, one-tenth of natural gas use, and one-twentieth of refined petroleum use. Closer inspection of the goods that account for embodied energy imports, however, shows that relatively few imports—steel, autos, and chemicals are the three most important—account for a very large share of the embodied fossil fuels. It would not seem particularly difficult to levy import duties on these goods in proportion to their estimated carbon emissions.[18]

Taxing Emissions versus Subsidizing Carbon Sequestering

The carbon tax raises the cost of adding carbon dioxide to the atmosphere. It does not, however, provide similar incentives for all methods of altering the global carbon balance. A notable omission is that a carbon tax does not reward activities that *remove* carbon from the atmosphere; tree planting is an obvious example of such a carbon-sequestering policy. Just as advocates of tradable permits in more standard pollution contexts have long argued for equating the marginal costs of each alternative method of changing the ambient level of various pollutants, there is an argument for subsidizing projects that reduce the level of global carbon.

A number of administrative issues make the implementation of carbon-sequestering subsidies difficult, however. The net private cost of some sequestering activities, such as tree planting, is small relative to the potential public subsidy. If the subsidy assumes that trees live for many years and draw CO_2 from the atmosphere over their lifetime, tax cheats could plant trees, collect their subsidy, destroy the trees, and collect another subsidy. There are of course ways to minimize these problems: subsidies could be tied to the land on which the trees are planted, limiting each property to no more than one subsidy each fifteen or twenty years. Alternatively, the subsidy could be provided incrementally in each year the trees are alive.

A workable system of subsidies for carbon sequestering might be devised, but it would require a higher degree of administrative organization than a carbon tax. Rather than burdening a relatively simple carbon tax plan with the complexities associated with policing carbon sequestering, policy in this area might begin with a relatively small carbon tax and then address issues of carbon sequestering at a later date.

Carbon Taxes versus CFC Taxes

The carbon tax is not the only fiscal instrument that affects the emission of greenhouse gases. A number of nations have already adopted

Table 3.9
Chlorofluorocarbon (CFC-11 and CFC-12) tax rates, United States

Year	Tax rate (dollars/pound)	Implied carbon tax (dollars/ton)
1990	1.37	1.16
1991	1.37	1.16
1992	1.67	1.41
1993	2.65	2.24
1994	2.65	2.24
1995	3.10	2.62
1996	3.55	3.00
⋮	⋮	⋮
2000	5.35	4.52

SOURCE: Column 1: U.S. Congress, Joint Committee on Taxation (1990). Column 2: Author's estimate using Nordhaus's (1990b) calculations of the equivalent CO_2 emissions per ton of CFC-11/12 gas. I use the Nordhaus estimate of this ratio assuming a discount rate of 1 percent per year.

limits or taxes on CFC emissions; they are currently taxed in the United States according to the sliding rate scale shown in table 3.9. One policy design issue that can readily be addressed involves setting appropriate relative tax rates on CFCs and fossil fuels. This requires data on the relative contribution of the various gases (per unit emitted) to greenhouse warming; in turn, information on the time profile of greenhouse effects for the various gases, as well as the social time preference rate, is required. Nordhaus (1990a) explores the links between the relative greenhouse effects of different emissions and finds that with a social discount rate of 1 percent per year, 1 pound of CFC-11/12 has the same ultimate greenhouse effect as 1.184 *tons* of carbon emitted as CO_2 (4.34 tons of CO_2).[19]

If the only justification for taxing both carbon emissions and CFCs is to avoid long-run global warming, then the tax rates on the two gases should be set in proportion to their greenhouse effects. The second column of table 3.9 shows the carbon taxes associated with current U.S. CFC tax levels. If a carbon tax were adopted, some attempt to bring the rates of CFC and carbon taxation into rough agreement would clearly be useful.

Other Issues

There are many questions concerning carbon tax design and implementation, such as the phase-in rules that would be adopted, the treatment of exports (can firms claim rebates for fossil fuels used in exported products?), and the procedures for handling claims that some firms or households use fossil fuels in ways that reduce CO_2 emissions relative to standard estimates. These and other issues would need to be addressed if a carbon tax were enacted. Relative to many other fiscal instruments, however, the carbon tax seems straightforward to specify and enforce.

Conclusions: General Principles to Guide Policy

This paper has analyzed a variety of issues associated with the design and implementation of a carbon tax. Several findings emerge. First, if implemented without any offsetting changes in transfer programs, the carbon tax would be regressive. There are many ways to reduce this regressivity—for example, with offsetting changes in either the direct tax system or transfers. Second, the efficiency costs of small carbon taxes, such as a tax of $5/ton of carbon, are relatively small. For the United States, immediate implementation of such a tax would impose annual efficiency costs of less than $1 billion. Although some analyses have called for taxes at this level until further information on global warming becomes available, other proposals suggest far higher taxes. Stabilizing U.S. carbon dioxide emissions at their 1988 levels by the year 2000, for example, would require a carbon tax of close to $100 per ton. This tax, which would more than triple the producer price of coal and nearly double the producer prices of petroleum and natural gas, would have much more significant efficiency effects. Implementing such a policy might also affect the level of real output unless the monetary authority fully compensated for the tax by raising the money supply. Third, a central issue of carbon tax design is harmonization with other fiscal instruments designed to reduce greenhouse warming. Ensuring comparability between tax rates on chlorofluorocarbons and fossil fuels is particularly important in order to avoid unnecessary distortions in production and consumption decisions.

   Although this chapter concentrates on rather narrow issues involving carbon taxes, several broader issues of policy design should also be recognized. First, concerted international action in adopting carbon taxes would avoid some of the administrative difficulties and distortionary effects of unilateral carbon tax adoption. If all nations participate in a carbon tax treaty, then the tax can be implemented by taxing all fossil fuel production at mine mouth or wellhead. If a single country adopts the tax, however, it becomes necessary to tax both imported fossil fuels and other products that may embody fossil fuels. The multilateral approach, while solving this problem, raises additional questions concerning compensation and the appropriate distribution of revenues across nations.

Second, the current uncertainties regarding the future course of the global environment suggest the need for policy flexibility. It is important to avoid substantial efficiency costs or output losses *today* in pursuit of uncertain future benefits.[20] Because much new information is likely to accumulate in the next decades both on the scientific basis of the greenhouse effect and on the economic costs of countermeasures, current policy should avoid irreversible decisions. Losses in real output from high current taxes *are* irreversible. There is relatively little doubt that sharp increases in energy prices from a carbon tax large enough to stabilize CO_2 emissions near current levels would have significant adverse effects on real GNP. A strong case for the benefits of such a tax burden is therefore needed to outweigh these costs.

Third, it is important to recognize that economic policy toward reducing greenhouse emissions is part of a broader fabric of fiscal policy to encourage economic growth, promote equitable distribution, and internalize external effects. Some of these concerns operate directly with respect to the appropriate levies on fossil fuels, and optimal tax rates on these fuels should not be determined solely by reference to carbon emission levels. The current concern with greenhouse emissions may, however, provide a long-needed stimulus for attempting to calibrate and implement these tax policies.

Notes

I am grateful to the Istituto San Paolo di Torino, the NSF, the MIT Center for Energy Policy Research, and the John M. Olin Foundation for research support. Hilary Sigman provided outstanding research assistance. I am grateful to Peter Diamond, Paul Joskow, Lester Lave, Nancy Rose, Lawrence Summers, John Whalley, and especially William Nordhaus for helpful discussions.

1. Nordhaus (1990a) uses a different metric for converting different greenhouse gases into equivalent units from the estimates by the World Resources Institute (WRI) in table 3.1. The Nordhaus approach suggests that total CO_2 emissions account for 69 percent of current greenhouse emissions, compared with 63 percent in the WRI tabulations.

2. The other important source of carbon dioxide is deforestation, which is not significant in developed nations.

3. This point is developed in more detail by Davies, St.-Hilaire, and Whalley (1984), Kasten and Sammartino (1988), and Poterba (1989).

4. Poterba (1991) describes the data sample in more detail, and uses a similar approach to study the distributional burden of higher gasoline taxes in the United States.

5. Given concerns about the macroeconomic effects of instituting a carbon tax, it is unlikely that such a plan would be instituted without a significant phase-in period. The distributional results presented here, however, are likely to provide some evidence on the long-run effects of such plans.

6. These estimates of fuel shares of total kilowatt-hours generated are drawn from the U.S. Department of Energy (1988). The data on the various fuels' shares of costs are based on data in the Edison Electric Institute (1984).

7. Johnson, McKay, and Smith (1990) present similar calculations for the United Kingdom, showing somewhat greater regressivity of energy taxes even using the expenditure incidence basis.

8. Such indexed transfers are also important for households in the second expenditure decile, where they constitute 46 percent of income, but they decline at higher expenditure levels.

9. The analysis assumes no preexisting taxes in any markets, but this assumption is not quite accurate for the fossil-fuel markets in many developed nations. The problem of preexisting taxes will be addressed in a future work.

10. A general-equilibrium analysis of a world carbon tax by John Whalley and Randall Wigle, recognizing the effects on producing countries and also the changes in world fossil-fuel prices, is presented in Chapter 7 of this book.

11. The sensitivity of the estimated deadweight losses to changes in the demand elasticities may be more complex than this discussion suggests. If the policy being analyzed is simply a given specific tax on carbon content, then lower elasticities will translate into lower deadweight burdens. If the policy is a requirement for a given percentage reduction in carbon emissions, however, lower elasticities will in turn require higher tax rates; this effect will take the deadweight burden.

12. The preliminary results in table 3.7 assume away any preexisting taxes on fossil-fuel use. For petroleum, the presence of gasoline taxes in most developed nations make this assumption suspect. Recognizing these preexisting taxes would raise the estimated deadweight burdens on oil.

13. These estimated deadweight burdens compare favorably with those from other revenue sources; see, for example, Ballard et al. (1985).

14. Studies that simulate the long-run effects of a carbon tax on economic activity include Manne and Richels (1989), Hogan and Jorgenson (1990), and Congressional Budget Office (1990).

15. This analysis draws heavily on the more general discussion in Poterba, Rotemberg, and Summers (1986).

16. This figure is based on data in U.S. Congress, Joint Committee on Taxation (1987).

17. The table shows refined petroleum only, since the input-output table treats crude as an input to refined petroleum and the refined petroleum as the input to all other activities.

18. This is the approach adopted under current U.S. law with the excise tax on CFCs. The Treasury is empowered to estimate the CFC content of imported goods, and, in cases where this estimate is impossible, can levy a tax of up to 5 percent on imports. See U.S. Congress, Joint Committee on Taxation (1990).

19. If the discount rate were zero, then 1 pound of CFC-11/12 is the equivalent of 0.79 ton of carbon from CO_2; with a discount rate of 4 percent per year, the equivalence factor is 1.42.

20. This point has been made in many previous analyses of policy response to global warming; examples are Lave (1988) and Nordhaus (1990b).

References

Anderson, Robert C., Hoffman, Lisa A., and Rusin, Michael. 1990. The use of economic incentive mechanisms in environmental management. Mimeo, American Petroleum Institute.

Ballard, Charles, Fullerton, Don, Shoven, John, and Whalley, John. 1985. *A General Equilibrium Model for Tax Policy Evaluation*. Chicago: University of Chicago Press.

Bernow, S., and Marron, D. 1990. *Valuation of Environmental Externalities for Energy Planning and Operations, 1990 Update*. Cambridge, MA: Tellus Institute.

Bohi, Douglas R. 1981. *Analyzing Demand Behavior: A Study of Energy Elasticities*. Baltimore: Johns Hopkins University Press.

Congressional Budget Office. 1986. *Curbing Acid Rain: Cost, Budget, and Coal Market Effects*. Washington, DC: U.S. Government Printing Office.

Congressional Budget Office. 1990. *Carbon Charges as a Response to Global Warming: The Effects of Taxing Fossil Fuels*. Washington, DC: U.S. Government Printing Office.

Davies, James, St.-Hilaire, France, and Whalley, John. 1984. Some calculations of lifetime tax incidence. *American Economic Review* 74:633–649.

Edison Electric Institute. 1984. *Statistical Yearbook*. Washington, DC: Edison Electric Institute.

Flavin, Christopher. 1990. Slowing global warming. In Lester R. Brown, ed., *State of the World*. Washington, DC: Worldwatch Institute.

Hogan, William W., and Jorgenson, Dale W. 1990. Productivity trends and the cost of reducing CO_2 emissions. Mimeo, Harvard University.

Johnson, Paul, McKay, Steve, and Smith, Stephen. 1990. *The Distributional Consequences of Environmental Taxes.* Institute for Fiscal Studies Working Paper 23. London.

Kasten, Richard, and Sammartino, Frank. 1988. *The Distribution of Possible Federal Excise Tax Increases.* Washington, DC: Congressional Budget Office.

Lave, Lester B. 1988. The greenhouse effect: What government actions are needed? *Journal of Policy Analysis and Management* 7:460–470.

Manne, Alan S., and Richels, Richard G. 1989. CO_2 emission limits: An economic analysis for the USA. Mimeo, Stanford University.

Nordhaus, William D. 1990a. Contribution of different greenhouse gases to global warming: A new technique for measuring impact. Mimeo, Yale University.

Nordhaus, William D. 1990b. Global warming: Slowing the greenhouse express. In Henry J. Aaron, ed., *Setting National Priorities: Policy for the Nineties.* Washington, DC: Brookings Institution.

Pindyck, Robert S. 1979. The characteristics of the demand for energy. In I. C. Sawhill, ed., *Energy Conservation and Public Policy,* 22–45. Englewood Cliffs, NJ: Prentice-Hall.

Poterba, James M. 1989. Lifetime incidence and the distributional burden of excise taxes. *American Economic Review* 79:325–330.

Poterba, James M. 1991. Is the gasoline tax regressive? In D. Bradford, ed., *Tax Policy and the Economy* 5.

Poterba, James M., Rotemberg, Julio J., and Summers, Lawrence H. 1986. A tax-based test of nominal rigidities. *American Economic Review* 76 (September):659–675.

Sandmo, Agnar. 1975. Optimal taxation in the presence of externalities. *Swedish Journal of Economics* 77:86–98.

U.S. Congress, Joint Committee on Taxation. 1987. *Description of H.R. 2497 (Sulfur and Nitrogen Emissions Tax Act of 1987).* Washington, DC: U.S. Government Printing Office.

U.S. Congress, Joint Committee on Taxation. 1990. *Present Law and Background Relating to Federal Environmental Tax Policy.* Washington, DC: U.S. Government Printing Office.

U.S. Congress, Office of Technology Assessment. 1990. *Background paper: Energy Use and the U.S. Economy.* Washington, DC: Government Printing Office.

U.S. Department of Energy, Energy Information Agency. 1988. *Annual Energy Outlook.* Washington, DC: Government Printing Office.

U.S. Department of Energy, Energy Information Agency. 1990. *Annual Energy Outlook*. Washington, DC: Government Printing Office.

Comments

Lester B. Lave

Are Economists Relevant? The Efficiency of a Carbon Tax

Judging from the *New York Times, Science,* and similar publications, the efficiency of a carbon tax is not perceived to be a critical issue. Rather, the greenhouse debate is focused on the "recognition" and "equity" aspects—human actions ruining the Earth or making the planet a hostile place for future generations. If the debate gets beyond these points, it becomes bogged down in estimating the qualitative and quantitative changes that might arise from global climate change.

The debate can be influenced, as exemplified by the growing consideration given to uncertainties surrounding the scientific conclusions. A few people have even talked about the costs of abating greenhouse effects, but costs are regarded as a rude subject that only people like accountants and economists would be concerned with; the future of the Earth is viewed as entirely incompatible with discussion of costs—that is, the future of the Earth versus a few pieces of green paper.

Only among professional economists is there discussion of the least expensive way to achieve abatement. I must confess to wondering whether examining efficiency and costs of abatement are the most important issues or whether economists are simply doing what they are trained to do.

Environmental World Views

Before settling down to focus on the issue that I was asked to discuss, I want to remind us of the debate that is shaping policy. Few people have addressed issues of global climate change within a benefit-cost framework, and few seem inclined to do so, even after the framework is brought to their attention. Not only do we not control the debate, but the language and framework have been defined by people who see a balancing approach as unnatural, even wrongheaded, in thinking about these issues.

If we are going to engage a more general audience, we need to give more attention to the "world views" of the public and those who dominate the debate. Samuel Hays (1987) has characterized the history of the environmental movement in the United States as divided into three views. The first is a "frontier" mentality that viewed the environment as being either hostile or not worth attention; the environment is infinite and inexhaustible—no care need be taken to preserve it.

A second view arose around 1900, the "conservation" mentality. In this view the environment is limited and exhaustible. Humans must use the environment carefully in order to get the greatest level of environmental services. In this view, humans must constantly balance the good and harm they do in their environmental actions.

In the third view, the environment must be "preserved." Humans have no right to use exhaustible resources or degrade the environment. We "borrow the Earth" for a short period from the generations to come. This view is the only one of the three that is not anthropocentric. The other two views are from the perceptions and desires of humans; the environment has no role other than to serve the wishes of people (although these wishes can include preserving a wilderness area so that people can hike and camp there or preserving the wilderness for future generations). In this third view, the environment has standing apart from the desires of even the most environmentally conscious people; humans have no right to disturb the environment in more than trivial ways.

In this third view, there is no role for balancing benefits and costs; there is no need to inquire whether global climate change is beneficial or harmful or how much it would cost to mitigate the damages done by change. Change per se is bad and must be prevented; humans have no right to change the Earth, even if we think that the change would be helpful.

Anyone with a frontier or preservationist mentality who is reading these papers has already discovered that the authors are crazy. The authors are focused on "irrelevant" questions. Why waste time examining the size and nature of greenhouse effect or the cost of abatement programs? To a frontiersman, no actions are needed. To a preservationist, the only issue is how to get on with abatement as quickly as possible to prevent further climate change.

I am a conservationist; our training teaches economists to see decisions as requiring balancing, as getting things right on the margin, and as needing to accomplish goals as efficiently as possible. I have no apology for this approach, but think it is essential to remind both the economists and noneconomists of the different positions we start from and why many of us are saying things that appear to be complete nonsense. If you already know the answers concerning how much abatement is desirable, then you will be interested in Poterba's discussion of the carbon dioxide tax, since it is the most efficient way of accomplishing the desired goal. More likely, you think that speed of abatement and assurance of abatement are much more important than the efficiency of abatement. I see Poterba's discussion as premature, since it assumes that a careful benefit-cost analysis would find abatement to be desirable.

The Large Costs to Low-Income Nations

My own analysis leads to the conclusion that Nordhaus states in Chapter 2: Climate change of the magnitude described will have a trivial effect on the rich countries. These countries have the resources, intellectual and financial, to adapt to the changed climate. I doubt that most people would notice that climate had warmed by an average of 2.5° C.

However, the effects on the poor countries are likely to be more important for several reasons: (1) Between one-third and two-thirds of their GDP comes from agriculture, much of which is subsistence or partial subsistence farming (Lave and Vickland 1989). Furthermore, subsistence agriculture can be expected to adjust to changed climate and other factors much more slowly than will commercial agriculture. For a family raising their own food, there is no cash for new seeds, irrigation, fertilizer, or implements. The family will be reluctant to introduce new crops or even new cultivars, since the taste of their crops must be acceptable. The family is reluctant to change farming practices, such as when crops are planted, since the consequence of crop failure is starvation. These impediments to change result in an alarming likelihood of decreasing yields that gradually ruin the prosperity and health of the farmers if subsistence farms experience climate change. (2) These nations do not have the intellectual or financial resources to build large irrigation projects or otherwise adapt to change. (3) It is difficult to transport food or to move populations from an area that is no longer capable of feeding them.

Even with the best of intentions, the rich nations may be incapable of helping the poor ones in the event of crop failures and other disasters. Many dedicated men and women have worked to help the poor countries. The record during the past forty-five years is anything but reassuring. Much time and effort has been spent with little success. Should disasters occur in these countries, the rich nations might be able to do little other than feed the starving people and promote long-term problems in the economies. Even our willingness to ship food does not ensure that we could prevent starvation.

Taken to its logical conclusion, this line of thinking indicates that the rich nations might have to prevent greenhouse warming simply because there is no alternative in helping the poor countries. If there is an alternative, it requires help now to get these countries to become more flexible in anticipation of future climate change.

The Carbon Dioxide Tax

Poterba shows that the deadweight loss from a carbon dioxide tax is small—a conclusion relevant for the benefit-cost analysis. We need to know the deadweight loss in calculating how much abatement is worthwhile. The size of the loss helps determine whether the carbon dioxide tax really is the most efficient approach.

He shows that, if the basis is expenditures rather than income, there is hardly any regressivity in the tax. If there is a problem, it is the same problem for all government tax and spending programs: The poorest people in America are far too poor. No new taxes should be imposed on them; indeed, programs ought to be transferring income to them. While the carbon dioxide tax is a tax, it is a better tax than the vast majority faced by the poor.

My quick calculation is that burning a ton of coal in the Ohio Valley with no pollution control should generate about $200 in social costs (and thus potentially in effluent fees). A $200 per ton tax on coal use would all but eliminate the use of coal and hasten the switch to nonfossil fuels, in the long run. However, in the short term preventing pollution leads to more, not less, carbon dioxide emissions. Running a flue gas scrubber and electrostatic precipitator requires more than 10 percent of the energy from the coal. Thus efforts to abate air pollutants from coal combustion add to greenhouse effects.

In the long term, abating current environmental pollution will also result in abating greenhouse gases. As the effluent fees for sulfur oxides, nitrogen oxides, and particles are increased and a carbon dioxide tax is imposed, coal will become less attractive than other fuels. Given time to build new facilities, coal plants will be retired in favor of nonfossil fuels, especially nuclear. However, in the short term, abating current environment pollutants serves to increase greenhouse gas emissions.

Poterba observes that a carbon dioxide tax is likely to slow economic growth, at least in the short term. If greenhouse effects are large and disruptive, they would impede future growth more than would expenditures to abate emissions of greenhouse gases. But there is more involved here than simply a trade-off between rapid current growth and future growth.

Jorgenson and Wilcoxen (1990) have estimated that the high petroleum prices from 1974 onward slowed economic growth. A carbon dioxide tax would be expected to do the same. However, the carbon dioxide tax and efforts to abate other pollutants reflect recognition of the social costs of rapid growth, at least in terms of the spillovers from current technology. This recognition implies that productivity growth is less desirable than it would be in the absence of environmental externalities. Thus the carbon dioxide tax appears to be sending the correct signal, at least qualitatively, concerning the desire to slow economic growth unless or until technologies can be developed that have less damaging effects on the environment than those currently available. Rather than lament the slowdown in economic growth, we should recognize that society appears to believe that growth with current environmental externalities is undesirable. Even accounting for the greenhouse externality with a carbon dioxide tax does not take full account of the environmental externalities. Thus slowing economic growth is entirely desirable, at least to some extent, until the most important externalities have been managed satisfactorily.

What Should We Do Now?

Without attempting to comment systematically on policy, I want to set out a few steps that economists ought to be taking. The first concerns research to resolve the overwhelming uncertainty that haunts greenhouse issues. Economists need to play a central role in formulating an R&D agenda that sets out the most important issues, sets priorities, and ensures coordination among researchers. Current greenhouse research is characterized by individual research teams pursuing topics of greatest interest to them.

Some of us are naive enough to treat the various general circulation models as independent attempts at research. In fact they take quite similar approaches; their general agreement is more a comment on the technical capabilities of the various groups than independent confirmation of the same basic truth. If three (or more) global circulation models are to be supported in the United States, the research should be designed to give a wider exploration of the issues.

Since we want to know what will happen to agriculture and plants in the less managed environment, agronomists and biologists must get better characterizations of future climate; they need answers concerning the dates of the last freeze in spring, the first freeze in fall, total precipitation, when the precipitation occurs, whether there will be a series of terribly hot days during the growing season, and so on. Even if they cannot get estimates of all these parameters, at least they need to know what climate descriptors they can get. Climate modelers need to know what climate descriptors are needed by biologists and others.

Everyone needs to know when others will produce the promised outputs. At present there is no systematic attempt to coordinate what the agronomists need to know with what the climate modelers are committed to deliver. There is no mechanism for ensuring that the output from carbon cycle modelers will be available when climate modelers need the results. When one modeler gets an unexpected result, there is no mechanism for exploring the implications for each relevant researcher, or even for determining which researchers should be informed first.

A group of colleagues and I are at work on providing such an integrated model, at least to a first order. We believe that it will be invaluable in setting research priorities and in coordinating research.

At the 1990 White House Conference on Greenhouse Effects there appeared to be an irreconcilable difference between the European and American positions. The Europeans argued that we should proceed immediately to commit ourselves to reducing carbon dioxide emissions to 80 percent of their 1988 level by 2005 and to stabilize emissions at that level. The Americans argued that greenhouse effects are uncertain (see Solow, Chapter 1) and that abatement is costly and potentially disruptive. They wanted to wait for more definite confirmation of the magnitude of possible greenhouse effects before making a large commitment of resources.

In my conversations with European delegates I learned that their position was not what we seemed to understand them to say. They were not expressing their willingness to incur large costs now to abate greenhouse gas emissions. Rather, they were willing to make a commitment to start taking action—that they did not expect to be terribly expensive. Sometime in the future, they would come to grips with whether to take costly steps, if required.

Thus the positions of the two groups were much more similar than the rhetoric seemed to indicate. The Americans needed to make a moral commitment to worry about greenhouse effects, and both sides needed to coordinate their language on what they proposed to do during the next half decade.

The official U.S. position was somewhat different from that of most American participants. The official position did not go beyond endorsing research, while most delegates favored taking steps that would abate carbon dioxide emissions as long as the costs were low.

Buying Climate Change Insurance

One of the analogies that I and several others have used over the years is that abating greenhouse gases is buying an insurance policy in case the resulting climate change turns out to be harmful and important. To date, global climate change has been largely the concern of the rich nations; even within the rich nations, the concern has been concentrated in people in the top part of the income distribution.

That these groups favor buying insurance is not surprising. Those who voluntarily purchase other types of insurance—life, health, flood, earthquake—are in the top part of the income distribution; it is the affluent who elect to spend money today to protect themselves against possible future loss. Persuading poor people to buy flood or earthquake insurance is extraordinarily difficult. I predict that it will be difficult to persuade poor people in the rich countries to sacrifice for preventing possible climate change. At the White House conference, Mrs. Gandhi, the environmental minister of India, made an eloquent statement that however much India agreed that the environment should be protected, there were no funds available for abating greenhouse gases.

The insurance analogy is revealing in several ways. It presents a good reason for the rich and educated to support abatement expenditures despite current uncertainties. And it provides insights into which groups and countries are unlikely to support purchasing this insurance now, since they feel they have more pressing needs.

Finally, I have a note of caution for myself and my fellow economists. A well-done benefit-cost analysis will tend to underestimate benefits and overestimate costs, because an analysis must be based on fact and must be defensible. The unknowns on the benefit sides tend to be new benefits that have not been measured or quantified; when they are estimated, benefits will rise. The unknowns on the cost side are new technologies that will make abatement cheaper; when they are quantified, costs will fall.

Well-done economic analysis has a tendency to echo Voltaire's Dr. Pangloss: Everything is best; any change is likely to be for the worst. I want to caution myself and my colleagues to keep this bias in mind, lest we oppose any program to prevent global climate change.

References

Hays, Samuel P. 1987. *Beauty, Health, and Permanence: Environmental Protection in the United States, 1955–1985,* New York: Cambridge University Press.

Jorgenson, Dale W., and Wilcoxen, Peter J. 1990. Environmental regulation and U.S. economic growth. *The RAND Journal of Economics* 21:314–340.

Lave, Lester B., and Vickland, Kathleen Heffernan. 1989. Adjusting to Greenhouse Effects: The Demise of Traditional Cultures and the Cost to the USA. *Risk Analysis* 9:283–291.

Comments

Lars Bergman

Professor Poterba provides a broad and interesting analysis of several issues raised when a tax on CO_2 emissions is to be designed. Thus the issues dealt with in his chapter include efficiency, income-distribution, macroeconomic, and public-finance aspects of a carbon tax. The chapter convincingly shows that all these aspects clearly are relevant, and thus that CO_2 emission control should not be discussed only in a narrow environmental policy context. In my comments I will focus on some issues not dealt with in the chapter, although I also have a few minor comments on what is in it. In particular I will comment on the economics of CO_2 emission control against the background of the Swedish discussion of these issues.

My first comment is related to the choice of "reference case." In the chapter the impact of a carbon tax is measured in relation to a no-policy base case. However, assume that a certain constraint on total U.S. CO_2 emissions for one reason or another is regarded as necessary. The policy goals can then be attained by means of various instruments such as detailed regulations, tradeable emission permits, and various combinations of emission or fuel taxes and these instruments. The analysis of the impact of a carbon tax would then in effect be a comparison of various policy alternatives. I do not suggest that such an analysis would be easy to do or that the conclusions would be much different from those we find in the chapter. However, I guess that the carbon tax would produce efficiency gains rather than efficiency losses when it is compared with most policy alternatives.

My second comment is related to the general equilibrium effects of a carbon tax and the implications for the design of the tax. Here I think that the Swedish case provides an interesting example, and perhaps some perspective on the paper's focus on the United States. Let me therefore briefly summarize some of the findings from analyses based on a computable general-equilibrium model of the Swedish economy:

In Sweden a significant share of total CO_2 emissions originate in a few energy-intensive, export-oriented industries such as the paper and pulp industry, the iron and steel industry, and the chemical industry. Private cars, trucks, and fossil-fueled heating systems in homes and commercial buildings are other important sources of CO_2 emissions. Electricity production is currently almost entirely based on hydro and nuclear power, but additional capacity will most likely be based on coal or natural gas. Thus a carbon tax in Sweden would affect the marginal cost of electricity.

According to current policy goals, Swedish CO_2 emissions should by kept constant at the 1987 level. (In addition the emissions of SO_2 and NO_x should be significantly reduced, and the existing nuclear power plants should be phased out before 2010.) Numerical general equilibrium analyses suggest that the implementation of this goal will have quite significant effects on the structure of production and foreign trade as well as on domestic factor prices. More precisely the energy and emission-intensive industries lose international competitiveness, and factor prices are adjusted downward so that the manufacturing industry can make sufficient international market-share gains, and thus maintain current account equilibrium. In other words, the general-equilibrium effects, as well as the total income losses, of far-reaching constraints on CO_2 emissions can be significant. At least that is the case in a small economy specialized in energy- and emission-intensive production.

As a result of the calculated general equilibrium effects, the recently adopted tax on CO_2 emissions in Sweden is subject to a number of exceptions. Thus for each firm the sum of "ordinary" energy tax and carbon tax is maximized to 1.7 percent of the total value of output. The result is that neither the energy-intensive industries nor future power production based on fossil fuels has to pay the carbon tax. In other words, the carbon tax is essentially a tax on gasoline and fossil fuels for residential and commercial heating purposes.

This design of the Swedish carbon tax obviously is motivated by the expected impact of a uniform carbon tax on certain industries and regions in the country. However, it raises a general issue in relation to unilateral taxes on transboundary pollutants affecting global commons. A CO_2 tax on energy-intensive Swedish industries may not only seriously affect these industries, but it may also have very limited effects on CO_2 emissions. Reduced production and CO_2 emissions in Sweden are likely to be compensated by increased production and CO_2 emissions in other countries. Thus the net effect on the global climate is negligible, and the "global" cost-benefit ratio is most likely to be unfavorable.

In the chapter this problem is discussed in connection with taxes on CO_2 "embodied" in imported goods. The Swedish example suggests that exemptions for CO_2 "embodied" in exports is equally important in a unilateral strategy aimed at reducing CO_2 emissions. The design of the Swedish carbon tax clearly limits the international relocation effects of the tax, but at the same time the incentives to reduce CO_2 emissions per unit of output are eliminated. It seems to me that one important "design issue" is to reduce the output and international relocation effects of carbon taxation without significantly destroying the incentives for technological change.

In addition to these general remarks I have a few minor specific comments on the chapter:

1. If one accepts the idea that CO_2 emissions lead to real environmental costs, and the carbon tax reflects the marginal environmental cost of CO_2 emissions, the impact of the tax is an efficiency gain

rather than a loss. Thus the calculation of the "excess burden" of the carbon tax implicitly assumes that CO_2 emissions do not represent any real external costs.

2. The same argument also suggests that, in a revenue-neutral policy package, a carbon tax that is offset by a cut in other, probably distorting, taxes will produce efficiency gains in the form of reduced excess burden of taxation.

3. In connection with the discussion in the chapter about optimal taxation when there are several environmental effects related to the use of a particular fuel, it might be useful to observe a difference between CO_2 and, for instance, SO_x. In both cases the policy should aim at taxing the *emissions* rather than the fuel as such. In the case of CO_2 emission, taxation and fuel taxation is equivalent, but in the case of SO_x the relation between emissions and fuel use can be affected in many ways. Thus, unlike the optimal CO_2 tax, the "first best" optimal SO_x tax is not a fuel tax.

4. Finally, a minor aspect of carbon taxation not discussed in the chapter: Any type of policy aimed at reducing CO_2 emissions tends to increase the marginal cost of attaining other environmental policy goals. For example, the constraints on Swedish CO_2 emissions have significantly increased the cost of phasing out nuclear power and thus reducing a certain set of environmental risks. In fact, this aspect of a tax on CO_2 played an important role when the Swedish parliament made its decision about the carbon tax; the decision was made against the will of the government and was supported by a temporary coalition of "green" parties and parties who are against the previously decided phasing out of nuclear power.

4

Technological Substitution Options for Controlling Greenhouse Gas Emissions

Edward B. Barbier,
Joanne C. Burgess,
and David W. Pearce

This chapter is concerned with technological options for *greenhouse gas substitution*.[1] We interpret the term "substitution" to *exclude* energy conservation/efficiency measures, investments in afforestation (sinks), and greenhouse gas removal or abatement technologies. Our working definition of greenhouse gas substitution includes (1) *replacement technologies*, for example, substituting a greenhouse gas technology with a nongreenhouse gas technology; and (2) *reduction technologies*, for example, substituting a greenhouse gas technology with an alternative technology that reduces greenhouse gas emissions. Essentially, replacement technologies involve 100 percent reduction in CO_2; reduction technologies involve a partial reduction in CO_2.

Of the man-made sources of greenhouse gases, energy is the most important and is expected to contribute to at least half of the global warming effect in the near future.[2] The majority of this impact is from fossil fuel combustion as a source of carbon dioxide (CO_2), although fossil fuels also contribute significantly to methane (CH_4), to nitrous oxide (N_2O), and to low-level ozone (O_3) through production of various nitrogen gases (NO_x) and carbon monoxide (CO).[3]

Nonenergy sources of some greenhouse gases are also significant. For example, industrial production of solvents, refrigerator and air-conditioning fluids, foaming agents, aerosol propellants, and other products are virtually the only sources of CFC emissions. As a result of the Montreal Protocol, countries that produce CFCs are now seeking ways to phase out these gases and introduce substitutes. However, developing countries, who for the most part did not ratify the protocol, account for approximately 12 percent of the world's CFCs consumption. Agriculture—principally from livestock raising and rice paddies—accounts for around 50 percent of world man-made methane emissions and for around one-third of nitrous oxide emissions, notably from nitrogen fertilizer applications and land conversion.

Efforts to control future greenhouse gas emissions should be based on efficient strategies to ameliorate adverse climatic changes. Efficiency implies actions to reduce global warming that are cost-effective, meaning that the costs of adjustment are minimized, and that maximize net benefits—that is, at the margin the costs to society of any actions to avert global warming are more than compensated by the benefits from reducing the damages from climatic change, including the risks and uncertainties attached to the future damages.[4] From this approach an "acceptable," or "optimal," level (and rate) of global warming may be determined, and the role of technology substitution in greenhouse gas abatement can be assessed.

However, there are few cost-benefit evaluations to determine even an approximate estimate of acceptable greenhouse gas emissions.[5] Most policy options have instead been developed around target "stabilization" levels based on some judgment of acceptability, that is, the greenhouse gas reductions needed to stabilize at some predetermined level of emissions. For example, to stabilize emissions in 2005 at 1980s levels, CO_2 emissions would have to be reduced by 50–80 percent, methane by 10–20 percent, N_2O by 80–85 percent, and CFCs by 75–100 percent.[6] Carbon monoxide and NO_x would need to be frozen at 1980s levels. These stabilization levels have become the basis for global negotiations on actual targets for reducing greenhouse gases.

For example, the CFC Montreal Protocol was reached without a proper benefit-cost analysis being carried out on a global scale. In the United States, however, such studies were carried out.[7] On this basis, it was decided that a global study could be avoided. In any event, the data required to carry it out were simply not available.

An analysis of technological options for greenhouse gas substitutions and their relative costs is therefore essential to both targeting and cost-benefit approaches to controlling global warming. The following sections analyze the available greenhouse gas substitution options and their costs. We concentrate particularly on substitutions for *fossil-fuel combustion* and *CFC production and consumption*. We conclude by summarizing the potential for greenhouse gas substitution, the cost-effectiveness of the various options and the design of incentives for substitution.

Substitution Options and Their Costs

No detailed attempt is made to aggregate the combined effects of all the substitution options and to derive a *global* "marginal cost" function of the possible measures to reduce greenhouse gases. There are several reasons limiting such an approach:

First, the analysis of substitution options is not comprehensive. Because of the lack of data, some important supply and end-use technologies have not been considered. We rely mainly on data from OECD countries—although analysis of developing countries is included where appropriate.

Second, all the technical options, as well as their relative cost-effectiveness, are extremely location-specific. It is more instructive to show how the cost-effectiveness of each option varies by country and region than to derive aggregate cost functions for a global economy.

Third, to derive an aggregate marginal cost curve for the combined effects of all options requires assumptions concerning the *feasibility* of substitution over a specific time horizon. Establishing such a substitution scenario for a single country or region is difficult enough; deriving a global scenario for all feasible options and across all countries is probably impossible. This is the case even if we limited the analysis to current rather than future substitution options.

Finally, an aggregate cost function indicating the cumulative effects in terms of reducing greenhouse gas emissions of all options may give a misleading impression of the actual aggregate economic costs of these reductions. Each option is likely to have significant second-round economic impacts on its own if it is adopted on a large scale. For example, a significant expansion in nuclear power electricity generation may actually reduce the demand for fossil fuels. Any resulting fall in fossil-fuel prices may make other greenhouse gas replacement and reduction options less attractive, and could increase the demand for fossil fuels in other sectors of the economy (e.g., transport). Such impacts will be further compounded, and be more difficult to predict, because of the cumulative effects of a combination of substitution options. A more comprehensive analysis of costs should involve general equilibrium analysis.

Where possible, our assessment of the cost-effectiveness of each substitution option will be in terms of its *levelized costs*—that is, costs that are averaged over the lifetime of a plant, representing the uniform revenue required over the life of a project to recover all costs. However, these costs include only the *direct resource costs* (i.e., fuel, capital, and maintenance) of each option, which do not represent the full economic costs of introducing the technology. *Indirect benefits and costs,* such as any diversion of capital resources, the impact on overall demand for the final product and the effects on labor productivity, are not included. Similarly, the *external benefits and costs,* such as the positive or negative impacts on the pollution damages incurred by society, are excluded. We indicate how calculation of these full economic costs would influence adoption of a substitution option.[8]

Fossil-Fuel Substitution Options

Important substitution options for fossil fuel use may occur in the electricity-generation, buildings/industrial, and transport sectors. The cost-effectiveness of all fossil-fuel substitution options will be highly sensitive to energy supply and demand and price projections, notably the price of oil and other fossil fuels. For example, in electricity generation, all the levelized cost calculations for different generating technologies are based on a projected price for oil. If actual prices differ, then the relative cost-effectiveness of the various options will also differ.

For substitution options involving renewable energy technologies, cost-effectiveness will be highly sensitive to the maturity and proven capabilities of the technologies, as well as economies of scale. Table 4.1 indicates the current state of technological development of renewable energy technologies. Only hydro power, hydrothermal, some biomass applications, passive solar, and small remote photovoltaic (PV) systems are mature technologies today with proven capabilities.[9] These are likely to be the most cost-effective systems currently. However, renewable technologies are responding rapidly to research, development, and demonstration efforts. Some of these technologies— wind, solar thermal, ethanol, active solar heating, advanced hydrothermal, and larger remote PV systems—are already in a transition phase of development and capable of penetrating the market. In the medium to long term—that is, in the next ten years or more—some advanced renewable technologies will show significant potential. These will include advanced applications of wind, solar thermal, and geothermal, as well as ocean thermal conversion, energy crops for

Table 4.1
Renewable energy potential

Proven capability[a]	Transition phase[b]	Future supplies[c]
Hydro power	Wind	Advanced wind
Geothermal	Solar thermal	Advanced solar thermal
Hydrothermal	Ethanol (corn)	
High-temperature electric	Active solar in buildings	Transportation fuel from energy crops
Low-temperature heat	Geothermal	Ocean thermal
Biomass	Hydrothermal	Advanced geothermal
Direct combustion	Moderate-temperature electric	Hot dry rock
Gasification	Remote PV	Geopressure
Passive solar in buildings		Magma
Small, remote photovoltaic (PV)		Grid-connected PV
		Wave
		Tidal

Source: Idaho National Engineering Laboratory, Los Alamos National Laboratory, Oak Ridge National Laboratory, Sandia National Laboratories, and Solar Energy Research Institute, *The Potential of Renewable Energy: An Interlaboratory White Paper* (Golden, CO: Solar Energy Research Institute, March 1990).
a. Mature technologies.
b. Has or is entering market as technology develops, often preferential tax or rate considerations.
c. Advanced technologies that show potential.

transport, and grid-connected PV. Other future energy supplies that might become available include tidal power and wave energy.

Electricity Generation

For electricity, *replacement* technologies would involve the substitution of fossil fuels in power generation by nuclear energy and renewables—hydropower, wind, tidal, wave, geothermal, solar/photovoltaics, and refuse incineration. *Reduction technologies* would involve substituting one fossil fuel source of electricity with an alternative that lowers greenhouse gas emissions. The options here include changing the fuel mix (e.g., from coal to natural gas or biomass) and developing advanced fossil-fuel technologies, such as fluidized bed combustion of coal and combined cycle gas turbines. Combined heat and power (CHP) is another important reduction technology, but we will discuss this option more thoroughly in the next main section, "Building/Industrial and Other Stationary Users."

The potential role of renewable energy in electricity generation is particularly dependent on the suitability of these technologies to large-scale grid generation (i.e., whether the source of energy is *dispatchable* or *intermittent*). The *dispatchable sources* include hydro power, biomass, geothermal, and ocean energy. Hydro power contributes the largest single input into electricity generation from all renewable resources and, although costs vary significantly from site to site, they often compete favorably with conventional fossil fuels. Power production from *intermittent* generating technologies such as solar thermal, wind power, and photovoltaics is highly dependent upon the natural forces from which they derive their energy and is extremely vulnerable to the periodic fluctuations of these natural forces. These intermittent sources of power generation can be used in integration with other sources of power to ensure the continuity of power availability or be combined with storage facilities to reduce the need for other sources of power.

The technology for fossil-fuel-powered electricity will also be changing rapidly in the next few years (see table 4.2). Assessing the potential contribution of these new technologies in terms of *reducing* CO_2 emissions is difficult. The development of fluidized bed coal combustion and advanced gas turbines are among the most promising alternatives to conventional fossil-fuel plants. The greater efficiency of these technologies will yield lower greenhouse gas emissions per output of delivered electricity. However, a recent U.S. review notes that these substitutes alone are insufficient to achieve a 10 percent reduction of U.S. CO_2 emissions from 1985 levels by 2010.[10] A U.K. study suggests that deploying advanced coal and advanced gas technologies might be mutually exclusive options for abating CO_2 emissions.[11] Unless the price of gas rises substantially relative to coal, the economics of building new efficient coal capacity to displace generation from existing conventional coal stations are unlikely to compare favorably with advanced gas plants. *Substantial* deployment of advanced coal and gas could increase the price of gas, limiting substitution and hence CO_2 savings.

OECD

The projected levelized costs for electricity generation for conventional compared to renewable energy sources across OECD countries are shown in tables 4.3 and 4.4. Coal and nuclear power appear

Table 4.2
Advanced fossil-fuel power-generation technologies

Technology	Efficiency (% ECF)[a]	Status
Conventional Rankine plant + FGD[b]	36–37	Deployed
Advanced Rankine plant + FGD	38	Under deployment
AFBC[c] + sulfur removal	39	Near deployment
PFBC[d] + sulfur removal	40	Near deployment
CCCG[e] + sulfur removal	38–43	Near deployment
Topping cycle—PFBC	44.5	Future deployment
Topping cycle—AFBC	45.5	Future deployment
Combined cycle gas turbine (CCGT)[f]	42–46	Deployed
Intercooled STIG[g]	47	Future deployment
Advanced CCGT	47–50	Under deployment
Magnetohydrodynamics	48	Future deployment
Molten carbonate fuel cell	49	Future deployment

SOURCE: U.K. Department of Energy, *An Evaluation of Energy Related Greenhouse Gas Emissions and Measures to Ameliorate Them*, Energy Paper 58 (London: HMSO, October 1989), Table 5.2.12; and J. A. Edmonds, W. B. Ashton, H. C. Cheng, and M. Steinberg, *A Preliminary Analysis of U.S. CO_2 Emissions Reduction Potential from Energy Conservation and the Substitution of Natural Gas for Coal in the Period to 2010*, Prepared for the U.S. Department of Energy (Washington, DC: February 1989), Table 10.
a. Energy conversion factor.
b. Fluidized gas desulfurization.
c. Atmospheric fluidized bed combustion.
d. Pressurized fluidized bed combustion.
e. Combined cycle coal gasification.
f. Combined cycle gas turbine.
g. Steam turbine injected gas.

to offer the least-cost generating options. New coal plants are less competitive in importing regions with full emission controls imposed, and the nuclear plants are less competitive with higher discount rates and longer lead times. However, the main obstacles to nuclear power expansion may be more political and social: in addition, the costs of nuclear power include decommissioning costs but not any calculations of environmental risks, hazardous waste transport and disposal, or the external costs of location policies.[12] Few renewable alternatives compete favorably with the conventional fuels, either currently or in the near future. The exceptions may be wind, geothermal, and some biomass applications. Hydroelectric power may also be a cost-effective alternative, although the availability and costs of generating electricity from hydro power tend to be very site-specific and may vary considerably. Photovoltaics (PV) are currently expen-

Table 4.3
Electricity generating costs of conventional fuels, OECD countries (1989 U.S. cents/kWh)[a]

	Oil (2 × 600 MW)	Coal (2 × 600 MW)		Gas (2 × 600 MW)	Nuclear (2 × 1,100 MW) (lead time = 10 years)
		Importing region ($60/ton)	Low-price region ($40/ton)		
1. Base (5%)	5.3	3.6	3.1	4.6	3.7
With FGD[b]	5.7	4.1	3.5		
With FGD and SCR[c]	5.8	4.5	3.9	4.7	
2. Base (10%)	5.8	4.5	3.9	5.0	5.7
With FGD	6.3	5.0	4.5		
With FGD and SCR	6.5	5.4	4.9	5.1	
3. Middle load (5%)	5.8	4.2	3.6	4.9	
With FGD	6.3	4.8	4.2		
With FGD and SCR	6.5	5.2	4.6	5.0	

SOURCE: International Energy Agency, *Emission Controls in Electricity Generation and Industry* (Paris: IEA/OECD, 1988), Annex 4.
a. Establishment of new plants, 1995 conditions, 5 percent and 10 percent discount rates.
b. Flue gas desulfurization.
c. Selective catalytic reduction.

Table 4.4
Electricity generating costs of renewables, OECD countries
(1989 U.S. cents per kilowatt-hour)[a]

	Current		Future	
	Minimum	Maximum	Minimum	Maximum
Wind (60 MW)	5.3	9.0	4.1	4.9
Geothermal (50 MW)	4.1	10.9		
Municipal solid waste[b]	4.9			
Tidal[c] (6–7 GW)	6.7	24.8		
Solar thermal (CRS,[d] 100 MW)	15.3	26.6	13.5	
Photovoltaics (<500 kW)	56.9	101.2	5.9	6.8
Wave	7.9	9.4		
Hydro power[e]	5.7	17.1		

a. Unless indicated, source is International Energy Agency, *Renewable Sources of Energy* (Paris: IEA/OECD, 1987), Annex 2.
b. Mass combustion of municipal solid waste (MSW) with a capacity of 5 MW, from Japan.
c. U.K. Department of Energy, *An Evaluation of Energy Related Greenhouse Gas Emissions and Measures to Ameliorate Them*, Energy Paper No. 58 (London: HMSO, October 1989).
d. Central receiver system.
e. The data for hydro power are based on estimates made in West Germany: G. Kolb et al., *CO_2 Reduction Potential through Rational Energy Utilization and Use of Renewable Energy Sources in the Federal Republic of Germany* (Kernforschungsanlage Julich GmbH, 1989).

sive, but decreased capital investment, extended system life expectancy, and improved conversion efficiency, coupled with economies of scale, could enable PV systems to penetrate into the field of central power station applications by the late 1990s.[13]

The estimated costs of achieving reductions in greenhouse gas emissions by the various substitution options for electricity generation in the OECD region are given in table 4.5.[14] The two left-hand columns are used to calculate the additional costs of each reduction or replacement option over the coal base case. The next two columns indicate, in terms of metric tons (t) of CO_2 *gas* equivalents, the amount of greenhouse gases emitted per gigawatt-hour (GWh) generated by each option and the amount of greenhouse gas emissions saved per GWh by the option over the base case. For each option, the ratio of the additional costs to the amount of greenhouse gases saved gives the additional costs incurred in saving a unit of

Table 4.5
Costs of substituting for GHG emissions from electricity generation, OECD countries (1989 U.S. dollars)[a]

Technology	Energy generation costs (U.S. cents/kWh)	GHG intensity (tCO$_2$/GWh)	GHG saved (tCO$_2$/GWh)	Additional costs of GHG savings (US\$/tC)[b]
Base				
Coal (average)[c]	3.3	1,440.1	base	base
Reduction—fossil fuels				
Coal (modern)[d]	3.8	1,184.0	256.1	71.7
Gas	5.0	548.3	891.8	70.0
Oil (average)[e]	5.3	1,144.6	295.5	248.4
Oil (modern)[f]	5.7	1,144.6	295.5	298.1
Reduction				
Municipal solid waste	4.9	1,620.5[g]	−180.4	NA
Replacement—nuclear				
Nuclear (6-year lead)	5.2	0.0	1,440.1	48.4
Nuclear (10-year lead)	5.7	0.0	1,440.1	61.2

Table 4.5 (continued)

Technology	Energy generation costs (U.S. cents/kWh)	GHG intensity (tCO$_2$/GWh)	GHG saved (tCO$_2$/GWh)	Additional costs of GHG savings (US$/tC)[b]
Replacement—renewables[h]				
Geothermal	4.1/10.9	0.0	1,440.1	20.4/193.7
Wind, current	5.3/9.0	0.0	1,440.1	51.0/145.3
Wind, future	4.1/4.9	0.0	1,440.1	20.4/40.8
Hydro power	5.7/17.1	0.0	1,440.1	61.2/351.7
Tidal	6.7/24.8	0.0	1,440.1	86.6/547.9
Wave	7.9/9.4	0.0	1,440.1	117.2/155.5
Solar thermal, current	15.3/26.6	0.0	1,440.1	305.8/593.8
Solar thermal, future	13.5	0.0	1,440.1	259.9
Photovoltaics, current	56.9/101.2	0.0	1,440.1	1,366.0/2,494.9
Photovoltaics, future	5.9/6.8	0.0	1,440.1	66.3/89.2

SOURCE: Calculated from Tables 11, 12, and 13 in Barbier, Burgess, and Pearce, *Slowing Global Warming*.

a. 5 percent discount rate used.

b. Greenhouse gas (GHG) expressed as CO$_2$ (in carbon units).

c. No emissions technology assumed, average of importing and low-price region for coal.

d. FGD emissions technology assumed, average of importing and low-price region for coal.

e. No emissions technology assumed.

f. FGD emissions technology assumed.

g. S. Piccot, J. Buzun, and H. Frey, "Emissions and Cost Estimates for Globally Significant Anthropogenic Combustion Sources of NO$_x$, N$_2$O, CH$_4$, CO, and CO$_2$," Report for U.S. Environmental Protection Agency, Washington, DC, May 1990.

h. Estimates separated by slashes indicate minimum and maximum values.

greenhouse gas. In the far right-hand column we translate this amount into *carbon* units—that is, U.S. dollars per metric ton of carbon-equivalent emissions saved.

Of the reduction options, switching to oil generation (both with and without emissions technology) is an expensive option for lowering greenhouse gas emissions, with costs in the region of US$250 to US$300/tC. Gas or modern coal plants, on the other hand, are less expensive choices, with additional costs of reducing greenhouse gas emissions of around US$70/tC. As greenhouse gas emissions would be more than halved, substituting gas for coal in electricity generation may be a relatively effective, as well as cheap, way of lowering these emissions. In comparison, introducing modern coal plants achieves less than a 20 percent reduction in greenhouse gas emissions. Burning municipal waste instead of coal actually increases greenhouse gas emissions.[15] This option should not be considered as a means for reducing these emissions from electricity generation.

The replacement technologies for electricity generation in table 4.5 all have the advantage of not emitting any greenhouse gases.[16] Replacing coal-generated electricity by nuclear power appears to incur relatively low additional costs per metric ton of carbon removed (US$48 to US$61/tC). However, as noted previously, employing this substitution option may be constrained by concern for other social costs. There exists a wide range of renewable replacement technologies that have a substantial potential for cost-effectively reducing greenhouse gas emissions, both currently and especially in the future. Of the renewable replacement options currently available, the minimum costs per ton of greenhouse gas removed of geothermal, wind, hydro power, tidal, and wave lie at the lower end of the cost spectrum (from US$20 to US$120/tC). However, the estimated maximum costs of tidal are more than six times greater than its minimum costs, and the maximum costs of reducing greenhouse gases by hydro power double its minimum costs.

Currently, the most expensive method for reducing CO_2 emissions is photovoltaics (PV), with costs ranging from US$1,366 to US$2,495/tC, followed by solar thermal (US$306 to US$594/tC saved). It is predicted that PV costs will decrease dramatically in the future to less than US$100/tC saved, making it a relatively attractive substitution option. The costs of wind power are also expected to decline to levels that make substitution more attractive. In general, economies of scale and future technological breakthroughs could make switching from conventional electrical generation options to alternative, renewable methods more financially viable.

As the costs of substitution differ considerably across the OECD region, we examine in more detail the costs of reducing greenhouse gas emissions in a few selected countries—the United States, the United Kingdom, West Germany, and Australia.

United States

Table 4.6 reviews various options for reducing CO_2 emissions through fuel switching in the United States. As gas is a cheaper option for generating electricity than pulverized coal, the costs of reducing CO_2 emissions by switching from coal to gas are negative, from −US$68 to −US$231/tC saved. Carbon emissions per GWh generated would be reduced by about 63 percent if gas turbine combined cycle plants were deployed. Although switching from coal to oil would also be economically attractive, the amount of CO_2 savings would be much less, around 32 percent per GWh. However, the long-term potential for switching from coal to gas in the United States may be limited. The United States currently consumes around 28 percent of total world gas supplies. Power generation accounts for 16 percent of total U.S. gas consumption—slightly less than the OECD average. The United States has only 4.7 percent of the world's proven reserves, and if current U.S. production is maintained, its reserves will last for only 11.2 years.[17]

Municipal solid waste (MSW) is an expensive substitution option and does not yield any savings in per-unit greenhouse gas emissions. In addition, further assessment of MSW needs to address the problems of removing dioxins, chlorinated gases, and other toxins that are emitted during the combustion process. Wood generation is more economically attractive, but also produces high *direct* emissions of greenhouse gases (2,335 tCO_2/GWh). However, the overall impact of wood on greenhouse gas emissions may be a net reduction on these emissions as wood grown for fuel would extract carbon from the atmosphere. The capacity of wood generation is severely constrained by the availability and high delivery costs of wood and wood wastes. Currently, installed capacity of total biomass energy for electricity generation stands at 8,000 MW. If trends continue, this could reach over 30,000 MW by 2030, and with increased research, development, and demonstration it could amount to almost 38,000 MW by 2030.

Table 4.6
Costs of reducing GHG emissions from electricity generation, United States (1989 U.S. dollars)[a]

Technology	Electricity generation costs (U.S. cents/kWh)	GHG intensity (tCO$_2$/GWh)	GHG saved (tCO$_2$/GWh)	Additional costs of GHG savings US$/tC)
Base				
Pulverized coal	3.91	1,349.42	base	base
Reduction—fossil fuels				
Fluidized bed coal	3.91	1,310.54	38.88	0.00
CCFB[b] coal	5.15	1,044.48	304.94	148.74
Oil	2.76	922.41	427.01	−99.14
Gas turbine	0.41	793.91	555.51	−231.34
Gas boiler	2.64	658.01	691.41	−67.79
GTCC[c]	1.77	498.69	850.73	−92.41
Reduction—municipal solid waste				
Mass feed	15.65	1,774.36	−424.94	NA
Refuse	15.65	1,620.45	−271.03	NA
Reduction—biomass fuels				
Wood	5.36	2,335.01	−985.59	NA

SOURCE: S. Piccot, J. Buzun, and H. C. Frey, "Emissions and Cost Estimates for Globally Significant Anthropogenic Combustion Sources of NO$_x$, N$_2$O, CH$_4$, CO, and CO$_2$," Prepared for U.S. Environmental Protection Agency, Washington, DC, May 1990.
a. Levelized costs for each technology exclude fuel costs. CO$_2$ equivalents for various greenhouse gases calculated using the weightings in Barbier, Burgess, and Pearce, *Slowing Global Warming*, Table 13. Greenhouse gas emissions are from generation only.
b. Combined cycle fluidized bed.
c. Gas turbine combined cycle.

In table 4.7 renewable and nuclear technologies are compared against the baseload coal electricity-generating costs and greenhouse gas emissions.[18] Given the very optimistic projection of nuclear energy costs for the United States (5.5 U.S. cents per kWh), the additional costs in terms of CO_2 savings appear very low—around US$7/tC saved. However, the additional costs associated with nuclear power—waste treatment, transport and storage, environmental and health risks, and other social impacts—have made this option less attractive in the United States in recent years. Nuclear power construction costs in the United States have also been consistently underestimated in the past.[19]

The current additional costs of CO_2 savings from substituting hydro power for baseload coal are US$16/tC, although these are likely to fall in the future and become negative (around US$11/tC by 2030). In 1988 the aggregate capacity of all existing hydroelectric facilities was 88 gigawatts. It is estimated that added capacity will only reach 8 GW (i.e., total capacity 96 GW) in 2030; however, if research, development, and demonstration are intensified, added capacity may reach 37 GW (i.e., total capacity 125 GW) by 2030. But environmental and social considerations may severely hamper investments and may even lead to reductions in existing hydro power capacity.

Geothermal systems also have potential as substitutes for fossil fuels in electricity generation, although the systems are highly location-specific. There now exists a range of small (1–5 megawatt), medium (25–60 MW), and large (over 100 MW) hydrothermal plants with a total capacity of 2,800 MW. The additional costs of switching from coal to hydrothermal electricity generation to reduce CO_2 emissions are currently negative ($-$US$16/tC). These savings are expected to increase further in the future, and the supply of geothermal electricity is likely to increase depending upon the success of advanced geopressured, hot dry rock, and magma systems.

Although no commercial ocean thermal energy conversion (OTEC) plants are currently in operation, they have significant potential for the future, especially if all additional benefits are included (water, mariculture, and cooling). No major wave energy projects are being undertaken in the United States at present, but current costs are estimated to be high (US$133–399/tC saved). Other future sources of ocean energy for electricity generation include ocean currents, tidal power, salinity gradient conversion systems, and marine biomass.

Table 4.7
Costs of replacing GHG emissions from electricity generation, United States (1989 U.S. dollars)

Technology[a]	Electricity generation costs[b] (U.S. cents/kWh)	GHG intensity[c] (tCO$_2$/GWh)	GHG saved (tCO$_2$/GWh)	Additional costs of GHG savings[b] (US$/tC)
Base				
Baseload coal (c)	5.21	1,440.10	base	base
Baseload coal (f)	6.26	1,440.10	base	base
Replacement—nuclear				
Nuclear (c)	5.50	0.00	1,440.10	7.29
Replacement—renewables				
Hydropower (c)	5.84	0.00	1,440.10	15.95
Hydropower (f)	5.84	0.00	1,440.10	−10.63
Geothermal (c)				
Hydrothermal	4.59	0.00	1,440.10	−15.95
Geopressured	7.82	0.00	1,440.10	66.44
Hot dry rock	6.78	0.00	1,440.10	39.86
Magma	22.84	0.00	1,440.10	449.12

Table 4.7 (continued)

Technology[a]	Electricity generation costs[b] (U.S. cents/kWh)	GHG intensity[c] (tCO$_2$/GWh)	GHG saved (tCO$_2$/GWh)	Additional costs of GHG savings[b] (US$/tC)
Geothermal (f)				
Hydrothermal	3.13/4.69	0.00	1,440.10	−79.73/−39.86
Geopressured	4.59/5.11	0.00	1,440.10	−42.52/−29.23
Hot dry rock	3.44/4.80	0.00	1,440.10	−71.75/−37.21
Magma	4.28/6.26	0.00	1,440.10	−50.49/0.00
Ocean thermal (c)	8.34/22.94	0.00	1,440.10	79.73/451.78
Ocean thermal (f)	4.17/12.51	0.00	1,440.10	−53.15/159.45
Wave energy (c)	10.43/20.86	0.00	1,440.10	132.88/398.63
Solar thermal (c)	16.48	0.00	1,440.10	287.01
Solar thermal (f)	4.17	0.00	1,440.10	−53.15
Wind energy (c)	8.66	0.00	1,440.10	87.70
Wind energy (f)	3.23/4.17	0.00	1,440.10	−77.07/−53.15
Photovoltaics (c)	33.37	0.00	1,440.10	717.53
Photovoltaics (f)	4.17/5.21	0.00	1,440.10	−53.15/−26.58

SOURCE: Idaho National Engineering Laboratory et al., *Potential of Renewable Energy*. For nuclear power: B. Keepin and G. Kats, "Greenhouse Warming: Comparative Analysis of Nuclear and Efficiency Abatement Strategies," *Energy Policy*, December 1988.

a. c = current, f = future (2030).
b. Minimum = business as usual, maximum = research, development, and demonstration. Estimates separated by slashes indicate minimum and maximum values.
c. Greenhouse gas intensity (tCO$_2$/GWh) for coal taken from Table 13 in Barbier, Burgess, and Pearce, *Slowing Global Warming*.

Existing solar thermal systems (with and without storage facilities) are high-cost options for reducing greenhouse gas emissions (US$287/tC saved). Future solar thermal systems are expected to be used for peak load, either without the use of storage or with an integrated thermal storage facility for intermediate and base-load plants. Greenhouse gas reductions may then be achieved at a substantial economic saving (−US$53/tC). However, this potential is highly dependent upon technical improvements in storage facilities.

Wind power currently contributes more than 2 terawatt hours (TWh; tera $= 10^{12}$) of electricity generation in the United States, primarily in California. The potential contribution of wind energy is significant. If current trends continue, wind power could expand to 3.3 quads (967 TWh) by 2030, and with increases in research, development, and demonstration to as much as 10.65 quads (3,120 TWh). Wind power is therefore a relatively cost-effective method of reducing greenhouse gases, with current additional costs around US$88/tC. This figure could fall to −US$77/tC saved by 2030.

Although at present PV systems are an expensive choice for reducing greenhouse gas emissions at over US$700/tC removed, by 2030 these costs of removal may even be negative (−US$27 to −53/tC saved). The potential penetration of PV into the total U.S. electric power market is 0.8 GW of primary energy by 2000, and 114 GW by 2030 assuming that current trends continue. If research, development, and demonstration are intensified, then by 2000 PV supply may reach 3.6 GW, and by 2030 as much as 266 GW. For further market penetration, improved storage or new hybrid facilities are required.[20]

United Kingdom, West Germany, and Australia

A study of the practical technical options to curtail emissions of greenhouse gases from energy-related activities has been undertaken for the United Kingdom.[21] For each option, the *capacity* for electricity generation is projected, and the costs are calculated on the basis of the amount of CO_2 emissions reduced at each additional level of generation.[22] The relative cost-effectiveness of the options depends significantly on whether future fossil-fuel prices are expected to be high or low and on the time horizon—2005 or 2020. For example, in the case of nuclear energy, higher fossil-fuel prices lower substantially the marginal costs of CO_2 savings; in the 2020 scenario, the marginal costs would actually be negative—implying that switching to nuclear not only reduces CO_2 emissions but also saves on costs.

Other substitution options seem limited by either capacity or cost constraints. Landfill gas appears the most attractive option, as virtually all of its marginal costs of substitution are negative, but its maximum capacity in the United Kingdom would be limited to 3.2 TWh per year. This would only reduce annual CO_2 emissions by 0.36 MtC. Wind power initially has negative and low marginal costs of CO_2 savings, but the costs rise sharply as capacity increases. The study assumes that the best sites available for wind generation are limited and will be used up quickly, and it assumes no economies of scale. Advanced gas turbines could have a substantial impact on CO_2 emissions in the near future by displacing oil and coal. However, substitution capacity is probably limited by costs to around 20 GW. Power generation from gas turbine plants in the future is only cost-effective as a CO_2 abatement measure at very low levels of capacity (less than 8 GW) and only in the high price scenario.

Straw combustion is also a relatively low-cost technological alternative but has only a small potential capacity. The marginal costs of reducing CO_2 emissions by other options appear prohibitive. The costs of photovoltaics are extremely speculative because of the high level of technical uncertainty; however, more recent cost estimates suggest that photovoltaics are likely to be an attractive substitute for fossil-fuel electricity generation in the future.[23]

A similar assessment of the costs of substitution options to reduce CO_2 emissions in the energy sector has been undertaken in West Germany.[24] In the study, only hydro power, wind energy, and photovoltaic cells were compared as substitutes for fossil fuels (coal) in electricity generation. Of these substitutes, hydro-power plants have the lowest additional costs over coal, which are actually negative at the lower range of generation costs. However, further expansion of hydro-power capacity is severely constrained in West Germany. Wind energy may have the greatest potential for replacing CO_2 emissions. This option has a potential primary energy contribution of 40 TWh per annum, could reduce CO_2 emissions annually by 13.2 million tons of CO_2 (3.6 MtC), and only incurs additional costs ranging from US\$62–250 per ton of carbon saved. At present photovoltaic cells are not attractive because of the high and uncertain electricity-generating costs, but in the future, given expected technological improvements and economies of scale, this substitution technology may be a more cost-effective method of reducing CO_2 emissions from electricity generation.

Substitution options for electricity generation in Australia were examined as part of a study analyzing the potential effects of achieving a 20 percent economy-wide reduction in 1988 CO_2 emissions by 2005.[25] Options for reducing CO_2 emissions per unit of power generated vary significantly across Australia. Victoria is the highest per-unit CO_2 emitter, as it relies principally on brown coal. Other states, such as Tasmania (mainly hydro), South Australia, Western Australia, and Northern Territory (mainly natural gas) have relatively lower per-unit CO_2 emissions. For these states, the unit costs of reducing emissions will be higher than for coal-burning states.

The least expensive way of reducing emissions is to switch from brown- to black-coal plants, a change which actually incurs negative costs per ton of CO_2 saved. However, the amount of CO_2 saved per unit of power (170 tCO_2/GWh) is limited. Switching from brown coal to burning gas in an advanced turbine or a combined cycle plant would reduce CO_2 emissions further, but at a higher cost. Methane recovery would involve collecting and using the methane gas that escapes from coal mines and landfill sites. Not only would this substitution option reduce CO_2 emissions from fossil-fuel power generation, but it would also yield additional benefits in reducing the amount of methane escaping into the atmosphere. The costs of methane substitution are estimated to be US\$2.86 to US\$17.20/tC saved; however, serious doubts exist about the technical feasibility of recovering and using methane. Similarly, cogeneration (combined heat and power) could be a cost-effective means of reducing CO_2 emissions, but its maximum capacity is thought to be around 2 percent of total electricity demand.

Only those renewable energy technologies currently near commercialization—hydro power, wind, and photovoltaics—were considered by the Australian study as likely to have a potential impact on CO_2 emissions by 2005. Of these technologies, hydro power and wind appear the most attractive, but hydro power in particular is limited in new capacity. Although the cost-effectiveness of PV technology is rapidly improving, it is not expected to be economically feasible for large-scale power generation even by the turn of the century.

Developing Countries

Developing countries will be highly dependent on the transfer of replacement and reduction technologies applied to electricity genera-tion from OECD countries.[26] However, the relative cost-effectiveness of the substitution technologies will vary significantly from country to country in the developing world, depending on differences in population growth and distribution (e.g., rates of urbanization), economic development, levels of income and growth, government budget constraints, and institutional structures.

All substitution options, but especially renewable energy technol-ogies, in developing countries are highly sensitive to changing inter-national oil prices and the location and scale of the generation facility. Renewable technologies for large-scale generation will be located mainly near urban centers, whereas the smaller, stand-alone technol-ogies (e.g., small-scale biomass and photovoltaic systems) are often used in rural and remote applications. As fossil-fuel prices are rela-tively higher in rural than in urban areas, the economic viability of remote rural systems may be greater than the large-scale urban sys-tems, and the rural systems may be less sensitive to falls in interna-tional oil prices. In addition, supplies of fossil fuels tend to be more reliable in urban than in remote areas.[27]

Biomass options are particularly sensitive to varying feedstock costs. These costs fall into two main categories—those which have minimal or zero resource costs, such as on-site waste products found at wood or agricultural processing plants, and those which have a market value, such as plantation-based wood and cash crops. Waste products—crop residuals, agricultural wastes, and human or animal wastes—are competitive with fossil fuels when used on-site, in areas away from a central grid, or compacted to reduce unit transport costs. Large-scale and commercial biomass applications tend to be attractive only when feedstock costs are low; however, such low costs often depend on (1) depressed primary commodity markets (e.g., wood, sugar), (2) fewer alternative by-product uses, or (3) an unlimited or on-site resource supply.[28]

Finally, distortionary government pricing policies for fossil-fuel generation of electricity in developing countries may affect the adop-tion of substitution options. Such distortions also vary significantly from country to country and within a country. Uncontrolled retail prices for small-quantity fossil-fuel purchases in remote areas may be well above regulated prices and far above economic fuel costs for many small-scale rural energy systems. In contrast, the regulated fossil-fuel prices for large-scale urban electricity generation subsidize the generation costs of such systems.[29]

For example, a study comparing the long-run marginal costs of wind to conventionally generated electricity in ten developing countries indicates that wind may be a cost-effective substitute in most cases.[30] However, a World Bank study suggests that a 50 percent drop in diesel and fuel-oil import prices could reduce electricity generation costs by 30 percent, thus making wind a less attractive option.[31] Many biomass generating options currently promoted for developing countries, including dendrothermal power systems (a wood-burning power plant and a dedicated plantation of short-rotation trees), "bagasse" systems (a sugar-mill power plant burning the fibrous residue from cane crushing) and biomass power gasifiers (wood, charcoal, rice husks, or coconut husks), are also sensitive to prevailing diesel and fuel-oil prices. Feedstock prices, which can vary significantly, also tend to be an important determinant of economic viability. For example, estimates from Thailand indicate that quadrupling wood fuel prices up to typical plantation costs of US$20 per ton (wet weight) results in wood generation systems that are no longer competitive with coal or oil plants.[32] On the other hand, small-scale rural applications of these and other renewable energy technologies, including wind and photovoltaic water pumping, may continue to be economically viable because of the scarcity and unreliability of fossil fuels and their relatively high prices.

The role of nuclear energy as a substitution option illustrates the technical and financial difficulties facing developing countries. To replace coal with nuclear power generation by 2025 would require existing capacity in developing countries of 14 GW today and 38 GW projected for 1999 to reach 2,330 GW by 2025.[33] Building this capacity would result in an annual capital cost of US$64 billion and electricity-generation costs of US$170 billion each year (1987 U.S. dollars). Such a financial commitment is infeasible for most developing countries, as many would not have the access to capital to finance nuclear reactors, technology transfers, imported fuel and expertise, and investments in infrastructure and training. Many major developing countries with nuclear programs have already been forced to reduce or phase them out because nuclear plants have been too costly or slow to build.

Building/Industrial and Other Stationary Uses

For space and water heating and industrial process heat, reduction technologies would involve changing the fuel mix—for example, introducing combined heat and power (CHP) or switching from coal and oil to gas or biomass. The main replacement technologies are the various renewable energy options for both space and water heating and industrial process heat, passive and active solar heating systems, geothermal processes, and solar thermal energy.

Fuel Switching—Selected OECD Countries

The applications and economics of space/water heating and industrial process heat vary significantly from country to country. Table 4.8 illustrates these differences by examining the costs per unit of greenhouse gas saved for fuel switching in heat generation for selected OECD countries.

In Canada, coal is a relatively cheap source of energy for industrial process heat; therefore, switching to oil or gas is an expensive option. The most attractive options would be to switch to gas boilers, kilns, and dryers (ca. US$40–120/tC equivalent saved). However, in the residential and commercial building sector, the substitution of gas for oil can lead to some reductions in greenhouse gas emissions with substantial economic gains (i.e., − US$750 to − US$2,300/tC saved). In Germany, some reductions in greenhouse gas emissions from industrial process heat could be achieved through switching from coal to oil, but the cost would also be high (around US$300–470/tC saved). However, in Germany's residential and commercial sector, switching from coal to oil would produce CO_2 savings with economic gains (i.e., − US$145 to − US$160/tC saved). In Italy, the best options for the industrial, residential, and commercial sectors would be to switch from coal to gas, although the additional costs would be significant (from US$65–425/tC saved).

In Japan, coal is a relatively cheap source of energy, which makes switching to oil or gas expensive options for industrial process heat and residential/commercial heating. Gas is the cheapest option for reducing greenhouse gas emissions from boilers and dryers; however, oil is a marginally less expensive substitution option for coal cement kilns. In the United Kingdom, switching from coal to gas in both the industrial sector and the residential/commercial sector in-

Table 4.8
Costs of fuel switching to reduce GHG emissions, selected OECD countries[a] (1989 U.S. dollars per ton of carbon)

	Canada	West Germany	Italy	Japan	United Kingdom	United States
Industrial						
Oil boilers	716	415	734	999	477	610
	(49)[b]	(49)	(49)	(49)	(49)	(49)
Oil cement kilns	807	468	827	1,125	538	687
	(43)	(43)	(43)	(43)	(43)	(43)
Oil dryers	529	307	542	737	352	450
	(66)	(66)	(66)	(66)	(66)	(66)
Gas boilers	57	—	208	636	63	167
	(83)		(83)	(83)	(83)	(83)
Gas cement kilns	117	—	425	1,296	127	340
	(41)		(41)	(41)	(41)	(41)
Gas dryers	43	—	155	474	47	124
	(111)		(111)	(111)	(111)	(111)

Table 4.8 (continued)

	Canada	West Germany	Italy	Japan	United Kingdom	United States
Residential/commercial[a]						
Oil furnaces	—	-158 (35)	645 (35)	—	523 (35)	—
Oil boilers	—	-145 (39)	593 (39)	—	481 (39)	—
Oil heaters	—	-152 (37)	620 (37)	—	503 (37)	—
Gas furnaces	-2,299 (9)	—	97 (45)	2,675 (9)	193 (45)	-1,549 (9)
Gas boilers	-755 (28)	—	65 (67)	879 (28)	130 (67)	-509 (28)
Gas heaters	-1,929 (11)	—	90 (48)	2,244 (11)	180 (48)	-1,299 (11)

SOURCE: Adapted from Barbier, Burgess, and Pearce, *Slowing Global Warming*, Table 21.

a. For all countries, the base technologies for industrial process heat are coal furnaces, boilers, and heaters. In Canada, Japan, and the United States, the base technologies for residential/commercial heating are oil furnaces, boilers, and heaters, whereas in West Germany, Italy, and the United Kingdom the base technologies are coal furnaces, boilers, and heaters.

b. Figures in parentheses are the amounts of GHG emissions reduced, in kilogram CO_2 equivalents per million Btu.

curs substantially lower costs per unit of greenhouse gas saved (US$45–195/tC saved) than switching from coal to oil. In the United States, gas is again the least expensive substitution option. In the industrial sector costs of switching from coal to gas are low, ranging from US$124–340/tC saved. Switching from oil to gas in the residential sector yields an economic gain, from around −US$508 to −US$1,548/tC saved.

Other Substitutions—United States and United Kingdom

Of the replacement renewable options for industrial heat processes in table 4.9 for the United States, geothermal technologies currently incur relatively low additional costs for reducing greenhouse gas emissions. These costs are expected to fall further in the future. However, applications of geothermal energy to industrial heat processes are limited because sufficient resource sites may not be located near main industrial demand centers. At present, solar thermal industrial process heat is an expensive substitute for conventional coal technologies, with costs ranging from US$190 to US$725/tC equivalent saved. Future applications of solar thermal power to industrial processes may benefit from developments in parabolic dishes and solar trough systems for solar thermal electricity generation. The main constraints on industrial applications of solar thermal energy remain the need for high direct insolation, storage capacity for photolytic detoxification, and durable collectors that track the sun.[34]

In the U.S. residential/commercial sector, replacing oil with geothermal heat resources leads to substantial savings, from −US$90 to −US$280/tC saved. However, reservoir temperatures and flow rates, as well as depths of the resource, vary greatly among geographic locations, thus affecting regional costs. Greater development is expected initially in the Northeast, followed by the West, with the South and North Central regions providing only minimal contributions by 2030. A significant proportion of this development is expected to be heat pumps, with an annual increase of 10–18 percent in their use during the next twenty years.[35]

Some passive solar designs can be incorporated into building design at little or no added cost, replacing oil heating/cooling systems with substantial gains (−US$533 to −US$107/tC). However, passive heating technologies face some constraints, including greatest heat requirements in northern latitudes and winter months when insola-

Table 4.9
Costs of substituting for GHG emissions in heat processes, United States and United Kingdom (1989 U.S. dollars per ton of carbon)

	United States		United Kingdom, Current
	Current	Future	
Industrial			
Small-scale CHP[a]	—	—	−73
Small-scale CHP[b]	—	—	−101
Geothermal[c]			
Boilers	99–209	36–154	—
Cement kilns	41–86	15–64	—
Dryers	65–138	24–102	—
Solar thermal[c]			
Boilers	460–722	—	—
Cement kilns	190–298	—	—
Dryers	303–476	—	—
Residential/commercial[d]			
Geothermal			
Furnaces	(−259)–(−100)	(−350)–(−180)	—
Boilers	(−233)–(−90)	(−315)–(−162)	—
Heaters	(−277)–(−107)	(−375)–(−192)	—
Active solar			
Space/water heat	84–1,169	(−303)–(−65)	—
Cooling	169–1,169	(−303)–(−1)	—
Passive solar			
Heat/cooling	(−532)–(−107)	—	—
Orientation	—	—	−340
South windows	—	—	−265
Roof collector/fan	—	—	89
South windows (maximum)	—	—	170
Conservatory	—	—	362
Double-glazed wall	—	—	642

SOURCE: Adapted from Barbier, Burgess, and Pearce, *Slowing Global Warming*, Tables 22 and 23.

a. Replaces coal power plus heat from coal/oil boilers.
b. Replaces coal power plus heat from gas boilers.
c. Replaces coal power.
d. Replaces oil power in the United States and coal heat in the United Kingdom.

tion is lowest, and limited availability of south-facing potential glazing area. Further research into advanced windows with reduced thermal loss, improved ventilation, incorporating thermal storage into building materials, and integrating passive with active solar systems may improve the use of passive solar in residential/commercial buildings in the future.[36]

Active solar heating and cooling systems use pumps or fans for heat distribution and solar collectors that are distinct from the building structure. They are currently more expensive than conventional oil-fired systems in residential/commercial buildings, with great variations in costs (see table 4.9). Active heating shares similar constraints with passive heating, in that the greatest heat requirement is in northern locations and winter months where insolation levels are lowest, as well as suffering high heat losses when the load is the greatest. Active cooling systems are constrained by the need for cooling subsystems and higher operational temperatures that reduce collector efficiency, and by competition from efficient conventional chillers/heat pumps. Improving construction materials, such as glazers, absorbers, and desiccant materials, and developing central storage systems and integrated heating and cooling systems will make active solar systems more attractive.[37] In the future, they are expected to be economically competitive with conventional oil fired systems ($-US\$1$ to $-US\$303/tC$ saved).

In the United Kingdom, combined heat and power (CHP) systems are believed to offer substantial savings in fuel use compared to the usual combination of boiler plant for heating and conventional thermal generation for electricity. The thermal output that is harnessed from an electricity-generating plant in a CHP can replace fuels that would otherwise be consumed in heat-only boilers. When allowance is made for heat recovery, CHP systems can run at an efficiency of at least 80 percent given good utilization of the thermal output. Conventional coal-fired electrical power stations currently operate at 33 percent efficiency. The costs and emission levels of small-scale combined heat and power systems (40–60 kW capacities) are compared to conventional systems in table 4.9, although viable installations could range from 15 kW in small commercial buildings to over 50 MW on large industrial sites.

Gas-fueled combined heat and power stations save 1,027 tCO_2 equivalent emissions per GWh when replacing coal-powered electricity-generation and gas boilers, and 1,420 tCO_2/GWh when replacing coal-generated electricity with coal or oil boilers. The additional costs of reducing greenhouse gas emissions by this substitution option are negative, ranging from − US$73 to − US$101/tC equivalent emissions saved.

In the residential/commercial sectors in the United Kingdom, passive solar heat systems compete with conventional coal heaters. There is a wide variety of passive solar technologies that are available, some of which are less expensive than coal heaters, others that are more costly. Of the cheaper passive solar options, building orientation and south-facing windows incur negative additional costs for reducing greenhouse gas emissions, from − US$265 to − US$340/tC equivalent saved. The most expensive option is double-glazed walls, with additional costs of around US$642/tC saved.

Developing Countries

The ability of developing countries to reduce greenhouse gas emissions from the industrial and residential/commercial sectors will again depend on the transfer of technologies from OECD countries, domestic and international factors, including the price of oil, government intervention in fuel prices, and specific site conditions.

China is distinct among developing countries in that it has significant heating loads over much of the country. Total consumption of energy in China has been growing rapidly from 293 million metric tons of coal equivalent (mtce) in 1970 to 845 mtce in 1987 and is expected to increase to between 1.3 and 2.4 billion tce by 2000.[38] China is currently the third-largest energy-consuming country in the world, and up to 75 percent of its primary energy requirement is derived from coal. Around 60 percent of primary energy in China is consumed by the industrial sector. At present, space heating use, excluding that for hotels and offices catering for foreigners, is constrained by mandated coal allocations resulting in partially heated buildings with indoor temperatures significantly below design conditions.

Inefficiencies are also caused by a pricing structure that does not reflect the true costs of energy production in China. Distortions in energy pricing may impact severely upon the choice of substitution options in heat generation. For example, switching from conventional boiler generation in Beijing to cogeneration or the use of clean coal in boilers reduces annual coal consumption by 110,000 and 74,130 tons, respectively. The additional costs per kilogram of greenhouse gas emissions reduced range from yuan (Y) -5.67 to Y4.78/kgC equivalent saved for cogeneration and around Y31/kgC equivalent saved for clean coal.[39] (The official exchange rate in 1989 was Y3.73 = US$1.00.) However, large government subsidies for coal consumption are making both substitution options less financially attractive, although they also hide the opportunity costs of the electricity output forgone from cogeneration. For example, in 1984 electricity prices in China were only 58 percent of the long-run marginal cost of electricity supply.[40]

A recent study of the potential for energy conservation in residential/commercial buildings in China also includes estimates of some "passive solar" technologies in terms of the cost of coal conservation (the ratio of the annualized cost of investment to amount of coal saved annually).[41] Translated into tons of carbon saved, the costs of these substitution options amount to Y2.12/tC and Y7.56/tC saved for north and south wall insulation respectively, and Y4.11/tC saved for double glazing.

Biomass heat gasifiers are used widely for industrial and commercial process heat applications in Brazil, Southeast Asia, and the South Pacific. In large-scale industrial processes, biomass heat gasifiers (100kW–10MW capacity) are substitutes for fuel oil to provide process heat for drying (e.g., tea, grain, lumber), manufacturing glass, tiles, and bricks, producing cement, processing food, and so on. Smaller biomass heat gasifiers are used for crop drying, baking, and similar applications. These systems are extremely sensitive to oil prices, wood fuel prices, and gasifier capital cost estimates. For example, with a drop in fuel oil prices from US$30 to US$15 per barrel (bbl) (1986 prices) the break-even fuel wood price for a moderately priced heat gasifier system (US$25,000/GJ/hr) drops from US$30/ton to near zero.[42] The economic feasibility of large-scale biomass gasifiers tends to be more constrained by high oil, biomass, and capital costs than the smaller, remote, rural systems.

Active residential and small commercial solar water-heating systems operate in many developing countries. Large industrial applications of solar water heating are more constrained by economic costs and are highly sensitive to the price of oil. For example, Kenyan residential solar heating installations remained economically attractive even when fuel oil prices fell from 5.5 U.S. cents per kilowatt-hour to 4.4 cents (1986 prices) between 1985 and 1986.[43] Similarly, when the price of displaced fuel oil rises above US$150/ton of oil equivalent (toe) (1986 prices), existing solar water heaters in high insolation areas may be cost-effective for industrial process heat in Kenya; however, when the price of fuel imports drops well below US$150/toe, many industrial solar water-heating systems are no longer viable alternatives to oil-based heating systems. Given that in Kenya electrical power costs range from 3–10 U.S. cents per kilowatt-hour for hydro power to 5–20 cents for thermal generation, solar water heating systems in high insolation areas are often more economical than conventional electric systems for heating water. Similar factors are likely to affect solar cooling systems for buildings in the industrial, commercial, and residential sectors of developing countries.

Transport

The clean fuel substitution options for replacing greenhouse emissions from the transport sector include biomass-based fuels (e.g., ethanol, methanol, gasoline), hydrogen (H_2), and electricity from non-fossil-fuel sources. Although progress has been made to develop cost-effective clean fuels, technological and financial constraints often undermine their economic attractiveness. For example, electric cars are currently constrained by their limited range and dependence upon fossil-fuel-generated electrical power. The remaining alternative fuels are reduction substitutes; that is, they reduce rather than replace greenhouse gas emissions per unit of energy substituted.

Table 4.10 compares the level of CO_2 equivalent greenhouse gas emissions from gasoline and diesel from crude oil with clean-fuel and other substitutes. The effect of efficiency improvements in vehicles is also included as a benchmark. In some cases, such as switching from gasoline to methanol derived from natural gas, the reduction in emissions may be relatively small (3%). In comparison, methanol derived from coal almost doubles CO_2 equivalent emissions. Similarly, electric vehicles from the current fossil-fuel power mix would only marginally reduce emissions. Although compressed natural gas (CNG) and liquified natural gas (LNG) could lead to 19 percent and 15 percent reductions, respectively, in greenhouse gas emissions when substituted for gasoline, problems of fuel storage as well as the limited range of natural-gas-fueled vehicles constrain their potential.

Hydrogen and electric vehicles from non-fossil-fuel sources are a

Table 4.10
Greenhouse gas emissions for alternative fuels for vehicles

Fuel/feedstock	Total CO_2 equivalent emissions[a] (billion tons per year)	Percentage relative to petroleum
Hydrogen, nonfossil power	0	-100
EVs, nonfossil power[b]	0	-100
Methanol from biomass	0	-100
Ethanol from biomass	0	-100
Gasoline from biomass	0	-100
Double fleet efficiency	0.668	-50
CNG from natural gas[c]	1.081	-19
LNG from natural gas[d]	1.135	-15
Methanol from natural gas	1.293	-3
EVs, current power mix	NA[e]	-1
Gasoline/diesel from crude oil	1.336	base
Methanol from coal	2.639	$+98$
Liquid hydrogen from coal	3.240	$+143$

SOURCE: D. Sperling and M. A. DeLuchi, "Transportation Energy Strategies and the Greenhouse Effect," IEA/OECD Expert Seminar on Energy Technologies for Reducing Emissions of Greenhouse Gases, OECD, Paris, April 12–14, 1989.
a. Total CO_2 equivalent emissions include production, distribution and end-use emissions of the fuels. Greenhouse gas emissions included in calculation are CO_2, CH_4, and N_2O. The CO_2 equivalent weighting used for CH_4 is 11.6, and for N_2O it is 175 (75-year time horizon assumed).
b. EV = electric vehicles.
c. CNG = compressed natural gas.
d. LNG = liquified natural gas.
e. Depends upon the level of penetration assumed possible for electric vehicles.

long-term substitution option. Problems with hydrogen include the weight of storage tanks, which are currently 15–20 times the weight of the stored hydrogen, complications in production from nuclear and photovoltaic sources, and difficulties with leakage and safety. However, a study in the United States has shown that, if the production cost of amorphous silicon PV modules are reduced from their current cost of US\$1.50–1.60 per peak watt (W_P) to US\$0.2–0.4/W_P, then PV hydrogen could become comparable in cost to other liquid synthetic fuels. The levelized life-cycle costs for owning and operating cars on PV hydrogen compared to other fuels also show that, assuming storage and range limits are solved, PV hydrogen cars could become an economic option.[44]

Electric-powered vehicles are constrained by range limitations and development of sufficiently light, compact, and powerful batteries at a low cost. The most promising option in the near term is a "hybrid" car, which combines an electric engine with a conventional internal combustion engine. The electric engine could be used in short trips in urban areas, as it is more efficient and less polluting, and the conventional engine could be used for longer journeys and recharging.[45]

Considerable attention has been given to biofuels—the liquid fuels for transportation produced from biomass feedstocks—as the most attractive clean-fuel substitution option in the near term. Ethanol can be produced from sugar, starch, or cellulose feedstocks (wood, energy crops, and municipal and other wastes). Methanol is made from biomass by first gasifying the feedstock to form a "syngas" mixture of CO, H_2, CO_2, higher hydrocarbons, and tar. Gasoline can also be produced from biomass by either producing first an intermediate biocrude liquid product or by isolating the hydrocarbon portion of oils derived from rapeseed, sunflowers, oil palms, or even aquatic plants. In the United States, it is estimated that through intensive research and development biofuels could increase their present contribution of 0.07 quads (1 quad $= 10^9 \times$ MBtu) to 2.4 quads in 2010 (over 2% of total U.S. energy demand) and to 8.4 quads in 2030 (almost 6% of total energy demand).[46]

However, given current relative fuel prices, wide-scale adoption of biofuels is still limited. Unless the recent oil price rises are sustained, environmental standards are changed, biofuel subsidies or petroleum taxes are imposed, or significant cost reductions occur for biofuel technologies, then petroleum gasoline and diesel fuel will remain the only transport fuels available on a large scale and at low prices. Table 4.11 indicates the current competitiveness of biofuels in the United States, the United Kingdom, and West Germany. In none of the countries are the prices of these fuels comparable to those of petroleum gasoline.

Perhaps the best lessons to date on the economics of biofuel development comes from Brazil's sugarcane-to-ethanol program. Since 1975, Brazil has been committed to increasing its use of ethanol as an extender for petroleum-derived gasoline. Ethanol production costs in the mid-1980s were estimated to be US$0.18 to US$0.48 per liter. However, these costs have been highly subsidized in the past— through a guaranteed floor price of US$0.25 per liter, by providing

Table 4.11
Gasoline and biofuel prices in the United States, United Kingdom, and West Germany

Fuel	Cost (U.S. dollars per liter)[a]
United States	
Gasoline, from biomass	0.42
Ethanol, from corn	0.34
Ethanol, from cellulose	0.33–0.36
Methanol, from biomass	0.16–0.45
Gasoline, from petroleum	0.16
United Kingdom	
Ethanol, from beet	0.63
Ethanol, from wheat	0.46
Gasoline, from petroleum	0.15
West Germany	
Gasoline, from rapeseed	0.50–0.55
Ethanol, from biomass	0.53
Methanol, from natural gas	0.18
Gasoline, from petroleum	0.15

SOURCE: Calculated from Idaho National Engineering Laboratory et al., *Potential of Renewable Energy*, Appendix B; J. E. Marrow, J. Coombs, and E. W. Lees, *An Assessment of Bio-Ethanol as a Transport Fuel in the UK*, Energy Technology Support Unit (London: HMSO, 1987); and G. Kolb, G. Eickhoff, M. Kleemann, N. Krzikalla, M. Pohlmann, and H. J. Wagner, CO_2 *Reduction Potential through Rational Energy Utilization and Use of Renewable Sources in the Federal Republic of Germany* (Julich, West Germany: KFA, 1989).
a. All prices are ex-refinery.

large ethanol investment loans at negative real interest rates, and by subsidizing the industry's capital costs. The rationale for subsidies stems from low international prices for sugar, high unemployment in agricultural areas, and vulnerability to world oil price fluctuations. Although the ethanol program has enabled Brazil's sugarcane industry to expand and strengthen, the program still provides only 3 percent of agricultural jobs in Brazil, mainly through temporary and seasonal labor demand. Moreover, domestic price distortions bias the competitiveness of the ethanol program. If the savings from the recent declines in world oil prices were passed on to the Brazilian economy, the ethanol program would be economically infeasible on a production cost basis at 1987 oil prices.[47]

Based on U.S. data, it is possible to indicate the cost-effectiveness of biofuels and PV hydrogen as substitutes for petroleum-derived gasoline (see table 4.12). Of the three replacement biofuel options, ethanol is currently the most expensive substitute for gasoline and incurs additional costs of US$350/tC equivalent of greenhouse gas emissions saved. Gasoline derived from cellulose feedstock is marginally less expensive than ethanol, and in turn methanol is marginally less expensive than gasoline. However, the costs of ethanol and biomass gasoline are projected to fall more rapidly in the future than the costs of methane, and may become much more attractive.

A major constraint for biofuels is that the economic reliability of feedstock production must be demonstrated if farmers and landowners are to commit large land areas to long-term production of energy crops. Monoculture herbaceous and woody energy crops must be produced on a large scale over an extended time to demonstrate the economic viability of several species under a variety of climatic conditions, exposure to pests and diseases, and responsiveness to inputs. In countries where there is surplus arable land, such as the United States, the opportunity costs of diverting land to biofuel feedstock production may be low. However, in the more densely populated European economies, such as the United Kingdom and the Netherlands, these costs may increase. In developing countries, the impact on agricultural production, particularly food, must be examined. For example, even in land-abundant Brazil the price incentives for the sugarcane ethanol program may have displaced food production.[48] Also, the net impact of biofuel feedstocks on greenhouse gas emissions will depend on the previous land use. If biofuel crops replace a forest, the difference between the amount of forest carbon released from forest clearance and the proportionately smaller amount of carbon-fixing crops results in a one-time net emission of CO_2. In addition, there would be a release of CO_2 from the cleared soil, and a large release of N_2O.[49] On the other hand, the national economic benefits of expanded biofuel use include the development of new domestic fuel and agro-industry markets, more efficient utilization of basic commodity by-product markets, rural employment generation, and foreign exchange savings through imported fuel displacement.

The future substitution of PV hydrogen for gasoline could be a relatively cost-effective way of reducing greenhouse gas emissions, with additional costs ranging from US$35–226/tC saved (see table 4.12). As noted previously, however, these low additional costs

Table 4.12
Costs of substituting for CO_2 equivalent emissions of GHG in transport fuels, United States (1989 U.S. dollars)

Fuel type	Fuel costs (US$/MBtu)	GHG intensity (kgCO$_2$/MBtu)	GHG saved (kgCO$_2$/MBtu)	Additional costs of GHG savings (US$/tC)
Gasoline, petroleum	8.66	99.28	base	base
Replacement—biofuels[a]				
Ethanol (c)[b]	18.14	0.00	99.28	350.78
Ethanol (f)[c]	7.51/10.43	0.00	99.28	−42.40/65.33
Methanol (c)	14.39	0.00	99.28	212.01
Methanol (f)	10.64	0.00	99.28	73.24
Gasoline (c)	16.16	0.00	99.28	277.54
Gasoline (f)	7.30/8.86	0.00	99.28	−50.11/7.71
Replacement—PV hydrogen[d]				
Fuel (f)	9.61/14.78	0.00	99.28	35.23/226.47

a. Idaho National Engineering Laboratory et al., *Potential of Renewable Energy*, Appendix B.
b. c = current (1990).
c. f = future (2010).
d. S. Piccot, J. A. Buzun, and H. C. Frey, *Emissions and Cost Estimates for Globally Significant Anthropogenic Combustion Sources of NO$_x$, N$_2$O, CH$_4$, CO, and CO$_2$,* Prepared for U.S. Environmental Protection Agency, Washington, DC, May 1990.

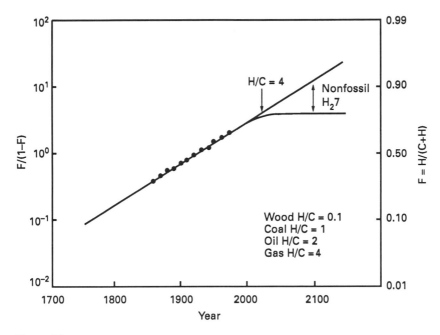

Figure 4.1
The ratio of hydrogen to carbon in the world fuel mix

SOURCE: J. H. Ausubel, A. Grubler, and N. Nakicenovic, "Carbon Dioxide Emissions in a Methane Economy," *Climate Change* 12 (1988): 245–263.

NOTES: Evolution of the ratio hydrogen (H) to carbon (C) in the world fuel mix. The figure for wood refers to dry wood suitable for energy generation. If the progression is to continue beyond methane, production of large amounts of hydrogen fuel without fossil energy is required.

require substantial breakthroughs on the costs of this substitute technology.

Switching to a Hydrogen/Methane Economy

Figure 4.1 indicates that the long-term evolution of the world energy system has been away from energy sources that have a low ratio of hydrogen to carbon, such as wood, coal, and oil, toward energy sources with an increasing ratio of hydrogen to carbon, such as natural gas (methane). From this perspective, methane could be the transitional hydrocarbon. By the turn of the century, the share of gas in the world primary energy demand could exceed the shares of coal and oil, peaking at close to 70 percent of world primary energy supply, and gas could remain the primary source of world energy for fifty years.[50] Natural gas emits only about 40 percent as much greenhouse gases per unit energy as coal, and because natural gas is more efficient than coal for many applications, this emission ratio may be even lower. Switching to a methane-based economy has important implications for global warming.

Total demand for hydrogen is also expected to increase by 12–17 percent between 1985 and 2025, with the majority of this growth from indirect energy demand.[51] Currently the main uses of hydrogen in the economy are in ammonia synthetics, methanol synthetics, and oil refining. In the petroleum and coal industries hydrogen is increasingly required to improve yields through upgrading the hydrogen-carbon ratio of the fuels. The demand for hydrogen as a fuel for domestic and commercial heating is likely to emerge and become significant in the future. For example, in Denmark, hydrogen has been added to natural gas supplies, up to about 10 percent of volume, without the need for major modifications to existing appliances. Hydrogen may also have an important role in the future as an energy carrier because it can be stored and transported relatively easily and may have a lower transmission cost than electricity. The use of liquid hydrogen in aircraft may be economically attractive, since it is likely to have superior technical characteristics over conventional fuels, resulting in lower direct operating costs for aircraft. Hydrogen could also be used as a vehicle fuel in most conventional internal combustion engines with only minor modifications, and could become competitive with alternative synthetic fuels in the future (see section on transport and table 4.12).[52]

Hydrogen can be produced from a range of sources, including hydrocarbons, electrolysis of water, direct use of nuclear heat by thermochemical cycles, and catalytic photolysis using solar energy. As noted in the section "Transport," if hydrogen is produced by electrolysis from PV electricity, no carbon dioxide gases would be emitted in its production or combustion. Given advances in thin-film solar technology, the cost of producing hydrogen from PV (US$10.1–15.5/GJ, 1990 U.S. dollars) is cheaper than from nuclear-based electrolytic hydrogen (US$26.7/GJ), from hydroelectric sources (US$23.4–28.9/GJ), and from wind sources (US$18.9–22.3/GJ).[53] If these technological advances are realized, then PV hydrogen could potentially become a cost-effective economy-wide way of controlling greenhouse gas emissions.

CFC Substitution Options

Under the terms of the Montreal Protocol, signatories have agreed to reduce the consumption of five major chlorofluorocarbons (CFCs) and three important halons with effect from January 1989. The consumption, defined as production plus imports minus exports, is to be progressively reduced so that by 1998 it will be only 15 percent of its July 1986 level. These terms apply to signatories that are generally regarded as developed countries, whereas "developing countries" are permitted ten years to arrive at the same reduction in consumption.[54]

Chemical companies are actively involved in developing substitutes to CFCs at the present time. In some applications (e.g., aerosols), the substitutes are already there and are cheaper than the CFCs they replace; in others (e.g., solvents) the substitutes exist but are more expensive than the CFCs they replace; and in some applications such as refrigeration, adequate substitutes have yet to be developed. Table 4.13 gives the existing costs of substitutes as of 1989. Existing CFCs currently cost about $1.5 a kilo for CFC-11 and CFC-12.

As with all new chemical products, the price is expected to fall over time as production increases. One elasticity estimate indicates

Table 4.13
Incremental costs of substitutes for CFCs and dates of availability

	Additional cost[a] ($/kg)	Available dates
Aerosols	nil	available now
Industrial refrigerants	0.95	1995
Solvents	1.15	1993
Nonrigid foam blowing agents	1.75 → 0.8	1990 → 1998
Rigid foam blowing agents	1.75 → 0.8	1990 → 1998
Comfort air conditioning	1.45 → 0.95	1990 → 1998
Domestic refrigeration	14.60 → 11.90	1995 → 1998
Mobile air conditioning	13.25 → 10.95	1994 → 1998

SOURCE: McKinsey & Co., "Protecting the Global Atmosphere: Funding Mechanisms," Second Interim Report to the Ministerial Conference on Atmospheric Pollution and Climate Change, The Hague, Netherlands, 1989.

a. Where more than one figure is given, the cost is expected to fall from the higher to the lower figure. The dates at which the two figures apply are given in the second column.

that for every doubling of cumulative production of CFC-11 and CFC-12, price fell by about 20 to 30 percent. Hence there is an incentive to wait for prices to fall before moving production to the substitute. Recent research results confirm that it is not generally desirable to focus on substituting the cheapest alternatives first, leaving the most expensive to the last.[55] The least-cost substitution profile depends, among other factors, on the size of each market, the relative initial cost differentials, and the expected rate of fall in price.

Table 4.14 shows the main industries that use CFCs and the technological possibilities for substitution within them. These will necessarily entail costs, arising from changes in maintenance practices, in production processes, and in operating costs of the new equipment used (mainly energy costs). At present it is difficult to say how large these costs will be, although they need not all be incurred initially. For example, there would not normally be any need to retrofit much of the air-conditioning or refrigeration equipment if new equipment operating on substitutes could be brought into use quickly enough. This approach would imply higher costs in new manufacturing and faster amortization of existing equipment, but lower costs on retrofitting. In some of the earlier research it was argued that equipment using substitutes, particularly in refrigeration, would involve higher energy costs of operation.[56] However, this view has been challenged, and the current consensus is that there probably would not be much in the way of additional energy costs involved in the transfer. In fact, some of the prototype refrigerators are more energy-efficient than the ones they replace.

In developed countries with manufacturing facilities for CFCs (principally France, Germany, Italy, U.K., U.S.A.), the lead time in arriving at the Montreal Protocol has been long enough that there is no need to amortize plants faster than would otherwise have been the case. In any event, many of the new plants are "swing plants" capable of switching to the production of unbanned materials. This is also the case with some of the new facilities set up in India and China. In other developing countries with such facilities, there may be a need for earlier closedown, but it is not likely to amount to a large figure. If plants have an economic life of twenty-five years and the terms of the agreement would allow them production for the next eighteen years, the maximum shortening of the life could be seven years. As substitutes develop and become cheaper, the economic life will be shortened by more than that anyway.

Table 4.14
Technological substitution possibilities with CFCs

Sector	Savings possible with existing equipment	Prospects of substitutes for CFCs	Changes use of CFC substitutes will entail
Domestic refrigeration	Recycling of CFCs possible; costs under investigation.	Several alternative refrigerants should be available by 1995. But they will be costly.	New equipment required; will probably reduce energy efficiency.
Commercial refrigeration	Minor technical adjustments to reduce CFC use or emission. Recycling of CFCs upon disposal of unit. Substitution of CFCs with alternative refrigerants possible but costly.	Two costly refrigerants should be available by 1995.	New equipment required for optimal use of CFC substitutes. Cost increase for new equipment estimated at 10–20%. Drop in operating costs expected.
Refrigerated transport	Minor technical adjustments, recycling.	Good. Several alternative refrigerants now in testing. Available late 1990s.	New equipment required. No certain cost estimates available. Effective replacement costs high because of extended lifetime of existing equipment.
Cold storage	Minor technical adjustments, recycling, use of CFC substitutes.	Good. Several alternative refrigerants now in testing. Available late 1990s.	New equipment will be more energy efficient but costly. Effective replacement costs high, again due to extended lifetime of existing equipment (average 15 years).
Comfort air conditioning	Recycling, leakage reduction, and use of CFC substitutes possible but costly.	Good. Several alternative coolants now in testing. Available early 1990s.	New equipment required for optimal use of CFC substitutes. No certain cost estimates available.

Table 4.14 (continued)

Sector	Savings possible with existing equipment	Prospects of substitutes for CFCs	Changes use of CFC substitutes will entail
Industrial refrigeration	Improved maintenance, recycling, and use of CFC substitutes.	Alternative refrigerants now in testing. Available mid-1990s.	No further information available.
Heat pumps used for heating	Improved maintenance.	Good. CFC substitutes should be available by 1993.	New equipment required. No cost estimates available.
Mobile air conditioning	Technical adjustments (some major), use of CFC substitutes (some options very costly).	Good. CFC substitutes should be available by 1995.	New equipment required for optimal use of CFC substitutes. Added cost $30–100 per vehicle.
Rigid and flexible foams	Use of CFC substitutes (including water).	Good. CFC substitutes should be available by early 1990s.	New equipment required for total elimination of CFCs.
Electronic degreasing and dry cleaning solvents	Recovery of solvent losses, use of CFC substitutes (including water).	Good. Many alternative cleaning solutions already in use.	New equipment required for some industrial uses (i.e., dry cleaning). Costs significant but not specified.
Aerosols	Use of CFC substitutes.	Excellent. Many non-CFC gas propellants or pumps now available with few technical impediments.	New equipment required in many instances, but not significantly costly. Cost of final aerosol product generally less than corresponding CFC-using product.
Sterilants	Use of CFC substitutes, technical adjustments.	Excellent. Many CFC substitutes now available, others in development.	Few changes required, total CFC replacement feasible using already-existing technology.

SOURCE: A. Markandya, *The Costs to Developing Countries of Joining the Montreal Protocol* (Nairobi: UNEP, 1990).

Costs to Developing Countries

As part of the attempt to encourage nonsignatories to the Montreal Protocol (notably India, China, and Brazil), estimates were made of the costs to developing countries of meeting the terms and reducing their use of CFCs by 2008 in the prescribed manner. The results of these studies showed the following: (1) For all developing countries, the discounted present value of costs of the more expensive substitutes would amount to around $1.8 billion. However, it is possible that the total cost would be much less than this. (2) For the next three years the costs of restructuring industry and training personnel in the use of alternative technologies would amount to between $210 million and $280 million.[57]

Conclusions and Policy Recommendations

Cost Curves and Cost Analysis

Policymakers seek guidance not just on emission targets but also on the *sequencing* of control measures. For this reason, it is essential to identify cost functions and to seek the minimum cost combination of ameliorative measures. The minimum cost requirement can be stated more formally as one of minimizing the present value of the costs of achieving target reductions, although the present value formulation raises issues of intergenerational fairness.[58] Technically, the relevant cost function needs to be defined in terms of *social* costs, not resource costs alone. Strictly what is required is a multisectoral general equilibrium model in which it is possible to identify cost impacts beyond the immediate resource costs of technology substitution. Such models exist and some have been supplemented by environmental benefit estimates.[59] As far as we know, however, no model has yet been "run" with technology substitution scenarios, although this procedure would seem to be feasible.

Some fairly simplistic attempts have been made to estimate cost functions, employing direct resource costs alone. Two U.K. cost functions are shown in figures 4.2 and 4.3. Figure 4.2 represents a government viewpoint, and figure 4.3 an environmentalist group's viewpoint.[60] Clearly, as might be expected, official and environmentalist estimates diverge markedly. The official view on nuclear power has changed, however, and the marked preference for nuclear tech-

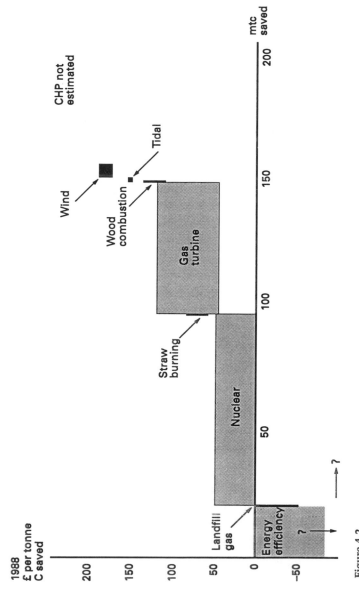

Figure 4.2
An official view of GHG substitution costs, United Kingdom

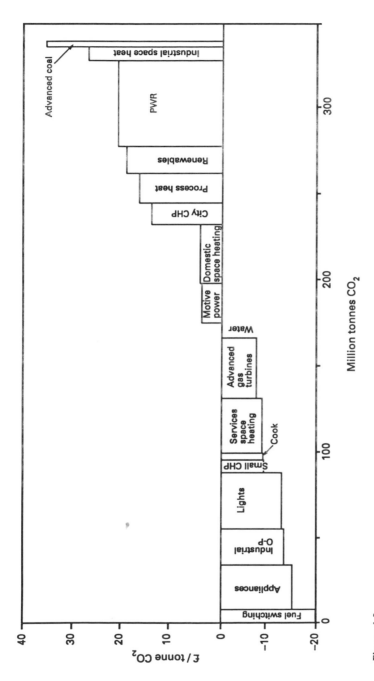

Figure 4.3
An environmentalist view of greenhouse gas substitution costs, United Kingdom

nology is perhaps not as strong as is shown in figure 4.2. Note also that figure 4.3 contains energy conservation technologies in considerable detail, whereas figure 4.2 has energy conservation in general (at an agreed negative cost) but with substantial uncertainty about cost and scale of potential penetration.

Conclusions on Greenhouse Gas Substitution Options

The results of this study confirm that technology substitution options for greenhouse gas abatement are likely to remain relatively expensive in the near term. The exceptions may be fossil-fuel switching—for example, from coal to advanced gas technologies, passive solar, and CFC substitution. Indeed, our findings suggest that some of these options may actually yield economic savings. Given the rapid changes in the technology and costs of various substitution options, a wide spectrum of greenhouse gas substitution options may become economically attractive abatement strategy in the long run.

Significant substitution technologies are on the verge of achieving market penetration on a large scale, as indicated, for example, in tables 4.1 and 4.2 for many critical energy technologies. Once market penetration is assured, both economies of scale and improved reliability may lead to substantial cost reductions in many advanced technologies at a rapid rate. However, technologies with high social costs, such as nuclear power and possibly tidal energy, will benefit less from economies of scale, as these obviously impact only on direct resource costs. Suitable land availability may affect some technologies, such as photovoltaic power, biomass, and wind energy.[61]

Costs will vary significantly from country to country and even from region to region within countries, making some substitution options more cost-effective in certain countries or locations than in others. Rational greenhouse gas abatement strategies should take advantage of geographic-specific potentials for substitution.

Current cost estimates for substitution technologies are necessarily based on projections of future prices and policy interventions. Most projections are conservative. For example, for the energy sector, future fossil-fuel prices are assumed to remain constant in real terms, or rise slightly, and current energy policies are assumed to continue. However, in the long run, future scarcity or market imperfections for fossil fuels—or political events like the Persian Gulf crisis and subsequent war that began in mid-1990—may lead to more substantial price rises.

Although substitutions will phase in gradually as the long-run marginal cost of substitutes declines relative to fossil-fuel costs, market forces alone are unlikely to secure the "optimal" rate of substitution given environmental costs. The imposition of a carbon tax or of significant quantitative restrictions on the use of fossil fuels may be necessary to change relative prices to favor substitution and conservation. Greenhouse gas substitution options must consequently be considered a necessary component of any strategy for controlling global warming. Moreover, the cost-effectiveness of these options will invariably be affected by any resulting policy interventions—carbon taxes and emission permits, phased reductions in greenhouse gas emissions and subsidies for the research, development, and deployment of the substitution technologies. Further research is therefore required to (1) improve estimates of the current and future cost-effectiveness of the relevant substitution options for different regions of the world; (2) extend these estimates to include not just the direct resource costs but all the economic and social costs (and benefits) of the various options; (3) incorporate this "micro" analysis into multisectoral general-equilibrium models to examine the impact of appropriate policy instruments in abating greenhouse gas emissions; and, (4) based on the above analysis, design incentive structures to encourage the appropriate level of research, development, and deployment of greenhouse gas substitution technologies.

Further consideration must be given to the specific capital and technology constraints facing developing countries. For example, to assist developing countries in meeting these costs of CFC substitution, a technical assistance fund with an initial allocation of US$10 million for the first two years has been recommended. The fund would also lend US$200 million over three years to increase manufacturing capability using new technologies with CFC substitutes and US$10 million for systemic collection of information on the production, consumption, and use of CFCs and their substitutes by country.[62] Similar financial assistance will be required for a wide spectrum of greenhouse gas substitution options, which any negotiations leading to international agreements and policy measures must consider.

Notes

This paper is a summary version of a paper prepared for the Conference on Economic Policy Responses to Global Warming, sponsored by the Instituto

San Paolo di Torino in Rome on October 5–6, 1990. We are grateful to the Instituto for their financial support.

The section of this chapter entitled "CFC Substitution Options" was written by our colleague Anil Markandya. We would also like to acknowledge the comments and support provided by Dennis Anderson, Nick Eyre, Beth Taylor, Connie Smyser, Gerry Leach, Stewart Boyle, and the U.K. Energy Technology Support Unit. We are also grateful to all participants at the Rome conference for their helpful comments, in particular John Martin and James Poterba. Any errors or omissions are, of course, our responsibility alone.

1. The original and more detailed version of this chapter presented at the Rome conference now appears as E. B. Barbier, J. C. Burgess, and D. W. Pearce, *Slowing Global Warming: Options for Greenhouse Gas Substitution*, LEEC Discussion Paper 90-05 (London, November 1990). For further information on substitution options and costs, interested readers should consult this London Environmental Economics Center paper.

2. CO_2 and CO_2 equivalents can be expressed either in units of *gas* or in units of *carbon*. These two units can be easily equated; i.e., the standard conversion is that 1 gigaton of carbon (GtC) will produce 3.67 gigatons of carbon dioxide (GtCO$_2$). In this chapter we will use units of *carbon* as far as possible.

3. For further details on these trends see IEA and OECD, *Greenhouse Gas Emission: The Energy Dimension*, A Working Paper Submitted to the White House Conference on Science and Economics Research Related to Global Change, April 17–18, 1990.

4. E. B. Barbier and D. W. Pearce, "Thinking Economically about Climate Change," *Energy Policy*, January/February 1990, pp. 11–18.

5. One exception is the study by W. D. Nordhaus, "To Slow or Not to Slow: The Economics of the Greenhouse Effect," mimeo, Yale University, New Haven, CT, February 1990. The study concluded that major reductions in CFCs are the most effective control option, although the relative cost-effectiveness of different options was not analyzed.

6. Intergovernmental Panel on Climate Change (IPCC), *Policymakers Summary of the Scientific Assessment of Climate Change*, Working Group 1, Third Draft (Geneva: World Meteorological Office and United Nations Environment Program 1990).

7. See, for example, Environmental Protection Agency, *Regulatory Impact Analysis: Protection of Stratospheric Ozone*, vols. 1–3 (Washington, DC: 1987).

8. For an interesting discussion of these issues in relation to U.S. studies of CO_2 emissions reduction, see J. A. Edmonds, W. B. Ashton, H. C. Cheng, and M. Steinberg, *A Preliminary Analysis of U.S. CO_2 Reduction Potential from Energy Conservation and the Substitution of Natural Gas for Coal in the Period to 2010*, Prepared for the U.S. Department of Energy (Washington, DC: February 1989), pp. 40–41.

9. Assessing biomass substitution options offers particular problems. In most studies only the *direct impact* of biomass combustion on greenhouse gas emissions is included, which can often be as high as for fossil fuels. However, the full impact of biomass as a substitute for fossil fuels should also include the indirect impacts of carbon fixing by biomass when it is growing, which in most cases will yield a net reduction in carbon emitted into the atmosphere.

10. Edmonds et al., *Preliminary Analysis*.

11. U.K. Department of Energy, *An Evaluation of Energy Related Greenhouse Gas Emissions and Measures to Ameliorate Them*, Energy Paper 58 (London: HMSO, October 1989), p. 62.

12. For an interesting discussion of some of these issues and costs, see D. Chapman, "The Eternity Problem: Nuclear Power Waste Storage," *Contemporary Policy Issues* 7 (July 1990): 1–15; and B. Keepin and G. Kats, "Greenhouse Warming: Comparative Analysis of Nuclear and Efficiency Abatement Strategies," *Energy Policy*, December 1988, pp. 538–561.

13. IEA, *Renewable Sources of Energy* (Paris: IEA/OECD, 1987).

14. For details on the calculations of CO_2 equivalent emissions of greenhouse gases, see Barbier, Burgess, and Pearce, *Slowing Global Warming*.

15. In this case, combustion of municipal solid waste is not considered as part of any biomass carbon cycle, so only the direct impact of combustion on greenhouse gas emissions is relevant. Most of this impact was in terms of CO_2 emissions.

16. However, in their construction stage, the generation plants employing replacement technologies indirectly involve emissions of greenhouse gases. Such emissions are relatively small. For example, a plant using solar thermal emits 3.6 t/GWh of CO_2 in its construction stage, photovoltaics 5.4 t/GWh of CO_2, wind 7.4 t/GWh, hydro power (depending on size) from 3.1 to 10 t/GWh, nuclear 1.0 t/GWh, and geothermal 1.0 t/GWh of CO_2. A geothermal plant also emits 0.3 t/GWh of CO_2 in its fuel extraction stage, and a nuclear plant 1.5 t/GWh. See R. L. San Martin, "Environmental Emissions from Energy Technology Systems: The Total Fuel Cycle," in OECD/IEA, *Energy Technologies for Reducing Emissions of Greenhouse Gases*, vol. 1, Proceedings of an Experts' Seminar, Paris, April 12–14, 1989. As these indirect emissions from replacement technology plants are relatively insignificant, they are not included in our calculations.

17. *BP Review of World Gas* (London: British Petroleum Company, August 1989).

18. The following discussion draws on tables 4.6 and 4.7 and Idaho National Engineering Laboratory, Los Alamos National Laboratory, Sandia National Laboratories, and Solar Energy Research Institute, *The Potential of Renewable Energy: An Interlaboratory White Paper*, prepared for the Office of Policy, Planning and Analysis, U.S. Department of Energy, and published by Solar Energy Research Institute, Golden, CO, March 1990.

19. For example, construction costs increased from US$200/kW installed in the early 1970s to over US$3,200/kW in 1986/87—a sixfold increase in real terms—and construction lead times have increased to more than twelve years for large plants (Keepin and Kats, "Greenhouse Warming").

20. PV is a research-driven technology and should respond with great sensitivity to an intensified research and development budget. The figures of future costs of PV systems for generating electricity may be *pessimistic* and higher than may actually occur. Taking more optimistic assumptions with greater cost reductions and improved market penetration, PV generation costs fall faster, to 13 U.S. cents per kWh in 1995, 8 cents in 2000, and 5 cents in 2010. Consequently, PV systems may supply as much as 80 GW by 2010, 240 GW by 2020, and 480 GW by 2030. See the discussion in Idaho National Engineering Laboratory et al., *Potential of Renewable Energy*, Appendix G.

21. U.K. Department of Energy, *An Evaluation of Energy Related Greenhouse Gas Emissions and Measures to Ameliorate Them*, Energy Paper Number 58, U.K. Country Study for the Intergovernment Panel on Climate Change Response Strategies Working Group Energy and Industry Sub Group (London: HMSO, October 1989).

22. Unusually, in this study the two biomass options (wood and straw combustion) have included the additional impacts on net CO_2 reductions of any carbon-fixing by these crops.

23. For example, the costs for grid-connected PV systems in the study were based on a 1988 cost range of UK£0.08–0.67/kWh and 2025 cost range of UK£0.02–0.37/kWh. More recent analysis suggests that the current likely achievable cost range for centrally generated PV power is UK£0.11–0.17/kWh, and future costs could be in the range of UK£0.06–0.09/kWh. See *Review of Solar Energy Technologies*, Part 3: *Photovoltaic Power*, Draft Paper, Energy Technology Support Unit, Harwell, U.K., November 1989.

24. G. Kolb, G. Eickhoff, M. Kleemann, N. Krzikalla, M. Pohlmann, and H. Wagner, *CO_2 Reduction Potential through Rational Utilization and Use of Renewable Energy Sources in the Federal Republic of Germany* (Kernforschungsanlage Julich GmbH, 1989).

25. McLennan Magasanik Associates, *The Feasibility and Implications for Australia of the Adoption of the Toronto Proposal for Carbon Dioxide Emissions* (Victoria, Australia, 1989).

26. Lawrence Berkeley Laboratory et al., *Energy Technology for Developing Countries: Issues for the US National Energy Strategy* (Berkeley, CA: Lawrence Berkeley Laboratory, 1989).

27. See E. Terrado, M. Mendis, and K. Fitzgerald, *Impact of Lower Oil Prices on Renewable Energy Technologies*, Industry and Energy Department Working Paper, Energy Series Paper No. 5 (Washington, DC: World Bank, 1989).

28. M. M. Gowen, "Biofuel v. Fossil Fuel Economics in Developing Countries: How Green Is the Pasture?" *Energy Policy*, October 1989, pp. 455–470.

29. See Terrado, Mendis, and Fitzgerald, *Impact of Lower Oil Prices*, and J. C. Burgess, "The Contribution of Efficient Energy Pricing to Reducing Carbon Dioxide Emissions," *Energy Policy*, 1990, pp. 449–455.

30. E. Tasdemiroglu, "The Energy Situation in OIC Countries: The Possible Contribution of Renewable Energy Resources," *Energy Policy*, December 1989, pp. 577–590.

31. Terrado, Mendis, and Fitzgerald, *Impact of Lower Oil Prices*.

32. Gowen, "Biofuel v. Fossil Fuel."

33. Keepin and Kats, "Greenhouse Warming."

34. Idaho National Engineering Laboratory et al., *Potential of Renewable Energy*, Appendix H.

35. Ibid., Appendix C.

36. Idaho National Engineering Laboratory et al., *Potential of Renewable Energy*.

37. Ibid.

38. Yu Joe Huang, "Potentials for and Barriers to Building Energy Conservation in China," *Contemporary Policy Issues* 8 (July 1990): 1–18.

39. Derived from estimates by W. O. Spofford, "Least-Cost Alternative of Space Heating Alternatives in Beijing: The Case of Cogeneration at Shijingshan Power Plant," working draft, Resources for the Future, Washington, DC, March 1990.

40. M. Kosmo, "Commercial Energy Subsidies in Developing Countries: Opportunity for Reform," *Energy Policy*, June 1989, pp. 244–253.

41. Yu Joe Huang, "Potentials and Barriers."

42. Terrado, Mendis, and Fitzgerald, *Impact of Lower Oil Prices*.

43. Ibid.

44. J. M. Ogden and R. H. Williams, "New Prospects for Solar Hydrogen Energy: Implications of Advances in Thin-Film Solar Cell Technology," IEA/OECD Expert Seminar on Energy Technologies to Reduce Emissions of Greenhouse Gases, OECD, Paris, April 12–14, 1989.

45. OECD/IEA Expert Panel on Low Consumption/Low Emission Automobile, Summary Report, OECD, Paris, February 14–15, 1990.

46. Idaho National Engineering Laboratory et al., *Potential of Renewable Energy*.

47. Gowen, "Biofuel v. Fossil Fuel." Despite the poor economics suggested by the Brazilian ethanol program, other developing countries such as Argentina, Costa Rica, Kenya, Malawi, Swaziland, and Zimbabwe have also committed themselves to ethanol production.

48. Ibid.

49. D. Sperling and M. A. DeLuchi, "Transportation Energy Strategies and the Greenhouse Effect," IEA/OECD Expert Seminar on Energy Technologies for Reducing Emissions of Greenhouse Gases, OECD, Paris, April 12–14, 1989.

50. J. H. Ausubel, A. Grubler, and N. Nakicenovic, "Carbon Dioxide Emissions in a Methane Economy," *Climatic Change* 12 (1988): 245–263.

51. K. F. Langely, "The Future Role of Hydrogen in the UK Energy Economy," Energy Technology Support Unit, Harwell, Oxford.

52. Ogden and Williams, "New Prospects."

53. Ibid.

54. In addition, developing countries have a few other concessions, such as production above the 1986 level being permitted in the interim phase.

55. A. Markandya and M. Pemberton, "Dynamic Optimization and Control in the Use of CFCs," mimeo, University College London, 1990.

56. See for example, United Nations Environment Program, *Economic Panel Report: Pursuant to Article 6 of the Montreal Protocol on Substances That Deplete the Ozone Layer*, vols. 1–3 (Nairobi, 1990). Also, U.S. Congress, *An Analysis of the Montreal Protocol on Substances That Deplete the Ozone Layer* (Washington, DC: Office of Technology Assessment, 1988).

57. A. Markandya, *The Costs to Developing Countries of Joining the Montreal Protocol* (Nairobi: UNEP, 1990). Individual country case studies are still being reviewed, and their results are not as yet available. In addition, the figures referred to are not based on domestic production but on importation from the cheapest source.

58. Thus, under the present-value approach, costs borne by future generations are discounted back to the present. If low-cost measures are adopted first, future generations will face possible high-cost solutions to further contain global warming. Offsetting this trend, technological change should keep future costs down, and, of course, future generations are the primary beneficiaries of current policies to contain global warming.

59. See, for example, S. Glomsrad et al., "Stabilization of Emissions of CO_2: A Computable General Equilibrium Assessment," Norwegian Central Bureau of Statistics, Oslo, Discussion Paper No. 48, April 1990.

60. Figure 4.2 is derived from data in U.K. Department of Energy, *An Evaluation of Energy Related Greenhouse Gas Emissions and Measures to Ameliorate Them*, Energy Paper 58 (London: HMSO, 1989). Figure 4.3 is taken from T. Jackson and S. Roberts, *Getting Out of the Greenhouse* (London: Friends of the Earth, 1989).

61. However, D. Anderson, "Photovoltaics: A Review of Costs," Draft Paper, University College London, indicates that photovoltaic generation may be less constrained by land availability than previously thought. Less than 0.5 percent of the land surface in areas with high insolation is in theory

required to meet the world's energy demands, assuming 15 percent photo-voltaic conversion efficiency.

62. Markandya, *Costs to Developing Countries*.

Comments

John P. Martin

I would like to begin my remarks by making an apology to the authors. I find it extremely difficult to do justice to their chapter, since I am neither a technologist nor a specialist in energy economics. In partial mitigation of my difficulty, I would add that this is not an easy chapter to digest. There must be several hundred estimates of the costs of reducing CO_2 equivalent emissions of greenhouse gases (GHGs) cited in this chapter, and it is extremely hard for the reader to form a good overview of plausible ranges of costs for the main substitution options in different countries.

At the same time, everyone working in this field owes a debt of gratitude to the authors. They have summarized a vast amount of material, covering not only the major OECD countries but also the much sparser literature on the less-developed countries too. This chapter will prove a valuable reference source on the direct resource costs of different substitution options. People who have to undertake modeling work in this area will be particularly grateful, and I expect that many of these cost estimates will be cited in future studies as if they were Holy Writ.

That being said, it is inevitable that there will be great skepticism about many of these estimates. At several points in the chapter the authors rightly stress the difficulties in making good cost estimates for substitution technologies, especially for those which are still in laboratory development. Nonetheless, they plunge on ahead to cite estimates and make judgments about the economic feasibility of these technologies. It would be very helpful to other analysts and policy-makers if they were to devote some attention to the key issue of the reliability of such estimates. How should policymakers deal with such uncertainties? This question is actually posed in the chapter but is never answered.

The authors are very careful in pointing out that the cost estimates cited cover the direct resource costs only and ignore many important general equilibrium repercussions that would necessarily result from large-scale substitution. They call for a multisectoral applied general-equilibrium (AGE) approach to this issue. I am pleased to assure them that the OECD Secretariat has taken up this challenge.

The GREEN Model

The remainder of my comments will (1) provide some information on the ongoing project that I and my colleagues Jean-Marc Burniaux and Giuseppe Nicoletti are undertaking to develop a multisector, multicountry, dynamic AGE model to quantify the medium- and long-term economic costs of reducing GHG emissions on a global basis; and (2) mention some preliminary results that throw light on the substitution options issue. The project is called the GeneRal Equilibrium ENvironmental Model, hereafter referred to as the GREEN model. At this stage the model only covers CO_2 and ignores other GHGs such as CFCs and methane.

As the authors' note in passing, there are several national AGE models that have addressed this issue in a single-country context. But the problem is a global one and, aside from the Whalley-Wigle model presented in Chapter 7, there is no other *consistent* global model that can tackle this issue. It is intended that GREEN will fill this gap. The model will be used to simulate the economy-wide and global costs of alternative policies, including different types of international agreements, to restrict emissions. In this way, it is hoped that the model will provide useful information to the negotiations on this issue that are now getting under way.

Overview of the Structure and Specification of GREEN

Some key features of the model are as follows:
1. It contains eight production sectors, four consumer goods, and eight regions. Agriculture, a sector that is particularly vulnerable to global warming, is distinguished separately, as are the main fossil fuels and energy-producing sectors. The OECD area is represented by three main zones—North America, Europe, and the Pacific—while the non-OECD area is represented by five regions including OPEC and China.

2. GREEN is an explicitly dynamic model in that changes in savings and investment affect the capital stock and output in future periods. In the present version, the model simulates over a period of thirty-five years through a sequence of interdependent temporary equilibria for each five-year period. It is our intention to lengthen this time period to the year 2050 and beyond at a later stage. In the present version, consumers and producers are assumed to be myopic in their behavior.

3. The model is calibrated to 1985 data, that being the latest year for which input-output tables, an essential source for building the GREEN data base, are available for most of the OECD countries.

Progress to Date

We have successfully built and simulated models for North America, Europe, and the Pacific area. At this stage, the model is rather straightforward:

• Capital and labor are assumed to be perfectly mobile between sectors.

• Domestic and imported goods are assumed to be imperfect substitutes, while domestically sold goods and exported commodities are assumed to be perfect substitutes.

• There is a constant supply elasticity for each energy source. The sources are primary "greenhouse" (coal, oil, natural gas) and "non-greenhouse" (nuclear, hydroelectric, backstop) energies. In addition, supply responses are assumed to be asymmetric: Primary energy sectors are assumed to keep their prices fixed by adjusting supply when output falls, while finite supply elasticities are specified when output increases.

Finally, the models have been calibrated to the benchmark data set at this stage using arbitrary values of the key exogenous parameters. A literature search to pin down the values of these elasticities more precisely is currently under way.

Preliminary Results on Substitution Options

We have undertaken a series of simulations in which a "carbon tax" is applied in 1990 in order to cut annual CO_2 emissions in the year 2000 to 80 percent of their 1990 level and to stabilize them thereafter.

Among the key results so far, I would highlight the following as being particularly relevant to this paper:

• The authors attempt to quantify the long-run "carbon tax" required to achieve a given emissions reduction target by analyzing the marginal costs of various substitution options. This is an important task because up to now we have few estimates of this tax for different countries. Manne and Richels (in press) put the long-run equilibrium tax in their Global 2100 model at $250 per ton of carbon; this estimate is determined by the requirement that synthetic fuels and nonelectric backstop technologies be equally attractive to the consumer. But this $250 tax is uniform in *all* regions in Global 2100. One of the main contributions of this paper is that the authors show that the long-run carbon taxes are likely to differ across countries. Preliminary results with GREEN come to a similar conclusion. With unilateral action by each of the three OECD regions, we find these differences require carbon taxes in the year 2020 of $180 in North America, $230 in Europe, and $290 in the Pacific. This conclusion implies that, if any international agreement were to contain a provision for tradable permits, countries would want to avail themselves of this possibility. For example, our results suggest that Europe and Japan would want to buy emission permits from North America if a global carbon constraint were applied across the OECD area. Such trade in emission rights in turn would have significant impacts on the terms of trade and real income in the participating countries.

• If it is assumed that the supply of nuclear power is inelastic over the next thirty years, because of the political and social concerns cited by the authors, the economic costs of achieving a given emissions reduction target, in terms of the impacts on real GDP and consumer welfare, are significantly larger than in our reference scenario, which assumes that the supply of nuclear power expands moderately. This result is in line with those reported by Manne and Richels: It implies an almost fourfold increase of the coal price in the United States compared with its simulated level in 2020 when the carbon limit is not applied.

• The timing of introduction of backstop technologies and their likely costs are another key element in understanding the economic effects of carbon taxes in GREEN. Manne and Richels emphasize the potential role of synthetic fuels based on coal or shale oil as a key backstop technology that serves to pin down the long-run equilibrium carbon tax in their model. This issue is not treated in the chapter, whereas the option of biomass fuels is. Since the marginal cost of backstop technologies plays a crucial role in the determination of the equilibrium carbon tax, the neglect of the synthetic fuels option is a major oversight in the chapter.

• The chapter argues that substitution from coal to gas is the most cost-effective option for most countries. However, reserves of natural gas and other fossil fuels are not unlimited, and the impact of this crucial resource-depletion issue is not discussed by the authors. This aspect seems to be crucial for understanding the outcomes in GREEN. You could take the view that in the long run the greenhouse gas issue is primarily a coal problem for two reasons. First, coal is the fossil fuel that is the greatest emitter of carbon. Second, it is also the fossil fuel for which the earth has the largest proven reserves. When one adds the fact that well over 90 percent of current global reserves are concentrated in only five countries—the United States, China, Australia, South Africa, and the Soviet Union—the potential for strategic bargaining over the terms of any international convention are obvious. One must also take into account the fact that the price of coal, like other fossil fuels, is heavily influenced by government intervention. For example, the price of coal in many European countries is significantly above the world price as a result of a web of subsidies and import restrictions. Removing these distortions in the context of a carbon tax would provide an additional source of welfare gains to consumers.

Note

These comments represent the author's own views and should not be taken to represent those of the OECD.

Reference

Manne, Alan S., and Richels, Richard G. In press. Global CO_2 emission reductions: The impacts of rising energy costs. *Energy Journal.*

5   Economic Responses to Global Warming: A European Perspective

Emilio Gerelli

The Purpose of This Chapter: Understanding the Hero and the Villain (If Any . . .)

Recent discussions at the political level show a difference of official attitude between the United States and the European Community on the subject of climate change. The role of the hero on the international scene is being played by the EC, which has been issuing statements and documents about an active preventive policy to reduce adverse climate change impacts. The apparent villain is the United States, which is advocating the gathering of more scientific evidence before taking action and has been trying to challenge the application of the principle of preventive action when climate change damage is uncertain. The purpose of this chapter is to illustrate and analyze these views.

Summary and Conclusions

On the basis of our analysis we summarize certain features of the climate change problem and the EC-U.S. confrontation on such a problem.

Because of the *global* (or planetary) "public bad" character of climate change, decentralized decision making by single countries would not determine an appropriate reduction of the adverse effects of climate change, particularly because of "free-riding" behavior. A world government (or agency) would in theory be necessary to make efficient decisions. Since this is not possible, recourse must be made to international agreements, which are rather difficult to reach, as we shall see.

A more philosophical but nonetheless real reason for uncertainty and difficulty is the fact that climate change is seen as linked to the preservation of human life. Deciding about climate change is therefore a so-called tragic choice for which it is difficult to act in a rational way because of conflicts of values.

All this is further complicated by the fact that there are uncertainties about the causes, the timing, and the possible consequences of climate change.

A possible formal instrument to find a practical and flexible solution to these problems is a so-called framework convention, consisting of a series of general statements that summarize the scientific positions and the concerns of the international community. The task of setting quantitative objectives is left to subsequent protocols negotiated in the framework of the convention.

This type of instrument should provide the flexibility to cope, even if probably through high transaction costs, with these general problems and with more specific ones—for example, the fact that there are many sources of greenhouse gases (GHGs), sizeable per capita differences among countries in the production of such gases, and high marginal control costs.

It is thus no wonder that conflicts arise about the way to deal with climate change. In this chapter we have focused on the EC and U.S. positions, which are apparently opposite. The EC has in fact been claiming repeatedly that "a response should be made without further delay, irrespective of remaining uncertainties on some scientific aspects of the greenhouse effect" (Council of Environment Ministers 1989). On the contrary, "The United States believes that uncertainties associated with the timing and magnitude of possible global change mean that policies will vary in their appeal as uncertainties are reduced; *an appropriate strategy to address possible global change based on today's knowledge and in light of today's economic environment may be wholly inappropriate within a decade*" (White House Conference 1990, question 1.2, italics added).

Both such rather extreme views are open to criticism, and it is doubtful to what extent they really represent the positions of the two parties. The apparently strict wait-and-see position of the United States is unacceptable in principle, because many social decisions are taken under high degrees of uncertainty, which in certain cases may be even higher than with regard to climate change. It is, therefore, rather difficult to accept the statement that just for the case of climate change the lack of complete scientific evidence makes prevention policies unacceptable. In fact, U.S. officials are careful to point out that their administration has already instituted a number of policies that will reduce greenhouse emissions while being fully justified for other reasons. The American "nyet" may therefore very well be a negotiating and temporary position.

On the other hand, the EC active position is characterized by the fact that up to now it has been only verbal. No specific measures have been taken, and the recent Environment Council of June 1990 did not approve a resolution on policy targets on the greenhouse issue. A few member countries disagree on certain aspects of the proposal, and unanimous agreement has yet to be reached. Therefore, it will take some time also for the EC to pass from words to facts, particularly since the question of the specific instruments to be used has not yet been tackled. To sum up on this point, the EC position up to now reflects a moral commitment but lacks the muscle of a clear strategy about goals and instruments.

We note furthermore that the reasons stated by the EC and the United States may not be the real ones to justify their attitudes. With regard to the United States, most observers believe that the question of scientific evidence is to a certain extent a formal one. According to this opinion, the real reason for not undertaking climate change policies is their cost. The revised Clean Air Act will in fact be costly, and further cost increases are foreseen with regard to solid waste and other environmental problems. For this reason, an additional increase of the economic burden due to global problems is not accepted, particularly since the United States is by far the largest emitter from fossil carbon combustion both per capita (see figure 5.3) and in absolute terms (figure 5.2). We could thus interpret the U.S. position not as a disregard for the environment, but rather as an option in favor of national and local problems to the detriment of global ones.

On the other hand, the present ambitious EC position is explained in our opinion by institutional characteristics, that is, by the fact that up to now only EC environment ministers have declared their position, not the Community as such. On the contrary, the U.S. position reflects the administration as a whole. We suspect that when the EC decision-making process on climate change involves other sectors of the Community (e.g., finance ministers with regard to a possible carbon tax) the situation will change.

Whatever its causes, the present situation of conflict we have been describing is neither new nor surprising. In the political arena, and particularly at the international level, there are no automatic optimum decisions. A *tâtonnement* (trial-and-error) process is needed, and paradoxically we may consider a positive factor the existence of initially opposite positions between two partners, the EC and the United States, which are used to fruitful (even if sometimes harsh) negotiations. By successive moves, through understanding and luck, this process may very well lead to an intermediate position that may not be far from a theoretical optimum (however calculated). During this process both parties will be able to better take into account their starting position. For the United States, in particular, their low energy efficiency in comparison to the EC would justify higher energy prices in the United States. For the EC, the fact that on the whole (and beyond verbal declarations) their environmental policy is probably weaker than in the United States, particularly in certain Mediterranean countries where such policies really began only at the time of their joining the Community, and where in any case the enforcement of public policies is rather inefficient.

The *tâtonnement* process just mentioned will take time, particularly since at the time I am writing (August 1990) Kuwait's invasion by Iraq makes it even more difficult than in "normal" times to have a clear view about policies to deal with climate change. As in the period after the first oil shock due to the Yom Kippur war of 1974, the rise in oil prices will exert a positive influence on energy saving and therefore, in general, on the reduction of CO_2 emissions. It will be recalled, in fact, that the sharp rise in oil prices (the so-called oil tax), generated for a few years (particularly in the 1975–1979 period) in advanced countries a decoupling between growth and energy consumption.

Of course, there are negative effects of the present situation. First, if climate change and more generally air pollution, together with other problems like resource conservation, are real issues, advanced countries should take action without implicitly relying on external (and inimical) action to help solve these problems by creating at the same time unnecessary human and economic troubles. Perhaps the only useful message of such episodes as the Yom Kippur war and Kuwait's invasion by Iraq is that we do achieve important results by introducing relevant changes in our prices. One is indeed amazed by the conviction of many even cultivated people that appropriate price changes do not exert an important influence in changing people's behavior also for environmental protection. However, by now we should have learned enough the hard way. The energy price changes we need also for environmental protection should be brought about in a rational way, and not because of local wars in the Middle East.

If the rise in oil prices is a (mixed) blessing from the environmental point of view, a negative consequence of the external and abrupt way in which it is being brought about is the fact that an "external" oil tax makes it more difficult (or even impossible also for political reasons) to introduce more sophisticated instruments like a carbon tax, which would exert a more selective influence on climate change reduction.

To conclude, controlling climate change will be a long story because of large uncertainties and costs that to a certain extent justify different starting positions. Difficulties, however great, cannot be used to cancel the problem. The parties involved should not only discuss, but they should also take action beginning with those measures which have a moderate cost or which not only reduce climate change but also reach other useful results—for example, energy efficiency and non-renewable resource conservation. Time would thus be gained to acquire better knowledge and to adopt more ambitious policies, if necessary.

The EC Position

We first of all analyze in some detail the EC position. An initial document is a communication of the Commission of the European Communities (1988) to the Council of Ministers. In this document it is admitted that the various impacts of climatic change and their socio-economic consequences cannot be reliably assessed in detail at present. "However the preliminary works made on this subject show that the risks are alarmingly high and the likely direct and indirect consequences potentially disruptive. . . . It has come out clearly that this is the time to work out viable strategies while accelerating research efforts." Therefore, the Commission states that they will take the initiative to launch a substantial policy-options study program to evaluate the feasibility, costs, and likely results of possible measures to limit greenhouse gas emissions.

This initiative of the Commission is accepted in a Council of Environment Ministers resolution (1989). The main areas of such a program should be as follows:

• Identification and technical assessment of measures and technologies that can help reduce emissions of greenhouse gases, in particular CO_2, or other measures, including afforestation and prevention of forest fires, that can otherwise combat the greenhouse effect.

• Analysis of environmental, economic, industrial, energy, social, agricultural, and institutional implications of possible measures and technologies.

• Evaluation of likely benefits of different policy options by use of a decision-analysis framework.

• Identifying measures, such as further coastal protection, necessary to adapt to new situations that the decision analysis demonstrates are likely to arise as an unavoidable result of the greenhouse effect and drawing up, where necessary, Community policies to implement such measures.

The Council invited the Commission to submit a report by the end of 1990.

The resolution further states a position of principle which will literally become a leitmotiv of EC documents on climate change—that is, that "a response should be made without further delay, irrespective of remaining uncertainties on some scientific aspects of the greenhouse effect."

The year 1990 was a fairly active one for the EC on climate change. Three documents are of particular importance here. First, a communication from the Commission to the Council on energy and the environment (1990a). The topic of climate change is dealt with in this document in conjunction with other questions concerning the energy-environment relationships. Of particular interest is figure 5.1 which shows a forecast of CO_2 emissions to the year 2010 (in millions of tons per year).

It can be seen that CO_2 emissions from fossil-fuel combustion decreased slightly up to 1986 but would increase again gradually up to the year 2010. (It is interesting to note that over the same period 1980–2010, SO_2 emissions from fossil fuel use will decline substantially, about 70%, and also NO_x emissions will be reduced, though at a more modest rate of about 20%.) As worldwide CO_2 emissions are estimated to amount to about 21 billion tons, the Community share is in the order of 13 percent. With regard to carbon emissions from commercial energy consumption, figure 5.2 shows that the EC is the third-largest emitter after the United States and the U.S.S.R.

According to the Commission document, actions in the field of energy efficiency improvements seem to be the most promising single policy tool with the most significant CO_2 reduction potential showing immediate results. However, the Commission confirms the main

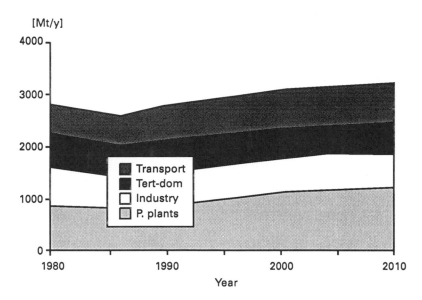

Figure 5.1
European Community CO_2 emissions by sector

SOURCE: Commission of the EC, *Communication to the Council: Energy and the Environment*, COM (89) 369 final, Brussels, February 8, 1990, p. 13.

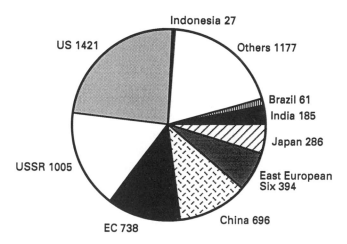

Figure 5.2
Fossil carbon emissions, commercial energy consumption only (million tons of carbon)

SOURCE: Derived from *BP Statistical Review of World Energy*, June 1989.

findings of its review of member states' energy policy, which clearly highlight that if no new policy measures are introduced at Community or national level it now seems to be clear that the achievement of a minimum 20 percent energy efficiency improvement by 1995 will not be realized.

This is probably one of the main reasons why a subsequent communication from the Commission is devoted to establishing policy targets, and takes a more aggressive position (1990b).

First, the document confirms that EC member states were among those industrialized countries considering that stabilization of CO_2 emissions should be achieved by the year 2000, as stated in the conference on atmospheric pollution and climatic change at Noordwijk (the Netherlands, November 6–7, 1989). Second, the document contains a fairly sharp criticism that seems directed to the U.S. position:

Progress towards definition of an effective policy to deal with the greenhouse issue and towards taking an effective action in particular in the field of CO_2 emissions seems to be affected, at this stage, by hesitations shown by important industrialized countries, which play a major role in the IPCC (Intergovernmental Panel on Climate Change) process.

Those countries have failed until now to take the lead and to show the way by declaring clearly their willingness to undertake commitments for concrete and urgent action especially in the field of CO_2 emissions. This in spite of the fact that significant reductions on CO_2 emission trends in the industrialized countries could be achieved without important social and economic impacts.

Last, we must refer to a draft Council resolution on policy targets on the Greenhouse Issue, which was discussed in the EC Environment Council on June 7, 1990. The purpose of this draft resolution is to transform in operational terms the suggestions contained in the communication quoted above. The Commission is in fact invited to include in its proposals for concrete action, which were requested by the council by the end of 1990, measures that should lead to stabilization of CO_2 Community emissions at present levels by the year 2000. Furthermore the Commission is invited to present by the end of 1991 a strategy for achieving a subsequent reduction of Community CO_2 emissions.

However, the approval of the Council resolution was postponed to a subsequent meeting, since a number of countries had various reservations about the document. We also note that specific instruments to abate GHG emissions have yet to be chosen by the EC. Therefore, the most painful part of the story is still to be faced.

Description of a Conflict

The White House Conference on Science and Economic Research Related to Global Change (Washington, DC, April 17–18, 1990) provides perhaps the best evidence to introduce the different U.S. and EC attitudes.

With regard to the United States, a very clear statement can be found in the reply given to a questionnaire submitted to all participating countries in preparation for the conference. The question was, "What potential conflicts, if any, between your interest in continued economic progress and your interest in arresting possible undesirable global change have been identified by your existing research?" Here is the relevant part of the reply:

The United States believes that uncertainties associated with the timing and magnitude of possible global change mean that policies will vary in their appeal as uncertainties are reduced; *an appropriate strategy to address possible global change based on today's knowledge and in light of today's economic environment may be wholly inappropriate within a decade.* (White House Conference 1990, question 1.2, italics added)

The fact that conflicts exist was clearly recognized by the chairman of the U.S. Council on Environmental Quality, M. R. Deland: "Let me be candid. This Conference will not lead to unanimity. We have disagreed on the question of global change, and we will disagree again" (1990, 3). In fact, several top-level U.S. officials use all possible arguments to justify their wait-and-see position. The tone was set by President George Bush with an ironic remark in his opening address: "Perhaps it's not surprising when the problem is global change that the debate often generates more heat than light." The chairman of the Council of Economic Advisers (CEA) stresses the question of costs and of their impact on developing countries:

When the costs of a policy are small relative to the size of the overall economy, as a CFC phaseout by the industrialized nations would be likely to be, it would be adequate to think about those costs in purely monetary terms. But when costs are large enough to be measured in percentages of GNP or in significantly slower economic growth, that simply will not do. . . . Current emissions projections suggest that India, China, and other developing countries will become increasingly dominant sources of carbon dioxide and other greenhouse gas emissions over the coming decades. For developing countries, slower economic growth does not mean making do with last year's model car—rather, it is a goal worth life itself to many (Boskin 1990, 4–5).

The cost issue is also taken into account when stressing that the United States is already bearing a heavy burden for the protection of the environment: "The United States comes to this conference as a leader in environmental action in both the domestic and global arenas," proudly states the chairman of the CEA, and goes on to mention that the revised Clean Air Act would already impose costs of about $20 billion annually on the U.S. economy when its provisions are fully phased in (ibid., p. 1). In a similar vein, the assistant to the president for science and technology states that "the Bush Administration has already instituted a number of policies that will reduce greenhouse emissions while being fully justified for other reasons" (Bromley 1990, 5). As a matter of fact, according to the administrator of the Environmental Protection Agency, "The measures already underway, including the phaseout of CFCs, reforestation and conservation, will reduce the US contribution to climate-altering gases by more than *15 percent* below what they otherwise would have been by the year 2000" (Reilly 1990, 12).

The EEC attitude differs in principle from that of the United States particularly on the question of decision making under uncertainty about the control of climate change. As mentioned, the U.S. position was that present knowledge on global change is insufficient for rational decision making, except with regard to increased research. On the contrary, European Community delegations in their short "Concluding Remarks" state:

The European Community reiterates the importance it attaches to taking effective and prompt action to deal with global change and underlines the global dimension of the greenhouse effect and the need for the Community and Member States to play their full part in the definition and implementation of a global response to the problem. *Such a response should be made without further delay, irrespective of remaining uncertainties on some scientific aspects of the greenhouse effect.* . . . It is incumbent on industrialized countries to take the lead.

This rather drastic statement—which reflects the attitude of previous documents—may be partly considered a reaction to the not always tactful way in which the conference was organized; EEC ministers resented, for instance, the fact that they were not allowed to speak in plenary sessions, so that, in the word of the French minister for environment, they had come to Washington to *faire tapisserie* (to be wallflowers). Before the conference the attitude was in fact more moderate. The EEC reply to the already quoted question on potential conflicts between economic progress and undesirable global change was in fact:

Where conflicts eventually arise will depend on the stages and level of actions considered. For instance, in the short and medium term, significant reductions in CO_2 emission trends are feasible in many of the most industrialized countries, without important socioeconomic costs. In the longer term and in a broader context it is inevitable that there will be some conflicts between some economic variables and the obligation to preserve and protect the environment. (White House Conference 1990)

Among EEC countries the Netherlands is particularly sanguine about immediate action:

The two objectives of continued economic progress and arresting undesirable global change have a symbiotic relationship and to sustain economic progress we have to avoid climate change. . . . The existing goal of CO_2 emission stabilization and reduction can be achieved without major conflicts between diverse objectives. The additional cost of investments to meet this goal will be compensated by the savings in the national energy bill and by other benefits for the environment such as on acidification, waste management, water pollution, and for society such as reducing risk, increasing energy security, improving land use, etc.

Furthermore we think that a cost benefit analysis has limited applicability in guiding policy formulations especially when dealing with global intergenerational problems. This is not only due to our limited understanding of global geospheric/biospheric processes, but also due to our limited capability to predict the future. Besides, other considerations point to the need of taking action now. These include the decreasing efficiency in time of actions to limit global change, the need for a precautionary approach when facing risks. . . . Therefore, the Netherlands focuses on cost effectiveness to decide whether the short term goals are economically viable. (ibid.)

The Reasons for Conflict

The different attitudes described in the preceding sections can be justified on several general grounds.

The Lack of an Appropriate Government Level

Climate change is a typical global environmental problem: the climatic changes throughout the world depend only on worldwide aggregate emissions of climate gases, and not on how emissions are distributed among countries. The consequences of climate change may of course differ among different countries. We shall assume here, however, that such differences do not exist, first of all for simplicity's sake, secondly because information is uncertain, and thirdly because even for the areas (e.g., Siberia) for which global warming may exert positive impacts, adaptation costs may be relevant.

For the reason just stated, from the economic point of view the control of climate change may be defined as a global (or planetary) public good. The point is that if there is a reduction of adverse overall climate change, once such reduction becomes available to one country, it is also available to others. Avoidance of climate change is thus a public good because its benefits extend to all countries in the world. A public good is in fact one that by its nature is enjoyed jointly and in the same quantity by all concerned.

We must, therefore, ask whether a system of decentralized decision making is likely to result in the efficient reduction of climate change—in other words, whether individual countries, each assumed to maximize the welfare of its own citizens, end up providing a level of climate change control such that the cost, say, of a marginal CO_2 emission not being released is equal to the sum of the values placed on that emission by the citizens of all countries.

The answer to these questions is in the negative. The reason is that each country in determining whether it will or will not reduce its emissions by an additional unit considers only the benefits its own citizens will receive from the marginal reduction. For this reason, the full social value of an additional reduction in emissions is not taken into consideration. Each country pays in fact the full cost of the planetary public good "control of climate change" but gets only a fraction of the benefits of the collective good. This means that individual members of an international organization like the United Nations have an incentive to stop providing climate change control long before the efficient world level of such control is provided. This is particularly true of the countries (e.g., developing ones) which for various reasons would value less the total benefits accruing from the control of climate change, and which find that they have little incentive to provide additional amounts of the collective good, with the result that the burdens are shared in a disproportionate way.

In conjunction with the situation just described there is likely to be "free-rider" behavior stemming from the incentive to have others provide or pay for a country's benefit deriving from the control of climate change. If a country can consume units of a good provided by other countries it has reason to try to get others to provide the good.

In conclusion, our global public good will be underproduced in a system of decentralized decision making. A world government, working perhaps in a federal framework, would therefore provide a better approximation to the efficient level of output of a public good that benefits the citizens of all countries. Since this is quite far from the present possibilities, conflicting views and decision making will take place, through which suboptimal solutions will be reached (for a general analysis of this economic problem, see in particular Oates 1972).

"Tragic Choices" and Climate Change

Another reason why decisions about the control of climate change are conflicting is that climate change is seen—rightly or wrongly—as causing possible catastrophes. For example, according to a not particularly terroristic description of the anticipated changes due to the phenomenon:

Rainfall and monsoon patterns could shift dramatically, upsetting agricultural activities world-wide. In summer, the Great Plains of the United States, Central Europe, and parts of the Soviet Union could experience Dust Bowl conditions. Sea level could rise from one to four feet, flooding coasts and allowing salt water to intrude into water supplies. Ocean currents could shift, altering the climate of many areas and disrupting fisheries. The ranges of plant and animal species could change regional, endangering protected areas and many species whose habitats are now few and confined. Record heat-waves and other weather anomalies could harm susceptible people, crops, and forests. (Speth 1987)

In the same vein it was also stated that climate systems are complex, nonlinear systems, rife with mathematical chaos. Catastrophic changes cannot therefore be ruled out (Nordhaus 1990, 22).

The relevant fact is that climate change is seen as very much linked to welfare and health, and even to the preservation of human life. For the purpose of our analysis, satisfactory scientific evidence about the negative impact of climate change is not necessarily relevant, at least for a certain period. What matters is the perception at the popular and political level. Also of relevance is not only the value assigned to the risk about human life per se, but also anxiety (or the fear of an important negative event).

The link just mentioned between climate change and human life is very relevant for social decision making because it relates to the central (though often hidden) issue of the social value given to the life of people. It is a very thorny issue for the society because this valuation entails a conflict of values for which there is no easy "rational" solution. There is, in fact, a conflict between society's wish, or illusion, to give life an infinite value and the hard fact that it is impossible to do so in a world of scarce resources. Such a conflict of ethical values underlies the so-called "tragic choices"—among which we would put the case of the level of control of climate change as the phenomenon is perceived by politicians and the public at large—for which no resource allocation method is fully satisfactory (see Calabresi and Bobbitt 1978). When dealing with such choices, more than in other cases, we are in fact forced to eschew the assumption that, in resource allocation, efficiency is "the" criterion. We are forced to take into account other conflicting values that are sometimes but a subterfuge or an illusion, such as the "infinite" value of life. There is thus no optimum solution to a tragic choice, but a mere dwindling from one solution that is consistent with certain values and inconsistent with others to another solution where the situation is changed or reversed.

By complex mixtures of approaches, various societies attempt to avert tragic results, that is, results which imply the rejection of values which are proclaimed to be fundamental. These may succeed for a time. But it will become apparent that some sacrifice of values has taken place; fresh mixtures of methods will be tried, structured . . . by the shortcomings of the approaches they replace. . . . When we have observed this recurrence and continuity of tragedy, it becomes apparent that a special type of mixture is being used by societies over time, namely the mixture or alternation of mixtures. Such a strategy of successive moves comprises an intricate game which better than any other method or set of methods reflects appreciation of the tragic choice.
It is the most subtle of methods because it depends on methodology being constantly replaced; yet alone among mixtures and methods, cycle strategy does not depend, for its success, on subterfuge. It may represent a forthright way of facing tragic choices since it accepts the fact that society faces the paradox of being forced to choose among competing values in a general context in which none can, for long, be abandoned. (ibid., pp. 195–196)

The cycle strategy in decision making holds not only to explain the dwindling behavior in time of a specific society about a tragic choice. It is our contention that the interpretation just given is also useful to understand the contrasting attitudes that different societies bear at the same time about a tragic choice, such as climate change. Because of the difficulty in choosing among contrasting ethical values, it may very well happen that one country, like the United States in the case of climate change, advocates cost minimization and efficiency at least in the short run, whereas others, like the EEC, favor environmental values. These attitudes may change in time, for the reasons stated in the quotation from Calabresi and Bobbitt. Furthermore, the attitude about climate change may appear inconsistent with decisions taken even on related environmental questions. In particular, the contrasting attitude between the United States and Europe with regard to climate change is by and large reversed when we look at the problems of local air pollution. In this area, in fact, taking into account the revision of the Clean Air Act, it is the United States that appears to give priority to the protection of health and life although costs appear relevant.

Uncertainty about the Causes and the Possible Consequences of Climate Change

There are several types of uncertainties that characterize climate change. First, the future mix of greenhouse gases that will be emitted into the atmosphere is difficult to forecast (with the exception of the CFC phaseout, although already-emitted CFCs will go on to exert a sizable impact on climate). Second, even if the emissions of greenhouse gases were known, their impact on climate would still be uncertain particularly because feedback effects may delay even for decades the reaching of a new condition of climate equilibrium (especially because of the interaction of oceans, glaciers, clouds, etc.). Third, even if the questions about "when" and "how much" *global* climate change had an answer (which they have not), there is a perhaps even greater uncertainty about the regional impact of climate change. Of course, this level of information is of particular interest for decision making by specific governments.

The Cost Problem

According to Professor Nordhaus, potential damage from global warming is an annual flow on the order of 0.25 percent of U.S. GNP, with a ceiling of 2 percent. This order of magnitude is considered relatively low by Nordhaus and by others (see Chapter 2 by Nordhaus and Chapter 6 by Schelling in this volume), although this is not the opinion of the U.S. government, as noted previously. Apart from the simplifying assumptions mentioned by Nordhaus, there are, however, value judgments and debatable aspects that underlie the optimistic position about climate change costs.

One of the reasons why the damage of climate change is considered to be relatively limited is that such damage occurs particularly in the agricultural sector, the share of which in the GNP of advanced countries is rather low (e.g., about 3 percent in the United States and 4.4 percent for Italy). This argument of course neglects the fact that agriculture is the most important sector in many poor countries. Even without speaking about solidarity, brotherhood, and all that, limiting the horizon of our analysis to rich countries does not seem to be a good example of statesmanship in an interdependent world.

Another cost that appears to be neglected in Nordhaus's evaluation is the cost (including important psychological disamenities) of moving from regions becoming too warm to cooler ones. This cost may very well be relatively negligible in the U.S. social and economic environment, but the situation is different in Europe and, we suspect, even more in certain developing countries.

We finally mention the question of the time horizon. Estimates about impacts and damage costs of climate change generally refer to estimates of the Intergovernmental Panel on Climate Change (IPCC) that a doubling of CO_2-equivalent trace gas concentration in the atmosphere will occur by the year 2025 and that such doubling will cause in subsequent decades a global warming of 2.5 to 3 degrees centigrade. However William R. Cline shows in this volume (Comment, Chapter 6) that by extrapolating IPCC's "business as usual" scenario to 2200, average global warming would reach 10 degrees. This increase would of course change the scenario, particularly with regard to sea-level rise. Of course a time horizon of about two centuries may be considered irrelevant because of its length, but in our view this would be myopic because of the long-term characteristic of climate change.

Summing up on this point, important uncertainties also characterize the evaluations of damages due to climate change. Economic evaluations produced up to now seem, however, to disregard in their cost concepts the framework of sustainable growth, which is based on solidarity with developing countries and with future generations.

Having discussed some general problems that justify the different positions on climate change, it is now appropriate to discuss these questions in the light of different types of international agreements and of alternative instruments to implement them.

International Agreements in Theory and in Practice

The first step is the examination of different types of international agreement to protect the atmosphere of the earth from GHG emissions. Such examination is necessary to determine which types of convention provide a satisfactory degree of efficiency and fairness to make them acceptable and lasting in time.

The agreements we shall consider concern prevention measures for the stabilization of atmospheric concentrations of GHG through appropriate targets for the reduction of such emissions; they do not take into account adaptive policies, since the latter are generally considered a responsibility of specific governments (although in extreme cases international help may be necessary). Although no clear analysis of benefits and costs of alternative approaches is available now, it is generally considered that world-wide preventive policies are to be preferred to locally oriented curative policies. This belief is based on the pervasive and "public bad" character of climate change, such that in the long run everybody may be a victim.

Nonetheless, even when the main objective of the reduction of GHGs is accepted, there remain many obstacles to overcome to reach an international agreement based on protocols that explicitly determine how to implement it. Such obstacles are caused in the end by the equity-efficiency problem and by the way in which these two terms are harmonized in the agreement.

A relevant cause of conflict in negotiations is the per-capita production of GHG. There is in particular a relevant difference between the EC and the United States. Furthermore, industrial countries for years have been surpassing LDCs in per-capita emissions of CO_2. Therefore, the former are held responsible for the increase of atmospheric concentrations of CO_2. However LDCs are now becoming the major potential producers of CO_2. If the industrial plans of such countries were to be implemented disregarding environmental impacts, CO_2 reductions already being achieved in OECD countries would be rapidly compensated. For this reason, agreements must contain compensation or "bribing" clauses.

The umbrella convention is an agreement designed to cover simultaneously all aspects of a problem through general rules (see Grubb 1989). An example of such convention is the Law of the Seas, which requested no less than fifteen years of negotiations ending in 1982. However, the situation concerning the right to exploit the oceans is

different from that concerning the atmosphere, because the former
is characterized by a lesser degree of uncertainty and because already
established interests are weaker, whereas the latter has more scientific uncertainties coupled with a pollution level that is strictly linked
to economic activity. Furthermore, this type of agreement generally
has little flexibility.

I consider next the case of the "framework convention." The most
recent example of such a convention is the Vienna Convention of 1985
on the protection of stratospheric ozone, followed by the Montreal
Protocol. This type of agreement consists of a series of general statements that summarize the scientific positions and the concerns of the
international community. The task of setting quantitative objectives
is left to subsequent protocols negotiated in the framework of the
convention.

The characteristic of framework conventions is a more flexible,
case-by-case approach that allows dealing with the problems posed
by different gases and by different economic sectors. Examples of
initiatives that may pave the way to a world convention on climate
change (which is planned in 1992, twentieth anniversary of the UNEP
Stockholm Conference) are the Hague Declaration of March 1989, the
Noordwijk Declaration of November 1989, the Toronto Conference
of June 1988 setting the goal of a 20 percent reduction by the year
2005, and the Hamburg Conference of November 1989 setting the
goal of a 30 percent reduction by 2000.

Before concluding this section it is useful to criticize two approaches that could be used in a future framework convention:

1. The Montreal Protocol takes into account the different situations
of industrialized countries and LDCs. However, such a protocol is
based on the notion of "equivalent percentage reductions," which
imposes specific limitations on each country. This approach does not
provide enough flexibility, since the costs for the reduction at the
margin of GHGs differ in a relevant way from country to country, as
may be shown in the Montreal case. Listing in increasing order along
a cost curve economic measures to reduce GHG emissions, EC countries like Italy and the United Kingdom would be found at a cost
level near to zero, since they could comply with the Montreal
agreement simply by banning CFCs in aerosols. On the contrary,
the United States should use more costly measures, since they have
already introduced such a ban. These differences in marginal costs
make the Montreal protocol inefficient, since the abatement level,

which is equal for all countries, is collectively realized by the contracting parties at a total cost that is higher than the minimum.

2. Another suboptimal approach can be found in the EEC directive on large combustion plants. This directive entails a trade-off among member countries taking into account their initial situation; different objectives of emission reductions are set at different dates. Countries are thus given a wrong incentive because during negotiations they will tend to overstate their difficulties in accepting the agreement to get more favorable conditions. The stability of the agreement is thus compromised.

An Example: The Montreal Protocol

Because of the number of countries involved and because of the abatement objectives, the Montreal Protocol of 1987 is the only example of legal international instrument that can be a reference model for a future framework convention on atmospheric pollution.

The Montreal Protocol, which has been subscribed to by fifty-six countries, had initially set the objective of a 50 percent reduction by 1999; a ten-year "bonus" was granted to LDCs. These targets have been revised in a restrictive way by the June 1990 London Conference, where some countries have declared themselves to be able to unilaterally reach a complete ban of CFCs in a much shorter time than the one foreseen (e.g., the Federal Republic of Germany has indicated a 1994 date). This is a "virtuous" target, but it conceals certain risks for the stability of the agreement. On the other hand, countries like China and India have difficulties in signing the treaty.

Apparently the effects of the Montreal Protocol are positive. It is estimated that the destruction of stratospheric ozone will be reduced from 50 percent to about 2 percent by 2075. As mentioned before, however, the specific characteristics of the agreement make it a model that is difficult to copy in future negotiations on the atmosphere. The consensus of industry to the agreement is linked to specific circumstances. In October 1988, one year after the signing of the protocol, but before the United States and EC decided to completely ban CFCs, Du Pont announced its support to a total ban by the year 2000. British ICI followed suit a few months later. The favorable attitude of industry was probably linked to an attempt to gain advantages in the opening market of substitutes with the aim of also discouraging free riding of potential competitors in the LDCs. In any case, such a favorable attitude by industry was surely an important factor for the approval of the agreement by governments.

To sum up, the reasons for the success of the Montreal Protocol are the following:

• The number of producers in the world, including potential ones, is limited.

• CFC uses are also limited to relatively few sectors, and there are already substitutes on the market.

• The benefits of the agreement are greater than those that can be obtained through unilateral action; they are also fairly clearly defined and well distributed among countries.

• Abatement costs are fairly low, which explains the acceptance by a few countries that had already adopted unilateral action.

• However, the fifty-six signatory countries are a number which is far smaller than the number of countries that should sign the convention on the atmosphere.

In the GHG case the situation is much more complex. There are many sources, and they are often difficult to monitor; the regional distribution of the effects is uncertain; abatement and transaction costs are high; it is foreseen that the time span for negotiations will be long.

In the absence of a world authority the only solution for the management of a common property like the atmosphere is an international agreement. However, there are strong incentives for governments to get a free ride. As in the case of CFCs, also for GHGs an agreement is more likely when through some benefit-cost evaluation countries decide that they would also be prepared to take some action on their own. This decision will be particularly difficult for LDCs.

Economic Instruments: A Brief Reference

The feasibility of an international agreement on GHGs very much depends also on the type of mechanisms that will be used to implement such an agreement. From the economic point of view, it is interesting to consider the application of tradable-permit schemes, as proposed, for example, by Grubb (1989). Each country would be allotted a certain share of CO_2 (or more generally GHG) permits up to an upper limit based on a per-capita average negotiated internationally. This share should be proportional to adult population for two reasons: (1) the moral principle according to which each human being has equal right to the atmosphere and (2) the necessity to provide for financial resources to third world countries. The advantages of this approach are summarized as follows:

The approach of using leasable carbon-emission permits allocated in proportion to adult population solves many problems simultaneously. It creates a logical basis for a long-term emissions control regime. It provides the flexibility and incentives needed to find the best way of limiting carbon emissions. It is a simple solution, compared with other approaches; if the basic principle is accepted, the scope for dispute over other major issues is limited, since the real bargaining occurs in subsequent bilateral deals. It creates a mechanism for ensuring a real transfer of resources from rich countries which are overexploiting the atmospheric resource to poor countries which need technical assistance if they are to minimise further exploitation as they develop. And it provides a continuing downward pressure on all carbon emissions, irrespective of whether individual countries are meeting predetermined targets. (Grubb 1989, 37–38)

An alternative economic instrument that could be applied is taxation. One may consider either an energy tax or a CO_2 tax—that is, a tax related to the carbon content of different fuels. The results of the two forms of taxation are different. In the case of energy taxation there will be energy conservation and new technologies; in the case of a CO_2 tax there will be a substitution effect among different fossil fuels and also between such fuels and alternative energy sources (nuclear, hydroelectric, etc.).

An international carbon tax may be introduced using three organization models. It may be managed and applied by an international agency; it may be introduced at the national level according to an international agreement; or it may be levied on each country by an international agency according to the quantity of emissions, and the agency would manage a fund to make back-payments according to appropriate parameters.

The first solution (direct management of the tax by an international agency) entails the creation of a fairly large international bureaucracy, which makes political costs rather high. The second solution (international agreement) entails a free-riding risk. Since countries and their economic systems are heterogeneous, those with heavily subsidized energy sectors in particular may reduce value-added or sales taxes on fuels, subsidize road transport, and the like.

According to M. Hoel (1990) the third case (each country paying the carbon tax to an international agency) is an economically efficient solution. In order to minimize costs, CO_2 emissions of each country would reach that level for which the marginal cost of emission reduction in each country equals the international rate per unit of CO_2 emitted, which is the same for all countries. The fund financed by the tax would redistribute the money raised through the tax according to the following parameters: (1) the level of costs that has to be met by each country in order to reduce CO_2 emissions; (2) the magnitude of the damage costs to be borne by each country because of climate change.

The first criterion would take into account the unfavorable situation of many LDCs and of countries with large coal reserves. The second criterion would probably entail rather large net transfers from industrialized countries to LDCs.

It is not easy to evaluate what would be the negotiating position of the EC and of the United States with regard to the possible use of economic instruments, since each of them may be applied in different ways. For instance, in the case of tradable permits, very different situations would arise if, instead of a per-capita average for the initial allocation of emission shares, "grandfathering" were used—that is, an initial allocation geared to previous emission levels. As shown in figure 5.3, this criterion would favor the greatest polluters—that is,

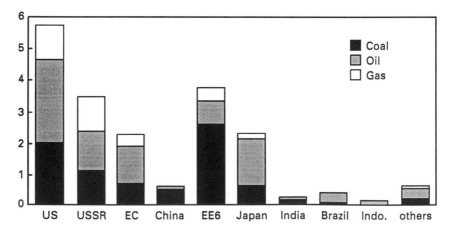

Figure 5.3
Fossil carbon emissions in tons per capita (1989)

SOURCE: M. Grubb, *The Greenhouse Effect: Negotiating Targets* (London: Royal Institute of International Affairs, 1989).

first of all and with a rather large "advantage" the United States, followed by the six Eastern European countries (EE6), the U.S.S.R., and the EC.

From a general point of view one can note furthermore that the United States uses a greater quantity of energy in proportion to income than the average of European countries, which are less energy-intensive. Therefore, there appears to be more room for greater energy-efficiency in the United States than in the EC. Since, as we have seen, energy-efficiency is linked to a reduction of climate change, a plea for higher energy prices in the United States would seem justified. We are considering in fact a typical situation in which a reduction of the adverse effects of climate change would be coupled to the attainment of other useful objectives, like cost savings, resource conservation, and the development of new technologies. This may in fact be, as already stated in the "Summary and Conclusions" section, the more suitable way to tackle for the moment the climate change problem—that is, through the so-called no-regret policies.

References

Boskin, M. J. 1990. Economics and global change: Links to the policy process and science research. Mimeo. White House Conference on Science and Economics Research Related to Global Change, Washington, DC, April 17–18.

Bromley, D. A. 1990. Uncertain change: The scientific and economic research challenge. Mimeo. White House Conference on Science and Economics Research Related to Global Change, Washington, DC, April 17–18.

Calabresi, G., and Bobbitt, P. 1978. *Tragic Choices*. New York: Norton.

Commission of the European Communities. 1988. Communication to the Council: The Greenhouse Effect and the Community. COM (88) 656 final, Brussels, November 16.

Commission of the European Communities. 1990a. Communication to the Council: Energy and the Environment. COM (89) 369 final, Brussels, February 8.

Commission of the European Communities. 1990b. Communication from the Commission on Community Policy Targets on the Greenhouse Issue. SEC (90) 496 final, Brussels, March 16.

Council of Environment Ministers. 1989. Council Resolution of 21 June 1989 on the Greenhouse Effect and the Community, 89/C 183/03. *Official Journal of the European Communities*, 20.7.89.

Deland, M. R. 1990. Remarks. White House Conference on Science and Economics Research Related to Global Change, Washington, DC, April 17–18.

Grubb, M. 1989. *The Greenhouse Effect: Negotiating Targets*. London: Royal Institute of International Affairs.

Hoel, M. 1990. *Efficient International Agreements for Reducing Emissions of CO_2*. Department of Economics, University of Oslo.

Nordhaus, W. D. 1990. Count before you leap. *The Economist*, July 7–13. 22–25.

Oates, W. E. 1972. *Fiscal Federalism*. New York: Harcourt Brace.

Reilly, W. K. 1990. Global Change: A commitment to action. Mimeo. White House Conference on Science and Economics Research Related to Global Change, Washington, DC, April 17–18.

Speth, J. G. 1987. Foreword. In I. M. Mintzer, *A Matter of Degrees: The Potential for Controlling the Greenhouse Effect*. Washington, DC: World Resources Institute.

White House Conference on Science and Economics Research Related to Global Change. 1990. *Delegate Information Book*. Washington, DC, April 17–18.

Comments

Thorvald Moe

Professor Gerelli's chapter gives us a very competent and thorough description of present positions, notably those of the European Community and the United States. Furthermore, the challenges and difficulties we face regarding solutions to the problem of global warming are ably elaborated.

At the outset, I may add one difficulty or conflict not explicitly mentioned by him. That is the strategic conflict of interests *between producers and exporters of petroleum on the one hand and (large) importers on the other*. It is understandable that Saudi Arabia does not favor carbon taxes. Coming from a country that is a large net exporter of petroleum, my colleagues at the Ministry of Petroleum tell me that Norway stands to lose large export revenues if a global system of carbon taxes is implemented. On the other hand, we possess large reserves of natural gas, and we export hydroelectricity, which may increase in value.

I will argue that questions regarding economic policy responses to global warming should be seen in the context of implementing long-term structural policies, and that they are not entirely different from the problems we face in international economic policymaking more generally. As global economic interdependence keeps increasing, it is well recognized that the need for coordination of macroeconomic and structural policies grows.

During the 1980s structural policies gained in importance and a consensus on the key role of neoclassical economics was emerging. Tax and price systems are being reformed in many countries, and *the need for establishing credible strategies* to guide the expectations and behavior of the household and business sectors is a key element in policymaking. I think the problem of improving the environment generally, and addressing the global warming problem specifically, could be seen in the context of an ongoing need for such long-term structural changes. If so, some simple economic principles of taxing externalities established long ago, for example by Pigou, could be useful guidelines for practical policies.

Efficient International Agreements

Articles in the economic literature are already emerging on efficient international agreements for reducing the emissions of greenhouse gases. Hoel (1990) shows that both systems—an international CO_2 tax and tradable CO_2 quotas—are efficient under certain conditions. These are appealing themes to theoretical economists, and such agreements should certainly be the ultimate goal of international negotiations.

A well-known condition for reaching environmental standards at minimum cost is that emissions be distributed so that all sources under consideration should have *equal marginal costs of further emissions reductions.* A uniform percentage reduction of emissions from all sources will normally lead to an emission pattern that makes marginal costs of emissions differ between sources. This rule is true whether "sources" are interpreted as different firms or consumers within a country (i.e., national efficiency) or as different countries (i.e., international efficiency). Uniform percentage reductions of emissions is therefore not a cost-efficient way to achieve environmental goals, be it nationally or internationally. Furthermore, national efficiency in all countries (or regions) will not necessarily lead to international or global efficiency. Uniform percentage reductions of greenhouse gases (GHG) would therefore not seem to be an optimal point of departure for a convention on greenhouse gases.

At present, as far as I know, no comprehensive empirical study explicitly analyzing different ways of reducing worldwide emissions of CO_2 has been carried out. However, some empirical studies of other emissions may be indicative. We now have estimates suggesting that further reductions in Norway's sulfur dioxide emissions could cost ten times as much as similar reductions in Poland. By the Helsinki protocol, which is based on equiproportional cuts in the emission of pollutants, we are nevertheless committed to cut our emissions further. However, the effect on both acid rain in Scandinavia and local pollution problems in Poland would be much larger if we instead could contribute the same amount of money to cutting Polish sulfur emissions.

Furthermore, results for domestic problems regarding other emissions and Mähler's studies of emissions of SO_2 in Europe suggest that uniform reductions of CO_2 emissions from all countries participating in an agreement may be very costly and reduce the probability of an agreement in the foreseeable future.

Muddling Through toward a Framework Agreement: A Gradualist Approach

On the one hand we have the economists' notion of efficiency. On the other we have the experience of environmental policies in the 1970s and 1980s dominated by "command and control," and a number of international agreements have been established that are more or less inefficient. Clearly, there is room for improvements during the 1990s and beyond.

Experience from national and international policymaking indicates that such processes do not change overnight. Efficient global agreements to reduce greenhouse gases may be some time ahead. Active participants in the coming negotiating processes, referring to the preventive principle, may prefer an inefficient agreement to no agreement at all. As we muddle toward a framework agreement, could we as economists—in addition to acting as noble proponents of efficiency—suggest certain simple propositions in order to improve on present processes?

First, we should at the outset be able to agree on avoiding equiproportional reductions of emissions among nations or a panicky recourse to quick-acting but economically inefficient regulatory instruments. In a scenario suggested to us by Nordhaus, inefficient policy could cost 0.5 percent of GNP growth per annum for a twenty-year period.

An alternative strategy would, given large uncertainty and different preferences among countries, be a *gradualist approach:* Start now or soon, and spread the adjustment out over a longer period, perhaps into the next century (see Emerson 1990). This implies *both* clear long-term signals on the part of the authorities in the form of stated objectives and gradual changes of relative prices *and* giving the economy and technology time to prepare. In the terminology of Professor Manne, this could be seen as an "act then learn" strategy, rather than the U.S. position of "learn then act" (Manne and Richels 1990).

This approach involves, inter alia, a *closer integration of environmental and economic policies.* For whatever it is worth, let me give an example of how this is done in Norway. We regularly project emissions of major air pollutants in connection with the government's long-term macroeconomic policy documents. These projections are made on the basis of the energy accounts and air pollution emission accounts linked to a general-equilibrium model (MSG-TAX) that we use for long-term analytic purposes (Central Bureau of Statistics 1990). By means of these calculations, the Ministry of Finance presents a fairly comprehensive view of the outlook for key economic and environmental indicators. Economic costs and environmental benefits in money terms are indicated. In recent simulations one arrived at the shadow price of reaching a national objective of stabilizing CO_2 emissions in the year 2000. It indicated, for example, a user price of gasoline ten years from now roughly 75 percent higher than today (or 100 percent higher twenty years from now if stabilization should take place in 2010). This was signaled to the household and business sectors as a long-term guideline in policy documents recently presented to the Parliament. Such policy analyses must of course be revised regularly as circumstances such as oil price developments change.

Similar work has been carried out in other countries. But as Gerelli points out in his chapter, the EC has not at the time of writing come up with a pricing strategy or concrete measures to show how they will stabilize CO_2 emission in Europe. Maybe similar simulations using regional, or indeed global, models would be useful in this context. I refer to John Martin's paper on the modeling work being undertaken by the OECD.

Within a gradualist approach, there might in several areas be scope for *considerable overall improvements of efficiency* that could at the same time increase future options and flexibility. This approach would seem likely to be particularly fruitful with regard to activities and market conditions closely tied to potential environmental degradation, such as the following:

• *Increased taxation of the perceived external costs of air pollution* and—if tax revenues were to remain constant—a consequent decrease in other tax rates. If applied gradually and on a general basis, a shift in taxation toward charges on proven externalities ("Pigovian" taxes) could result in overall efficiency gains and increase the potential for and profitability of innovations in "clean" technologies.

• *A standardization of tax rates across fuels* according to their environmental impact, so as to minimize distortions in consumption patterns due to tax differentials—for instance, between close substitutes such as gasoline and diesel fuel or coal and gas.

• Reforms in sectorial policies in such fields as *agriculture* and *urban congestion and related transport policy incentives* that, if applied consistently, could provide overall efficiency gains and at the same time reduce emissions of pollutants, including emissions of CO_2.

Adopting a gradualist approach would call for *acting soon* so as to allow time for adjustment while preventing concentrations of greenhouse gases from reaching too high a level. At the same time one should initiate work to *learn* more about the dimensions and the uncertainties of the problem. We could act now and at the same time learn more before initiating policies that would lead to major structural changes. More drastic policies might, in the event, be sensible at the point when it is possible to identify future damage with more confidence.

Without taking a firm stand in favor of either of the two alternative response strategies that are now debated internationally—reaction or preemption—I think there is no reason to neglect the possibility of significant future environmental damages. Buying no insurance against possible future damage, as indicated by Nordhaus, seems to me not to be a fully rational or credible approach. To safeguard against potentially large future damage costs, the *international community* could prepare, if not immediately implement, further contingent steps to curb environmental pressures. Appropriate measures could thus be implemented if further information suggested they were necessary. Pursuing this strategy, *the sequencing of policies* could, as suggested by the OECD Secretariat (1990), be divided into three stages:

1. *Enhancing internal efficiency* through structural policies aimed at improving overall economic performance. This could involve making corrections to those environmental policies with negative effects on the allocation and degradation of capital.

2. *Enhancing transnational measures* to prevent further environmental degradation or encourage technological diversity. Beyond those first steps that would be justified on the grounds of national efficiency or environmental preferences, steps could be taken to impose increased charges on global environmental degradation. By their nature, such policies would need to be conducted within a transnational framework, as we attempt to move toward framework agreements.

3. In the longer term, policies to deal with global problems would require *incentives to third parties* (developing countries) not included in an agreement or convention. Otherwise, global feedbacks caused by the "free-rider" problem might seriously undermine any agreement. It may be important to give incentives to developing countries to cooperate in global conventions. If the costs are large, as is likely, one would have to ask whether other problems in developing countries, like the population problem, would be more pressing (see Schelling's discussion on this point in Chapter 6).

The first and second stages could be initiated gradually as we move toward a framework agreement.

Summing Up

The EC seems to have a nobler starting point than, for example, the United States by attempting to adopt CO_2 stabilization as a (soft?) goal. But a strategy including concrete measures and how it is to be implemented by EC members has not been presented at the time of writing. Furthermore, how do we set in motion a reasonably cost-efficient *long-term European strategy*, including Eastern European and perhaps EFTA countries? This question poses difficult problems and requires further work.

While having the goal of cost-efficiency as a starting point, I have argued that a *gradualist policy strategy* may be to start now with a number of steps that many countries may agree to. Furthermore, I have supported some elements and stages suggested by the OECD that may be implemented as part of such a strategy in the coming process of reaching a framework agreement. And while it seems necessary that all participants move in the same direction, the timing of each step may not have to be identical.

Within such a strategy, individual countries could "act then learn" without necessarily waiting for a framework agreement. For example in the case of Norway, stabilization of CO_2 by the year 2010 might, according to calculations made by the Central Bureau of Statistics, require a doubling of the user price of gasoline. This could lead to, inter alia, a level of GNP that is 2.7 percentage points lower than a baseline without CO_2 charges, but still 80 percent above the level of GNP in 1988, *and* yearly environmental and health benefits of the order of magnitude of 20 billion Norwegian kroner. Norway's share of global CO_2 emissions is some 0.2 percent. Clearly, without international agreements stabilization of CO_2 emissions in Norway would make no contribution to reducing global warming. Nevertheless, in a period of learning in coming years, and as part of an international gradualist approach, such measures could be justified as part of a domestic "act then learn" strategy.

References

Central Bureau of Statistics. 1990. *Natural Resources and the Environment 1989.* Oslo.

Emerson, M. 1990. Europe after 1992: Economic and monetary policy aspects. Paper presented at the European Economic Association, Lisbon.

Hoel, M. 1990. Efficient international agreements for reducing emissions of CO_2. Paper prepared for the Ministry of Finance in connection with their preparations for the conference Actions for a Common Future, Bergen, May 8–16.

Mähler, Karl Gøran. 1989. The acid rain game. In H. Folmer and E. van Ireland, eds., *Valuation Methods and Policy Making in Environmental Economics.* Amsterdam: Elsevier.

Manne, A. S., and Richels, R. G. 1990. Buying greenhouse insurance. Mimeo. Stanford CA: Stanford University, September.

Organization for Economic Cooperation and Development. 1990. *Economics and Environment: Issues and Policy Responses.* Paris, March.

6

Economic Responses to Global Warming: Prospects for Cooperative Approaches

T. C. Schelling

I am going to confine my discussion to carbon dioxide. The reasons are simple:

1. The CFCs are potent greenhouse gases that are emitted in sufficient volume to be a substantial part of the problem, but efforts to curtail emissions globally are proceeding with remarkable success. There appears to be adequate motivation without greenhouse arguments; the time horizon of abatement is short compared with any such horizon for carbon dioxide; and an initial rudimentary system for burden sharing is in development. Linkage with carbon dioxide could slow down or complicate a process that is already working. The by-product of greenhouse abatement should be welcomed but not put back on the bargaining table.

2. Methane is a serious greenhouse gas, but it cannot currently be monitored by country. Too little is known about the sources, and less about how to bring them under control (except possibly for natural gas leakage). Fortunately, methane residence time is so short that emissions over the next thirty years will have no influence on the greenhouse effect in the middle of the next century; if in two or three decades we know what to do about methane, that is soon enough.

3. Nitrous oxide, like methane, cannot currently be monitored nationally; somewhat like methane, the sources are not well known, nor are the means for abatement known. (Carbon dioxide also cannot be monitored nationally, but carbon fuel can be monitored as an input.)

4. Deforestation, especially in Brazil and a few other tropical countries, receives increasing attention for several environmental reasons, including the carbon in burnt and decomposed vegetation and topsoil. However, the countries involved are few and poor; the extent of deforestation, especially as measured in carbon, is not well measured;

deforestation may not respond readily to national policy; and concern with deforestation is not limited to carbon. Not for lack of greenhouse importance, deforestation has to be dealt with separately.

Several characteristics of the greenhouse problem make it especially daunting:

1. It is truly a problem of the global common. No single nation will find it in the purely national interest to engage on its own in substantial abatement on account of greenhouse warming. (The arguable exceptions might be the United States and a collective European Community.)

2. The magnitude of potential abatement costs would be perceived as immense. I say "perceived" because estimates invite comparisons with something like the federal budget of the United States. At the present time 2 percent of GNP is 100 billion dollars per year, a currently unmanageable amount politically, even though a 2 percent loss of GNP through reduced productivity, phased in over a decade or two and maintained in perpetuity, would not be much noticed.

3. There is a severe mismatch between an optimal distribution of abatement among nations and any equitable distribution of costs. It is the poorest countries of the world where carbon emissions are increasing most rapidly; they account now for somewhat more than a quarter of the total and will pass half the total before the middle of the next century.

4. To be worth the bother, any international regime to bring carbon emissions into line with agreed quotas or agreed efficiency standards, or to impose taxes on fuels, will have to appear capable of surviving for at least a half century and be dynamically flexible to cope with a world in transformation.

5. The number of nations that consume fossil fuel is the number of nations that there are. The number that produce some fossil fuels, for consumption or for export, is very large. There are no national "nonparticipants" in greenhouse activities.

6. The mix of gas, oil, coal, nuclear, hydro, and solar differs drastically among countries. The industrial mix differs widely among countries in energy intensity, as do technologies, climate, geographical density and distribution of populations, consumption styles, habits, and customs, and other determinants of carbon dioxide production and of costs of conserving carbon. (A few decades ago, half of all the coal produced in the Soviet Union was consumed in transporting coal

from the mines to where it was to be burned, and I am told distance remains a main determinant of Soviet coal use.)

7. Countries differ not only in the ability to pay for carbon emissions abatement but also in their abilities to induce or coerce consumers, businesses, and farmers to change their household and business and farming technologies, styles, and behavior.

8. Countries differ drastically in their prospective rates of growth in population and in GNP per capita, in their prospective increase of fossil fuel use, and in the particular fossil fuels they have available.

9. Nuclear power, the main alternative for electricity and perhaps eventually for liquid fuels, is not only expensive but also unpopular in many countries. New "inherently safe" power reactors may not begin to come on line for at least another two decades. Many fuel-using technologies, from electric power plants to home heating, are embedded in capital equipment with mean lifetimes ranging from one to three decades.

10. Uncertainties are huge, and most of them will persist. These are uncertainties about the changes in climate to be expected, about the impact of climate change, about the costs and problems of adapting to climate change, and about the costs of reducing carbon emissions. Embedded in many of these uncertainties will be uncertainties about the way people will live and work a hundred years from now, how they will transport themselves and house themselves, what they will eat and where they will live, and what will be the threats to public health of any changes in climate.

The Trade-off between Abatement and Adaptation

At the outset, any cooperative approach to global warming will have to reach some rough consensus on two sets of magnitudes and the marginal trade-off between them. One set of magnitudes relates to CO_2 production and abatement. It is the cost and difficulties of reducing energy use by households, farms, and industry, and of switching to cleaner fossil fuels or converting to nonfossil energies. These are the kinds of things that economists and engineers, sometimes sociologists and architects, have been working on with special motivation since 1973. The uncertainties remain great, and they increase many-fold when projected to the middle of the next century. But these estimates do receive attention.

The other set of magnitudes has to do with the impact of changing climate on economic productivity, on health and comfort, on the quality of life in general, and on the differential rates of progress among countries. These estimates, on which virtually no work was done until recently, and only very little recently, are doubly uncertain. They are uncertain, first, because the climate changes to expect are exceedingly uncertain. There is uncertainty about the extent of greenhouse emissions even in the absence of efforts to abate them; there is uncertainty about influences on the radiation balance other than carbon dioxide; there is uncertainty about the extent of "warming" to be associated with those changes in the radiation balance; and then there are the uncertainties of translating a mean surface global warming into climates around the world. About all that seems to be known with certainty is that there is a potential for serious climate change because the estimates of the likely warming that will drive the changes in climate are large in relation to any mean temperature changes recorded in the last 10,000 years, and this warming will put the earth into a mean surface temperature regime outside any experience to which we have access.

The other set of uncertainties is at least as great and possibly greater. If we knew what the regional and local climates would be all over the earth seventy-five or a hundred years from now, it would be hard to resist the temptation to superimpose those altered climates on today's cultures and economies. If life, culture, technology, and economics change as much in the next ninety years as they have changed since the turn of the century, we may be no better able to imagine, for Europeans or for Asians, what the significance of alternative climates would be. Even barely more than a half century ago, computer and other electronics were not dreamed of, nor nuclear energy or nuclear medicine, nor genetics, antibiotics, or modern plastics.

I belabor the point because it is hard to imagine any international cooperative regime doing anything serious about greenhouse warming without arriving at some notion of the order of magnitude of effort that may possibly be justified by the consequences of failure to abate emissions at all, or of lesser or greater abatements. In the section that follows I shall offer a judgment about the magnitude of the consequences of failing to reduce CO_2 emissions drastically below what they would be in the absence of such an effort. I shall take "drastic" to mean anything between an emissions growth rate half of what it would otherwise be and an emissions growth rate of zero beginning one or two decades from now—that is, annual emissions leveling off within a decade or two. That level would still leave emissions growing at the maximum achieved rate. (There is nothing particularly significant or attractive about "stabilizing" emissions; it is an arbitrary choice of a particular rate of increase of concentration, one that brings about a doubling of CO_2 concentration a little faster than a 0.05 percent per year reduction of annual emissions and a little slower than a 0.05 percent annual increase of emissions.)

The Trade-off between Climate Change and Abatement

It might appear exceptionally difficult to estimate the impact of a change in climate on economic activity without knowing what the change in climate is going to be. But that would be the case only if climate really made a significant difference. The estimates I have seen for the impact on the U.S. economy make sense to me. They are based on no esoteric methodology. They are based on a moderately detailed examination of economic activities in the United States that are dependent at all on the weather. The estimates assume the *present* economy functioning in future climates, and thus do what I warned against in the previous section. But the results strike me as robust.

To a first approximation, or even a second, the changing climate makes no difference. I believe this result is better spelled out by William Nordhaus in Chapter 2. The reason the climate change appears to make no difference is that there are very few productive activities in the U.S. economy that are affected by climate. When Toyota chooses to locate an automobile assembly plant in Michigan or Alabama or California, there are important geographical differences to take into account, but climate apparently is not one of them. Most manufacturing and mining, transportation and communications, finance, wholesaling and retailing, education, and medical care are not visibly affected by climate. Milder climates may have a benign impact on construction in some parts of the United States; rain, snow, ice, and fog can have a minor effect on transportation. (Technical progress in instrument flying in the past few decades clearly overwhelms the climate differences that air traffic experiences in different parts of the United States.)

It is agriculture, together with fishery and forestry, that can be affected. They are almost too small to matter in the overall picture of climate changes around the country. Even if agricultural productivity declined by one-fifth, which is beyond any expectation, the effect would be less than 1 percent of a gross national product that per capita may be double, triple, or quadruple what it is today.

Not everything that matters shows up in the GNP. But it seems unlikely that in the United States there would be adverse effects on health more serious than those that may be incurred when we exchange jobs in different parts of the country; what we eat, drink, and smoke continue to have vastly more effect than climate on our health and comfort. As to comfort, if the net result should be a warming, it is worth noticing that in North America and Europe most people go south for vacations both summer and winter, and if they move upon retiring tend to go south, not north. As to outdoor recreation, snow-making machinery must have done more in the last twenty years to improve ski conditions than climate change can possibly offset, and that is the kind of thing we have to keep in mind.

I conclude that for the United States it will be exceedingly difficult to demonstrate serious adverse impacts of climate change. I see no reason why the same should not be true of Japan and Western Europe. To reformulate this conclusion: The countries that can afford to take serious measures to reduce carbon emissions may not be able to perceive any narrow national interest in doing so.

That is a strong conclusion, much stronger than the conclusion that the atmosphere is a global common and no individual nation has purely national reasons for engaging in costly abatement on its own. This is the conclusion that they may not perceive good reasons even for going ahead collectively.

I continue this first step toward identifying motives for international cooperation by observing that virtually all the rest of the world is too desperately in need of economic improvement to penalize itself with reductions in energy use or with investments in lower carbon emissions for their own sake. I think we cannot expect China, India, the Soviet Union, the countries of Eastern Europe, or the rest of the developing world to burden their current economic growth for the sake of a possibly more benign climate fifty, seventy-five, or a hundred years from now than they should otherwise anticipate. Nor would I urge them to.

At the same time I recognize that agriculture plays an immensely larger role in the economic life of developing countries, and their potential susceptibility to climate change is at least an order of magnitude greater than that of the industrial nations. It is important, of course, that they become less dependent on agriculture over the coming seventy-five years; maintaining maximum rates of economic improvement may have a lot to do with how vulnerable they are in another seventy-five years to the vagaries of climate. But they probably are susceptible in a way that the richer countries are not.

An additional point is that many of these same countries—notoriously Eastern Europe and the Soviet Union, as was publicized during 1990—have been poisoning their drinking water, the air they breathe, and their topsoil, so much that any economic penalties they are prepared to incur to clean up emissions should, for at least a generation, concentrate on immediate threats to health and child development. Carbon dioxide will appear benign by comparison.

So in searching out the national interests around the globe that may motivate countries to participate in cooperative approaches to global warming, I conclude that most of the countries that can afford to do anything may perceive very little interest of their own, and most of the countries that perceive themselves potentially vulnerable have urgent needs that leave no resources to invest in greenhouse abatement.

If we couple this conclusion with my earlier observation that some of the most egregious carbon-fuel inefficiencies are in places like China, India, and Eastern Europe, it looks as if any successful cooperative scheme will have a couple of salient characteristics. One is that whatever is done will be financed by the industrial countries with high income. The second is that any efficient utilization of the resources that those high-income countries may be willing to contribute will entail massive resource transfers from the industrial to the less-developed world. Economically that second conclusion need not matter much; the scale of capital movements is not large in relation to the world economy. Politically and organizationally I see it as a great complication.

Other Motivations for Greenhouse Abatement

To this point I have been trying to identify the motivations that national governments around the world will bring to the search for a cooperative approach to global warming. But these motivations that

I impute to the different national governments are based on my assessment of what a few studies show about the likely impact of climate change on the quality of life in different parts of the world. My assessment can be perceived as very optimistic; it can be perceived as very pessimistic. It is optimistic in suggesting that there is no call for alarm in the developed world. It is pessimistic in suggesting that when governments come to look seriously into the potential damage resulting from climate change and the costs of severe abatement programs, they are unlikely to embark on anything very ambitious. That conclusion is pessimistic, of course, only if there are strong grounds for preferring an ambitious program of abatement. Are there such grounds?

There are several arguments for being concerned. Their appeal is different for different individuals and different populations. The one that appeals most to me is that there may be discontinuities, or *catastrophes*, that today's meteorological dynamics cannot discover or produce. The general circulation models predict change that is gradual in time and in space; the climate of Nebraska in the course of 100 years may become like that of Oklahoma or like that of North Dakota, but not like that of Oregon, Massachusetts, or Louisiana. But what comes out of the models may be gradual and continuous only because of what goes into the models; there may be, for example, oceanic phenomena not yet understood that could produce sudden drastic changes.

An example, fortunately now dismissed but only in the past dozen years, was the possibility that grounded ice in Antarctica could glaciate or break away rapidly into the ocean, raising sea level by some 6 meters, within the coming century. Something like that possibility could be discovered that does not yield benignly upon further examination. A switch of North Atlantic ocean currents can be neither predicted nor confidently ruled out, as best I can tell from the literature, but there is nothing in the general circulation models that can test the possibility. Similarly, there has been allusion to the possibility of some kind of runaway positive feedback, possibly involving the release of arctic methane in increasing quantities. If another decade's research into these matters cannot put us at ease, a risk-averse insurance policy of vigorous CO_2 abatement may recommend itself.

A second argument for proceeding vigorously with abatement is that the poorer three-quarters of the world may be in serious jeopardy from climate change. These are more vulnerable economies. If the climate models become able to yield reasonably confident forecasts for different regions of the world within the next decade, projecting those specific changes and projecting the corresponding economies fifty or seventy-five years into the future may indicate the magnitude of the problem of climate change. If such forecasting does not prove feasible, a "sensitivity analysis" for different regions for plausible changes in climate may help to assess the magnitude of the problem of adapting to climate change.

If the developed high-income nations are now prepared to make substantial investments of their own resources in the standard of living and quality of life fifty to seventy-five years from now in the now-developing countries, there will be two competing routes to pursue. One is to invest in greenhouse gas abatement; the other is to invest directly in economic growth and improvement. If the contribution were to be on the order of 1 percent of GNP over the next half century or more, it has to be determined whether such an investment would yield greater returns in the future if plowed into consumption, investment, education, public health, and population control in the developing countries. (I would expect that if the issue were formulated explicitly in these terms, the preference in developing countries would be for the immediate direct investment; but institutionally and politically issues like this rarely get formulated as such an explicit choice.)

A third set of values that can motivate economic sacrifices in favor of abatement is "the environment." There is scientific interest but also economic interest in preserving what has come to be known as biological diversity—the genetic legacy of billions of years of biological evolution. There is popular interest in endangered species. There is the belief that the earth itself deserves our respect. How powerful these motivations will be when faced with the price of CO_2 abatement remains to be seen; my expectation is, not very powerful. The American aversion to even the most modest rise in motor-fuel or heating-fuel prices has had another opportunity to show itself as I write this, during the latest Persian Gulf crisis. President Jimmy Carter's proposal during the energy crisis of the late 1970s to phase in gradually a fifty-cent tax on motor fuel got nowhere; and when the price of diesel fuel jumped less than twenty cents, through no fault of the U.S. government, drivers from all over the country blockaded the nation's capital.

The Momentum for Action

There is currently the appearance of vigor and enthusiasm in the international scientific community and even among many governments, especially those of Western Europe, in moving toward some kind of internationally agreed greenhouse abatement effort, or at least toward international institutions to facilitate reaching eventual commitments on abatement. The George Bush administration has come under criticism, both in the United States and in Western Europe, for its cautious approach; administration officials expressed the position that drastic action now would be premature. How deep the concern is among West European governments is hard to gauge; there is little evidence that they have studied the trade-off between abating emissions and adapting to change. When they do face up to that trade-off they may back away somewhat, as the Bush administration did. In any event it seems likely that an international effort cannot go forward without strong U.S. participation, if not strong U.S. leadership. That leadership does not appear forthcoming, nor even strong participation. Prospects for serious abatement in the near future are not good.

But all this great diplomatic effort probably must culminate in something in two or three years. If it cannot culminate in serious commitments to shares in an abatement program, it will probably lead to some kind of "framework convention," one that establishes some permanent organization and that anticipates specific protocols to be subsequently negotiated, protocols that will spell out obligations toward CO_2 and possibly toward some of the other greenhouse gases.

I expect, in other words, that the current momentum will not lead to serious greenhouse abatement commitments but will become absorbed in institutional arrangements. There will then occur the long, slow process of examining the hard facts that underlie the greenhouse dilemma, both in the international organizations set up for such a purpose and, more importantly, within national governments. And then will begin the arduous process of negotiating commitments to certain goals, criteria, or quantitative schedules and targets. There is every indication that this initial stage, leading to something like a framework convention, will be universalist or nearly so, involving at least the thirty-four members of the Economic Commission for Europe, most of the larger developing countries—Brazil is the host country for the 1992 conference—and very possibly most of the membership of the United Nations.

Action on the Greenhouse Problem

Ultimate progress in the second stage, that of determining what actually to do rather than how to organize it, will depend on realistic judgments on the part of the main industrial Western countries of what can be expected with any likelihood of realization. And, as I have argued, there should be no expectation of more than token contributions from the developing world or from the formerly socialist nations of Eastern Europe.

What I foresee as the most favorable outcome for greenhouse abatement is an understanding among the European Community, the United States and Canada, Japan, and a few other nations that can afford to participate and will insist on it (Finland, Australia) that they will have to bear the cost of all greenhouse-motivated changes in energy use. These costs will take two forms, and the two forms will be politically and diplomatically disjunct. The first and most straightforward of the two will be national undertakings for the reduction of carbon emissions. The second will be the financing of efforts to reduce carbon emissions in the rest of the world.

A special problem will be the participation of the Soviet Union. The Soviet Union has been a major participant in international environmental scientific activities; it is accustomed to being a major participant in international affairs. As I argued earlier, the Soviet Union cannot be expected to incur significant sacrifice to curtail greenhouse emissions. It would be acutely embarrassing for the Soviet Union to plead "underdeveloped" status to be excused from an international greenhouse regime. The dilemma is that the Soviet Union cannot significantly participate and cannot afford to be perceived as not participating.

The only resolution to this dilemma may be to hope that as the Soviet Union reorganizes its economy—and this observation may apply to other East European countries—the incentives and opportunities for more efficient use of energy will lead to reductions in carbon emissions significantly below what would otherwise have been projected, allowing the U.S.S.R. to take credit for greenhouse abatement even though the abatement was a result of market prices and elimination of subsidies. Without any net investment for the sake of greenhouse abatement the Soviet Union thus may be able, with the acquiescence of the other industrial countries, to claim the status of full-fledged participant.

Structures of Cooperation

What is the likely structure of a regime that the developed higher-income countries may adopt? I think a carbon tax unlikely. An international carbon tax does two things. It provides the right kind of incentive for fuel conservation, fuel switching, and expanded production of noncarbon or lower-carbon fuels. And it transfers income to some taxing authority. A sufficient excise tax to provide much incentive would produce more revenue than any international taxing authority would be allowed to manage, and it would inflict financial penalties that many nations would find intolerable. Domestically, carbon taxes may be among the preferred policy instruments of some participating countries and may deserve to be promoted enthusiastically, but the proceeds of domestic carbon taxes remain at home. Some countries may find popular logic in using the proceeds of fuel taxes or carbon taxes to promote greenhouse-efficient energy; and some countries will probably find the social costs of greenhouse-efficiency more willingly accepted by voters and taxpayers if they show up as the economic burdens of regulation rather than as visible taxes.

The only international carbon tax that I can envisage as being both effective and acceptable would be a carbon tax used in conjunction with agreed carbon quotas. A marginal tax on carbon in excess of quota (preferably negative within the quota) levied on quotas that were deliberately set 5 or 10 percent below the negotiated targets, could be several times as high as a tax on total consumption without yielding excessive revenues. The net taxes in such a scheme would be less embarrassingly large, while the incentives would be much larger.

Participation would probably have to be voluntary. And any nation that earned negative taxes over several successive years would likely be challenged to renegotiate its quota downward. So I consider even this marginal tax on national excess emissions not very promising.

What are some other structures that this industrial-nation greenhouse regime might take? I can imagine limited use of something like "best available technology," or specific efficiency standards. Something like the fleet mileage average for automobiles and buses might be proposed to be administered not company by company but nation by nation. Uniform efficiency standards for household electric equipment might be proposed. I think the scope for these is essentially opportunistic; they might be more readily accepted within the European Community; they would depend on popular appeal; and they would probably be voluntary among nations rather than enforceable.

What is left is some variant of national carbon-emission quotas or allowances. (The European Community might well be treated, in the international negotiations, as a single "bubble.") Several pertinent questions are (1) How are the quotas arrived at? (2) How are they phased in? (3) How are they managed or enforced?

There are several ways that quotas might be arrived at. Ideally a quota might be arrived at by formula. The formula would take into account GNP and population density, climate, industrial mix, hydroelectric resources, and inherited technology in construction, manufacturing, transport, and household energy use, along with other pertinent factors. I consider this approach to be out of the question; even if technicians could econometrically determine an appropriate formula, including a formula for phasing in the quota in light of embedded technology, the formula would have to be negotiated; and the negotiations would be of a remarkably perverse sort. Intercountry comparisons would have to be formulated in the language of econometrics, in the pretense that it was the formula that mattered, while all that any government cared about was the quotas that the formula determined.

A second possibility would be to choose a baseline year or years, perhaps a period immediately preceding the initiation of negotiations, and to set annual quotas numerically calculated uniformly from each nation's baseline emissions. This plan would clearly not be acceptable to other countries for the United States, which would enjoy the fruits of high baseline emissions; it might be unacceptable to France, which has already eliminated more than half its fossil-fuel power production and would get no credit.

The final alternative is simply to negotiate quotas. (Again, the international negotiation might involve the European Community as an entity, with EC members negotiating their own shares of the EC international quota.) But negotiations have to begin somewhere, and there has to be some notion of what the allowable arguments and criteria are. This kind of negotiation has to be substantive. What are

the substantive elements that go into the negotiations? I believe they
are precisely the things that I mentioned previously as ingredients in
a formula and dismissed as a pure system but now retrieve as a
basis for negotiation. Obviously the main focus of attention will be
"baseline." Baseline may be of more than one dimension. Emissions
in, say, 1990 are bound to be a focus for quota negotiations in the
1990s. But a growth trend may also be a part of baseline. While
baseline may be a point of departure, the critical arguments may
include the other characteristics I mentioned, such as climate, inherited technology, industrial mix, population density, domestic nonfossil energy resources, and all of those determinants of emissions, or
emissions per capita, or emissions per unit GNP.

A Model for International Negotiation

My only models are negotiations among the countries of the Organization for European Economic Cooperation (OEEC) in 1948 for distribution of Marshall Plan dollars among fifteen potential recipient
countries and the negotiations beginning in 1951 on "burden sharing" in NATO. There was never a formula for distributing Marshall
Plan dollars; there was never an explicit criterion, such as equalizing
living standards, equalizing growth rates, maximizing aggregate output or growth, or establishing a floor under levels of living. Baseline
dollar-balance-of-payments deficits were a point of departure, but the
negotiations took into account investment needs, traditional consumption levels, inherited technologies and industry-agriculture mix,
war-induced capital needs, opportunities for import substitution and
export promotion, and opportunities to substitute intra-European
trade for trade with hard-currency countries.

These were multilateral negotiations. The United States insisted
that the recipient countries argue out and agree on their shares in
the total available. In the end they did not quite make it; the United
States made the final allocation. But all of the submission of data and
open argument led, if not to consensus, to a reasonable appreciation
of each nation's needs. The United States was able to arrive at its
own distribution based very much on the critical examination of each
other's needs that had taken place in the OEEC.

With NATO burden sharing much the same occurred. As this was
oriented again toward the allocation of U.S. aid, the United States

was decider of last resort but could demand a procedure of critical examination, comparison, and debate, in the course of which there emerged consensus on what the relevant variables were and what criteria were legitimate.

These negotiations were somewhat simplified by the existence of a predetermined total to divide. In greenhouse negotiations, agreeing on something like a total may be as difficult as agreeing on shares in some abatement total. But the negotiations were not just about the division of U.S. aid. Each government's macroeconomic policies, investment plans, trade policies, financial policies, and levels of consumption of critical materials and foodstuffs were subject to multilateral examination. Bilateral and multilateral trade commitments were undertaken. So it was not all make-believe with the United States standing ready to divide the pie once the recipients had agreed that they could not agree.

In the kind of greenhouse negotiations that I am envisioning, the final output need not be as simple as carbon-emissions quotas or carbon-emission trajectories. The results might look more like detailed programs for energy use and conservation projected over five or ten years or more, with carbon emissions the ultimate scoring system but with the negotiated commitments being to the program as a whole and not just to carbon in the bottom line.

These negotiations were remarkably professional and decorous. They were assisted by a proficient secretariat. The resources involved for most recipient countries were immensely important. Good relations were observed throughout, and proficiency in debate, acceptance of criteria, and negotiating etiquette steadily improved.

That is the only model I find plausible, and I believe distribution of Marshall Plan and defense-support funds to Europe is the only model of multilateral negotiation involving resources commensurate with, and probably exceeding, the cost of greenhouse abatement. In the first year, Marshall Plan appropriations were about 1.5 percent of United States GNP and—adjusting for overvalued currencies—probably 5 percent of OEEC GNP (and more than that for some countries).

What is lacking in the greenhouse case, of course, is any ultimate arbiter corresponding to the United States in the 1940s and 1950s. That lack makes my model imperfect, but nevertheless it is the best we have.

A Possible Outcome of Negotiations

The outcomes of negotiations—what I would call the quotas or targets or agreed-on overall plans—will themselves have several components. One will be the trajectory for coming into line with some agreed plan for carbon emissions. The period for coming into line may be so long—a decade or two—that programs may have to be renegotiated even before they have been approximated. That possibility raises the second feature, namely, that quotas will have to be renegotiated. Quotas will have to be expressible in terms of a very few variables—a baseline, a GNP projection, an investment schedule. Quotas will have to be accepted in the absence of experience in how to get within the quotas. Quotas will rest on assumptions that may prove obsolete within a decade or two, or within a year or two, and the greenhouse community cannot wait a decade or two to come to grips with whether countries are getting on line in accordance with schedule. Progress will have to be monitored and argued and negotiated either continuously or, say, quadrennially. A main function of the secretariat will be to monitor, critique, and report on national performance.

I expect no enforcement other than publicity and persuasion. For the first decade or so I would expect no financial levies or penalties.

I have used the word "quota" to conform to the language being used. But probably a word like "target," "plan," or "program" would better characterize the concept. "Quota" suggests something that is assigned; what I have in mind is something that would be negotiated, and would represent a kind of agreed "best effort" on the part of the participating country. Each country's willingness to commit itself to reduced emissions will be contingent on the reciprocity of other countries; but if consensus is arrived at through negotiation, the emission numbers associated with each nation will probably only represent the emissions bottom line in a government's overall energy plan. The plan might or might not look like a set of input-output accounts, with carbon emissions arrived at by accounting and arithmetic.

The plan could detail such things as proposed taxes, subsidies, technologies, and regulations, with implied carbon emissions that would have to be estimated. An example might be a proposal to tax automobiles by weight or by gasoline mileage; unlike a rationing scheme, such a tax does not "add up to" some level of automobile emissions. Consumer demand elasticities would have to be estimated and revised as the years go by; negotiations would concern not only whether the taxes represented an impressive effort to reduce emissions, but also whether the emissions estimate was optimistic or reasonable. A decade later, if the country's overall emissions are greater than the plan had called for, the country might not be said to have exceeded a "quota" but either to have failed to fulfill the original plan or to have overestimated in advance the impact of its plan on emissions.

As the years go by and countries are found emitting more carbon dioxide than their original plans indicated, renegotiation may again concentrate on the overall plan rather than simply on a comparison of actual emissions with those originally in the plan.

An implication of this approach may be that nations will not begin by negotiating a collective emissions total and then negotiate "shares" or "quotas" within the overall total; they may simultaneously discuss overall totals and national programs. The word "quota" may thus not be very descriptive of what will actually be the object of negotiations.

An important point to keep in mind is that some governments, notably the government of the United States, are in no strong position simply to make things happen where carbon emissions are concerned. Consider nuclear electric power in the United States. The U.S. government could propose to put large resources into the development of a new generation of "inherently safe reactors." It could have a plan in which all new power-plant construction beginning fifteen years from now would be nuclear. Its estimate of the time to completion of the research, development, and demonstration could be off by many years; and when the time comes the government would have to find some way to induce electric utilities to invest in the new technology. For the government of France or China, an investment decision is all it takes to make the conversion to nuclear happen. The United States does not have the kind of government that can order all electric utilities to shift completely to nuclear, or to nuclear except for auxiliary peak load supply, or to nuclear for all stations exceeding 500 megawatts. It could try to tax coal high enough, as well as oil and gas, to make nuclear power the only competitive source; taxing the fuel in old power plants would be resisted for its distributional effects and would not serve much of an allocative purpose.

Similarly, the U.S. government could impose fleet mileage standards on new automobiles, but it would be a decade before the entire fleet embodied the new standards, and the effect on miles driven could only be roughly estimated.

This proposal is a loose system and a flexible procedure. I can imagine the Soviet Union participating. Ultimately each nation's quota has to be voluntarily accepted. The price of participating is to have the nation's economic performance scrutinized, to have its energy policies and patterns of use come under examination and cross-examination, and to have to argue the macroeconomics of fluctuations in carbon emissions due to economic expansion and contraction. And if developing nations, especially major nations like China, India, and Brazil, wish to participate, this mechanism becomes the forum in which negotiation over technology transfer, and possibly financial transfer, from rich to poor countries can begin to emerge.

Carbon Taxes and Tradable Quotas

I dismissed briefly two kinds of proposals that are currently receiving so much attention, and make such good sense, that I owe some further justification for giving them no place among the arrangements I foresee. One of them, an excise tax on the carbon content of fuels, plays a major role in the discussions in this volume. The other, tradable permits (quotas, rights) is popular among economists as an alternative to a universal carbon tax and has received favorable attention in the U.S. administration.

The argument in favor of a carbon tax I need to touch on only briefly; other chapters in this book present it in more detail. The argument that most appeals to economists is that a uniform tax on the carbon content of fuels provides users of those fuels with an incentive to conserve energy, to substitute noncarbon energy for coal, petroleum, and gas, and to substitute oil for coal and gas for oil and coal because of the relative carbon intensities of those fuels. The carbon tax rewards the development of technologies that conserve carbon. The uniformity of the tax provides incentives for carbon to be burned in those uses and locations where conserving carbon would be most expensive and for conservation and substitution to occur where it is most cost-effective. A somewhat more ambitious argument is that if the environmental damage caused by carbon dioxide emissions can be estimated, putting the carbon tax at the estimated marginal damage minimizes the combined aggregate cost of emissions abatement and environmental damage. (The estimate is difficult because the marginal damage has to be integrated over a century and discounted back to the present.) Finally, in terms of "property rights," with the carbon tax the damage to the environment is "paid for" by the perpetrators (although the sufferers from the damage may not receive the proceeds as compensation).

If the issue were domestic policy I would pursue the advantages of a carbon tax with some enthusiasm despite its unpopularity, at least in the United States. But my topic is not optimal internal policies for compliance with an international regime, but a carbon tax that is part of an international regime.

So the interesting tax for our purpose is one that is levied by an international taxing authority. It should be on all carbon burned, not merely carbon passing through international trade. For constitutional reasons the tax would have to be levied on national governments. They in turn could tax carbon internally at a higher rate, at a lower rate, or at different rates for different uses, or not tax carbon at all. The tax thus becomes a national financial penalty on the combustion of carbon. A crucial question for my purpose is whether the tax would be large or small.

There are two main purposes of a carbon tax. One is to provide incentives on national governments to discourage the domestic burning of fossil fuels. The other is to raise revenue. For the former purpose, the tax can be adopted as the unique international means of coping with greenhouse emissions or as a financial penalty superimposed on a system of quotas.

I believe any tax proposal commensurate with the perceived seriousness of the greenhouse problem would at a minimum have to be equivalent to fifty cents a gallon on motor fuel. But the United States is currently consuming 250 billion gallons per year of petroleum products, and if it were all subject to the tax, the total would be $125 billion, not counting coal and gas. I utterly dismiss the possibility that the United States would contribute in any fashion, let alone through taxation, upwards of $100 billion per year, or that the Senate would ratify any treaty incurring such financial commitments. Reduce the figure by an order of magnitude and we are in the realm of the possible, but for greenhouse purposes the tax is then trivial.

The only way I can see to reconcile the need for acceptably modest revenue and a powerful inhibition on carbon consumption would be to couple a high marginal carbon tax to the system of national quotas.

As mentioned earlier, taxing carbon in excess of 95 percent of quota at a rate equivalent to a dollar per gallon of motor fuel might yield revenue from a country like the United States in billions (not tens of billions) and would provide significant budgetary incentives on national governments. But to many people the beauty of the carbon tax is that it solves everything; there is no need to negotiate and renegotiate quotas and argue about excesses over quotas; you pay your tax—at the same rate as everybody else—and that is all that is required. Superimposing a marginal tax on top of quotas means that the quotas have to be negotiated about as they would have to be in the absence of the carbon tax, and the carbon tax is merely a strong marginal incentive that replaces some other mechanism of enforcement and adjudication.

The marginal tax, though elegant in principle, is in several ways more complicated than the tax on carbon consumed. The latter can be levied currently—monthly, quarterly, annually—but an excess carbon tax, especially if construed as a penalty for failing to abide by a commitment, might have to be averaged over a period of two years or more. Many things can happen in a single year that increase the needs for fuel; policies to reduce the use of fossil fuels can be uncertain as to effectiveness and timing and may need a protracted period to be adjusted on to target. Very significant excesses over quota may result in a demand to renegotiate a quota. So the marginal tax may lack some of the neatness and automaticity that are usually among the attractions of such a tax.

The marginal tax, especially if it is negative for performance under quota, is approximately equivalent to a system of tradable quotas. The idea of a tradable quota is that, assuming an enforcement mechanism makes the quotas effective, countries that find it most difficult to avoid going over quota can purchase (or lease over some period) a portion of the quota of a country that, at that price, does better to accept the compensation and correspondingly reduce its own fuel consumption. Two or more countries might permanently institutionalize an arrangement by declaring themselves a "bubble" and combining their quotas officially. If quotas were tradable in a common market at a common price, or through a clearinghouse to which all countries subscribed, the effect would be that of a marginal carbon tax, with the tax rate continually adjusted to try to keep net revenue at zero and aggregate carbon consumption equivalent to the sum of the quotas.

Alternatively, the marginal tax could be set at a rate intended to produce some agreed positive net revenue that could be used to finance research and development, technology transfer, amelioration of hardship, or other purposes agreed through whatever procedures and mechanisms the international organization had established.

My skepticism about the viability of a system of marketable quotas, whether managed bilaterally or through a common clearinghouse, rests on three premises: that any viable international regime concerned with greenhouse emissions has to appear capable of lasting at least a half century, that rates of economic growth and population will differ among nations in ways that cannot be forecast decades in advance, and that technology and energy prices will change unpredictably and with different impact on different countries. Therefore, no system of negotiated quotas can be considered permanent. No agreed formula for recalculating quotas periodically can be expected to survive. Even in a peaceful and harmonious world carbon quotas will have to be renegotiated every five or ten years. (If the quotas are serious, if real commitments to reduce carbon consumption are undertaken, the minimum of five years may be required for experience to show whether quotas are realistic.)

But if I am correct, the differential abilities of countries to live within their quotas are likely to be handled through renegotiation rather than trading at the margin. Indeed, for a country to sell part of its quota to other countries is to demonstrate that its quota was lenient to begin with, and countries that have sold off parts of their quotas will bear the brunt of quota renegotiation. (Public and private agencies and their subdivisions are usually aware that if they return a surplus at the end of a fiscal year they may lose not only the surplus but part of their budget for the coming year.)

The Developing World

The Montreal Protocol of 1987 on Substances That Deplete the Ozone Layer is no harbinger for suppression of CO_2. Economically, what is at stake is two or three orders of magnitude greater for fossil fuels than for CFCs, and the prospects for technological replacement of CFCs are much brighter. (The ozone protocol does illustrate the need for worldwide collaboration to make restrictions worthwhile: the treaty takes effect only when ratified by nations representing two-thirds of world consumption.) But in one respect it may be revealing.

Developing countries successfully insisted on more than $200 million of help from several developed-nation contributors.

President Bush originally declined to participate. It was reported that his administration was afraid that the modest amount, $20 million, asked of the United States would be a precedent for much larger transfers in connection with greenhouse gases, which at the time were the subject of much busy scientific and political activity. He probably need not have worried: when it is time to deal with greenhouse gases the developing world will not need such a modest precedent.

A small beginning may already have been made in dealing with carbon emissions in developing countries. The World Bank a few years ago was uninterested in the greenhouse problem but has recently indicated that loans for energy development will take environmental issues into account. Bilaterally there have appeared at least a few international resource transfers for environmental protection. Even before there was any prospect of German unification, West Germany had agreed to help East Germany finance the abatement of sulfur and other stack products; analysis had shown such investment in East Germany was more cost-effective in cleaning West Germany's atmosphere than the marginal improvements that the money could buy if invested in West Germany. Sweden, Norway, Finland, Denmark, and Iceland have made similar arrangements with Poland to protect the Baltic fisheries. In what used to be East Germany, environmental investment will undoubtedly accelerate on a permanent basis; bilateral and multilateral aid to other East European countries may be somewhat directed at cleaning the air and drinking water and even decontaminating soil. Carbon will undoubtedly not itself be a target, but cleaner fuels and better fuel efficiency will probably do all that economically should be done to reduce carbon emissions in those countries.

In China, India, and the other big current and future producers of carbon dioxide I see two obstacles to overcome before any great effort can get under way to curtail carbon emissions. The first is simply getting the high-income countries to commit resources and to begin fulfilling the commitments to large and visible changes in their consumption of fossil fuels. Developing countries are unlikely to take any initiative. Any apparent initiative will be rhetorical. They may demand of developing countries, but not of each other, severe measures to save some atmospheric capacity for the carbon that it will be their privilege to emit as they industrialize further in decades to come. They will not be shamed into taking measures of their own until the developed countries are demonstrably incurring painful sacrifices.

Under these circumstances there is no hurry in seeing or planning how the developing countries might eventually be brought into participation. But at least the second obstacle can be sketched.

The second obstacle is the need for criteria and institutions by which rich countries can finance poor countries' transformation in their sources and uses of energy. To have a significant impact on midcentury concentrations of CO_2 would probably require resource transfers, for that purpose alone, greater than all of the foreign aid, multilateral and bilateral, in current programs. A third-world carbon abatement effort would be totally different from foreign aid as we have known it since the end of World War II. In principle it would all be directed, from whatever sources and through whatever channels, to protecting that same global common. There would be, for the first time, a single criterion—economizing carbon. In the abstract, aid recipients in the war on greenhouse gases would not compete; they would not be envious; would not make India-Pakistan, Arab-Israel, Poland-Czechoslovakia comparisons. All would in principle benefit equally from maximum carbon conservation wherever it could be achieved.

It would not work that way. If nuclear power reactors are to be provided to developing countries that are intent on electrification, they will compete for reactors for the sake of more rapid electrification, cleaner local environments, and the sense of technological advance.

If the contributing developed countries manage to act together, their bargaining position is probably enhanced by the fact that cleaner fuels bring a number of benefits other than reduced carbon, and recipients of greenhouse aid will be actively interested parties and not merely neutral agents attending to the global atmosphere. At the same time, individual large nations like China and India will be aware of the extortionate power that resides in ambitious coal-development projects.

I can sketch the problem but not the solution. On a greatly reduced scale, however, there may be something constructive to do. There is a huge difference between transferring "technology" and transferring capital goods that embody technology or, going further, financing entire investments (local construction, etc.) in which the technology is embedded. The difference is at least an order of magnitude in cost. While the developed countries are feeling their way into some common attack on carbon emissions, a tangible expression of their interest and an effective first step would be to establish a permanent means of funding technical aid and technology transfer for developing countries, as well as research, development, and demonstration in carbon-saving technologies suitable to the developing countries. Eventually the rural Chinese household may cook more efficiently with nuclear-powered electricity, but for another generation or two what is important is less carbon-wasteful ways of cooking and heating.

Maybe here is a role for the carbon tax. Western Europe, North America, and Japan will be burning 3 or 4 billion tons of carbon per year for the next decade. Taxing themselves, that is, contributing in proportion to the carbon they consume, at one, two, or three dollars per ton, they could contribute to a fund that might begin at $3 billion a year and progress to $10 billion. Through the World Bank or through new institutions these funds could be used to prepare developing countries to conserve carbon. I conjecture this approach could be as cost-effective in reducing emissions as anything the developed countries might themselves do.

The carbon tax is a little arbitrary. The Norwegians and the French get off easily while Americans pay for the long distances they travel. But the symbolism is good. The Bush administration, or whatever administration will be in office when such a project is ready to go, may worry about the precedent when the carbon levy has to begin rising from $10 billion to $100 billion per year, but compared with alternative criteria for sharing costs it might not even be a bad precedent.

Postscript

I want to conclude with two points that are not part of my assigned topic but that deserve emphasis. The first one I mention only because some of the rhetoric of environmental alarmists makes a demand on developing countries that appears to have some audience appeal. It is that developing countries should be prepared to sacrifice some of their hopes for economic development in the interest of slowing down a climate change that may prove disastrous. As stated, the advice contains a contradiction. Any disaster to developing countries from climate change will be essentially a disaster to their economic development. What is desired is to optimize development by investing in greenhouse abatement only when that appears, subject to all the uncertainties, to contribute more to development in the future than the alternative direct investment in development now. It is not a question of economic growth versus environment; it is economic growth with environmental impact taken into account.

The second point is about population. Population growth is crucial to the prospects for climate change. It is crucial in two respects, a little like—but not quite like—supply and demand. One respect is that carbon emissions in developing countries are positively driven by population. Population growth does not merely dilute carbon emissions per capita; for a number of reasons more people means more carbon. If China succeeds in holding population growth to near zero for the next couple of generations, it may do as much for the earth's atmosphere as it would with a heroic anticarbon program and 2 percent per annum population growth.

The other relation between population and climate change is simply that the most likely impact of climate change on human productivity and welfare will be the impact on food production. In the poorest parts of the world the adequacy of food production depends on the number of mouths and stomachs. In a hundred years, adverse changes in climate for food production would be far more tragic if the countries we now associate with the developing world had populations totaling 12 billion than if they totaled 8 or 9 billion.

Considering the relative likelihoods of success and their relative costs, given a choice between vigorous international efforts to slow the growth of carbon dioxide and vigorous efforts to slow the growth of the world's population, I would probably elect the latter. This is not a question of values, only a question of means to enhance the quality of life in 2090 in what we now call the developing world.

Comments

William R. Cline

The crucial diagnosis in the first part of Thomas Schelling's paper is that for the industrial countries, "it will be exceedingly difficult to demonstrate serious adverse impacts of climate change." This view is consistent with Nordhaus's rough calculation that potential damage from global warming is an annual flow on the order of 0.25 percent of U.S. GNP, with a ceiling of 2 percent (Nordhaus 1990, 32). If the stakes are small on the benefit side, it is likely that there will be little interest among the industrial countries in undertaking the costs of abatement of global warming—although the intensity of feeling in Europe even in the absence of demonstrated economic damage from the greenhouse effect means that this conclusion may not follow.

My concern about the incipient stylized fact of minimal greenhouse damage is that the estimates not only omit important types of costs, but more important, they are premised on global warming of the conventional 2.5 to 3 degrees centigrade associated with the doubling of CO_2-equivalent trace gas concentration in the atmosphere. Yet that is just the start.

The Intergovernmental Panel on Climate Change (IPCC) estimates that the doubling of CO_2 will occur by the year 2025 (although the resulting increase of temperature would occur only decades later because of ocean thermal lag). The radiative forcing from doubling CO_2 is 4 watts per square meter ($W \cdot m^{-2}$). The IPCC calculates that under a "business as usual" scenario, radiative forcing by the year 2100 would reach 9.9 $W \cdot m^{-2}$. The gradient in the final decades shows little decline, so this analysis implies radiative forcing of something like 16 $W \cdot m^{-2}$ by the year 2200.[1]

If the feedback of water vapor, albedo, and clouds remains unchanged, total radiative forcing of 16 $W \cdot m^{-2}$ would cause average global warming of 10° C.[2] There is as much reason to expect feedback to intensify as to decline (for example, because of possible release of methane clathrates in permafrost and ocean shelves, and reduced ocean uptake of CO_2 from decreased biota activity associated with warming).

I would suggest, then, that the entire climate-change debate has been largely misspecified. It has become fixated on the impact of a doubling of carbon dioxide, primarily because the expensive simulations of the general-circulation models (GCMs) have focused on this benchmark. But the stakes of doing nothing are much larger. They probably involve eventual global warming of 10° C, not 2.5°. To cut off the analysis of CO_2 doubling is to commit the same mistake as the man who falls off the twentieth floor and concludes as he passes the sixteenth that all will be well.

Once a much higher range of warming is considered, the innocuous damage estimates currently in vogue become highly questionable. Consider sea-level rise, recently downgraded from 1 meter to about 40 centimeters for CO_2 doubling. The IPCC calculations are premised on no contribution to sea-level rise from the Antarctic, on grounds that its temperature remains in a range (below $-12°$ C) where warming increases rather than decreases glacier mass. (One reason is that warmer air is more moist, so it provides more snow for glacier buildup.) But warming of 10° C or more could cause the Antarctic to move into the domain where it contributes to sea-level rise. If so, the increase in sea level would be much higher— particularly if the West Antarctic ice sheet began to disintegrate.

Or consider agriculture.[3] The stylized fact at the moment is that increased carbon dioxide fertilization will largely offset the adverse effects of warming. But studies at the U.S. Department of Agriculture indicate that the beneficial fertilization effects become exhausted above atmospheric concentration of 550 parts per million—that is, somewhat below the doubling benchmark. So this favorable factor would plateau by about the year 2025, yet the adverse effects of warming (decreased soil moisture in particular) would continue to build up.

Up to a doubling of CO_2, an increase in precipitation (about 15 percent) tends to offset the rise in evapotranspiration. But as temperature continues to rise, evapotranspiration rises more than linearly, and eventually it overtakes the increase in precipitation. Moreover, simply the absolute level of temperature presents a physical barrier to crop growing. In a range of about 18° C to 43° C, crop yields are at a relatively flat optimum. Above 43° C, they drop off rapidly, and collapse to zero at 45° C. Summer days in Texas frequently exceed 100° F, or 38° C. Another 5° C, let alone 10°, could shut down Texan agriculture.

Even remaining within the conventional reference of a doubling of CO_2, there are reasons to believe the existing guesstimates of economic damage are understated. For example, the Nordhaus estimate does not include damage from increased frequency and severity of hurricanes. On the basis of Emanuel's (1987) estimate that the destructive potential of hurricanes would rise by 40 to 50 percent from a doubling of carbon dioxide, I have calculated that hurricane damage in the United States would increase by at least $750 million annually (Cline 1990). Similarly, dollar values are not placed on species and forest loss.

Damage estimates also make no allowance for a consumer's willingness to pay a fee for the amenity of avoiding warming, and another fee for the pleasure of staying where his ancestors lived. Schelling notes logically that people can move, and have tended to move toward the sunbelt. But changes in temperature on the scale that I have suggested would be likely to go far beyond any optimum for wide geographical areas. What would be the response to the following survey question in Washington, DC? "What percent of your income would you be willing to pay to avoid an increase of August temperature peaks from the current range of 100° F to a range of 118° F?" If the answer is even 0.25 percent, the Nordhaus central estimate of damage doubles.

In short, I fear that the damage side of the cost-benefit equation has been not only sorely neglected (with the important exception of Nordhaus), but also underestimated. I do not find it implausible that proper long-term damage estimates would easily reach the midpoint of the Manne and Richels (in press) range of 0.8 to 4.0 percent of GDP on the cost side for fossil-fuel limitation. So I am unprepared to commit to Schelling's premise that the underlying cost-benefit ratio of abatement action is unfavorable.

With respect to regional effects, Schelling endorses the judgment by Nordhaus that agricultural impact of global warming would have little effect on the U.S. economy (or by implication, those of other industrial countries) because agriculture is such a small share of GNP. I have been uncomfortable with this argument since I first saw Nordhaus's articulation of it. The argument would appear to ignore consumer surplus, as classically illustrated by the diamond/water paradox. Consider application of the proposition to a country that imports all of its food. In this case, even if global warming causes a dramatic reduction in world food production, the Nordhaus/Schelling approach would identify no loss whatsoever for the country in question. The reason is that they do not consider the welfare effect of loss of consumer surplus, which can be large for a class of goods with such highly price-inelastic demand as foodstuffs overall. Production share in GNP is an inadequate measure.

The implicit assumption that might permit nonchalance about consumer surplus could be the notion that there is a great excess of agricultural land in the world, and that the supply curve is nearly horizontal. Any reduction in yields would be made up by exploitation of currently unused land. However, it must be kept in mind that the planning horizon involves a world population more than double that of today. The fundamental point is that what now seems an abundant resource—agricultural land of good quality, soil moisture, and growing conditions—will become relatively more scarce from population growth alone, and there could be a high cost associated with reducing this resource even further by uncontrolled global warming. Theoretically, in transiting to much higher temperatures it might be possible to pass through a window of optimum global temperature, but the agronomists have yet to identify that optimum, and the political reality of global warming makes it unlikely that warming could be halted at the optimum through fine-tuning.

Having concluded in the first half of his chapter that there is an unfavorable cost-benefit ratio for global CO_2 reduction, Schelling proceeds in the second half to recommend how it might be achieved. The delicate transition is accomplished by invoking risk aversion to "catastrophe," although the reader receives the impression that the author considers the insurance premium too high.[4] I agree with the catastrophe-avoidance approach, although it is unclear that buying just a little insurance is meaningful because a modest deflection in the baseline emissions path is unlikely to suffice to avoid whatever catastrophes might be associated with warming under the baseline— just as a partial insurance plan against unwanted pregnancy through applying birth control methods 10 percent of the time provides no effective insurance.

Schelling begins the international discussion with the observation that the developing countries have the most to gain from avoiding global warming and the least capacity to finance abatement measures. His rationale rests on the share of agriculture in GNP, and as noted I have reservations that this approach is adequate.[5] I would add that the greatest temperature changes tend to be at the middle and higher latitudes, whereas temperature will rise relatively less in the tropics, and on this basis the developing countries would tend to be relatively less affected by warming.[6] There are other dimensions in which warming damage cuts across north and south, as in the case of sea-level rise (Netherlands and Bangladesh).

Schelling's treatment of the carbon tax is puzzling. He rejects such a tax on grounds that it would raise enormous amounts of revenue that national governments would never be prepared to entrust to an international entity. I agree that the sums would be large; my calculations using the Edmonds-Reilly carbon dioxide model indicate that it would take a consumer tax of 50 percent on natural gas, 100 percent on oil, and 150 percent on coal to cut global emissions from a baseline of 10 to 12 billion tons of carbon in the mid-twenty-first century to some 4 billion tons.[7] But there is no reason that the revenue from a carbon tax with an internationally agreed *rate* would need to accrue to an international entity rather than to national governments. It is much more realistic to expect that the bulk of the revenue would remain with the source country. Indeed, it could be appropriate for macroeconomic reasons to rebate most of the revenue, making the tax primarily an instrument for affecting relative prices rather than raising revenue. Perhaps 10 percent could be earmarked for international transfers (a level Schelling apparently considers reasonable) and another 10 percent channeled to research and development of alternative fuels.

Internationalizing the rate but not the revenue does raise the issue of enforcement. Here the moral commitment of the international agreement would provide some force (as in the case of the Montreal Protocol), but sanctions could also be added. In particular, special import duties could be imposed on imports from countries with low carbon taxation. Such trade penalties are present in the precedent of the Montreal Protocol on CFCs.

I also wonder whether international action will have the luxury of permitting developing and Eastern European countries to be free riders, as Schelling recommends. Simulations of the Edmonds-Reilly model suggest that without abatement measures, the share of developing countries in global carbon dioxide emissions will rise from 22 percent in 1975 to 57 percent in 2075. China alone will account for almost 19 percent of world emissions, double its present share. At the very least, conditionality in development lending linked to carbon dioxide impact of energy plans would seem appropriate. I agree that significant transfers to help developing countries develop alternative technologies should be available, as carrots. But it may eventually be necessary to consider negative reinforcement as well, by making developing countries subject to the same penalty tariffs or other sanctions applied to any noncooperating country.

At the same time, it should be kept in mind that if what is being asked of the developing countries is that they too impose carbon taxes at the international rate, there would be an important side benefit for their governments: potentially large domestic revenue, in a context in which chronic fiscal deficits have caused inflation, capacity underutilization, and forgone growth.

Schelling's discussion of national quota determination highlights how difficult the equity aspect of international abatement measures will be. I would be somewhat more sanguine about the utility of standard formulas. They have been instrumental in determining IMF–World Bank quotas (although a benefit rather than an obligation is being allocated).

The paper sets forth a plausible scenario for international action in the medium term. Instead of a full-fledged treaty with agreed targets, it is likely that within the next few years a framework will be established for verifying greenhouse science and working toward an eventual concrete program. In my view, that outcome would be appropriate. I would envision the proper policy implementation as following a logistic curve—with, for example, a carbon tax applied at a rate that is initially low but rising at an increasing rate until it subsequently decelerates and then plateaus at relatively high steady-state level. During the initial low-tax phase, if new scientific evidence sharply reduced the expected extent and damage of global warming, the tax and its timetable could be abolished or curtailed. In the meantime, it would greatly enhance the potential effect of the initially low tax to devote its revenue to research and development of alternative fuels.

One additional aspect of international bargaining warrants consideration. Sole reliance on taxation could mean large losses for exporters of oil and coal, as Whalley and Wigle point out in Chapter 7. It would seem possible to complement taxation (presumably at lower levels) with a producer-consumer commodity agreement for the purpose of sharing some of the rent with the exporters. Such an arrangement could provide a strong incentive to carbon exporters to refrain from selling at low prices to countries not cooperating with the international regime, thereby stiffening any sanctions already built into the system through penalty tariffs on trade with these countries.

Finally, I could not agree more with Schelling that the global warming problem is in considerable part a global population problem. Much as economists have sought to exorcise Malthus by appealing to technological change, the greenhouse effect reminds us that a strong kernel of truth remains in his original message.

Notes

1. Although the radiative forcing is logarithmic in CO_2 concentration, the buildup of the CO_2 is geometric, yielding a linear radiative forcing outcome.

2. That is, $2.5° C/(4 W \cdot m^{-2}) = 10° C/(16 W \cdot m^{-2})$.

3. The observations here draw on discussion with John Reilly, U.S. Department of Agriculture.

4. I agree with Schelling that consumer willingness to pay for environment for environment's sake is extremely limited, although recent polls suggest the public is prepared to make economic sacrifices for at least domestic and local environmental improvement.

5. There might be better grounds for invoking Engel's law (the greater share of foodstuffs in a low-income budget) as the basis for expecting relatively greater damage in developing countries.

6. However, at some critical thresholds, such as the limits to agricultural temperatures discussed previously, a smaller increment in temperature in a high-temperature country might do more damage than a large increase in a moderate-temperature country.

7. For discussion of simulations using this model, see Cline (1989).

References

Cline, William R. 1989. Political economy of the greenhouse effect. Mimeo. Washington, DC: Institute for International Economics, August.

Cline, William R. 1990. Global warming and the costs of hurricane damage. Mimeo. Washington, DC: Institute for International Economics, July.

Emanuel, K. A. 1987. The dependence of hurricane intensity on climate. *Nature* 326(2):483–485.

Manne, Alan S., and Richels, Richard G. In press. CO_2 emissions limits: An economic cost analysis for the USA. *Energy Journal.*

Nordhaus, William D. 1990. To slow or not to slow: The economics of the greenhouse effect. Mimeo. New Haven, CT: Yale University, February.

Comments

Lutz Wicke

International Burden Sharing: Prospects for Cooperative Approaches to Global Warming

There is only one way to tackle the global warming problem:

• By reducing CO_2 and other greenhouse gases by developed, less-developed, and developing countries.

• By protecting tropical and nontropical forests.

• By reforestation, especially in tropical countries.

It will be necessary to establish a worldwide plan (and for all nations at the end an obligatory plan) on the basis of an international treaty and by introducing the beneficiary-pays principle (BPP) in addition to the polluter-pays principle (PPP) with the following elements:

1. Zero production of chlorofluorocarbon gases from 1995 onward with help for developing countries to reject use of these gases.

2. Reduction of carbon dioxide emissions in the world by 50 percent by 2030. This goal may be achieved by the following means:

• Reduction of primary energy use by 15 percent (OECD, -27%; Eastern "bloc," -13%, third world, $+12\%$).

• Expanding renewable energy use by a factor of 4.

• Reducing coal use to 30 percent and crude oil use to 40 percent of the 1990 basis.

• Increasing gas use by about 30 percent.

• Increasing nuclear power production (without special help) by about a third as compared to 1990 (with strictest safety regulations and obligatory risk-oriented insurance, thus reducing speed of nuclear power increase).

3. Reduction of tropical forest loss to zero by 2000 and reforestation of wide tropical and nontropical country ranges.

4. Introduce an OECD and international CO_2 charge. This should be the financial basis for national CO_2-reduction measures and for international help to third and second world countries.

Especially points 2 and 3 mean enormous technical, socioeconomic, and financial changes and burdens in all countries of the world with different abilities to bear those changes and burdens.

The Ecological Marshall Plan

The OECD countries with the biggest burden of reducing CO_2 emission will only be willing to do so if they can be sure that other countries will do the same according to the international agreement (international collective-good problem: world climate). That's why we need an international and obligatory plan—which will be supervised and have international sanctions for countries that do not meet their obligations.

But there is no hope at all of getting agreement for such an international obligatory plan if there is no massive aid to the third and second world countries in order to help them overcome their especially big problems in achieving their greenhouse-gas reduction—and their tropical and nontropical forest obligations.

In the historical Marshall Plan, in which the United States spent $13 billion on the European countries, the motivation was not merely mercy but also the idea that the United States would gain profits or benefits by its help to the Europeans. The main benefit was that the Western Europeans did not become communistic but instead developed into good, sometimes too good, trading partners.

This underlying beneficiary-pays principle (BPP, the donor or payer country has the benefits of the help too) is the basic idea behind the Ecological Marshall Plan: If the OECD countries help the third and the second world countries to protect and expand their forests and to reduce (or not to expand) their greenhouse gas emissions, they and their OECD children and grandchildren will have the benefit. The worst ecological damage in the tropical rain forest will be avoided, and the world climate will stay within bearable temperature limits.

The Ecological Marshall Plan has two strategic aims: First, OECD and other countries should implement the polluter-pays principle (PPP) in a very effective way, strictly realizing command and control politics, and especially by using many more economic instruments of environmental and energy politics in their own countries. Second, the international ecological beneficiary-pays principle (BPP) should be implemented by helping the less-developed countries to protect the world environment. By this Marshall Plan idea (realized by a CO_2 charge, realistic international and national plans, and international funds for effective and supervised help for implementation of those plans) the financial donor countries will in the future be also the ecological receiver countries by protecting their own environment and that of future generations of their countries.

The Ecological Marshall Plan has been elaborated in great detail in a book by Lutz Wicke and Jochen Hucke, *Der Ökologische Marshall-Plan* (Berlin and Frankfurt: Ullstein-Verlag, 1989).

7   The International
Incidence of Carbon Taxes

John Whalley and
Randall Wigle

This chapter discusses how different countries may fare (because of international incidence effects) under any carbon-tax scheme that may be adopted in the next few years as part of efforts to limit global buildup of carbon dioxide and other greenhouse gases.[1] As such, the chapter makes no claims to provide an evaluation of the severity or otherwise of the greenhouse effect,[2] but instead makes the assumption that there will be a policy response to the risk of significant global warming over the next few decades. A component of such a response may be a tax on carbon use (carbon embodied in fossil fuels); we evaluate what the intercountry effects of such a measure could be.

International incidence effects from carbon-tax schemes reflect a number of factors. One is the sharply differing configuration of production and consumption of carbon-based energy sources (oil, coal, natural gas) across countries. Depending upon whether carbon taxes are passed forward in higher prices to carbon-based energy users or passed backward in reduced rewards to producers, effects across countries will differ. If supply elasticities of carbon-based energy products are low, producers (including OPEC countries) will finish up largely bearing the burden of any carbon taxes. If supply elasticities are high, more of the burden of the tax will be borne on the demand side by consumers (including OECD countries).

Another factor is how the revenues raised by such taxes are treated. These are potentially very large, and how they are disbursed (i.e., whether there is any international redistribution of revenues) makes a large difference. Yet another factor is trade in energy-intensive manufactures (primary metals, fabricated metal products, chemicals), since countries may bear some of the carbon-tax burden because they are importers. Hence consumption, production, and trade in energy and in products embodying energy, as well as tax revenue distribution, all need to be considered in evaluating international incidence effects from carbon taxes.

International incidence effects also need to be evaluated relative to a particular reference point, and that may or may not involve the full participation of all countries in the tax. Developing countries have long claimed that global environmental problems largely reflect the cumulative growth process of the developed countries over a 200-year or even longer period.[3,4] In their view, only the developed and not the developing world should be responsible for limiting carbon emissions. In contrast, some developed countries point to the more rapid growth of developing countries as the source of potentially major global environmental difficulties in the decades ahead. Combined with their perception of inefficient energy-conversion technologies that needlessly generate carbon emissions in such countries, their view is that developing countries should be involved.

In this chapter we report results from a global numerical general-equilibrium model that we use to investigate international incidence effects quantitatively. The model captures trade, production, and consumption of carbon-based and non-carbon-based energy products, as well as energy-intensive manufactures, and other goods between six major world trading areas. Demand and production functions are used with specified parameter values, and the model is calibrated to a 1990–2030 base-case scenario. A series of counterfactual equilibrium analyses with the model then allow various carbon tax schemes to be analyzed and their effects to be compared to the base-case model solution (no carbon tax).

Despite a number of weaknesses in the model,[5] a series of striking features emerge from our results. First, we show that both the base and revenues generated by such a tax are likely to be large. We estimate that a global carbon tax base in 1990 present-value terms could be $43 trillion over the period 1990–2030. This is about 10 percent of the projected 1990–2030 global value of product (gross world product). To meet an emission reduction target set at 50 percent of base-case emissions over the period, carbon-tax rates would need to be around 85 percent of the consumer (gross of tax) price of carbon-based energy products, or around $460 per ton of carbon. The tax revenues involved would be in the $40–$50 trillion range; that is, around 10 percent of gross world product would be raised by such a tax.

Perhaps not surprisingly, model results also show that what happens to these tax revenues is crucial for international incidence. If a significant portion is recycled to lower-income countries, then their benefit from participation in a global carbon tax scheme will be large, probably more than outweighing benefits they now receive from aid flows.

Model results also confirm elasticity assumptions as important for international incidence effects. Low supply elasticities for carbon-based energy products imply more redistribution away from producers (owners) of carbon-based energy, as well as higher tax rates in order to achieve emission reduction targets. With higher supply elasticity values, the converse is true. We survey literature elasticities in an effort to produce a best-guess assessment of carbon-tax incidence effects using the model. Interestingly, however, even though we use a wide range of elasticity values in sensitivity calculations we later report, international incidence effects seem substantially more dependent on the treatment of revenues under such a tax than they are on elasticity values.

The form that any carbon tax might take also turns out to be important in determining international incidence effects. There are, for instance, sharp differences between a production-based and a consumption-based tax, simply because some countries are in net export and others in net import positions. In addition, such features as a common, cross-country, per-capita emission target for the tax, instead of a common equiproportional emission cut, have sharply differing incidence effects. The former, for example, may induce relocation of manufacturing activity from high-emission (developed-country) regions to low-emission (developing-country) regions. Thus international incidence effects can also work through induced-capital-flow and production-relocation effects.

The model also captures international incidence effects operating through trade in energy-intensive manufactures. In the model, trade is differentiated between these and other products, and takes place between a number of developed and developing countries. Model results show that direct incidence effects from trade in energy products (oil) dominate those from trade in energy-embodying products.

In summary, two central themes emerge from the reported model results. The first is that international incidence effects of carbon-tax schemes will likely be large. The second is that their precise form depends crucially both on the design features embodied in such a tax

Table 7.1
Summary features of current carbon-tax proposals

Objective

• To achieve reduction in global emissions of carbon relative to some specified baseline projection (say, 20 percent reduction by 2020, and stabilize emission levels thereafter).

Features

• Tax base to include carbon-based energy products (oil, coal, natural gas).
• Taxes apply to carbon content of fuel (rates highest on coal, then oil, then natural gas).
• Tax rates typically in 50–100 percent range (around $250 per ton of carbon).

Ambiguities

• Consumption- or production-based tax.
• New tax or replacement for existing taxes.
• Revenues collected nationally or through a supranational agency.
• Revenue from the tax to finance global alternative technologies fund or to be recycled.
• All countries or subset of countries to participate.
• Common rate across all countries or country-variable rates.
• With or without annual exemption set at specified emission level per capita, or some other more beneficial treatment for low emitters (developing countries).

(revenue disbursement, and whether a production or consumption basis is used for the tax) and on key model parameters (supply elasticities).

The Carbon-Tax Proposal

As table 7.1 indicates, the idea underlying most carbon-tax proposals is to reduce consumption of carbon-based energy products (oil, coal, natural gas) and slow (or even stabilize) the buildup of atmospheric carbon dioxide. Most involve taxing the carbon content of individual fuels; hence different tax rates would apply to coal, natural gas, and oil.[6]

The tax is seen as one that would meet a specified target in terms of reduction in emission levels. Targets commonly discussed are between 20 and 50 percent of projected baseline levels (i.e., with no policy intervention to slow CO_2 accumulation) by some specified date.[7] Taxes are usually proposed as a fixed dollar (or currency) amount on a physical unit basis—say, $250 per ton of carbon embodied in each fuel.[8] Ad valorem equivalent carbon tax rates (which vary by fuel) are in the region of 50–100 percent (higher in some cases). The rate needed in any given carbon tax is thus dependent on a variety of factors, including the target emission reduction and assumed elasticity values for demand and supply functions. The latter will, in part, determine how closely the emission reduction target will be met by any given tax rate.

While carbon-tax proposals have been discussed for some time at an academic level,[9] the idea of responding to global warming in this way was popularized by the World Conference on the Changing Atmosphere held in Toronto in June 1988 (see Climate Institute 1988). The concluding conference statement proposed a 20 percent cutback in global CO_2 emissions (from their then current level) by 2005, with a larger 50 percent cut in emissions beyond 2005 to stabilize atmospheric CO_2 content.[10] To achieve these objectives, the conference called for a World Atmospheric Fund to finance the development of new technologies to help reduce carbon emissions, with industrialized countries to contribute to the fund, and new technologies focused on the developing world. The statement proposed that the fund be financed by a tax on fossil-fuel consumption in industrialized countries. Since this conference took place, such taxes have also been proposed by the U.K. environment secretary (in 1989) and by the West German Social Democratic Party.[11]

As can be seen from table 7.2, carbon use around the globe is highly concentrated, suggesting that significant intercountry effects may accompany the introduction of such a tax. Emissions per capita in developed countries are on average around 20–30 times those of developing countries; three countries (United States, U.S.S.R., and China) account for more than 50 percent of emissions. On the other hand, carbon use per dollar of GNP is typically much higher in developing countries, reflecting the use of relatively inefficient energy-conversion technologies.

However, despite the calls for a carbon tax, and as table 7.1 indicates, there is a surprising ambiguity and lack of specificity in the proposals currently under discussion. There is ambiguity in whether their main purpose is to finance schemes to develop new energy-efficient technologies (as in the Toronto Conference statement), with incentive effects on energy consumption viewed as of secondary consequence, or whether their primary aim is to use the price mechanism to reduce energy consumption, and hence carbon emissions.

The lack of specificity in current proposals reflects the many design

Table 7.2
Country characteristics of fossil-fuel carbon emissions, 1987

	Emissions per capita (tons/year)	Country emissions (percent of world total)	Grams of carbon per dollar of GNP
United States	5.03	21.9	276
Canada	4.24	1.9	247
Australia	4.00	1.1	320
Soviet Union	3.68	18.5	436
Saudi Arabia	3.60	0.8	565
Poland	3.38	2.3	492
West Germany	2.98	3.3	223
United Kingdom	2.73	2.8	224
Japan	2.12	4.5	156
Italy	1.78	1.8	147
France	1.70	1.7	133
South Korea	1.14	0.8	374
Mexico	0.96	1.4	609
China	0.56	10.7	2,024
Egypt	0.41	0.4	801
Brazil	0.38	0.9	170
India	0.19	2.7	655
Indonesia	0.16	0.5	403
Nigeria	0.09	0.2	359
Zaire	0.03	0.01	183
Average for the world	1.08		327

SOURCE: Information reported in this table has been extracted from Flavin (1990, Table 2-1, p. 19), who, in turn, uses a variety of primary sources in his calculations.

and implementation issues with such a tax. These are not clarified as far as we are aware in any recent literature. First of all, the definition of liability for the tax is greatly complicated by the integrated nature of production of refined energy products. As currently proposed, the carbon tax is not a sales tax and is in no way related to conventional retail sales, value-added, turnover, or even excise taxes. Any attempt to tax the carbon content, say, of oil used by an integrated producer/refiner who extracts and refines crude oil and then sells refined products will, for tax purposes, become involved with separating out, in some way, transactions internal to the firm. The same is true of natural gas, where natural gas producers convert gas into feedstock or into subsequent petrochemical production.

In addition, it is unclear whether carbon taxes as proposed are to apply to the consumption or production of carbon. The vocabulary commonly used is "carbon use," seemingly implying a consumption-based tax. However, among other things, if the tax were administered akin to a value-added or retail sales tax, this approach would involve taxing carbon as it crosses national borders, requiring customs officials to infer the carbon content of various imports. Such imports might include not only crude oil, but also other energy products at various stages of refinement, and even nonenergy products at higher stages of fabrication. If "carbon use" is defined to include carbon taxed in the origin country at lower stages of fabrication before entry into the destination country, such difficulties may be potentially soluble, but enormous problems in administering such a tax likely remain. The alternative of a production-based tax seems simpler, but then becomes an extraction tax rather than a tax on "use."

As pointed out earlier, this distinction between a production- and a consumption-based carbon tax is extremely important in any discussion of international incidence, because individual countries differ sharply in their net trade position in carbon. Under a production-based tax, OPEC oil exporters keep the tax revenues; under a consumption-based tax, oil importers keep the revenues. Also, the carbon content of fuels even within broad fuel groups varies substantially, making any application of the tax, at best, inexact.

The definition of the base for any carbon tax is especially crucial in any evaluation of its international incidence effects. In table 7.3, we present some calculations of the potential global and regional tax bases in present-value terms over the forty-year period 1990–2030, using the same data base employed in the general-equilibrium-model calculations we subsequently report. The base for such a tax is large, around $43 trillion in 1990 present-value terms (approximately 10 percent of gross world product over the period). Also, for individual regions the difference between the consumption and production tax base is substantial (EC, Japan, oil exporters). These data clearly suggest that a carbon tax will have major consequences for global economic activity, with potentially large intercountry effects.

Tax rates are also important to international incidence effects, and a variety of issues arise here. One is whether rates should be uniform or nonuniform across countries. Uniform rates by country are viewed as desirable, since they are nondistorting of trade and production

Table 7.3
Estimated global and regional carbon-tax bases for the period 1990–2030
(billions of 1990 dollars)

	Value of carbon-based energy production	Value of carbon-based energy consumption
European Community	3,078	6,060
North America	10,195	11,231
Japan	92	1,842
Other developed countries	999	1,053
Oil exporters	8,666	2,290
Developing/centrally planned	19,900	20,454
World	42,929	42,929

SOURCE: Data base constructed by the authors for general-equilibrium model discussed later.

location decisions. On the other hand, if environmental quality is a luxury good and if taxes are related to the country-specific benefits from emission reductions, then arguments in favor of nonuniformity of tax rates emerge. Developing countries concerned not to truncate their development, as well as countries for whom the cost of global warming seems small (Canada and the U.S.S.R., for instance), may argue that they should face lower tax rates.

A further issue, which is surprisingly important, if conceptually pedantic, is whether the tax rates at issue are on a gross or net basis. A $250 per ton carbon tax may imply an effective 500 percent tax on coal calculated on the net of tax price, but only an 80 percent tax when calculated on the gross of tax price. There seems to be confusion in the literature over the difference in these two rates, with incomplete discussion of which base particular proposals relate to.

The uses to be made of tax revenues generated by any carbon-tax scheme actually implemented are also crucial to international incidence effects. If the base is of the order of magnitude that we have suggested and if ad valorem equivalent rates are large, who gets the revenues (i.e., to whom they are distributed) becomes very important. Particularly crucial is whether the carbon tax is agreed to globally but left to be collected by national government agencies (i.e., revenues redistributed within nation-states) or whether the tax is instead a truly global tax, collected by a supranational agency (the World Atmospheric Fund, or WAF, or the UN). Under a true global tax, revenues would presumably be recycled to countries on some mutually agreed basis, perhaps an equal amount per capita. As the results of the model we present later clearly indicate, such a redistribution scheme, not surprisingly, is extremely beneficial to developing countries.

Even the preceding does not exhaust the list of design and implementation issues with the tax. Whether carbon taxes replace existing taxes within countries or are new taxes, and whether exemptions of a per-capita amount of carbon emissions are to accompany the tax (as developing countries seek), will affect international incidence effects. Complex international negotiation issues that also seem likely to be involved in agreeing on rates as part of any global carbon-tax scheme will come into play. Small countries will generally have an incentive to get a free ride—levy no taxes themselves and let large countries reduce their carbon emissions. Whether large countries will be able to force small countries to participate in a global carbon-tax scheme at full tax rates, without using other non-carbon-tax sanctions, such as trade measures, is thus a question.[12]

Beyond all these considerations, there are also uncertainties as to how successful a carbon tax would be in practice in achieving its objectives. If the tax is not passed on in higher prices but merely redistributes wealth away from owners of energy sources, it could have less than the intended effect (or even, in the limit, no effect) on consumption, and hence on emissions. Moreover, with underlying real growth in both the global and in individual regional economies, unless carbon-tax rates increase over time, any carbon-tax scheme will only have the effect of delaying atmospheric buildup of carbon dioxide, not preventing it. Nordhaus and Yohe (1983), for instance, estimated that a 60 percent carbon tax might only delay a doubling of atmospheric carbon dioxide content by fifteen years, a period which Edmonds and Reilly (1983), using somewhat higher tax rates, suggested could be even shorter, perhaps no more than ten years.

Because of this wide range of options, uncertainties, and ambiguities in actually implementing any carbon-tax scheme, our discussion of international incidence effects of carbon taxes in the later sections of this chapter considers a number of different variants for such a tax. Our model results, in part, emphasize that, beyond the potentially large effects from such a tax, the form the tax takes can be the key factor in determining its international incidence effects.

Table 7.4
Regions in the global-equilibrium model used to evaluate international incidence effects of carbon taxes

---

1. European Community (of the twelve)

2. North America: United States, Canada

3. Japan

4. Other OECD: Austria, Switzerland, Finland, Iceland, Norway, Sweden, Australia, New Zealand

5. Oil exporters (OPEC countries, plus major non-OPEC exporters): Algeria, Libya, Nigeria, Tunisia, Mexico, Venezuela, Indonesia, Iran, Iraq, Kuwait, Saudi Arabia, United Arab Emirates

6. Rest of the world (developing countries and centrally planned economies): This is a residual category containing all other countries, including the U.S.S.R., Eastern Europe, China, Brazil, India, and other developing countries not in category 5.

A Numerical General-Equilibrium Model for Assessing the International Incidence Effects of Carbon Taxes

To help make discussion of international incidence effects of carbon taxes more concrete, we have used a global general-equilibrium model[13] to generate a number of counterfactual calculations that we use to provide an indication of what could happen to the global economy after the introduction of carbon taxes of various kinds. The model incorporates trade, production, and consumption of both energy and nonenergy products for a number of countries (or groups of countries) over a single forty-year projection period of 1990–2030.[14,15] To keep the model manageable, we do not identify fuel types within the broader category of carbon-based energy products, even though in practice the various elements within this category (oil, coal, natural gas) would be taxed at different rates. We also have not incorporated existing taxes on energy products. In practice, these vary by region, and could also affect results.

In the model, the world is divided into six regions, as indicated in table 7.4. The European Community, North America, and Japan are separately identified. Oil exporters include all OPEC countries and major non-OPEC energy exporters. Most developing countries (those who are not oil exporters) are included in a residual rest-of-the-world category, along with the centrally planned economies. Data difficulties preclude a separation between the two groups (i.e., between centrally planned and other developing countries).

Nested functional structures are used in the model to represent production and demand in each region. Each region is endowed with four nontraded primary factors: (1) primary factors, exclusive of energy resources; (2) carbon-based energy resources (deposits of oil, gas, and coal); (3) other energy resources (hydroelectric capacity and nuclear); and (4) sector-specific skills and equipment in the energy-intensive manufacturing sector. Both energy resources are converted into the relevant energy products through a refining/extraction process, which uses other resources (primary factors). There are three internationally traded commodities in the equilibrium system: carbon-based energy products, energy-intensive manufactures, and other goods (all other GNP). Energy-intensive manufactures, other goods, and the composite energy product (carbon-based and non-carbon-based energy) are the commodities that enter final demands.

For each of five produced goods in each region, production is represented by a constant elasticity of substitution (CES) function. Carbon-based and non-carbon-based energy products use the respective energy resources and primary factors. Non-carbon-based energy products are nontraded, since hydroelectric, solar, and nuclear power are not traded in significant quantities between the regions as defined here.[16] A domestic energy composite is produced by a third (energy-conversion) industry, using inputs of the two energy products. The two final goods (energy-intensive manufactures and other goods) use primary factors and the composite domestic energy product as inputs. Perfect competition is assumed throughout for all sectors and in all regions.

Equilibrium in this model involves full global market clearing in the single forty-year period in all three traded goods (carbon-based energy products, energy-intensive manufactures, and other goods). For the two nontraded goods (noncarbon energy products and composite energy) there is domestic market clearing within each economy. Since prices in this system are treated as completely flexible, they will adjust to the levels required to clear the relevant international and domestic markets.

The introduction of a carbon tax into this system will raise prices of carbon-based energy products, and hence the price of composite energy to users, and reduce prices to producers. These price changes will have the effect of cutting both consumption and production of carbon-based energy products, with prices adjusting until the global market in carbon-based energy products clears. If prices to consumers increase fully by the amount of the tax, the tax will have been fully passed on to users of carbon. If prices to consumers change little, then the tax will have been passed backward to producers of carbon-energy-based products. Substitution will also occur between carbon and noncarbon energy products, and between the energy composite product and other inputs. The strength of all of these effects depends on the elasticity values used at the respective nodes in the nesting of substitution possibilities.

To evaluate international incidence effects of alternative carbon-tax schemes on the six regions, we use the model in what we term counterfactual mode.[17] This involves constructing a base (or reference) case solution to which the equilibrium model is calibrated (see Mansur and Whalley 1984); that is, parameters are chosen such that the model will reproduce the base-case data as a full-equilibrium solution prior to the introduction of any policy change. The base-case data thus fully describe a no-policy-change model solution. In this case, this is a general-equilibrium model solution covering the forty-year period 1990–2030 with transactions represented in present-value terms. Different carbon-tax schemes can then be introduced, with a new equilibrium (counterfactual equilibrium) solution computed for each. Using a pair-wise comparison (base case versus counterfactual), international incidence effects over the period 1990–2030 are evaluated after each such calculation.

Data

The model is benchmarked to a base-case equilibrium solution that has been constructed to represent the future evolution of the global economy over the forty-year period 1990–2030. The model is solved to yield a forty-year baseline solution representing the world economy in the absence of any response to global warming over the period 1990–2030 (in discounted present-value terms at 1990 prices, and in billions of U.S. dollars). Policy experiments are then evaluated against this baseline, with a comparison of the base and counterfactual equilibria.

To construct this base-case solution, Hicksian neutral growth is assumed to occur in each of the regions in the model at average growth rates reported in the 1989 *World Development Report* of the International Bank for Reconstruction and Development (IBRD). These are assumed to apply over the entire period under consideration, including the interim period 1982–1989. The oil-exporting region is assumed to grow at 2.5 percent, the "rest of the world" at 2.7 percent, and the remaining regions at 2.3 percent. Each region's endowment of nonproduced factors during this period thus reflects the present value of its resources (at constant prices) over the entire period. We assume that a 5 percent real discount rate applies for all years in the period.

The structure of the regional economies in the base data used to calibrate the model corresponds largely to data available for 1982. Data for regional population and GNP in 1982 (the benchmark year) are obtained from the 1987 *World Tables* of the IBRD (1988). Value added, production, and trade in energy-intensive manufactures (primary metals, glass, ceramics, and other basic manufactured products) are obtained from Nguyen, Perroni, and Wigle (1990). These are identified as those industries having the highest energy input requirements. Input ratios used in Ross (1989) are used to infer energy input requirements for energy-intensive and other industries.

Production, consumption, and trade in carbon-based energy products and non-carbon-based energy (for 1982) come from United Nations (1986) energy statistics. Raw data are in (metric) kilotons of coal equivalent. These are converted to determine the carbon content of production and consumption for the regions in the model using conversion coefficients from the CDIAC CO_2 glossary (Milleman 1988). To convert the data into value terms, we use price information from World Resources Institute (1990).

Some of the main features of the base-case data we use are displayed in table 7.5. Consumption and production of carbon-based energy over the period 1990–2030 are each around $43 trillion (in 1990 dollars), from a worldwide GDP figure over the same period of approximately $450 trillion. A carbon tax, therefore, will apply to approximately 10 percent of world product and will produce revenues potentially of a comparable order of magnitude. Put another way, the tax may yield a global policy instrument with the potential to redistribute 10 percent of global income (and, effectively, over a forty-year period 10 percent of global wealth).

Table 7.5 also gives details of the concentration by region in both population and emission-generating activities, and reports net trade by region. Because the model considers only net trades (rather than gross) and uses a highly aggregated product classification, the volume of trade relative to GDP is substantially reduced compared to

Table 7.5
Global baseline data for 1990–2030 used in the general-equilibrium model

A. Global production and consumption of carbon-based energy products[a] and GDP (billions of 1990 dollars)

	Production	Consumption	GDP
European Community	3,078	6,060	96,739
North America	10,195	11,231	127,480
Japan	92	1,842	39,879
Other OECD	999	1,053	21,362
Oil exporters	8,666	2,290	26,242
Developing/centrally planned	19,899	20,454	132,472
World	42,929	42,929	444,174

B. Trade in carbon-based energy products, energy-intensive manufactures, and other goods by region (net exports [+] or imports [−] over the period 1990–2030 in billions of 1990 dollars)

	Carbon-based energy products	Energy-intensive manufactures	Other goods
European Community	−2,982	638	2,300
North America	−1,036	36	985
Japan	−1,751	551	1,174
Other OECD	−54	246	−193
Oil exporters	6,376	−234	−6,049
Developing/centrally planned	−554	−1,237	1,783

C. Shares of population, GDP, and global emissions by region, 1990–2030 (percentages)

	Population	GDP	Emissions
European Community	7.1	21.8	15.0
North America	6.0	28.7	27.3
Japan	2.8	9.0	4.8
Other OECD	1.2	4.8	2.6
Oil exporters	8.7	5.9	4.1
Developing/centrally planned	74.4	29.8	46.1
World	100.0	100.0	100.0

a. These data on consumption and production are identical to those in table 7.3, which gives the carbon-tax base over the period 1990–2030.

actual and likely future trade. As there is relatively limited cross-hauling of trade in carbon-based energy products, the amount of netting out that occurs in this category is small.

Elasticities

In this model, the implied demand and supply elasticities for carbon-based energy products are important parameters as far as international incidence effects are concerned. The values of these elasticities are not directly specified in the model formulation, but instead reflect preferences and intermediate production technology on the demand side, and the relative importance of fixed and variable factors in carbon-based energy production (oil in the ground versus extraction costs) and the marginal productivity of variable factors in this production process on the supply side.

We are able to solve the model under varying carbon-energy product-supply elasticity assumptions relatively easily, since in the special case where the production function for carbon-based energy products is Cobb-Douglas, the supply elasticity is given simply as $(1 - \theta)/\theta$, where θ is the share parameter on the carbon resource input in the carbon-based energy-product production function. We use a central-case carbon-based energy supply elasticity of 0.5, with sensitivity analysis over the wide range 0.1 to 1.5.

Surprisingly, there are relatively few estimates of energy supply elasticities in the literature; most estimation is concerned with income and own-price elasticities on the demand side, or interfuel substitution elasticities (see Kouris 1981 and Pindyck 1979). The supply elasticities that have been estimated are mainly for OPEC countries and focus on strategic supply response over relatively short periods of time; not the longer-run elasticities at issue here that reflect exploration and extraction cost functions.

The ease with which the composite energy output can be produced from varying mixes of energy inputs (carbon- and non-carbon-based energy) and the ease of substitution between composite energy and the two nonenergy products in consumption are the model features that affect the elasticity of demand for energy. In the absence of any literature estimates of the elasticity of input substitution in composite energy production, we set this equal to 1.0. This value reflects two competing factors. First, for many industrial and home purposes (such as heating), it is relatively easy to substitute between fossil fuels and electricity. At the same time, substitution between fossil and nonfossil fuels is not as easy in transportation. Literature on elasticity estimation for industrial electricity demand (see Nainar 1989) provides some support for a range around the value we use.

In the final demand function involving composite energy and the two nonenergy final products, the CES function used has an elasticity of substitution set equal to 0.5. A demand elasticity for energy in this range is consistent with that suggested by several studies of the long-run demand for energy (see Pindyck 1979; Kouris 1981; Nguyen 1986; Hunt and Manning 1989; Considine 1989; and Estrada and Fugleberg 1989).

Since all of the traded goods produced in each of the three regions are perfect substitutes, the model does not employ the Armington structure of product heterogeneity by region for traded goods common in other applied general-equilibrium models (see Shoven and Whalley 1984).

Counterfactual Policy Experiments Using the Model

We have used the model to evaluate possible international incidence effects that would follow the introduction of alternative carbon-tax schemes. The results that follow initially evaluate a target of a 50 percent cut in carbon emissions relative to the baseline model solution over the period 1990–2030. We later report model calculations with different reduction targets for one of our tax options. A 50 percent cut in emissions from the baseline is on the high side of the range of targets currently used by other modelers evaluating carbon-tax proposals, but corresponds approximately to that called for in the 1988 Toronto Conference statement.

In all our model runs, we endogenously determine the ad valorem carbon-tax rate, which, in this structure, applies to all fuels at the same rate. We also calculate the implied carbon tax in dollars per ton of carbon. As emphasized earlier, the model does not capture the benefit side of reduced atmospheric CO_2 concentrations—that is, the benefits of reduced or slowed global warming.

The carbon tax variants we consider are as follows:

1. Production-based carbon taxes collected by national governments. The emission target assumed is a 50 percent reduction in each region's production of carbon-based energy. Under this scheme, tax rates will vary by region.

2. Consumption taxes collected by national governments. The emission target assumed is a 50 percent reduction in each region's consumption of carbon-based energy. Under this scheme, tax rates will vary by region.

3. A global consumption (or production)[18] tax collected by an international body such as the UN, with revenues distributed to countries according to population, and achieving a global 50 percent emission reduction. Under this scheme, tax rates are identical across regions.

4. A series of national consumption taxes designed to reduce global emissions by 50 percent by achieving the same per-capita consumption of carbon-based energy. Under this scheme, tax rates vary sharply across regions.

These tax schemes are each evaluated using the general-equilibrium model in counterfactual mode. The model is first calibrated to reproduce the original (benchmark) data as a baseline equilibrium solution over the period 1990–2030, with no policy changes in effect. The model is then re-solved with a carbon tax in place.[19] The international incidence effects attributable to any of the tax schemes are determined by comparing the original (benchmark) and the new (or counterfactual) equilibria.

Table 7.6 reports the central-case results from our model experiments. We consider three alternative forms of carbon tax: a national production-based tax, a national consumption-based tax, and a global tax. In each case, the target emission reduction is 50 percent relative to the base-case model solution for the period 1990–2030.

As part A table 7.6 indicates, the carbon-tax rates involved in meeting such emission reduction targets are high, in the range of 85–90 percent. Importantly, these are calculated on a gross-of-tax basis, meaning that from each dollar spent by carbon users on carbon-based products, 85 cents would go in taxes and only 15 cents directly on the purchase of carbon-based energy products. Thus, if calculated on a net-of-tax basis, these rates would be considerably higher.

We report required carbon tax rates for these targets in the range of $450 per ton of carbon. These tax rates are higher than other estimates in the literature in part because our model assumes a finite supply elasticity for carbon-based fuels. With a given quantity reduction target, required tax rates increase as the supply elasticity of carbon-based energy products falls.

Part B of table 7.6 reports our central-case estimates of the gains or

Table 7.6
Central-case model analyses of 50 percent reduction in global carbon use

A. Carbon-tax rates needed to meet emission reduction targets

Option	Tax rate[a] (percent)	Carbon-tax rate[b] (dollars per ton of carbon)
National production-based tax	88.7–89.6	448.0
National consumption-based tax	89.3–89.7	448.0
Global tax	88.6	439.0

B. Gain or loss by region under each option (Hicksian EVs over period 1990–2030 in billions of 1990 dollars; figures in parentheses are percent of GDP in present-value terms, 1990–2030)

Region	Tax option		
	National production-based tax	National consumption-based tax	Global tax
European Community	−3,840.5 (−4.0)	−1,006.1 (−1.0)	−3,724.5 (−3.8)
North America	−5,494.4 (−4.3)	−4,576.5 (−3.6)	−12,442.0 (−9.8)
Japan	−1,459.6 (−3.7)	215.3 (0.5)	−366.9 (−0.9)
Other OECD	−487.0 (−2.3)	−440.1 (−2.1)	−939.9 (−4.4)
Oil exporters	1,191.4 (+4.5)	−4,901.9 (−18.7)	−3,416.7 (−13.0)
Developing/ centrally planned	−9,392.3 (−7.1)	−8,994.4 (−6.8)	2,371.2 (1.8)
World	−19,482.4 (−4.4)	−19,704.1 (−4.4)	−18,516.1 (−4.2)

a. These are gross tax rates; that is, an 85 percent tax rate means that for each dollar spent by consumers, 85 cents is collected in tax. The equivalent net tax rate is 566 percent (i.e., 85/15%).
b. These are calculated by taking the present value of revenues raised by the tax and converting this to a dollar revenue flow for each year, including the 1990 base year. This is then divided by projected global carbon emissions for the year (5.038 billion tons of carbon in 1990), multiplied by one minus the emissions cut. We use data from Milleman (1988) and World Resources Institute (1990) to provide a base-year estimate of global carbon emissions from fossil fuel consumption of 5.038 billion tons.

losses for the regions identified in the model under each of the tax options. In making these estimates, we have calculated Hicksian equivalent variations (EVs) over the period 1990–2030 in billions of dollars (expressed in 1990 prices). These measures capture the combined gains or losses to regions from the production and sale of carbon-based products, as well as the consumption side gains associated with price changes. They also capture the economy-wide effects of energy price changes as they feed through the model.

As can be seen from table 7.6, the global implications of such taxes are large. For both a national production-based carbon tax and a global carbon tax, our results suggest the global economic cost to be in the region of $19 trillion over the period 1990–2030. With global economic product over this period of time valued at approximately $450 trillion, this represents a cost of approximately 4 percent of world product.

Effects by region differ dramatically across the various tax options. North America loses $12 trillion, or approximately 10 percent of the value of income, under a global tax, whereas the loss under a national consumption-based carbon tax is smaller: $4.5 trillion, or 3.6 percent of income. Developing and centrally planned countries lose more than $9 trillion (or 7 percent of income) under a national production-based carbon tax, whereas they gain $2.3 trillion (or 1.8 percent of national income) under a global tax. Oil exporters gain substantially from a national production-based tax, while they lose dramatically from either a global tax or a national consumption-based tax.

These results, therefore, strongly underline the point we have emphasized previously—namely, that the form any carbon tax takes will have major implications for the international incidence effects of the tax. Under a national production-based tax, energy producers collect tax revenues; hence oil exporters gain. Under a national consumption tax, oil importers collect revenues, and hence Europe gains, North America loses only marginally, and oil exporters lose. Under a global tax, the revenues from the tax are redistributed on a per-capita basis, and developing and centrally planned countries gain substantially.

Data reported in table 7.7 showing tax revenues collected and redistributed by region under each tax option reiterate the same theme. Under a global tax, the associated intercountry transfers are extremely large. The revenues raised are in the region of $46 trillion, slightly more than 10 percent of global income over the period 1990–2030. Under the first two tax options, taxes are both collected and

Table 7.7
Revenue redistribution under carbon-tax schemes in central-case model analyses
(taxes paid and revenues received by region under each tax option over the period 1990–2030; in billions of 1990 dollars)

Region	National production-based tax (taxes paid and received)	National consumption-based tax (taxes paid and received)	Global tax		
			Taxes paid	Transfers received	Net transfer
European Community	3,324.7	6,698.2	6,492.3	3,270.1	−3,222.2
North America	11,039.1	12,362.0	11,824.6	2,765.2	−9,059.4
Japan	98.7	1,998.2	1,957.6	1,273.8	−683.8
Other OECD	1,078.5	1,144.4	1,116.4	537.3	−579.1
Oil exporters	9,404.3	2,505.7	2,517.1	4,029.7	+1,512.6
Developing/centrally planned	21,681.2	21,950.1	22,410.8	34,442.6	+12,031.8
Global revenue raised	46,626.5	46,658.6	46,318.7	46,318.7	—

redistributed within countries with no international redistribution. Under a global tax, taxes are collected and redistributed to countries on an equal per-capita basis. In this case, developing countries receive $12 trillion over the period 1990–2030 (around 5 percent of income), with a majority of the transfer originating from North America, which loses $9 trillion. The revenue redistribution scheme accompanying any carbon-tax option is, therefore, crucial in determining international incidence results.

Table 7.8 provides more-detailed model results on the potential impacts of a global carbon tax. We report the percentage change in consumption and production of carbon-based energy products by region, consumption of non-carbon-based energy, and change in the consumption of the composite energy product. The impacts reported largely reflect the 50 percent emission target and the use of similar demand and supply side elasticity values by region in the central-case specification. Consumption falls approximately 50 percent in most regions, as does the production of carbon-based energy, with a much smaller response in consumption of non-carbon-based energy (solar and nuclear).[20] The percentage change in consumption of total energy is reported in the final column.

There are large changes in the prices of carbon-based energy products in this case. For the global tax scheme that we consider, the price of carbon-based energy for users increases by 140 percent, whereas the price for sellers falls by 70 percent, reflecting the substantial price wedge associated with approximately 85 percent tax rates (calculated on a gross-of-tax basis).

We have also examined the impacts of global carbon taxes on trade patterns between regions in the model, emphasizing those cases where there is a change in trade pattern as a result of the imposition of the carbon tax. For the six regions and the two products involved, changes in trade patterns occur in four out of the twelve possibilities. Both Europe and Japan become net importers of energy-intensive products, where previously they were net exporters. A change also occurs for oil exporters from a net import to a net export position for energy-intensive manufactures. Developing and centrally planned countries change from a net export to a net import position in other goods.

Table 7.9 presents results that show the impact of using a ceiling-emissions per-capita approach to implementation of a carbon tax. In this set of model calculations, emission levels within countries are

Table 7.8
More detailed model results for a global carbon tax

A. Results by region

Region	Change in consumption of carbon-based energy (percent)	Change in production of carbon-based energy (percent)	Change in consumption of non-carbon-based energy (percent)	Change in consumption of total energy (percent)
European Community	−48.6	−49.8	+3.1	−46.6
North America	−49.5	−49.1	+3.2	−52.9
Japan	−49.0	−50.3	+2.6	−46.1
Other OECD	−49.1	−50.0	+2.7	−41.1
Oil exporters	−47.3	−48.5	+4.7	−46.5
Developing/centrally planned	−47.4	−47.3	+5.5	−46.1

B. Global results

Change in the users' price of carbon-based energy	+145.4%
Change in the sellers' price of carbon-based energy	−72.7%
Change in the price of non-carbon-based energy (effects vary by region)	+17% to +25%

Table 7.9
Impact of a per-capita emissions ceiling implemented through national carbon taxes

A. Gain or loss by region (Hicksian EVs over period 1990–2030 in billions of 1990 dollars; figures in parentheses are percent of GDP in present-value terms, 1990–2030)

Region	National consumption-based carbon tax	
	Central-case results	Per-capita emission ceiling
European Community	1,354.3 (1.4)	−6,220.3 (−6.4)
North America	−1,529.8 (−1.2)	−23,698.5 (−18.6)
Japan	1,208.3 (3.0)	−985.0 (−2.5)
Other OECD	76.9 (+0.4)	−1,431.2 (−6.7)
Oil exporters	−4,374.5 (−16.7)	−3,959.8 (−15.1)
Developing/centrally planned	−5,948.0 (−4.5)	−1,549.9 (−1.2)
World	−9,212.8 (−2.1)	−37,844.7 (−8.5)

B. Carbon-tax rates by region (ad valorem, gross basis)

European Community	88.6	95.0
North America	88.6	98.0
Japan	88.6	93.2
Other OECD	88.6	95.1
Oil exporters	88.6	81.1
Developing/centrally planned	88.6	81.4

C. Changes in trade patterns involving energy-intensive manufactures[a]

European Community	NE → NI	NE → NI
North America	NC	NE → NI
Japan	NE → NI	NE → NI
Other OECD	NC	NE → NI
Oil exporters	NI → NE	NI → NE
Developing/centrally planned	NC	NI → NE

a. NC denotes no change in the direction of trade; NE → NI denotes net exporter changed to a net importer; NI → NE denotes net importer changed to a net exporter.

reduced to an equal per-capita level across countries. As might be expected under such a scheme, results are more dramatic than for the carbon-tax case presented in table 7.6. The global economic costs are four times larger. The losses in North America are approximately fifteen times larger; while losses in developing and centrally planned countries are nearly four times smaller. Carbon-tax rates by region are substantially higher, particularly if these are recalculated on a net-of-tax basis. Once again, the form of the tax makes a major difference to international incidence.

In table 7.10 we report model results showing the impacts of alternative supply elasticity assumptions for carbon-based energy products. We run our model with alternatively low (0.1) and high (1.5) carbon-based energy-product supply elasticities, examining a global carbon tax in both cases. Lower elasticities imply higher carbon tax rates, both in ad valorem terms and in dollars per ton of carbon. Gains and losses by region vary with these elasticity parameters, but not by as much as with changes in the form of the tax. These results also have the feature that the lower the carbon-based supply elasticity, the larger the welfare cost. At first sight, this result may appear counterintuitive, but with the constant emission (output) reduction target across all these cases, a higher tax rate is required in low-elasticity cases, implying larger costs in terms of economic dislocation for the global economy. Effects by region vary across cases in a similar way.

Finally, in table 7.11 we report model calculations of the tax rates and associated welfare costs involved in meeting alternative emission reduction targets for a global carbon tax. We consider emission reduction targets from 5 to 50 percent, with the welfare cost involved in meeting each increasing more than proportionally. This pattern of cost estimates by size of emission-reduction target reflects the well-known Harberger rule that welfare costs of taxes vary (approximately, depending on cross-price effects) with the square of the tax rate. The rapid increase then slowing rise in the ad valorem equivalent rate, in part, reflect our use of gross tax rates (rates are bounded from above by 100 percent), although a similar, if less pronounced pattern, comes through for carbon-tax rates.

These results suggest that a 50 percent cut, as we consider here (taking our lead from the Toronto conference), is a severe cut, and milder cuts would be less costly with less pronounced international incidence effects. Nonetheless, it is also worth reiterating that any

Table 7.10
Impacts of alternative supply elasticity assumptions on global carbon-tax model results

	Central-case model specification with carbon-based energy supply elasticities of 0.1	Central-case model specification	Central-case model specification with carbon-based energy supply elasticities of 1.5
A. Gain or loss by region[a]			
European Community	−4,331.7 (−4.5)	−3,724.5 (−3.8)	−3,394.5 (−3.5)
North America	−14,845.4 (−11.6)	−12,442.0 (−9.8)	−10,261.3 (−8.1)
Japan	−335.8 (−0.8)	−366.9 (−0.9)	−526.2 (−1.3)
Other OECD	−1,158.0 (−5.4)	−939.9 (−4.4)	−754.0 (−3.5)
Oil exporters	−5,080.2 (−19.6)	−3,416.7 (−13.0)	−1,744.0 (−6.6)
Developing/centrally planned	304.8 (0.2)	2,371.2 (1.8)	2,715.6 (2.0)
B. Carbon-tax rate ad valorem in dollars per ton of carbon	99.3% 484.0	88.6% 460.0	74.2% 380.0
C. Revenues raised globally from carbon tax (billions of dollars, 1990, over period 1990–2030)	50,399.7	46,318.7	39,529.3

a. Hicksian EVs over period 1990–2030 in billions of 1990 dollars; figures in parentheses are percent of GDP in present-value terms, 1990–2030.

Table 7.11
Global welfare cost estimates and tax rates for alternative emission
reduction targets (global carbon tax)

Emission reduction target (percent)	Global welfare cost (percent of global income)	Ad valorem carbon-tax rate (gross basis)	Carbon-tax rate (dollars per ton)
5	0.0	7.9	34
10	0.1	25.9	113
15	0.3	40.4	180
20	0.6	52.1	237
25	0.9	61.7	286
30	1.4	69.5	328
35	1.9	75.8	366
40	2.6	81.0	400
45	3.3	85.2	431
50	4.2	88.6	460

attempt to stabilize carbon emissions in the face of both population
and real GDP per capita growth would likely require ever-increasing
tax rates.

Concluding Remarks

This chapter discusses what the possible international incidence effects (which countries gain and which lose) from global carbon taxes
could be if they are used in the future to reduce carbon emissions
because of concerns over global warming.

We first emphasize that carbon-tax proposals, while discussed extensively at popular level in recent years, are lacking in specificity.
The treatment of the revenues raised by such a tax can make a major
difference to international incidence. In addition, the difference between production- and consumption-based taxes is of substantial
consequence.

Second, we try to help place future discussion of the international
incidence effects of such taxes in a quantitative context by using a
global general-equilibrium model covering six countries or regions
and capturing production, consumption, and trade in energy and
nonenergy products to evaluate a range of carbon-tax options. The
model is calibrated to a base-case scenario for the global economy
projected over the period 1990–2030 using current growth rates. Using this model, we introduce alternative carbon taxes, compute a new

model solution, and compare each of these to the base-case model solution.

A number of themes emerge strongly from our results. The first is that the effects of carbon taxes are potentially very large. The base and revenues involved could well account for 10 percent of global income over the period we consider (1990–2030). Tax rates needed to meet the form of emission targets that we consider will typically be high. The introduction of such a tax, therefore, has to be treated as one that potentially is of major consequence for global economic activity.

At the same time, our results show that the precise form of the tax will largely determine what international incidence effects will likely occur. Under global taxes collected supranationally (say, via the UN) and redistributed to countries on a per-capita basis, developing countries benefit. Under national production-based taxes, energy exporters (OPEC) do well. Under national consumption-based taxes, energy importers (OECD) do well.

Notes

An earlier version of this paper was presented to the conference Economic Policy Responses to Global Warming organized by the Istituto Bancario Sao Paolo di Torino, held at Palazzo Colonna, Rome, October 4–6, 1990. We are grateful to Ngee Choon Chia for comments and help, and to David Newbery, William Nordhaus, and Carlo Perroni for comments.

1. An earlier and more preliminary discussion of some of the issues taken up here can be found in Whalley and Wigle (1989), where calculations related to those presented here also appear.

2. See the discussion of the possible scientific dimensions of the greenhouse effect in Schneider (1989). A range of economic consequences are set out in Cline (1989).

3. See also the discussion of linkages between development and the greenhouse effect in Arrhenius and Waltz (1990).

4. We do not capture potential international incidence effects from carbon taxes via country growth performance in the calculations we report later. In many developing countries the growth process has involved moving resources first from agriculture to labor-intensive manufactures, then to heavy manufacturing, before moving on into consumer electronics and other higher-technology manufactured products. The argument is that carbon taxes may make the energy-intensive heavy industry phase of such development more difficult, potentially truncating the growth of the least-developed countries.

5. To simplify the model, we work with a single carbon-based energy product, and hence different tax rates by type of fuel are not explicitly considered. Also, existing taxes, and particularly excise taxes on gasoline and other energy products, are not explicitly captured. The time profile that carbon-tax rates may be expected to follow can also complicate the analysis in ways we do not capture. If carbon-tax rates are expected to increase through time, then the expectation of future tax changes will change the time profile of supply, and an analysis of international incidence effects of carbon taxes based on an assumption of fixed tax rates can be misleading. A final omission is macro dislocation and adjustment costs associated with carbon taxes. These may be large and asymmetric across countries, and contribute to shorter-run international incidence effects.

6. Edmonds and Reilly (1983), for instance, consider taxes at rates of 100 percent on coal, 78 percent on oil, 56 percent on gas, and 115 percent on shale oil. Flavin (1990, fn. 45) suggests tax rates proportional to the carbon content of fuels; with coal averaging 24.12 kilograms of carbon per gigajoule, oil 19.94 (82 percent of coal), and natural gas 13.78 (57 percent of coal).

7. Manne and Richels (1990), for instance, consider a target of a 20 percent reduction from baseline emission levels by 2020, with a stabilized level of emissions thereafter, until 2100. See also IEA (1990) and Nordhaus (1977, 1990).

8. Tax rates of this order are considered by Manne and Richels (1990) and Nordhaus (1990). They imply more than a fivefold increase in the price of coal and a doubling or more in gasoline prices.

9. See Nordhaus and Yohe (1983) and Edmonds and Reilly (1983), for instance.

10. Subsequent conferences at The Hague and in Cairo have focused on similar proposals.

11. See the discussion in Flavin (1990, 28), who also notes the West German SDP endorsement of the carbon tax as an "ecological redistribution of taxes," on the grounds that revenues could finance development of alternative renewable resources and energy conversion and efficiency improvements.

12. See also the early discussion of this issue in Kosobud and Daly (1984), who highlight the free-rider problems with reaching a global cooperative outcome on a carbon-emission-reduction scheme.

13. See also the presentation in Whalley and Wigle (1989) of earlier, preliminary calculations made using a simplified version of this model.

14. This has been chosen somewhat arbitrarily to capture the initial period and subsequent intermediate term during which a carbon tax would have its largest effects, since with discounting the significance in present-value terms of later-year effects recedes. It is relatively easy to run the model for a longer projection period (say, eighty or 100 years), and were this done we believe that the main themes of our results would remain.

15. A weakness of this forty-year projection period approach is that in the base-year data used for these projections, most carbon energy trade takes place in oil rather than in other carbon-based fuels. If, as some expect, trade in oil is slowly replaced by trade in coal into the next century, the data used here may be misleading because the countries that are potential future coal exporters (United States, U.S.S.R., Australia, China) are quite different from current oil exporters.

16. There is trade in radionuclides, but it is ignored.

17. This is a technical term used in the applied general-equilibrium modeling literature; see Shoven and Whalley (1984, in press) for more details.

18. In the case of a global tax, production and consumption taxes are equivalent. Revenues are distributed in the same way, and the divergence between consumer and producer prices is the same.

19. Each counterfactual equilibrium solution is computed using the MPS/GE code developed by Thomas Rutherford of the University of Western Ontario (see Rutherford 1988).

20. This result reflects their small share in production of the composite energy product, and the substitution elasticity used in the composite energy production function.

References

Arrhenius, F., and Waltz, T. W. 1990. The greenhouse effect—Implications for economic development. World Bank Discussion Paper No. 78, Washington, DC.

Climate Institute. 1988. Toronto conference calls for sharp cuts in carbon dioxide emissions. *Climate Alert* 1, no. 3 (Fall).

Cline, W. R. 1989. Political economy of the greenhouse effect. Mimeo. Institute for International Economics, Washington, DC, August.

Considine, T. J. 1989. Estimating the demand for energy and natural resource inputs: Trade-offs in global properties. *Applied Economics* 21 (7): 931–945.

Edmonds, J., and Reilly, J. 1983. Global energy and CO_2 to the year 2050. *Energy Journal* 4, no. 3 (July): 21–47.

Estrada, J., and Fugleberg, O. 1989. Price elasticities of natural gas demand in France and West Germany. *Energy Journal* 10, no. 3 (July): 77–90.

Flavin, C. 1990. Slowing global warming. In Lester R. Brown (ed.), *State of the World*. New York: W. W. Norton.

Hunt, L., and Manning, N. 1989. Energy price and income elasticities of demand: Some estimates for the U.K. using the cointegration procedure. *Scottish Journal of Political Economy* 36, no. 2 (May 1989): 183–193.

IEA. 1990. Follow-up to Noordwijk Ministerial Conference on Atmospheric Pollution and Climate Change. IEA/SLT(90)2, Paris.

International Bank for Reconstruction and Development. 1988. *The World Tables, 1988*. Washington, DC: International Bank for Reconstruction and Development.

International Bank for Reconstruction and Development. 1989. *World Development Report*. Oxford University Press.

Kosobud, R. F., and Daly, T. A. 1984. Global conflict or cooperation over the CO_2 climate impact. *Kyklos* 37: 637–659.

Kouris, G. 1981. Elasticities—science or fiction? *Energy Economics*, April 1981, pp. 66–69.

Manne, A. S., and Richels, R. G. 1990. Global CO_2 emission reductions—The impacts of rising energy costs. Mimeo. Revised version of a paper presented to the International Association of Energy Economics, New Delhi, February.

Mansur, A., and Whalley, J. 1984. Numerical specification of applied general equilibrium models: Estimation, calibration and data. In J. B. Shoven and H. Scarf (eds.), *Applied General Equilibrium Analysis*, 69–127. Cambridge University Press.

Milleman, R. E. (ed.). 1988. *A glossary for carbon dioxide and climate*. No. ORNL/CDIAC-22. Washington, DC: U.S. Department of Energy.

Nainar, S.M.K. 1989. Bootstrapping for consistent standard errors for translog price elasticities. *Energy Economics*, October 1989, pp. 319–322.

Nguyen, H. V. 1986. Energy elasticities under Divisia and Btu aggregation. *Energy Economics*, October 1987, pp. 210–213.

Nguyen, T. T., Perroni, C., and Wigle, R. M. 1990. A microconsistent data set for the analysis of world trade: Sources and methods. Working paper, Wilfrid Laurier University, Waterloo, Ontario, August.

Nordhaus, W. D. 1977. Economic growth and climate: The carbon dioxide problem. *American Economic Review*, Papers and Proceedings, February, pp. 341–346.

Nordhaus, W. D. 1990. A survey of estimates of the cost of reduction of greenhouse gas emissions. Mimeo. New Haven: Yale University, Department of Economics.

Nordhaus, W. D., and Yohe, G. W. 1983. Future paths of energy and carbon dioxide emissions. In National Research Council, *Changing Climate: Report of the Carbon Dioxide Assessment Committee*. Washington, DC: National Academy Press.

Pindyck, R. S. 1979. Interfuel substitution and the industrial demand for energy: An international comparison. *Review of Economics and Statistics* 61: 169–179.

Ross, Marc. 1989. Improving the efficiency of electricity use in manufacturing. *Science* 244 (April): 311–317.

Rutherford, T. F. 1988. General equilibrium modelling with MPS/GE. Department of Economics, The University of Western Ontario.

Schneider, Stephen. 1989. The greenhouse effect: Science and policy. *Science* 243 (February): 771–781.

Shoven, J., and Whalley, J. 1984. Applied general equilibrium models of taxation and international trade: An introduction and survey. *Journal of Economic Literature*, September, pp. 1007–1051.

Shoven, J., and Whalley, J. In press. *Applying General Equilibrium.* Cambridge University Press.

United Nations. 1986. *UN Energy Statistics Yearbook, 1984.* New York: United Nations.

Whalley, J., and Wigle, R. 1989. Cutting CO_2 emissions: The effects of alternative policy approaches. Paper presented to an NBER conference on Applied General Equilibrium Modeling, San Diego, September.

World Resources Institute. 1990. *World Resources, 1990–1991.* Oxford University Press.

Comments

David M. Newbery

John Whalley and Randall Wigle have analyzed the distributional consequences of differing formulations of a carbon tax designed to achieve a 50 percent reduction from reference levels. They have done so in a single-period computable general-equilibrium (CGE) model of a six-region world model. Taxes on carbon raise the price of carbon-based fuels relative to noncarbon fuels, and this price rise induces some substitution between them (though to a remarkably modest extent judging from table 7.8). The cost of energy rises relative to other factors of production, causing some further substitution away from energy. In turn, the price of energy-intensive goods and final energy rise relative to less energy-intensive goods, inducing a final substitution. The combined effect of all these substitutions is to reduce carbon consumption by the required amount. The authors have stressed the importance of specifying the design of the tax and the magnitude of the various elasticities in determining the outcome. I wish to comment on the modeling strategy, the choice of alternative tax scenarios, and the presentation of results.

Modeling Strategy

Students of global warming are more than usually dependent on models for their analysis. It is therefore important to examine their assumptions and limitations, as the past record is of limited help in their validation. There is an interesting similarity between the climate models of the scientists and Whalley and Wigle's economic model. It appears easier to predict equilibrium temperature changes than the time path of warming, and very hard to predict the geographical detail. Whalley's model attempts to predict the (static) equilibrium response to carbon-tax changes and to capture some of the geographical impacts. We should ask whether it is misleading to ignore the dynamics of the change, and how much confidence should be attached to the geographical impacts. On the face of it, the question is intrinsically dynamic. Carbon dioxide is a stock pollutant with a long lifetime. Carbon-based fuels are exhaustible resources, with oil and gas in modest total supply. Taking a very long-term view, when the fossil fuels are economically exhausted, man-made CO_2 emissions will then fall, and eventually the stock of CO_2 will decrease, unless adverse positive feedback mechanisms have been triggered. The problem is one of choosing the best time path of extraction of carbon fuel and hence of emissions. Once this is done, there is an implied time path for the shadow price (or tax) on carbon, as, for example, derived by Nordhaus (1982) and many others.

Several points follow from this intertemporal view of taxes and extraction rates. First, efficient carbon taxes should typically increase over time. In the special simple case in which CO_2 does no damage until it reaches a critical level and then has catastrophic effects, the rate at which the carbon tax should increase is equal to the real interest rate on goods plus the rate of disappearance of CO_2 (i.e., the ratio of the absorption of CO_2 to the stock) (Nordhaus 1982, 243). Second, if CO_2 emissions are to be reduced, then extraction rates for carbon-based fuels should fall. On a simple view of exhaustible resources, this statement implies that the time period of extraction must be increased, and so the current rent should fall. This approach allows one to focus on the determinants of the supply elasticity, which in turn will influence the division of the burden between fuel producers and consumers. Whalley and Wigle admit that there is little information on which to base supply elasticities and choose a central estimate of 0.5, with variants of 0.1 and 1.5. But how is one to judge whether these are reasonable?

Consider a very simple example. Suppose that the terminal price of oil at the moment of exhaustion is p^T, the extraction cost is constant per unit at c, the discount rate is r, the date of exhaustion is T, and the initial price is p_0. Then the response of the current price to a change in the duration of extraction T can be found from the standard arbitraged price path:

$$p_0 = (p_T - c)e^{-rT} + c.$$

Hence

$$\frac{T}{p_0}\frac{dp_0}{dT} = \frac{-rT(p_0 - c)}{p_0} = -\ln\left(\frac{p_T - c}{p_0 - c}\right) \cdot \left(\frac{p_0 - c}{p_0}\right).$$

Models like this can be used to obtain some feel for the response of the producer price to the imposition of a time path of carbon taxes that will, by reducing consumption, spread out the time period over which the fossil fuels are extracted. The supply elasticity is related to (and roughly equal to) the negative inverse of this elasticity. Of course, the model is oversimple, but it is easy to modify it to deal with fields of increasing extraction cost. Consider a very simple extension in which there are five fields, of unit costs (dollars per barrel) of $5, $10, $20, $30, and $60, with a backstop price of $100, and durations in years of sequential (efficient) exhaustion of each field of 30, 20, 20, 20, and 60 years. The initial price at 3 percent discount is $13, and the point elasticity of price with respect to total duration is -1.1 for a small increase. The arc elasticity for a 50 percent increase in duration is -0.7, and its negative inverse, which we might compare with Whalley and Wigle's elasticity of 0.5, comes to 1.4. These figures might not be unreasonable for oil (though they ignore the exercise of market power, which could be handled in a more elaborate model). In the case of coal, with extraction costs rising in increments of $5 a metric ton from $20 a ton to $40 a ton and reserve/production (R/P) ratios of 30, 40, 50, 60 and 70, the initial elasticity is -0.16, and the arc elasticity of an increase in duration of 50 percent is -0.11, suggesting a supply elasticity of 9, or very much higher than those assumed, and critically affecting the division of burden between producers and consumers.

These results are not surprising, given the simple formula. They indicate the importance of the size of rent $(p_0 - c)/p_0$ in determining the elasticity, as well as the discount rate and R/P ratio (or the terminal price). Given the relative dominance of coal in reserves (R/P = 682) to oil (R/P = 40) and gas (R/P = 60) compared with their consumption shares (which are not too dissimilar in tons oil equivalent), it seems plausible that the world will gradually shift from oil and gas to coal. This prediction itself implies that the supply elasticity is likely to be rather large, and the impact on producer prices rather small.

It now becomes rather complicated to predict what will happen to the producer prices of the various fuels. On the one hand, coal would be more heavily taxed than oil on a carbon basis, encouraging a switch into gas, then oil, out of coal. This high coal tax will tend to increase demand for oil and gas. On the other hand, total carbon consumption is planned to fall, which will tend to reduce the demand for oil. Depending on the relative magnitude of interfuel substitution elasticities and supply elasticities, the effect on the producer price of oil could go either way. Given the very different geographical distributions of coal and oil reserves, it would appear to be important to disaggregate fuels. The Whalley and Wigle model, which aggregates all carbon fuel and ignores intertemporal aspects (and much of the substitution will take place over time rather than at a moment in time), cannot therefore be relied upon to identify the geopolitical impact of reducing carbon consumption.

One might cavil at other features of the model. I am doubtful that the elasticity of substitution between carbon and noncarbon fuel can be taken as constant (equal to unity) over the whole range of carbon prices. The tax on carbon is about $460 a ton (table 7.6), and the consumer price of carbon is thus raised to $520 a ton, while the producer price is $60 a ton. One suspects that at a sufficiently high price of carbon, other technologies (e.g., hydrogen produced from nuclear fuel) suddenly become attractive, so that the elasticity suddenly becomes very high at some backstop price. I worry about the assumed lack of technical progress in improving energy efficiency, which has proceeded at some 1 percent per year over lengthy periods even without price rises. Intertemporal models typically deal with both issues rather differently.

The Choice of Tax Scenarios

Whalley and Wigle consider four tax scenarios: taxes to reduce each region's level of production or consumption, global consumption taxes to reduce total carbon emissions with revenues redistributed per capita, and taxes designed to reduce carbon emissions per head to the same level. I appreciate that in order to generate stark comparisons one must examine a variety of differing alternatives, but are these the most appropriate? I would start from the objective of achieving efficiency (which implies equal taxes per unit of carbon *emitted* worldwide) and then consider various constraints that will affect how the taxes are collected. The obvious problem is one of achieving agreement between nation-states, and this will obviously be easier to achieve if they keep a large fraction of their tax revenues. In other words, countries might agree on a tax rate on carbon emissions, but be free to use the revenue to reduce other taxes. This system should substantially reduce the cost of the tax as the revenue will be used to lower the deadweight losses of tax collection. Nevertheless, some countries might not be willing to impose these taxes, and the remaining countries might then consider various bribes, of the kind that have been considered for other pollution abatement.[1] The incentive effects of bribing for reductions and taxing increases in carbon emissions are the same, only the transfers differ. In the case of developing countries, for example, the first step might be to agree on a reference time path of carbon emissions (business as usual, or some improvement on that). Other countries would contribute on some basis, perhaps but not necessarily out of carbon-tax revenue to pay at the going rate of carbon tax per ton carbon emitted below this reference path. Such payments might be combined with the total aid package and allow further increases in aid transfers (or reductions for exceeding the reference path). The government of the country would then have an incentive to encourage reductions just as if it were to impose a carbon tax of the correct amount. As monitoring improves (and the European Monitoring and Evaluation Program, which measures acid rain emissions and depositions, is a model here), countries can be rewarded for increasing embodied carbon in biomass, as well as penalized for increasing methane releases from flatulent cows.

The case for this approach is strengthened by noting that carbon emitted per dollar of GNP is higher in low-income countries, so a carbon tax might be regressive internationally. Transfers from rich to poor countries to bribe them would offset this effect. By a suitable choice of reference path and by adjustments in aid transfers, the main distributional impacts would be largely avoided, and one would be left with the impact on carbon-fuel producers, as well as the differential impact on the heavy carbon emitters compared with others. The distributional issue would now show up within the income distribution, and it would depend on the income elasticity of energy-intensive commodity consumption. Even this could be partially offset within each country by adjustments to income taxes.

Presentation of Results

Several results are striking. In table 7.6 the tax rates on carbon are remarkably uniform across regions and tax regimes. This result may just reflect the high level of regional aggregation, but it suggests that the costs of uniform emissions reductions rather than uniform taxes may not be too severe. More likely it is an artifact of assuming identical elasticities across regions. A more worrying feature that causes me grave misgivings is that the efficiency costs of the global tax, which is the most efficient tax, are higher than those for the less efficient option of a national consumption-based tax. I understand that this arises because the deadweight losses are not measured using a money metric, but in that case it is hard to interpret the results for the costs.

Table 7.8 contains some curious results. Non-carbon-based energy increases by about 6 percent. Granted it may be hard to increase nuclear power appreciably in the near future, at the proposed increase in the user price of carbon fuels to $520 a ton, it might become economic to use nuclear energy for a wider range of uses than electricity production, and it must surely become economic to use a variety of nontraditional energy sources more intensively. I suspect that the problem may be that in order to produce noncarbon fuel an endowment of suitable resources is required, and this is presumably calibrated to the current low levels of use. While this assumption is fine for currently used resources like hydroelectricity, it is less suitable for unexploited resources such as wind, wave, and solar energy, and it ignores the fact that nuclear energy does not require locationally specific resources.

Table 7.10 is the only sensitivity analysis reported (and serious modeling using a rather nontransparent model surely requires more such sensitivity analysis than this). It suggests that the supply elasticity is not very important except for OPEC. This is not surprising given the large carbon-tax rates required relative to the rent on oil (and even more so on coal), so most of the required increase in the final price must be borne by consumers. In a more fully specified intertemporal model of the kind considered by Nordhaus (1982) the role of the rate of discount, the height of the backstop price, and the various R/P ratios would be natural candidates for sensitivity analysis. At the gaming level, the cost of bribing deviant countries relative to the gains of reduced warming would also enter into a determination of the feasible equilibria. One would also like to know the effect of varying the various elasticities of substitution within the industrial structures (and perhaps making them differ across countries).

Let me just single out two issues here. The first and most critical is that we have no idea of the degree of nonlinearity of the relation between the costs and the level of abatement. Typically costs increase as the *square* of the intervention (Newbery 1990b), making small reductions almost painless and large reductions very costly. It would be easy to have explored this by postulating differing levels of reduction of CO_2. The second is that one would like to know the value added of the modeling technique. How different is the answer if one just takes a composite demand elasticity for carbon fuel, and what would that need to be to mimic the effect of all the substitution elasticities? Admittedly this would affect the ability to predict changes in trade flows of energy-intensive goods, though that seems less central than the cost of the abatement and the level of the carbon tax.

Notes

These comments were prepared for the conference Economic Responses to Global Warming, Rome, October 4–6, 1990, and revised October 8, 1990.

1. I have discussed a similar proposal for dealing with acid rain in Newbery (1990a).

References

Newbery, D. M. 1990a. Acid rain. *Economic Policy* 11, October.

Newbery, D. M. 1990b. Growth, externalities and taxation. *Scottish Journal of Political Economy*, November.

Nordhaus, W. 1982. How fast should we graze the global commons? *American Economic Review* 72, no. 2: 242–246.

Comments

Gerrit Zalm

The chapter by John Whalley and Randall Wigle is a good example of the proverb "Different models for different purposes." Covering the whole world and using a model with a simple structure, the chapter gives an interesting insight into some of the consequences of a worldwide carbon tax.

Before coming to the more critical comments let me state the most important conclusions that are, in my opinion, not easily refuted:

1. The first conclusion has already been put into focus by the authors and is that the incidence of a carbon tax for the different country blocks depends heavily on whether the tax is levied on consumers or on producers and on whether the revenues are redistributed globally or not.[1]

2. The second interesting conclusion is that a carbon tax will decrease energy-prices net of tax. This point has received little attention up till now, and, although the decrease will probably not be as large as Whalley and Wigle calculate, it should not be overlooked.

3. The third conclusion we can draw from the study is that a uniform per-capita quota for emissions for the different country blocks creates far greater welfare losses for the world than a uniform tax rate on carbon. Setting quotas is quite popular in politics. One cannot exclude that also in the field of carbon emissions the idea of quotas per country will look attractive to politicians. The study, however, shows clearly that the world is better off with uniform carbon taxes than with uniform per-capita emission quotas. And if a redistribution of income is added, this statement can even be applied to all the individual country blocks (compare table 7.9, second column, with table 7.6, third column).

The more critical comments are centered on two questions: First, is a carbon tax of $460 per ton of carbon needed, as the authors conclude, to reduce emissions by 50 percent? Second, if such a large tax is introduced, will the global economic losses be of the magnitude that is calculated?

The Carbon Tax Needed to Reduce Emissions by 50 Percent

I will not spend much time on the baseline projection. I guess that the implied assumptions are that energy use will grow at the same rate as GDP and that real energy prices are constant. That supposition can be criticized, of course.[2] Given the character of the model, the baseline projection does not play a significant role in assessing the incidence of a carbon tax. If, however, price elasticities and substitution elasticities are not constant but depend on the price level, the baseline projection for real energy prices does become important. I will come back to this issue later.

I have several reasons to think that a far lower tax rate than $460 per ton of carbon would suffice to realize a 50% reduction of carbon emissions compared to the baseline. The shortest argument is that the authors have taken coal, oil, and natural gas together as one single carbon-based energy product. So the reduction of emissions resulting from changed relative prices of coal, oil, and natural gas is not taken into account, although such a reduction could be substantial. A quick calculation by the energy department of our Netherlands Central Planning Bureau results in the conclusion that the substitution from coal to oil alone, as a consequence of the carbon tax, could result in an extra 12.5 percent reduction of emissions above the 50 percent in the chapter.

The theme that I would like to discuss in a more elaborate way concerns the assumption of the constant elasticities. The price elasticities that are used in the study are in accordance with present knowledge. For the price elasticities of *demand* for oil, the range of findings for the long-term value is between -0.25 and -0.6, so the applied value of -0.5 is not unreasonable. For the price elasticity of *supply* the authors complain that besides short-term elasticities for OPEC supply there are hardly any estimates for long-run elasticities for the non-OPEC area. Perhaps it is of some comfort to mention that our energy division estimates a long-run price elasticity of 0.6 for oil supply for Europe and North America together (higher for Europe and lower for America). This is quite close to the 0.5 used in the model. Using these elasticities as the crucial parameters, the authors conclude that a carbon tax of $460 per ton of carbon will be needed to reduce the production and use of carbon-based energy by 50 percent in comparison to the baseline projection. In the context of the model the authors also rightly conclude that in order to stabilize carbon emissions after this reduction of 50 percent has been achieved, yearly further increase of the tax is needed, resulting in a yearly further increase of real user's prices and a yearly further decrease of producer's prices. This is a rather frightening conclusion.

If my interpretation of the figures is correct, the calculations imply that the 50 percent reduction of emissions will result in a tax of $50–$60 per barrel of crude oil, with a *producers'* price of $5–$6 per barrel and a *users'* price of $55–$65 per barrel. It can, however, be questioned whether the elasticities found by time-series analysis can be used at such extreme price levels. A producers' price of $5–$6 per barrel of oil could, I think, reduce production volume by much more than 50 percent, especially since baseline production is much larger than at present. The operating cost of North Sea oil is around $10 a barrel, and in most of the U.S. wells it is even higher. And for a long-term analysis one should not only look at operating cost but also take into account the fixed cost of extracting oil and the cost of exploration. I think that at a price of $5–$6 large parts, if not all, of the oil production in the U.S.S.R. and the OPEC countries would not be profitable anymore. Furthermore, if we take into consideration any strategic behavior of OPEC, whose market share will increase if oil prices fall, we may expect that the long-run bottom price of oil will be higher than it would be in a world of perfect competition. I think a comparable story can be told about natural gas and coal, if prices drop to 25–30 percent of their present levels. Below a certain price, nothing at all will be produced. So the assumption of a constant price elasticity of supply is rather dangerous and exaggerates the needed carbon tax.

A peculiarity of the same kind can be observed in the supply of non-carbon-based energy, probably because of the way the production function is formulated. The extra supply of non-carbon-based energy in reaction to the tax is extremely low: about 3 percent (see table 7.8). According to the researchers from the London Environmental Economics Center, even at the price levels prevailing in the late 1980s, significant substitution technologies will begin to achieve market penetration at a large scale, and once market penetration has been established, cost may fall rapidly because of economics of scale. This observation is not in harmony with the 3 percent increase in non-carbon-based energy production, while carbon-based energy prices rise 140 percent. This discussion, again, suggests that because of stronger substitution a lower tax rate will do and that there is a ceiling above which carbon energy prices will not rise. My final point on the issue of elasticities is that possibly also the traditional elasticities of demand will break down above certain levels of the energy price because previously unprofitable possibilities for energy saving will become profitable.

With the risk of overkill I will mention two other arguments that indicate that a lower tax rate would be sufficient to realize the 50 percent reduction of emissions. The first is that a strong rise in the price of energy could break down the assumption of Hicks-neutral technological development. A cost-induced energy-saving technological development is probable then.

A second point is that although it is debatable whether possibilities for costless or even profitable reductions of energy use exist in a market economy, we can be quite sure that if the formerly centrally planned economies switch to a market economy, quite an impressive reduction of the use of carbon-based energy can be realized just by efficiency measures or at little cost. And if their energy prices are set at world levels, the reductions will increase further.[3]

The Global Economic Losses of a Carbon Tax

Compared to the height of the tax, a loss of 4.4 percent of GDP (national consumption-based tax, table 7.6) for the world may seem rather limited. I was not much surprised by that figure because at our bureau we made calculations on the long-run effects for several harsh environmental programs for the Netherlands, and these were on the same order of magnitude. Of course, the calculations we made were quite different. The programs not only comprised a rise of energy prices, but they also included measures directed at restricting noise, manure, and waste disposal and at cleaning water and poisoned land, as well as subsidies for energy saving, expansion of public transport, and so on. The calculation was made with a sectoral model. Nevertheless, there are few striking comparisons in the results. The effects on production were limited, and behind those limited effects large sectoral shifts are present, just as the limited effect on world GDP in Whalley and Wigle's calculation is combined with large regional differences.

Getting back to Whalley and Wigle's calculations, it seems evident that a lower carbon-tax rate than they assume will also mean smaller negative effects on the world GDP. Apart from that, it is not easy to assess whether the calculated loss is probably too small, too large, or just about right.

The losses could be higher than the calculations in the model because of the fact that in the model capital is malleable while in reality it is not. The existing capital goods cannot easily be reshuffled. A drastic increase in the user price of carbon-based energy will make part of the existing capital good obsolete, and so will a drastic reduction in the producers' price of carbon-based energy. If the carbon tax is introduced gradually and with a known timetable, these capital losses may be limited, but, nevertheless, the putty-putty concept of capital probably flatters the results.

On the other hand, I would like to mention that in calculating the gains and losses, it is assumed that there is no change in the availability of the other production factors. Whether that will be the case depends among other things on what the different governments do with the revenues of the carbon tax. I suppose that in the calculations the assumption is made that the revenues are recycled in some lump-sum way, not affecting the availability of the production factors nor the shape of the production function. If, however, governments would use the revenues partly to increase the supply of savings, to increase the effective supply of labor, or to stimulate technological developments, the results will become less negative or even positive. I can make it more concrete in terms of practical economic policy. If the Americans used part of the tax revenues to induce higher savings, and the Europeans used it to correct the massive tax distortions on labor that restrict the effective participation of the labor force, and the Eastern Europeans used it to buy new capital goods and technological and managerial know-how, the picture would look brighter. The greenhouse problem—whether real or not—may even be a blessing in disguise if the carbon-tax revenues lead to practical possibilities to cope more easily with other structural problems that the different governments face. I know this is perhaps a bit optimistic, but at least it is a nice end to my comment.

Notes

1. Less clear, however, are the reasons that lead to the conclusion that for the world as a whole the effects are quite different depending on the form of the tax and on whether redistribution takes place.

2. There are several arguments that lead to the conclusion that energy use will grow less than GDP and that nevertheless real energy prices will rise.

3. As Lars Bergman noted correctly, this second point should be handled as a correction on the baseline projection and not as a correction on the results of the introduction of a carbon tax.

8

Global Warming Initiatives: The Pacific Rim

Hirofumi Uzawa

In the last fifteen years or so, we have been continuously warned by geophysicists and meteorologists of the existence of numerous symptoms indicating that the atmospheric equilibrium is disturbed on the global scale. The phenomenon of global warming is such a symptom, apparently one of the most serious, which will have enormous implications for virtually every aspect of human life on the earth, affecting not only the current generation but also all future generations. This chapter concerns itself with understanding the mechanisms through which the phenomenon of global warming occurs, with specific reference to the Pacific Rim, and proposes an incentive scheme that may be effective in restoring the atmospheric equilibrium.

Atmospheric temperature has continuously risen during the last 200 years, with an accelerated rate of increase in the last three decades. Within the next thirty years, the global average surface air temperature could rise to a level 1.8° C higher than the preindustrial level, accompanying an increase in rainfall and other climatic changes. One of the alarming outcomes is a rise in sea level. The common prediction is that sea level will rise about 20 cm by 2030 and about 45 cm by 2070. A sea-level rise on the order of 20–45 cm will have an almost catastrophic impact upon human life, since the majority of human settlements are located either near the seashore or by rivers. Climatic changes accompanied by a rise in atmospheric temperature will present serious problems for farmers, since the choice of crops has been made to suit climatic and soil conditions over many years.

The phenomenon of global warming is largely of anthropogenic origin. The primary cause for global warming is identified as the atmospheric concentration of carbon dioxide, mostly resulting from the combustion of fossil fuels and the depletion of tropical rain forests. Indeed, the atmospheric accumulation of carbon dioxide has reached such a level that, even if the anthropogenic emission of carbon dioxide were entirely prohibited, the global average surface air temperature would continue to increase in the foreseeable future.

The increase in atmospheric temperature is also caused by other chemicals such as methane, nitrous oxide, carbon tetrachloride, and chlorofluorocarbons (CFCs). A particularly powerful role is played by CFCs, which are estimated to be 20,000 times more powerful than carbon dioxide in their effect on the increase of atmospheric temperature. At the same time, CFCs are the principal agents responsible for the destruction of the stratospheric ozone layer.

It is now estimated that carbon dioxide contributes 55 percent of the rise in atmospheric temperature, methane 15 percent, nitrous oxide 6 percent, and CFCs 24 percent.

The combustion of fossil fuels is mostly responsible for the anthropogenic accumulation of atmospheric carbon dioxide. However, the depletion of land forests, particularly of tropical rain forests, has become another major source of the atmospheric concentration of carbon dioxide, now estimated roughly at one-third of those emitted by the combustion of fossil fuels.

A number of policy proposals have been advanced in recent years to arrest the process of atmospheric warming, with particular impacts upon industrial and agricultural activities in the Pacific Rim countries. These policy proposals, among others, call for a drastic decrease in the use of fossil fuels, the reduction and the eventual abolition of the production and use of CFCs, an effective preservation of tropical rain forests, the curtailment of slash-and-burn agriculture, and changes in agricultural techniques, particularly with respect to practices in irrigated rice fields.

These policy proposals have been mostly formulated in terms of quantity constraints concerning the production or use of greenhouse gases and are implemented through governmental intervention into the activities of individual citizens or business establishments. The actual levels of quantity constraints on the emissions of greenhouse gases or on the acreage of tropical rain forests to be preserved are to be determined by the process of intense negotiation between the governments involved. Since the evidence concerning the causal relationships between emissions of greenhouse gases and increases in the average global surface air temperature involves a significant degree of uncertainty, the result of international or regional negotiation tends to be influenced by factors of a largely political nature that have little or no relevance to the substantive issues involved. The outcome of such international negotiation tends to affect the process of economic development in less-developed countries adversely, thus making effective enforcement untenable from the domestic political point of view, as well.

I am also concerned with implications any international agreement on quantity constraints may have for the domestic political process. In certain countries in the Pacific Rim region, governments exert decisive, occasionally arbitrary, influence over virtually every aspect of economic, social, and cultural life. In these countries, the governments possess an unswerving propensity to serve industrial interests, particularly with respect to matters related to environmental disruption and other similar concerns. Any attempt by the governments to intervene in the activities of private citizens or business firms for the purpose of implementing an international agreement would destabilize the environmental equilibrium, as well as encourage despotic trends in these countries.

In this chapter an alternative system will be introduced effectively to stabilize atmospheric temperature whereby governmental intervention will be held down to the minimum. The method will be based upon the concept of imputed prices for atmospheric carbon dioxide, other greenhouse gases, and land forests. It will guarantee that the allocation of scarce resources, including the atmosphere and land forests, is approximately optimum, both from the static and dynamic points of view. At the same time, it will not unduly hinder the process of economic development in the developing countries.

First, each greenhouse gas is evaluated in terms of its effect on the average global surface air temperature, and the unit of measurement for each greenhouse gas is so chosen that it has an effect identical with the unit (metric ton) of carbon dioxide. Second, land forests are evaluated in terms of the capacity to absorb carbon dioxide through the process of photosynthesis, and an acre of land forests is converted to the equivalent amount of carbon dioxide. Thus deforestation and reforestation activities are assessed in terms of the amount of carbon dioxide emitted or absorbed. It may be noted that not only does the depletion of an acre of land forest have a direct effect on the atmospheric level of carbon dioxide, but it also indirectly affects the atmospheric level of carbon dioxide through the burning of paper pulp from the trees felled and through the decomposition of organic matter in the soil.

Third, a price is imputed to each type of greenhouse gas and land forest. Each economic activity—industrial, agricultural, or urban—is then assessed (positively or negatively) based upon the imputed price system.

The problem is how to define the concept of imputed price and how to compute the imputed price for each greenhouse gas and for an acre of each type of land forest. The analysis will be presented in the section "Theoretical Analysis," but a more detailed analysis will be referred to Uzawa (1990). The concept of imputed price introduced in the present chapter is developed within the framework of the theory of imputation, as originally formulated by Carl Menger (1871) and extended to the dynamic circumstances by Ramsey, Cass (1965), and Koopmans (1965). In this chapter, however, we are not concerned with obtaining an exact level of the imputed price for each greenhouse gas or land forest. Instead, we are satisfied with an approximation for exact levels of imputed prices, which, however, guarantees the long-run optimality of the process of accumulation.

Our approach differs from the more standard theory of optimum growth and imputation in that attention is paid to equity issues during the transient process. One of the more important results obtained in this study is that imputed prices of greenhouse gases and land forests in each country involved are determined in such a way that the ratios of imputed prices to the per-capita level of national income in each country take the same values for all countries in the Pacific Rim. Thus, in the illustrative example shown in the section "The Incidence of Carbon Tax in the Pacific Rim," the imputed price of carbon dioxide in the United States is $150 per ton of carbon emitted, while it is $4.00/tC for Indonesia and $5.00/tC for the Philippines.

General Background

The industrial revolution ushered in a new phase in the history of mankind. Scientific inquiries have stimulated the development of new technologies, which in turn have been effectively utilized by avid entrepreneurs for large-scale production of goods and services ostensibly to enrich the life of people. In spite of a number of breakdowns in the process of economic development, the living standard of the average person, at least those not residing in a despotic country, seems to have now reached an unprecedently high level. However, advanced technologies and their large-scale applications, if not properly managed, tend to do intense and irrevocable damage to natural environments.

The nature of the new technologies brought in by the industrial revolution is characterized by the massive consumption of fossil fuels, particularly of coal and oil. Recently, a large number of scientific studies have been made to demonstrate that excess burning of fossil fuels disturbs the atmospheric equilibrium and brings about a global warming of the Earth's surface.

The temperature on the Earth's surface is rather difficult to identify. It varies a great deal between the regions; the seasonal variations are large; and so are the yearly changes. However, the historical data show an evident long-run trend for an increase in global temperature. The global average surface air temperature has increased 0.3°–0.6° C in the last hundred years. Recent studies by Hansen and Lebedeff (1987, 1988) indicate that the rate of increase in the global average surface air temperature has increased from $-0.5°$ C in 1880 to 0.2° C in 1980, on a five-year moving average basis. A recent report published by a working group of the Intergovernmental Panel on Climate Change (IPCC) estimates that the global average surface air temperature in 2020 will be 1.8° C (1.3°–2.5° C) higher than the level of the preindustrial times, and the average rainfall will be increased by 3 percent. As suggested by Dickinson (1986), the actual warming equilibrium would be an increase in the magnitude 2.5°–4.5° C, which is comparable to the increase the Earth has experienced in the 10,000 years since the last Ice Age.

An immediate impact of global warming is a rise in sea level. Gornitz, Lebedeff, and Hansen (1982) report that the sea level has risen about 10 cm because of the increase in surface air temperature during the period from 1880 to 1980. The IPCC report predicts that sea level could rise about 20 cm (10–32 cm) by 2030 and about 45 cm (33–75 cm) by 2070.

The principal causes of global warming are atmospheric concentrations of "greenhouse gases," particularly of carbon dioxide (CO_2), methane (CH_4), nitrous oxide (N_2O), and chlorofluorocarbons (CFCs). Among them, carbon dioxide plays a major role in the phenomenon of global warming.

The atmospheric concentration of carbon dioxide has increased from the level of 280 ppm just prior to the industrial revolution to the current level of 350 ppm, as estimated by Neftel et al. (1985), Fraser et al. (1986), and From and Keeling (1986). More reliable measurements have been made at Mauna Loa and the South Pole since 1958. Keeling et al. (1976), Komhyr et al. (1985), and Conway et al. (1988), among others, report findings that the atmospheric concentration of carbon dioxide increased from 315 ppm in 1959 to 335 ppm in 1978. During the period from 1880 to 1958, it increased at the annual rate of 0.3–0.5 ppm, and from 1958 to 1988 it increased at the annual rate of 1.3 ppm, a significant increase over the last thirty years. If the current trend were to persist, it would reach the level of 560 ppm by 2070, a doubling from the preindustrial level of 275 ppm.

The extent to which the atmospheric concentration of carbon dioxide contributes to the increase in global temperature has been extensively analyzed. Hansen et al. (1981) estimate that an increase of 0.2° C is due to the atmospheric concentration of carbon dioxide during the period from 1880 to 1980, while Ramanathan et al. (1985) attribute an increase of 0.52° C during the same period. According to Dickinson (1986), the atmospheric concentration of carbon dioxide will reach a level twice as high as the preindustrial level of 280 ppm, and the resulting equilibrium warming will be 2.5°–4.5° C.

In order to understand the mechanisms by which the anthropogenic emissions of carbon dioxide disturb the atmospheric equilibrium, it would be advisable to draw a crude picture of the global carbon cycle, as suggested by Woodwell and Houghton (1977), Hampicke (1979), and Keeling (1983). There are three major reservoirs of carbon on the earth's surface, each roughly of the same capacity: the atmosphere, the surface ocean (0–75 m depth), and the terrestrial biosphere. The atmosphere contains 700–770 GtC (gigatons $= 10^9$ tons), the surface ocean 680 GtC, and the terrestrial biosphere 750–800 GtC. Land plants in "detritus" contain a much larger quantity of carbon, roughly of the magnitude 1,000–3,000 GtC.

The exchange of carbon between the atmosphere and the surface ocean is in equilibrium, exchanging 75–90 GtC annually. The mechanisms by which atmospheric carbon dioxide is absorbed into the oceans are complicated. They depend partly upon the extent to which the surface waters of the oceans are saturated by carbon dioxide and partly upon the extent to which excess carbon dioxide is accumulated in the atmosphere. The findings reported by Takahashi et al. (1980) and Keeling (1968, 1983) suggest that the rate of ocean uptake is closely related to the excess quantity of atmospheric carbon dioxide over the stable, preindustrial level of 275 ppm.

The terrestrial biosphere plays an important role in the global carbon cycle. It absorbs atmospheric carbon dioxide through the process of photosynthesis, approximately 60 GtC annually. Roughly the same amount of carbon is returned to the atmosphere through the processes of decomposition and respiration. Thus the exchange of carbon between the atmosphere and the terrestrial biosphere is in equilibrium, too.

The equilibrium in the global carbon system is disturbed by anthropogenic activities, of which the major sources are the combustion of fossil fuels and the depletion of land forests, particularly of tropical rain forests. According to the estimates made by Rotty (1987) and others, the combustion of fossil fuels emits into the atmosphere roughly 5.6 GtC of carbon dioxide annually. The largest contribution is made by the United States (23.9%), followed by the U.S.S.R. (19.8%), China (8.7%), and Japan (4.8%). These four countries contribute close to two-thirds of carbon dioxide emitted into the atmosphere. It may be noted, however, that the quantity of carbon dioxide emitted by the combustion of fossil fuels per unit of GDP varies a great deal between the countries. The Japanese figure is roughly half of that for the United States, suggesting a rather significant degree of substitutability for energy use.

The equilibrium between the atmosphere and the terrestrial biosphere is also disturbed by the depletion of land forests. Total acreage of land forests is estimated at about 4 billion hectares, including open and closed forests and woodland. According to the report recently published by the World Resources Institute, *World Resources, 1990–91,* the acreage of tropical rain forests annually lost is estimated at 16–24 million hectares, a magnitude much larger than the previous estimate of 11 million hectares, made by the Food and Agriculture Organization of the United Nations for 1980, which has been the basis of the current discussion on the preservation of tropical rain forests.

According to estimates made by Houghton et al. (1987) and Detweiler and Hall (1988), 0.4–2.6 GtC of carbon dioxide are released into the atmosphere because of changes in the pattern of land use. About 95 percent of carbon dioxide released is regarded as the result of deforestation of tropical rain forests. More than one-third of the increase in the atmospheric level of carbon dioxide is due to the depletion of land forests.

Methane is estimated to be responsible for about 20 percent of the anthropogenic increase in global temperature, a magnitude second only to carbon dioxide. The atmospheric concentration of methane has more than doubled since the industrial revolution began, and it is currently increasing at an annual rate of 1 percent. Methane remains in the atmosphere a relatively short period of time (ten years). However, it has a greenhouse effect twenty-five times more powerful than carbon dioxide, and a higher temperature implies a larger quantity of methane released into the atmosphere, since land plants in detritus decay faster at a higher temperature.

The mechanisms by which methane is released into the atmosphere are not exactly known. However, the major sources of the anthropogenic increase in atmospheric methane are identified as irrigated rice fields, animal husbandry, biomass burning, landfills and sewage facilities, and fossil-fuel production. According to the estimates made by Cicerone and Oremland (1988); Crutzen, Aselmann, and Seiler (1986); and Lerner, Matthews, and Fung (1988), the annual rate of methane emission is 0.6 Gt, of which irrigated rice fields are responsible for about 25 percent, domestic animals for 15 percent, biomass burning for 15 percent, landfills for 10 percent, and fossil-fuel production for 15 percent.

Nitrous oxide is now estimated to be responsible for about 6 percent of the increase in the atmospheric temperature. The atmospheric concentration of nitrous oxide has increased from the preindustrial level of 285 ppb to the current 310 ppb. However, most of the increase in atmospheric nitrous oxide has occurred in the last fifty years, as estimated by Pearman and Hyson (1986) and Khalil and Rasmussen (1983). In addition, it has a greenhouse effect 230 times more powerful than carbon dioxide. The major sources of nitrous oxide emissions are in the soil. A particularly important role is played by nitrogenous fertilizers and biomass burning. It is also emitted by the combustion of fossil fuels, and changes in the pattern of land use contribute to the atmospheric emission of nitrous oxide.

Chlorofluorocarbons (CFCs) are the greenhouse gases that are solely of anthropogenic origin. They were released into the atmosphere for the first time during the twentieth century. The most common CFCs are CFC-12 and CFC-11, with atmospheric concentrations of 392 ppt and 226 ppt, respectively, in 1986. Although the atmospheric levels of CFCs are low, their greenhouse effects are estimated as 20,000 times more powerful than carbon dioxide, currently responsible for

24 percent of global warming. Chlorofluorocarbons tend to remain in the atmosphere for a long period of time, almost permanently, and are responsible for the depletion of stratospheric ozone.

In view of the imminent danger to which CFCs have exposed us, an international agreement was reached in 1987. The Montreal Protocol to Control Substances That Deplete the Ozone Layer stipulates a substantial reduction and an eventual abolition of the production and use of CFCs. Even if the Montreal Protocol is successfully implemented, we have to face the atmospheric concentrations of CFCs that have been accumulated in the past and still remain in the atmosphere.

The Pacific Rim—Facts and Policy Proposals

The phenomenon of global warming has particularly intricate implications for the Pacific Rim, and some of the policy proposals that have been advanced to arrest the process of atmospheric warming seem either to be not feasible or to seriously impede the process of economic development of the developing countries in the region. Before I proceed with assessing the economic impacts of these policy proposals, I should like to provide a glimpse of the economic and environmental characteristics of the Pacific Rim.

It may be first noted that the Pacific Rim is not a well-defined concept, either from the economic point of view or from the cultural point of view. It is a concept of a political nature, where the United States, with the possible cooperation of Japan, tries to establish hegemony in the Pacific Ocean. The Pacific Rim is composed of countries, such as the United States, Canada, Indonesia, Japan, Korea, Malaysia, the Philippines, Singapore, Thailand, Australia, and New Zealand, where the degree of economic development and the cultural and social characteristics are so diverse as to preclude the possibility of any international cooperation or agreement on a purely voluntary basis. Yet the phenomenon of global warming offers a unique opportunity to the Pacific Rim. It is possible to search for an international agreement to stabilize the atmospheric equilibrium whereby, for both developed and developing countries, the prospect of a slower but more harmonious process of economic development is feasible.

Table 8.1 lists some basic statistical data concerning major countries in the Pacific Rim. The United States leads the list with the highest per capita GNP of $19,000, followed by Japan, Canada, Australia,

Table 8.1
Basic statistical data

Country	Population, 1990 (million)	Land area (million ha)	Population density, 1989 (per 1,000 ha)	Urban population as a percentage, 1990	Gross national product, 1987 (billion U.S. dollars)	Per-capita gross national product, 1987 (U.S. dollars)	Distribution of gross domestic product, 1987 (percent)		
							Agriculture	Industry	Services
United States	249	917	270	74	4,517	18,529	2.1	30.1	67.8
Canada	27	922	29	76	392	15,160	3.3	34.8	61.8
Indonesia	181	181	981	29	76	444	26.0	33.0	41.0
Japan	124	38	3,265	77	1,925	15,764	2.8	40.6	56.7
South Korea	44	10	4,366	—	113	2,689	11.0	43.0	46.0
Malaysia	17	33	516	42	30	1,820	—	—	—
Philippines	62	30	2,043	42	34	589	24.0	33.0	43.0
Singapore	3	0	43,836	100	21	7,992	1.0	38.0	62.0
Thailand	56	51	1,075	23	46	850	16.0	35.0	49.0
Australia	17	762	22	86	180	11,103	4.1	32.5	63.4
New Zealand	3	27	125	84	26	7,764	8.1	30.5	61.4

SOURCES: United Nations, *Statistical Yearbook for Asia and the Pacific, 1990*; World Resources Institute (1990).

Table 8.2
Land forests in the 1980s

Country	Forests and woodlands (1,000 ha)	Average annual deforestation (1,000 ha)	Average annual reforestation (1,000 ha)
United States	295,989	159	1,775
Canada	436,400	—	720
Indonesia	116,895	920	164
Japan	25,280	—	240
South Korea	4,887	—	84
Malaysia	20,996	255	25
Philippines	9,510	143	63
Singapore	—	—	—
Thailand	15,675	397	31
Australia	106,743	—	62
New Zealand	9,500	—	43

SOURCE: World Resources Institute (1990).

New Zealand, and Singapore. Indonesia, the Philippines, and Thailand form a group with low per-capita GNP. Indonesia has the lowest per-capita GNP, $444, which is one-fortieth that of the United States. In the United States and Japan the agriculture sector occupies 2–3 percent of GNP, while both Indonesia and the Philippines have an agriculture sector that constitutes roughly 25 percent of GNP. While in the United States, Canada, Japan, and other developed countries, more than three-fourths of the population live in the urban areas, developing countries are marked by a very low urban population, somewhere of the magnitude of 20–40 percent. All Asian countries are noted for a high population density.

Table 8.2 shows the extent of forests and woodlands and annual rates of deforestation and reforestation. Canada leads the list with more than 400 million hectares of forests and woodlands, followed by the United States, Indonesia, and Australia, each with acreage roughly three-fourths to one-fourth of the Canadian holdings. Tropical rain forests are concentrated in Indonesia, Malaysia, the Philippines, and Thailand, all of which have rather high rates of deforestation and low rates of reforestation, with serious implications to atmospheric warming.

Table 8.3 shows the sources of emissions of greenhouse gases. As for carbon dioxide, the largest amount is emitted by the United

Table 8.3
Emissions of carbon dioxide, methane, and CFCs (1987)

Country	Emissions of carbon dioxide				Emissions of methane						Emissions of CFCs (1986)	
	Fossil fuels (MtC)[a]	Land use change (MtC)	Carbon dioxide Total (MtC)	Carbon dioxide Per capita (t)	Rice paddies (Mt)[b]	Livestock (Mt)	Solid waste (Mt)	Fossil-fuel production (Mt)	Total (Mt)	Per capita (t)	Total (1,000 t)	Per capita (kg)
United States	1,221.6	6.0	1,227.6	5.0	0.5	7.0	16.0	18.7	52.2	0.17	197.4	0.8
Canada	110.1	0.0	110.1	4.3	—	0.8	1.7	8.0	10.5	0.40	20.7	0.8
Indonesia	35.0	220.0	255.0	1.5	4.9	0.4	0.4	0.4	6.1	0.04	5.4	0.0
Japan	247.5	—	247.5	2.1	1.2	0.3	2.4	—	3.9	0.03	57.5	0.5
South Korea	47.7	—	47.7	1.1	0.6	0.1	0.1	0.0	0.9	0.02	3.1	0.1
Malaysia	11.4	38.0	49.4	3.1	0.3	0.0	0.0	0.0	0.4	0.03	1.4	0.1
Philippines	9.9	68.0	77.9	1.3	1.8	0.2	0.1	0.0	2.1	0.04	0.0	0.0
Singapore	7.8	—	7.8	3.0	—	0.0	0.0	—	0.0	0.00	2.1	0.8
Thailand	15.5	94.0	109.5	2.1	4.5	0.5	0.1	—	5.1	0.10	2.0	0.0
Australia	64.7	0.0	64.7	4.0	0.1	1.9	1.0	1.3	4.4	0.27	12.0	0.8
New Zealand	5.8	0.0	5.8	1.8	—	1.0	0.1	0.4	1.4	0.43	2.0	0.6

SOURCES: Houghton et al. (1987); Lerner, Matthews, and Fung (1988); World Resources Institute (1990); and other sources.

a. MtC = million metric tons carbon.
b. Mt = million metric tons (methane).

States, some 1.2 gigatons of carbon from the combustion of fossil fuels alone. The emissions due the land-use changes, largely deforestation of tropical rain forests, are mostly done by Indonesia, Thailand, the Philippines, and Malaysia. The emission of carbon dioxide on a per-capita basis is United States 5.0 tons of carbon, Canada 4.3 tC, Australia 4.0 tC, Malaysia 3.1 tC, and Singapore 3.0 tC, followed by Japan and Thailand, each 2.1 tC. Among these countries, roughly 2.1 Gt of carbon dioxide are annually emitted into the atmosphere.

The emission of methane is estimated at 87 million tons annually. The United States emits 52 Mt, roughly 60 percent of the Pacific Rim total. The sources of the emission of methane are fossil-fuel production 29 Mt, solid waste 22 Mt, rice paddies 14 Mt, and livestock 12 Mt. On a per-capita basis, New Zealand is the largest with 0.43 t, followed by Canada 0.40 t, Australia 0.27 t, and the United States 0.17 t.

Total emissions of CFCs are estimated at 304,000 metric tons, of which the United States emits 197,000 tons, roughly 65 percent of the total, followed by Japan, 58,000 tons, roughly 20 percent. On a per-capita basis, the United States, Canada, Singapore, and Australia use the largest amount of CFCs, 0.8 kg each.

The most important source of anthropogenic emissions of greenhouse gases is the energy sector. It is estimated that the energy sector is responsible for 57 percent of the greenhouse-gas emissions, followed by the production of CFCs (17%), agriculture (14%), forestry (9%), and other industries (3%). Table 8.4 shows the production of electricity by the Pacific Rim countries in 1987. The largest producer is the United States, 2,686 million kWh, producing three-fifths of the regional total. Per capita, the United States produces 10,800 kWh, compared with Indonesia 200 kWh, the Philippines 400 kWh, and Thailand 500 kWh. The United States production of fossil-fuel-fired electricity is 1,961 million kWh, two-thirds of the regional total.

The end use of energy is predominantly by the industrial sector (44%), and the transportation and residential-commercial sectors use 27 percent and 29 percent, respectively.

The Pacific Rim is marked by divergence between developed countries and developing countries, both in terms of economic and social conditions and in terms of the extent to which they are affected by the phenomenon of environmental disequilibrium. At the left end of the spectrum, there are developed countries, such as the United States, Canada, Japan, and others, that use more than 90 percent of

Table 8.4
Production of Electricity (1987)

Country	Total production (10^6 kWh)	Per capita (10^3 kWh)	Fossil-fuel fired	
			Total (10^6 kWh)	Per capita (10^3 kWh)
United States	2,686	10.8	1,961	7.9
Canada	496	18.7	103	3.9
Indonesia	35	0.2	27	0.15
Japan	699	5.6	423	3.4
South Korea	80	1.8	36	0.8
Malaysia	17	1.0	12	0.7
Philippines	24	0.4	14	0.2
Singapore	12	4.0	12	4.0
Thailand	30	0.5	26	0.45
Australia	132	7.8	118	6.9
New Zealand	27	9.0	6	2.0

SOURCE: United Nations, *Energy Statistical Yearbook, 1987.*

energy resources in the region and emit 80 percent of greenhouse gases. They enjoy an apparently high living standard, having 80 percent of the population living in the cities. At the right end of the spectrum, there are a number of developing countries, such as Indonesia, Malaysia, the Philippines, and Thailand, each of which has a low per-capita national income, with a rather poor living standard. Most of the tropical rain forests are located in these countries. Tropical rain forests are depleted extensively, either for logging and slash-and-burn agriculture or for permanent land clearing. In the process, a significant amount of carbon dioxide is emitted into the atmosphere. A relatively large amount of methane is emitted by the developing countries, even though, in absolute terms, the United States is the largest emitter.

The phenomenon of atmospheric disequilibrium and the resulting increase in the average surface air temperature conduce to a much heavier burden upon agriculture, particularly in the developing countries. The effects of climatic changes upon agricultural conditions vary a great deal between the locations and the type of crops, and not much is known for certain. However, tropical rain forests are extremely vulnerable to climatic changes, and, once they are deforested, the soil is rather unstable and tends to be rapidly decomposed. Agriculture in these countries is rather difficult to sustain when a substantial change in climatic conditions occurs.

Agricultural and forestry practices in the developing countries of the Pacific Rim are particularly affected by the policy proposals that have been conceived to curb the emission of greenhouse gases.

Irrigated rice fields are estimated to emit into the atmosphere roughly 70 Mt methane annually. As indicated in table 8.3, they are responsible for approximately 20 percent of the methane emissions in the Pacific Rim, with a heavy concentration in Indonesia, Japan, the Philippines, and Thailand. Some of the drastic proposals call for a shift to the dry, upland method, because of the large amounts of methane and nitrous oxide released by the wet, lowland method.

Not only does the irrigated-field method result in the highest yield per acre, but it also offers the most stable and sustainable land use. It has been practiced in East Asian countries for many centuries, and has served as a symbolic activity, through which a significant portion of the social, cultural, and religious heritages have been transmitted. I share the view that some of these heritages and the accompanying ceremonial activities have to be reassessed in light of emerging economic, political, and social conditions, but the reassessments should not be made solely on the basis of the propensity for irrigated rice fields to emit greenhouse gases. As will be discussed in detail in later sections, an arrangement has to be devised whereby any economic activity, either agricultural, industrial, or otherwise, has to be assessed a levy that corresponds to the extent of the social cost such an activity imposes upon the society as a whole. Irrigated rice fields then would be assessed based upon the amounts of greenhouse gases released into the atmosphere. They will, however, have to be remunerated to the extent to which their symbolic, cultural, and social functions are evaluated by the society. In this connection, it may be also noted that irrigated rice fields perform an important function in preserving natural equilibrium in the sense that they serve as gigantic water reservoirs, stabilizing seasonal variations in water requirements and at the same time alleviating the summer heat.

Policy proposals concerning forestry practices to arrest the propensity for atmospheric warming have pertinent implications, particularly in the Pacific Rim. They call for, among other things, a significant curtailment of slash-and-burn practices. The slash-and-burn method has a double implication for the phenomenon of atmospheric warming—the release of carbon dioxide by the depletion and burning of forests and the emission of carbon dioxide and methane through the processes of decay and decomposition. The recent spread of slash-and-burn practices, particularly in the Philippines and Malaysia, is related to the increase in unemployment in the sugarcane and other industries. They are neither efficient nor stable practices from the agricultural point of view, and the introduction of sustainable soil-management systems on a large scale is desirable. It would be made possible by the assessment of the social cost associated with slash-and-burn practices, combined with a remunerative system for adopting sustainable soil-management techniques.

The second proposal on forestry practices is concerned with restraint on deforestation activities for commercial purposes, particularly by large multinational corporations. Deforestation on a gigantic scale has been done by these corporations, with finances from governmental and commercial banks, occasionally even with the finances from the World Bank, particularly in the 1970s and early 1980s. In order for measures of control to be effective, a compensatory arrangement has to be made for these developing countries, as will be discussed in a later section.

The third policy proposal on forestry practices calls for the management of forest land and its products. In the developing countries, particularly in the Philippines, Malaysia, and Indonesia, rapid population growth has put pressure on forestry lands for settlements, transportation corridors, arable land, and fuelwood. Calls for the reduction of deforestation activities related to these purposes are naturally justified. However, financial and administrative measures have to be spelled out in order for such a policy objective to become feasible. In this respect, the concept of natural forest management, introduced by McNeely (1988), seems to be suitable for forests in these countries. Natural forest management effectively utilizes the techniques of silviculture to maintain forests of small size on a long-run economic basis. It rejects the traditional notion of the economies of scale with a maximization of short-term profits. Natural forest management is not confined to a mere management of forests, but rather is concerned with the management of the whole village, whose people would derive work and income from the products of forests.

The depletion of the stock of forests for fuelwood presents a rather difficult problem in the developing countries in the Pacific Rim, particularly in Indonesia where roughly 50 percent of total energy use is extracted from forests in the form of fuelwood. The introduction of more efficient cooking techniques is called for, but current economic conditions seem to preclude the adoption of such techniques, unless certain financial incentives are provided. Another policy proposal is related to the disposable use of wood on a larger scale. Recycling of paper is particularly effective in reducing demand for wood. Disposable chopsticks, single-use wooden crates for shipping, and similar uses of wood or nonwood products of forests are easily eliminated, with an effect on the depletion of forests.

There exist a number of policy proposals concerning the management of temperate forests, such as an increase in yields from temperate forests, an expansion of tree planting in the temperate zone, and reforestation of surplus agricultural lands and urban areas.

These policy proposals have significant effects in reducing the rate by which the stock of forests, both tropical and temperate, is depleted, and some of them have been undertaken in the Pacific Rim region. However, in order for such policy proposals to be adopted on such a scale that the global warming trend may be effectively arrested, an incentive scheme has to be introduced whereby each country or each individual finds it preferable to adopt the measure advocated by these policy proposals. The simplest and most effective incentive scheme would be first to precisely evaluate the benefits that a marginal increase in the acreage of land forests confers on society as a whole and then to reward afforestation activities or to assess penalties for deforestation activities.

In the United States, financial incentives on the order of $125–$250 per hectare would be sufficient to encourage reforestation of harvested woodlands and surplus croplands on a large scale. In Japan, it is estimated, financial remuneration on the order of $300/ha would be needed to induce foresters to undertake reforestation activities, mostly because of the steepness of Japanese forests. In the developing countries in the Pacific Rim, much lower financial incentives would be sufficient for reforestation on a large scale. Whether or not such magnitudes of financial incentives to encourage reforestation match those of the benefits the society receives from land forests is the question I would like to take up in the next section.

Energy use is the crucial determinant for anthropogenic emissions of greenhouse gases, and the policy proposals for arresting global warming are much concerned with finding more efficient energy use.

As indicated earlier, transportation consumes roughly 30 percent of the energy used, and the relative efficiency of energy use in the transportation sector varies a great deal between countries. In the developed countries, automobiles, including both passenger cars and trucks, are responsible for more than 80 percent of total energy used in the transportation sector. Most of the policy proposals, therefore, are concerned with cost-effective efficiency measures to improve the energy performance of automobiles. These proposals themselves are extremely desirable in terms of the effects they have on the reduction of greenhouse gas emissions, particularly carbon dioxide and CFCs. However, more emphasis seems to have to be placed on the necessity of introducing alternative modes of transportation, particularly those of public mass-transit systems.

Automobiles are the largest consumers of oil. In the United States, more than two-thirds of oil is used by passenger cars and light trucks, while in Japan they consume roughly one-fourth, and in developing countries in the Pacific Rim roughly half of the oil is used by automobiles. In the United States, automobiles account for one-fourth of total emissions of carbon dioxide.

As for CFCs, air conditioners in automobiles emit one-seventh of the total. Automobiles are also the sources of the emissions of carbon monoxide (70%) and nitrogen oxide (50%), two of the major pollutants in the local atmosphere. Increasing the fuel-efficiency of automobiles and improving road-efficiency may be desirable, but they will have the effect of increasing the number of automobiles on the road, with an adverse effect on atmospheric warming. Instead, it seems to be preferable, both from the energy-efficiency point of view and from the environmental point of view, to redesign the structure of social overhead capital in urban areas in the United States so that transportation is basically done in terms of walking, bicycles, streetcars, subways, or urban mass-transit systems. In other words, cities in the United States should be restructured in such a way that the basic patterns of streets, communities, and means of transportation of the beginning of the twentieth century are restored, as persuasively argued by Jane Jacobs in her classic work *The Death and Life of the Great American Cities* (1961). However, the predominant pattern of city design and modes of transportation, both in the developed and developing countries in the Pacific Rim, has been to imitate the American pattern as faithfully as possible. The extreme case is presented by Japan.

Transportation in Japan has experienced a drastic change in the last thirty years. Freight traffic has increased from 180 gigaton-kilometers in 1965 to 500 Gtkm toward the end of the 1980s. Similarly, passenger traffic has increased from 380 billion passenger-kilometers in 1965 to 1 trillion. In 1965 roughly one-third of freight traffic was by railroad, and trucks had a share of one-fourth, the rest being by ship. In 1987 railroad traffic was less than 5 percent of total freight traffic, while more than 50 percent was by trucks. For passenger traffic, railroads had a 70 percent share in 1965, and passenger cars only 30 percent. In 1987 railroad traffic was less than 40 percent, automobiles more than 60 percent. The number of automobiles was 17 million in 1970, but in 1990 more than 60 million automobiles existed in Japan, the highest number of automobiles per acre in the world. The construction of highways and the expansion of existing roads have been carried out at enormous costs each year, but they have been unable to keep pace with the increasing number of automobiles. The Japanese cities are now suffocated by the overcrowding automobiles, with high concentrations of poisonous gases such as carbon monoxide and nitrogen oxide, as well as airborne particles. The extent to which automobiles conduce to human, natural, and physical damage in Japan is enormous. I made an attempt to measure the magnitude of the social costs of the automobile in Japan, which came out at 2 million yen per car per year, at the very minimum (Uzawa 1974a).

In spite of enormous social costs associated with the use of automobiles in Japan, the number of automobiles has been steadily increasing, and the share of passenger cars and trucks in transportation is increasing at an accelerated pace. A number of political, economic, and social circumstances have brought about the current chaotic situation in the Japanese cities. Some of the causes are specifically Japanese, but they may be generally applicable to other countries in the Pacific Rim, particularly to developing countries. One of the major causes is that the enormous social costs of automobiles are not properly assessed to those who benefit from the use of automobiles. In this chapter we are concerned with the extent to which the use of automobiles contributes to atmospheric concentrations of greenhouse gases and to devise ways to measure the magnitude of the social costs in relation to the emissions of greenhouse gases, to be levied upon those who benefit from the use of automobiles. Thus it would be possible to move toward the restructuring of social overhead capital in such a way that an optimum balance between economic merits and environmental disruption may be partly attained.

Theoretical Analysis

In order to analyze the mechanisms through which economic activities interact with the phenomenon of atmospheric warming, a simple dynamic model will be constructed in this section. The analysis to be developed in the subsequent section will be made within the framework of the model presented in this section.

In our analysis of the phenomenon of global warming, a central role is played by the concept of imputed price. It was originally introduced by Carl Menger in the construct of modern economic theory (1871) and has since served as one of the most fundamental concepts in price theory. Menger's concept of imputation was static, without explicitly taking the time element into consideration. Recent contributions in economic analysis, particularly in the theory of optimum economic growth (e.g., Cass 1965; Koopmans 1965; and Uzawa 1974b), have extended the concept of imputation to the dynamic situation where one inherits accumulating impacts from past human activities and tries to choose the current economic activities with the interest of future generations explicitly taken into account. The phenomenon of global warming offers us precisely the kind of dynamic situation the modern theory of imputation is aptly applied to, as explored by Mähler (1974) and Nordhaus (1980, 1982).

Since the theoretical analysis we intend to develop here is rather complicated, in spite of its simplistic and utopian nature, we begin with the discussion of the simplest case to illustrate the general nature of our analysis. The basic apparatus that is needed for the computation of various imputed prices in a later section, however, is included in this simple case.

We consider the world as a whole or a particular region, such as the Pacific Rim, where each country is closely interrelated with others through atmospheric and oceanic environments. In the simplest case, we proceed with our discussion by presuming that the whole region consists of one country. We also assume that carbon dioxide is the only chemical that has a greenhouse effect.

At each moment in time t, we denote by V_t the amount of carbon dioxide accumulated in the atmosphere. The quantity V_t may be measured either in the actual tons of carbon dioxide or in terms of density of carbon dioxide accumulated in the atmosphere. Our analysis naturally does not depend upon which mode of measurement we take. The following discussion will be carried out for the case where V_t is measured in terms of the actual tons of carbon dioxide in the atmosphere. We adopt as the origin of the measurement the stable preindustrial level of 600 Gt (approximately corresponding to the density of 280 ppm). Hence, the current level of 750 Gt (= 350 ppm) is represented by $V_t = 150$ Gt.

The atmospheric level of carbon dioxide changes over time, owing to anthropogenic and natural activities. Anthropogenic changes in the level of atmospheric carbon dioxide are primarily brought about by the burning of fossil fuels in connection with industrial, agricultural, and civic activities, as summarily discussed in the previous sections. We denote by v_t the rate of change in the atmospheric level of carbon dioxide V_t due to anthropogenic activities. The current rate is roughly of the magnitude of 5.6 Gt per annum; namely, $v_t = 5.6$ Gt.

A certain portion of carbon dioxide released into the atmosphere is absorbed by the oceans, roughly estimated to be 50 percent, and to a lesser extent by living land plants. It is assumed that a certain constant fraction of excess carbon dioxide in the atmosphere is absorbed by the oceans. As for an approximation of the first order, we assume that the annual rate of carbon dioxide absorbed by the oceans is given by μV_t, where the rate of absorption μ is a positive constant. The estimate for μ is rather difficult to obtain. According to the estimates made by Ramanathan et al. (1985) and others, carbon dioxide remains airborne seven to fourteen years on the average, and about half is absorbed by the oceans. The rate of absorption μ would be roughly of the magnitude 2–4 percent per annum. In what follows, we shall assume the value of $\mu = 0.02$.

The exchange of carbon between the atmosphere and living land plants is not taken up in the simplest model, but it will be discussed in the general model.

The change in the atmospheric level of carbon dioxide then is formally written as

$$\dot{V}_t = v_t - \mu V_t, \tag{1}$$

where $\dot{V}_t = dV_t/dt$ stands for the rate of change in V_t over time. Those who are not familiar with the mathematical notation may simply take $\dot{V}_t$ as the difference $V_{t+1} - V_t$ between the atmospheric levels of carbon dioxide V_{t+1} and V_t.

The rate v_t by which carbon dioxide is emitted into the atmosphere is closely related to the levels of production and consumption activities conducted during the year observed. In the simplest model, we assume that these economic activities are represented by the vector of final consumption x_t.

A vector of final consumption x describes the quantities of all the consumption goods finally allocated to the members of the economy in consideration. It is explicitly written as

$$x = (x_1, \ldots, x_n)$$

where $1, \ldots, n$ denotes all the consumption goods produced in the economy, and, for each i, x_i stands for the quantity of commodity i finally consumed. In the simplest model, we abstract from the complications that would arise when the distribution of final consumption goods among the members of the economy is brought into the picture, and instead the economy is assumed to consist of N identical persons.

In the simplest model, we assume that the amount of carbon dioxide emitted into the atmosphere is directly related to the vector of final consumption. The possibility of technology substitution is taken up in the general model. Let a_i be the amount of carbon dioxide emitted into the atmosphere in relation to the production of the unit of commodity i, $i = 1, \ldots, n$. Then the total amount of carbon dioxide emitted into the atmosphere in relation to the production of consumption vector $x = (x_1, \ldots, x_n)$ is given by $a_1 x_1 + \ldots + a_n x_n$, or, if we use the vector notation, by $ax = \Sigma_i a_i x_i$, where $a = (a_1, \ldots, a_n)$.

Hence, when the level of economic activities for year t is given by the vector of final consumption x_t, then the annual rate of carbon dioxide emitted into the atmosphere v_t is given by

$$v_t = ax_t. \tag{2}$$

We now have to turn our attention to the evaluation of the level of satisfaction given by the consumption of final commodities. It is assumed that such a level of satisfaction may be represented by a preference relation over the set of all feasible vectors of final consumption. The preference relation is assumed to satisfy all the conditions required for the standard analysis, generally postulated in the theory of consumer's behavior.

In the following analysis, we shall adopt a specific form to represent the preference relation concerning vectors of final consumption. We first specify prices of consumption goods, $p^0 = (p_1^0, \ldots, p_n^0)$, which will be used as terms of reference throughout the discussion. These prices may be indicated in terms of whatever currency is being used. For each vector of final consumption, $x = (x_1, \ldots, x_n)$, the utility index y is defined with reference to the standard price vector $p^0 = (p_1^0, \ldots, p_n^0)$ in the following manner: The index y is defined as the minimum expenditure evaluated at the standard price system $p^0 = (p_1^0, \ldots, p_n^0)$ that would enable the consumer to attain the level of satisfaction at least as high as $x = (x_1, \ldots, x_n)$. In mathematical notation, the definition of the index y is given by

$$y = \min \left\{ \sum_i p_i^0 x_i' : x' = (x_1', \ldots, x_n') \text{ is preferred, or indifferent to} \right.$$

$$\left. x = (x_1, \ldots, x_n) \right\}.$$

Such a y is uniquely determined by x; we may use the notation $y = y(x)$.

The utility index $y(x)$ thus defined is assumed to satisfy all the conditions required in the analysis of the consumer's behavior.

The level of utility index $y(x)$ may be influenced by factors that do not enter explicitly into the discussion of a market economy. We are particularly concerned with the implications of the climatic conditions brought about by the excess accumulation of carbon dioxide in the atmosphere. An increase in the atmospheric level of carbon dioxide brings about changes in natural and social conditions, which would appear as a decrease in the level of utility index $y(x)$. Namely, we take into account that the level of utility index $y(x)$ depends upon the atmospheric accumulation of carbon dioxide V. The utility index y now has to be written as $y = y(x, V)$. In the following analysis, we shall assume that the utility index $y = y(x, V)$ is separable in the sense that $y(x, V)$ may be written as $u(x)\phi(V)$:

$$y(x, V) = u(x)\phi(V). \tag{3}$$

In equation 3, $u(x)$ may be regarded as the standard utility function, expressing the utility level as a function of vector of final consumption, while the second factor $\phi(V)$ expresses the extent to which the atmospheric concentration of carbon dioxide, through an increase in the atmospheric temperature, exerts an undesirable impact upon the life of people. The value $\phi(V)$ will be simply referred to as the impact index. In what follows, we occasionally use a more concrete form for the impact index, namely,

$$\phi(V) = (\hat{V} - V)^\beta, \tag{4}$$

where $\hat{V}$ designates a certain critical level of the atmospheric concentration of carbon dioxide, beyond which drastic changes in environmental conditions brought about by an increase in atmospheric temperature are feared to exert serious, irrevocable damage on human life on the earth. The parameter β is a constant, between 0 and 1, expressing the intensity by which the negative impact of the atmospheric concentration of carbon dioxide is felt.

The phenomenon of global warming presents us with a problem of dynamic nature, where the choices we make today have significant influence on all future generations, and we have to explicitly take into account future paths of the economy concerning the levels of utilities and the extent to which the atmospheric level of carbon dioxide is increased. The degree of uncertainty involved with these considerations is too great to be subject to any rigorous analysis. We take here a rather drastic approach that all future time paths are known for certain and derive a number of institutional and policy arrangements to bring about a dynamically optimum solution, which, nevertheless, would be applicable to the circumstances governed by a high degree of uncertainty and unpredictability.

The foregoing discussion may be summarized as follows:

The change in the atmospheric level of carbon dioxide V_t is described by differential equation 1, where the annual rate v_t of carbon dioxide emitted into the atmosphere is related to the level x_t of final consumption by the technological condition of equation 2. Then the time path of the utility indices is described by

$$y_t = y(x_t, V_t) = u(x_t)\phi(V_t) \qquad (0 \le t < + \infty), \tag{5}$$

where $\phi(V_t)$ denotes the impact index associated with the atmospheric level of carbon dioxide.

The problem we now are faced with is this: Starting with the atmospheric level V_0 of carbon dioxide today $(t = 0)$, we have to choose the time path (x_t, V_t) that is feasible, in the sense that the conditions of equations 1 and 2 are satisfied, and for which the time path of vectors of final consumption (equation 5) is dynamically optimum.

The meaning of the concept of dynamical optimum may become clear during the course of the following discussion. It simply means that the discounted present value of future utility indices

$$\int_0^\infty y(x_t, V_t)e^{-\delta t}dt \tag{6}$$

is maximized among all feasible time paths. The discount rate δ is assumed to be a positive constant.

This problem of dynamic optimization will be solved by using the concept of imputed price, which in turn will be utilized to devise an effective policy instrument for stabilizing the atmospheric concentration of carbon dioxide.

The imputed price of atmospheric concentration of carbon dioxide expresses the magnitude of damage felt by the society due to a marginal increase in the atmospheric level of carbon dioxide. It not only takes account of the assessment by the present generation, but it also includes the assessments that the present generation infers future generations would make. It may be more precisely defined like this: Suppose the atmospheric level of carbon dioxide has been increased by a marginal amount ΔV_t. The corresponding marginal decreases in the levels of future utility indices would be given by

$$\Delta y_\tau = u(x_\tau)\phi'(V_\tau)\Delta V_t \qquad (\tau > t).$$

Then the imputed price of atmospheric carbon dioxide at time t is defined by

$$p_t = \int_t^\infty u(x_\tau)\phi'(V_\tau)e^{-\delta(\tau-t)}d\tau. \tag{7}$$

The imputed price of atmospheric carbon dioxide is first used in obtaining the allocation of scarce resources that is optimum from a static point of view. Namely, a charge is levied for the emittance of carbon dioxide evaluated at the imputed price p_t at each moment in time t. Second, the imputed price p_t will be adjusted over time so as to attain a time path (x_t, V_t) that is dynamically optimum.

In our simple model, the effect of the imputed price upon the allocation of scarce resources is seen as follows: Since the imputed price p_t is charged for the unit emittance of carbon dioxide, the vector of final consumption x_t is so chosen as to maximize the imputed national income

$$y_t - p_t v_t = u(x_t)\phi(V_t) - p_t v_t. \tag{8}$$

If the number of commodities is only one, the maximum condition would be simply written as

$$u'(x_t)\phi(V_t) = p_t a. \tag{9}$$

It is rather difficult to see how the imputed price of atmospheric carbon dioxide is determined, even for our simplest model. Therefore, it seems to be advisable first to explain a heuristic approach to derive an approximation for the imputed price. Suppose that the atmospheric level of carbon dioxide has been increased by a marginal amount ΔV_t from the present level V_t. If the atmospheric level were to remain at the current level V_t for the entire future, the magnitude of the marginal damage felt by the people would be $-u(x_\tau)\phi'(V_t)\Delta V_t$. If the future level of consumption were also to remain at the current level of x_t, the present value of the marginal damage caused by the marginal increase by the amount ΔV_t of the atmospheric level of carbon dioxide at time t would be given by

$$\frac{1}{\delta + \mu} u(x_t)[-\phi'(V_t)]\Delta V_t.$$

It may be noted that, since the atmospheric accumulation of carbon dioxide is absorbed into the oceans at the annual rate of μ, the effective discount rate becomes $\delta + \mu$. Hence, for the imputed price p_t of atmospheric concentration of carbon dioxide, we obtain the following formula:

$$p_t = \frac{1}{\delta + \mu} u(x_t)[-\phi'(V_t)]. \tag{10}$$

The precise formula for the imputed price of atmospheric carbon dioxide has to take into account that both the level of consumption and the atmospheric concentration of carbon dioxide will continuously change over time. In order to derive a general formula for the imputed price of atmospheric carbon dioxide, let us suppose that atmospheric carbon dioxide is a marketable (negative) asset and the imputed price is the market price. If one holds the unit of the asset of atmospheric carbon dioxide for a short period of time Δt, then he would have incurred the damage to be estimated at $-u(x_t)\phi'(V_t)\Delta t$, and he would have obtained capital gains by the amount Δp_t, while the loss due to the depreciation would be $\mu p_t \Delta t$. On the other hand, he would have incurred the interest cost (with the rate δ) for the investment by the amount p_t during the period Δt. Hence, if the market were perfectly competitive, the following condition would have to be satisfied:

$$-u(x_t)\phi'(V_t)\Delta t + \Delta p_t - \mu p_t \Delta t = \delta p_t \Delta t,$$

which, by rearranging, yields the following condition:

$$\frac{\dot{p}_t}{p_t} = (\delta + \mu) + \frac{u(x_t)\phi'(V_t)}{p_t}. \tag{11}$$

Equation 11 is often referred to as the Ramsey-Keynes formula, a disguised form of the Euler-Lagrange equations in the calculus of variations. The optimum time path (x_t, V_t) then will be obtained if one finds the solution time path (x_t, V_t) that satisfies the pair of differential equations 1 and 11 and at the same time possesses a stable property as time t goes to infinity.

We can now see that the heuristic formula (equation 10) for the imputed price of atmospheric carbon dioxide corresponds to the situation where the rate of change $\dot{p}_t$ of the imputed price p_t is equal to zero in equation 11. In fact, we can easily show that the heuristic solution (equation 10) for the imputed price of atmospheric carbon dioxide gives us a close approximation for the true imputed price, and, for any practical purposes, the heuristic solution for the imputed price may be used to achieve a dynamically optimum allocation of scarce resources.

We now look into the heuristic formula (equation 10) more closely to see how the imputed price p_t of atmospheric carbon dioxide may be utilized to determine the level of economic activities, which, in our simplest model, are summarized by the vector of final consumption x_t. First, we introduce a new variable to be defined by

$$\lambda_t = \frac{p_t}{\phi(V_t)}.$$

It is the imputed price of atmospheric carbon dioxide per impact index $\phi(V_t)$. The heuristic formula (10) now may be written as

$$\frac{\lambda_t}{u(x_t)} = \frac{1}{\delta + \mu}\left[\frac{-\phi'(V_t)}{\phi(V_t)}\right]. \tag{12}$$

It may be recalled that the level of economic activities, to be represented by x_t, is determined so that the imputed national income $y_t - p_t v_t = u(x_t)\phi(V_t) - p_t v_t$ is maximized, where the rate of increase v_t

in the atmospheric level of carbon dioxide is related to the vector of final consumption x_t by equation 2. Hence, it is equivalent to finding the vector of final consumption x_t that maximizes the imputed national income per impact index:

$$u(x_t) - \lambda_t v_t. \tag{13}$$

We can now see that the optimum vector of final consumption x_t is uniquely determined once the imputed price λ_t of atmospheric carbon dioxide per impact index is known, independently of the atmospheric level of carbon dioxide V_t.

It is also easily seen that an increase in the imputed price results in a decrease in the rate of anthropogenic increase in the atmospheric level of carbon dioxide v_t and at the same time in a decrease in the utility level $u(x_t)$ associated with the vector of final consumption. The last property is also seen from the marginality condition (equation 9).

Thus the left-hand side of the heuristic formula (equation 12) is determined solely by the imputed price λ_t, independently of the level of atmospheric carbon dioxide V_t, and it is increased when the imputed price λ_t is increased. Hence, for any given level V_t of atmospheric carbon dioxide, the imputed price λ_t is uniquely determined by the heuristic formula (equation 12).

The determination of the imputed price per impact index λ_t is illustrated in figure 8.1, in which, the imputed price per impact index of atmospheric carbon dioxide λ_t is measured along the abscissa in the second quadrant, while $\theta_t = \lambda_t / u(x_t)$ is measured along the ordinate. The relationships between these two variables are depicted by the upward sloping curve BB in the second quadrant.

The heuristic formula (equation 12) gives us information about the way the imputed price changes when the atmospheric level of carbon dioxide changes. We assume that the impact function $\phi(V)$ is of the type specified by equation 4. In this case, the right-hand side of the heuristic formula (12) is easily calculated:

$$\frac{-\phi'(V_t)}{\phi(V_t)} = \frac{\beta}{\hat{V} - V_t}. \tag{14}$$

The right-hand side of the heuristic formula (12) then is described by the curve AA in the first quadrant in figure 8.1, where the atmospheric level of carbon dioxide V_t is measured along the abscissa, while the ordinate measures the magnitude of $[-\phi'(V_t)]/[\phi(V_t)]$. The curve AA, as depicted in figure 8.1, approaches infinity as the atmo-

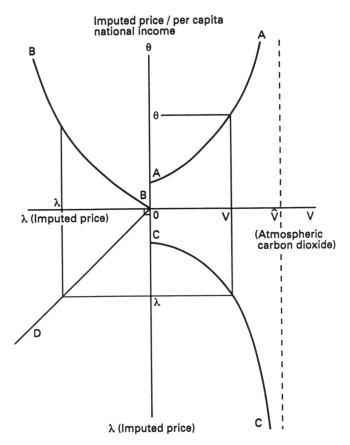

Figure 8.1
The determination of the imputed price of atmospheric carbon dioxide

spheric level of carbon dioxide V_t approaches the critical level $\hat{V}$. Figure 8.1 clearly shows how the imputed price per impact index λ_t is determined for a given level of atmospheric carbon dioxide V_t and how λ_t changes when V_t changes. The imputed price λ_t may be transformed from the abscissa in the second quadrant to the ordinate in the fourth quadrant, to derive the curve CC, which depicts the relationships between the atmospheric level of carbon dioxide V_t and the corresponding level of the imputed price λ_t. An increase in V_t increases the imputed price λ_t, and when V_t approaches the critical level $\hat{V}$, the imputed price λ_t approaches infinity.

The quantity $\theta_t = \lambda_t/u(x_t)$, which has been used to analyze the mechanism by which the imputed price per impact index is related to the atmospheric level of carbon dioxide, possesses a meaning of some importance, particularly from the practical point of view. It is written as

$$\theta_t = \frac{\lambda_t}{u(x_t)} = \frac{p_t}{u(x_t)\phi(V_t)} = \frac{p_t}{y_t}.$$

Thus θ_t stands for the ratio of the imputed price p_t over the per-capita level of national income y_t (evaluated at constant prices). The heuristic formula (12) now may be written in terms of θ_t, the imputed price per ton of carbon dioxide emitted into the atmosphere as a fraction of national income in constant prices:

$$\theta_t = \frac{1}{\delta + \mu}\frac{\beta}{\hat{V} - V_t}N, \tag{15}$$

where population N is explicitly brought in.

Equation 15 has been obtained for the case of the simplest model as a first approximation for the imputed price per constant-price national income. However, it will be shown later that equation 15 remains valid for the general situation where there exist a number of countries in the region and the possibility of technology and energy substitution is not excluded. It will also be shown that a similar formula will be applicable when other greenhouse gases are taken into account.

It may be noted here that equation 15 gives us information concerning the effects of changes in structural parameters such as δ, μ, β, and $\hat{V}$ upon the imputed price/national income ratio θ_t. An increase in the discount rate δ or in the rate of absorption μ results in a decrease in θ_t, while an increase in the sensitive parameter β increases the ratio θ_t. The lowering of the critical level $\hat{V}$ has the effect of increasing the ratio θ_t.

The analysis we have developed for the simplest model may be extended to more general circumstances. We first consider the case where the possibility of substitution for technology and energy use is permitted. First, we consider the situation where levels of economic activities may not necessarily be represented by vectors of final consumption. Let us now assume that x represents a vector of activity levels for the entire economy. Each component x_i of a vector of activity levels $x = (x_1, \ldots, x_n)$ denotes the level at which activity i is operated, where $1, \ldots, n$ exhaust all available activities in the economy. The quantities of scarce resources that are utilized when the economy is operated at $x = (x_1, \ldots, x_n)$ are specified in the following manner: It is assumed that the type of scarce resources available in the economy is generically denoted by $l = 1, \ldots, L$, and a_{li} denotes the quantity of scarce resources of type l that is required in order for the activity i to be operated at the unit level. Then, a vector of activity levels $x = (x_1, \ldots, x_n)$ utilizes scarce resources by the quantities

$$\sum_i a_{li} x_i, \quad l = 1, \ldots, L.$$

Hence, if the available quantities of scarce resources are given by $K = (K_1, \ldots, K_L)$, then a vector of activity levels $x = (x_1, \ldots, x_n)$ is feasible if and only if the following conditions are satisfied:

$$\sum_i a_{li} x_i \leqq K_l, \quad l = 1, \ldots, L, \quad x_1, \ldots, x_n \geqq 0.$$

In matrix notation,

$$Ax \leqq K, x \geqq 0. \tag{16}$$

The amount v of carbon dioxide emitted into the atmosphere associated with vector of activity levels x is similarly denoted by

$$v = ax = \sum_i a_i x_i. \tag{17}$$

If the imputed price of atmospheric carbon dioxide is given by p_t, the optimum levels of economic activities are expressed by the vector of activity levels x that maximizes the level of imputed national income

$$y_t - p_t v_t = u(x_t)\phi(V_t) - p_t v_t$$

subject to the constraints of equations 16 and 17. In this general case, however, the utility function $u(x)$ has to be defined as the utility level for the vector of final consumption that is obtained for the economy as a whole when the levels of economic activities are specified at the vector of activity levels x.

Then the heuristic formula (12) holds for our general case. Similarly, equation 15 holds for the imputed price per impact index λ_t. The exactly identical argument may now be applied to the present case to establish the relationships between the atmospheric level of carbon dioxide V_t and the corresponding imputed price λ_t. In particular, we can see that equation 15 holds for the ratio θ_t of the imputed price of atmospheric carbon dioxide over the level of national income in constant prices y_t.

When the economy comprises many individuals, our analysis may be applied if we take as y_t the per-capita level of national income in constant prices.

Our analysis now may be extended to the situation where atmospheric carbon dioxide may be absorbed by living land plants as well. The atmospheric amount of carbon dioxide that is absorbed by living land plants is assumed to be determined by the total acreage of land forests in the region, which will be denoted by R_t. It may be noted that R_t refers to nonstationary land forests. The absorbing capacity varies according to the type of land forests; there exists a significant difference—say, between tropical rain forests and temperate forests—in the rate per acre of forests to absorb atmospheric carbon dioxide through the process of photosynthesis. However, we will be satisfied here by assuming that the amount of atmospheric carbon dioxide absorbed by land forests per acre is a certain constant on the average, to be denoted by γ. Then the basic dynamic equation 1 may be modified to the following:

$$\dot{V}_t = v_t - \mu V_t - \gamma R_t, \tag{18}$$

where the rate of atmospheric carbon dioxide absorbed by land forests γR_t is explicitly brought out.

According to Dyson and Marland (1979), the carbon sequester rate for temperate forests is estimated at 7.5 tC/ha/yr. For tropical forests, it is estimated at 9.6–10.0 tC/ha/yr, according to Marland (1988) and Myers (1988). Our analysis will be carried out on the assumed rate of 5 tC/ha/yr for temperate forests and 15 tC/ha/yr for tropical rain forests.

The change in the total acreage of land forests R_t is related first to the level of afforestation and second to the extent to which land forests are depleted by various economic activities, particularly by the agricultural and lumber industries. Let us denote by r_t the annual rate of increase in the acreage of land forests due to the activities of afforestation and by s_t the acreage of land forests lost due to various economic activities during the year t. Then the change in the total acreage of land forests R_t is specified by the following dynamic equation:

$$\dot{R}_t = r_t - s_t. \tag{19}$$

We assume that the type of afforestation activities may be generically denoted by f, $f = 1, \ldots, F$, and m_f is the rate of increase in the forest acreage when afforestation activity f is operated at the unit level. Then r_t is given by

$$r_t = mz_t = \sum_f m_f z_{ft}, \tag{20}$$

where $m = (m_1, \ldots, m_F)$ and $z_t = (z_{1t}, \ldots, z_{Ft})$ is the vector of afforestation activities for the year t.

On the other hand, the acreage s_t of land forests lost by the economic activities during the year t may be expressed as follows:

$$s_t = \sum_i b_i x_{it}, \tag{21}$$

where $b = (b_1, \ldots, b_n)$ denotes a vector specifying the acreage of land forests lost by economic activities, and $x_t = (x_{1t}, \ldots, x_{nt})$ is the vector of activities for the year t.

Afforestation activities naturally have to utilize scarce resources available in the economy. The conditions (equation 16) for the resource constraints now have to be modified like this:

$$Bx_t + Mz_t \leq K, \qquad x_t \geq 0, \quad z_t \geq 0, \tag{22}$$

where M stands for the matrix specifying the resource requirements for afforestation activities.

The problem we have to solve now is this: Starting with the atmospheric level of carbon dioxide V_0 and the acreage of land forests R_0 at the beginning ($t = 0$), find the time path (x_t, z_t, V_t, R_t) that satisfies the constraints (equations 18–22) and yields a dynamically optimum time path of vectors of final consumption.

This optimum problem is also solved by using the concept of imputed prices. In the present case, we have to introduce the imputed price for land forests q_t, in addition to the imputed price for atmospheric carbon dioxide p_t. The imputed price q_t of land forests assesses the benefits the society as a whole receives when the acreage of land forests at time t is increased by the marginal unit. Since the only effect the acreage of land forests R_t exerts in our model is a decrease, from time t to the future, of the atmospheric level of carbon dioxide, the imputed price q_t of land forests at time t may be expressed by the following formula:

$$q_t = \frac{\gamma}{\delta} p_t. \tag{23}$$

Equation 23 may be obtained like this: The marginal increase of the acreage of land forests at time t implies that the atmospheric level of carbon dioxide is decreased by the amount γ for the entire future. That decrease in CO_2 causes an increase by γp_t in terms of imputed price p_t (assuming that the imputed price were to remain at the level p_t of time t). Since the rate of discount is δ, the discounted present value of γp_t is given by the right-hand side of equation 23. The imputed prices p_t and q_t are used in deriving the levels of economic activities, to be represented by x_t, and the levels of afforestation activities, to be represented by z_t, that result with an optimum allocation of scarce resources from the static point of view. Namely, (x_t, z_t) is so chosen as to maximize the imputed national income:

$$y_t - p_t v_t + q_t(r_t - s_t)$$

subject to the constraints of equations 20, 21, and 22.

A formula similar to equation 15 may be obtained for land forests. Namely, if we denote by η_t the ratio of the imputed price q_t of the unit acreage of land forests over the per-capita level of national income y_t, then

$$\eta_t = \frac{q_t}{y_t} = \frac{\gamma}{\delta(\delta + \mu)} \cdot \frac{\beta}{\hat{V} - V_t} N. \tag{24}$$

The dynamic structure of our model is specified by the pair of differential equations 18 and 19, which are repeated here in order to facilitate the exposition.

$$\dot{V}_t = v_t - \mu V_t - \gamma R_t, \tag{18}$$

$$\dot{R}_t = r_t - s_t. \tag{19}$$

We should like first to look into the situation where the atmospheric level of carbon dioxide V_t remains stationary, that is, $\dot{V}_t = 0$. This is the case if and only if the acreage of land forests R_t is the level satisfying the following condition:

$$R_t = \frac{1}{\gamma}(v_t - \mu V_t). \tag{25}$$

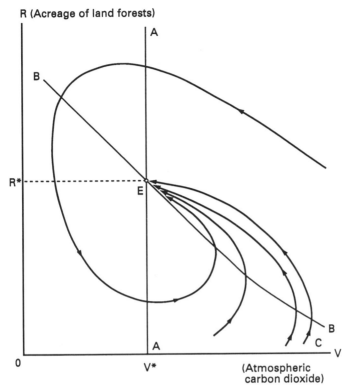

Figure 8.2
The atmospheric level of carbon dioxide and the acreage of land forests converge to the long-run optimum levels

An increase in atmospheric level of carbon dioxide V_t implies a higher imputed price p_t and hence a lower emittance rate of carbon dioxide v_t. The combination of (V_t, R_t) for which equation 25 is satisfied then is depicted by a downward sloping curve, as illustrated by the curve BB in figure 8.2. The atmospheric level of carbon dioxide V_t is measured along the abscissa, while the ordinate measures the acreage of land forests R_t. When (V_t, R_t) lies on the right, upper side of the curve BB, the atmospheric level of carbon dioxide V_t tends to be decreased; when (V_t, R_t) lies on the left, lower side of the curve BB, V_t tends to be increased.

On the other hand, the acreage of land forests R_t remains stationary $(\dot{R}_t = 0)$, if and only if the following condition is satisified:

$$r_t = s_t. \tag{26}$$

An increase in the atmospheric level of carbon dioxide V_t implies an increase in the imputed price p_t of atmospheric carbon dioxide, and hence a corresponding increase in the imputed price q_t of land forests. The rate of afforestation r_t then is increased, while the rate of forest depletion s_t tends to be decreased. This observation implies the uniquely determined level of atmospheric carbon dioxide V^* for which the stationarity condition (equation 26) is satisfied. In figure 8.2 the line AA is a vertical line with the distance of V^* from the ordinate. If (V_t, R_t) is on the right side of the line AA, the imputed price p_t of atmospheric carbon dioxide is higher than the equilibrium level p^*, implying that the acreage of land forests R_t tends to be increased, but on the left side of the line AA, R_t tends to be decreased.

The solution path (V_t, R_t) for the pair of differential equations 18 and 19 thus has the structure illustrated by the arrowed curves in figure 8.2. The point E, which is the intersection of the curve BB and the line AA, gives the equilibrium state (V^*, R^*), where both the atmospheric level of carbon dioxide and the acreage of land forests remain stationary.

The pair of differential equations 18 and 19 is easily seen to possess a pair of stable roots. Hence, the dynamic path (R, V) has a tendency to approach the stationary state (R^*, V^*) as time t tends to infinity. A cursory observation yields the following conclusions concerning the dynamic behavior of the optimum path (R_t, V_t). There exists a critical curve CE, representing the maximum acreage of land forests, corresponding to each level of atmospheric carbon dioxide, for which the optimum dynamic path monotonically converges to the stationary state (R^*, V^*). Namely, if, at the initial time $t = 0$, the state (R_0, V_0) lies on the curve CE, the optimum path (R_t, V_t) monotonically converges to the stationary state (R^*, V^*). When (R_0, V_0) lies below the curve CE, but on the right side of the line AA, then both R_t and V_t tend to be increased until (R_t, V_t) reaches the curve CE, and from then on V_t tends to be decreased, while R_t keeps on increasing. If the initial state (R_0, V_0) lies above the curve CE, but on the right side of the line AA, the stock of atmospheric carbon dioxide V_t tends to decrease while the stock of land forests R_t tends to increase until the atmospheric level of carbon dioxide V_t reaches the stationary level V^*. From then on, the stock of land forests R_t begins to decrease, while the atmospheric level of carbon dioxide V_t continues to decrease. However, at a certain critical point in time, the atmospheric level of carbon dioxide begins to increase, either to approach monotonically the stationary state E or to approach the stationary state after the economy has gone through the original phase where the atmospheric level of carbon dioxide V_t decreases while the stock of land forests R_t increases.

Multicountry Analysis

We now come to the next stage of our theoretical analysis, where the multicountry case is discussed. We consider the world as a whole or a particular region such as the Pacific Rim, where each country is closely interrelated with others through atmospheric and oceanic environments. Countries are generically denoted by v, $v = 1, \ldots, N$. Each country is assumed to possess the structure as specified in the previous analysis. Each country v is endowed with land forests by the acreage R_t^v at time t, while the atmospheric level of carbon dioxide for the whole region is given by V_t, as previously. Each country is also endowed with certain quantities of scarce resources, which will be utilized either for the production of final consumption goods or for afforestation activities. The burning of fossil fuels associated with economic activities increases the atmospheric level of carbon dioxide, while land forests absorb atmospheric carbon dioxide at a certain constant rate γ annually per acre of land forests. Atmospheric carbon dioxide also is absorbed by the oceans, at a certain constant fraction μ of the volume of atmospheric carbon dioxide V_t.

For each country v, the utility index y_t^v is defined in terms of the standard price system $p^0 = (p_1^0, \ldots, p_n^0)$. It is assumed that the utility index y_t^v for country v may be expressed as follows:

$$y_t^v = u^v(x_t^v)\phi(V_t),$$

where the impact index $\phi(V_t)$ is assumed to be identical for all countries, while the utility function $u^v(x_t^v)$ may differ between the countries.

Since we are concerned with the pattern of resource allocation over time that is both efficient and equitable, we adopt the optimum criterion that the minimum of the utility levels of all the countries is maximized among all feasible time paths of resource allocation. The problem again is solved by using the concept of imputed prices of atmospheric carbon dioxide and land forests. These imputed prices are obtained by the heuristic formulas similar to equations 15 and 24. We denote by p_t^v the imputed prices of atmospheric carbon dioxide at time t, and, for each country v, q_t^v stands for the imputed price of land forests at time t. We also denote the ratios of imputed prices over the utility level (as expressed by the per-capita level of national income in constant prices) by θ_t^v and η_t^v:

$$\theta_t^v = \frac{p_t^v}{y_t^v}, \qquad \eta_t^v = \frac{q_t^v}{y_t^v}. \tag{27}$$

Then the following formulas are obtained:

$$\theta_t^v = \frac{p_t^v}{y_t^v} = \frac{1}{\delta + \mu} \frac{\beta}{\hat{V} - V_t} N, \tag{28}$$

$$\eta_t^v = \frac{q_t^v}{y_t^v} = \frac{\gamma}{\delta(\delta + \mu)} \frac{\beta}{\hat{V} - V_t} N. \tag{29}$$

The static allocation of scarce resources at each time t is determined so that the imputed national income

$$y_t^v - p_t^v v_t^v + q_t^v (r_t^v - s_t^v)$$

is maximized subject to the constraints imposed by the availability of scarce resources for each country v, where v_t^v, r_t^v, and s_t^v are, respectively, the rate of carbon dioxide emitted into the atmosphere in country v, the rate of increase in the acreage of land forests in country v, and the rate at which land forests in country v are depleted because of economic activities. Such an allocation of scarce resources is obtained in a decentralized, perfectly competitive market economy, when the emittance tax evaluated at the imputed price of atmospheric carbon dioxide is levied, while the afforestation subsidy evaluated at the imputed price of land forests is paid.

Our optimum solution is obtained under the hidden assumption that produced goods are freely exchanged between the countries so as to attain the same utility level for all countries. Indeed, in equations 28 and 29, y_t^v are identical for all countries, and so are the imputed prices of land forests q_t^v. Hence, the crucial ratios θ_t^v and η_t^v, defined by the right-hand sides of equations 28 and 29, respectively, are identical for all countries. However, when we are concerned with applying our analysis to any practical situation, some of the conditions obtained for the optimum solution are not necessarily satisfied, particularly the identity of the utility level between the countries. In such circumstances, it is possible to obtain an approximation for the optimum solution. Namely, the imputed prices of atmospheric carbon dioxide and land forest in each country v, p_t^v and q_t^v, are defined by the following formulas:

$$p_t^v = \theta_t y_t^v, \qquad q_t^v = \eta_t y_t^v, \tag{30}$$

where the ratios θ_t and η_t are obtained from the right-hand sides of equations 28 and 29, respectively, and y_t^v is the *actual* level of per-capita national income for country v.

Our solution also will be found to be a good approximation for the situation where economic and afforestation activities are *fixed*, in the sense that changing the levels of these activities entails certain costs of adjustment.

Our theoretical analysis concludes with a remark concerning other greenhouse gases, such as methane, nitrous oxide, and CFCs. When we take into consideration the effect of these greenhouse gases, we have to modify the definition of V_t. The quantity V_t now is defined as the aggregate of these greenhouses in the atmosphere, where each type of greenhouse gas is so measured that it has an identical effect, comparable with carbon dioxide, upon the phenomenon of global warming. According to the estimates made by Ramanathan et al. (1985) and others, the effects of various greenhouse gases upon the increase in atmospheric temperature are roughly of the following magnitude (compared with that of carbon dioxide): methane, 25; nitrous oxide, 250; CFC-11, 17,500; and CFC-12, 20,000.

The calculation of the imputed prices for these greenhouse gases has to take into account the magnitude of the rate of absorption μ. In the case of carbon dioxide, we have taken $\mu = 0.02$ as a first approximation. For other greenhouse gases, the following would be bold estimates: methane, 0.10; nitrous oxide, 0; CFCs, 0. The imputed prices of these gases in reference to that of carbon dioxide then are given as follows: methane, 12; nitrous oxide, 350; CFC-11, 25,000; and CFC-12, 28,000.

The stabilization of the atmospheric disequilibrium may be efficiently attained through the device of the "carbon tax" evaluated at the imputed prices of greenhouse gases and land forests, at least in theory. The method described here is not quite satisfactory from the equity point of view, even though it has taken into consideration some aspects of the equity principle when the imputed price measured in terms of the per-capita level of national income in constant prices has been adopted. Suppose there exist two countries, A and B. Country A has a long history of industrial activities and has accumulated large quantities of scarce resources in the form of fixed factors of production, like factories, machinery, and urban infrastructures, but it is chiefly responsible for the accumulation of atmospheric carbon dioxide today. Country B, on the other hand, has only meager endowments of productive factors of production, having had virtually no industrial activity in the past. Since the atmospheric level of carbon dioxide has reached a high level, both countries A and B are levied a high imputed price per ton of carbon dioxide emitted into the atmosphere. In the method described in this chapter, the actual price country B has to pay for the unit discharge of carbon dioxide is much lower than that for country A. Still, the processes of economic development for country B are much more seriously hindered by the imposition of the carbon tax than country A. In the theoretical analysis we have introduced, an assumption was implicitly made that produced goods were all pooled together to be redistributed among the countries so that the utility level associated with per-capita national income is the same for all countries. The carbon-tax system has to be introduced in a situation where such a utopian hypothesis naturally is not applicable, and certain additional arrangements have to be introduced so that country B is not unduly handicapped in its economic development. The best method would be for some of country A's net receipts from the carbon-tax system to be transferred to country B, if country A is persuaded to do so. Such a method, however, would not be workable when more than two countries are involved, unless some sort of international agency is set up to administer the carbon-tax system.

The Incidence of Carbon Tax in the Pacific Rim

The dynamic theory of imputation, as outlined in the previous section, may be applied to solve the problem of atmospheric disequilibrium, especially for the Pacific Rim region. The Pacific Rim countries share the Pacific Ocean as a common reservoir that serves as a powerful absorber of carbon dioxide and other greenhouse gases as well as an effective circulator of the air. At the same time, the countries comprising the Pacific Rim are marked by an extreme degree of income inequality, at least in terms of nominal national income, and by diverse cultural characteristics. The concept of imputed prices, which was the main theme of the discussion in the previous section, is the device in terms of which the long-run optimum stationary state may be attained by an allocative mechanism that is equitable as well as efficient.

The imputed price of atmospheric carbon dioxide quantifies the extent of the damage the society as a whole incurs as the result of the marginal increase in the atmospheric level of carbon dioxide. It has been defined as the discounted sum, at a certain social rate of discount (usually of the order of 5%), of prospective future damages, measured in reference to the level of national income at constant prices, that society as a whole suffers because of the marginal increase in the atmospheric level of carbon dioxide today. The function of imputed price is twofold. The imputed price is used as an instrument through which efficient and equitable allocations of scarce resources, both private and public, may be attained. At the same time, it serves as the guideline that will guarantee that the allocative mechanism in terms of imputed price is optimum from the dynamic point of view. The actual computation of imputed price as introduced in the previous section differs from that of the standard analysis of the theory of optimum economic growth. It takes into consideration the presence of the inequality that exists in the transient process, without disturbing the optimum property from the long-run point of view.

The imputed price of atmospheric carbon dioxide p_t^v for country v is defined relative to the level of national income y_t^v at constant prices. Namely, if we denote by θ_t the ratio of the imputed price p_t^v of atmospheric carbon dioxide (per metric ton of carbon) over the per-capita level of national income y_t^v in constant prices for country v, then we have the following formula:

$$\theta_t = \frac{\beta}{\delta + \mu} \cdot \frac{N}{\hat{V} - V_t},$$

where δ is the social rate of discount, μ is the rate of ocean uptake, $\hat{V}$ is the critical level of atmospheric carbon dioxide, and V_t is the current level of atmospheric carbon dioxide.

Recent studies on the atmospheric equilibrium suggest that the rate of ocean uptake is on the order of 0.02–0.04 (i.e., 2–4% annually). We use the hypothetic value of $\mu = 0.04$. The critical level $\hat{V}$ of atmospheric carbon dioxide is assumed to be the level corresponding to 560 ppm; namely, $\hat{V}$ is assumed to be on the order of 1,100 to 1,200 GtC. Since the current level V_t of atmospheric carbon dioxide is somewhere between 700 and 770 GtC and the world population N is around 5.2 billion, the ratio of imputed price to per-capita national income θ_t may be assumed to take a constant value θ. If we assume that people are extremely insensitive to the consequences of atmospheric warming and the parameter β has a value $\beta = 0.1$, then the ratio of imputed price to per-capita national income will be assumed to be $\theta = 0.01$.

Imputed prices for other greenhouse gases, such as methane, nitrous oxide, and CFCs, are similarly computed. In order to compute the level of imputed price for each greenhouse gas, we have to take into account not only the degree of radiative forcing, but also the effect of the average time length each greenhouse gas remains in the atmosphere. Because of the availability of data sources, we confine ourselves to carbon dioxide, methane, and CFCs and disregard the effect of the difference in the average lifetime in the atmosphere. We take the values from the estimates of Ramanathan et al. (1985) and assume that the CO_2 conversion ratios for methane and CFCs are respectively 68.6 and 6,414.3, as in World Resources Institute (1990, 345–346).

Table 8.5 compiles the estimates for the imputed price of carbon dioxide for each country in the Pacific Rim. It may be noted that, because of an extreme degree of the inequality in per-capita national income, the imputed price of carbon dioxide varies to a significant extent, from \$30 per metric ton of carbon in the United States to \$0.80 in Indonesia.

In table 8.5 methane and CFCs are added to the net annual atmospheric increase in the level of greenhouse gases. It may be noted that the net annual atmospheric increases as compiled in table 8.5 differ from the emissions of carbon dioxide, methane, and CFCs listed in table 8.3. The dynamic theory of imputation as developed in the previous section suggests that the data on emissions of greenhouse gases would be more appropriate than net atmospheric increases. However, in the present analysis, a more conventional approach of using net atmospheric increases is adopted in computing the total assessment of greenhouse gas emissions, as in table 8.5. Table 8.5 also compiles the per-capita estimate for the assessment of greenhouse gas emissions. It again varies a great deal between the countries, from the highest value of \$120 for the United States to \$0.60 for Indonesia and the Philippines.

The dynamic theory of imputation as developed in the previous

Table 8.5
Imputed prices for greenhouse gases

Country	Per-capita national income, assumed (dollars)	Net annual atmospheric increase in CO_2 (million tons)	Net annual atmospheric increase in methane (million tons carbon)	Net annual atmospheric increase in CFC use (million tons carbon)	Net annual atmospheric increase per capita (tons carbon)	Imputed price (dollars per ton carbon)	Assessment per-capita (dollars)
United States	15,000	540	130	350.0	4.0	150	600
Canada	12,000	48	33	36.0	4.5	120	540
Indonesia	400	110	19	9.5	0.8	4	3
Japan	15,000	110	12	100.0	1.8	150	270
South Korea	2,600	21	29	54.0	0.7	26	18
Malaysia	1,800	22	1	2.5	1.5	18	27
Philippines	500	34	7	0.0	0.6	5	3
Singapore	7,000	3	0	3.7	2.4	70	168
Thailand	800	48	16	3.5	1.2	8	10
Australia	9,000	28	14	21.0	3.7	90	333
New Zealand	8,000	3	4	3.5	3.3	80	264

SOURCES: World Resources Institute (1990), Table 24.2, pp. 348–349; and others.

section provides us with the way to compute imputed prices of land forests. It may be recalled that the critical parameter is γ, the annual amount of carbon absorbed by land forests per acre. As mentioned in the previous section, carbon-absorbing capacity through the process of photosynthesis varies to a significant extent according to the type of forest. We assume that, for temperate forests, $\gamma = 5$ tC/ha, and for tropical rain forests, $\gamma = 15$ tC/ha, as an approximation of the first order. The basic formula we have derived relates the imputed price q_t^v of land forests to the per-capita level of national income y_t^v, for each country v, through the following relation:

$$\frac{q_t^v}{y_t^v} = \eta_t = \frac{\gamma}{\delta}\theta_t,$$

where p_t^v is the imputed price of atmospheric carbon dioxide and δ is the social rate of discount. Therefore, for temperate forests, the ratio of imputed price to per-capita national income η_t is roughly equal to 1.2, while for tropical rain forests, $\eta_t = 3.6$.

Imputed prices of land forests and the magnitude of the assessment are compiled in table 8.6. The imputed price of land forests again varies a great deal, from the highest value for the United States and Japan, $15,000 per hectare, to the lowest for Indonesia, $1200/ha. While for the developed countries the assessments for net annual reforestation are positive, the developing countries suffer from negative assessments for net annual reforestation, with the highest per-capita assessment of $73 for Malaysia. It is indicative of the extent to which deforestation of tropical rain forests of the developing countries in the Pacific Rim region contributes to an increase in atmospheric temperature.

Imputed prices of atmospheric carbon dioxide and land forests are used in deriving the carbon-tax base. Namely, each economic activity is levied a tax or paid a subsidy according to the extent to which such an activity aggravates or alleviates atmospheric concentrations of greenhouse gases, evaluated at the imputed price of each greenhouse gas. We have shown in the previous section that such a pricing scheme guarantees the convergence of the economy to a long-run optimum state, where the equilibrium between the atmosphere and the terrestrial biosphere is sustained. Various policy proposals have been advanced to stabilize the atmospheric disequilibrium. As we have discussed previously, most of these policy proposals will have significant impacts upon the process of global warming and will be

Table 8.6
Imputed prices for reforestation

Country	Forests and woodlands (million ha)	Net annual reforestation (1,000 ha)	Imputed price (per ha)	Assessment Total (million dollars)	Per capita (dollars)
United States	300	1,600	15,000	24,000	95.0
Canada	436	720	12,000	8,650	130.0
Indonesia	120	−800	1,200	−950	−5.5
Japan	25	200	15,000	3,000	−24.0
South Korea	5	80	2,600	200	4.5
Malaysia	20	−230	5,400	−1,250	−73.0
Philippines	10	−80	1,500	−100	−2.0
Singapore	—	—	—	—	—
Thailand	16	−370	2,400	−900	−16.0
Australia	110	60	9,000	550	32.0
New Zealand	10	40	8,000	30	105.0

SOURCE: World Resources Institute (1990), Table 19.1, pp. 292–293.

effective in restoring the climatic equilibrium. However, in order for such policy proposals to be effectively implemented in decentralized, entrepreneurial economies, it will become necessary to introduce an incentive scheme that internalizes the social costs associated with emissions of greenhouse gases. The carbon-tax system based upon the imputation principle offers us such a scheme, where a climatic equilibrium is attained without affecting the efficiency of allocative mechanisms inherent in decentralized economies, and administrative costs are held at a minimum.

Since the phenomenon of global warming has been scientifically established and has become one of the central issues, from economic, social, and political points of view, a number of international conferences and negotiations have been held by various governments and international agencies, some of which have particularly important implications upon the process of economic development for the developing countries in the Pacific Rim. The governmental negotiations mostly have a common trait that they try to agree upon a certain scheme whereby each country is obliged to curtail emissions of greenhouse gases to certain levels, typically as percentages of current emission levels, and to try to implement their commitment through administrative measures or otherwise. Typical examples are the International Conference on Atmospheric Changes, held in Toronto, June 1988, in conjunction with the Toronto Summit, which proposed a 20 percent curtailment of the emission of carbon dioxide by 2005; the Helsinki Agreement, July 1985, a 30 percent reduction in the emission of sulfur oxides from the 1980 level by 1993; the Sophia Agreement, November 1988, freezing the emission of nitrous oxides at the 1987 level by 1994; and the International Conference of Environmental Ministers, held in Holland, November 1989, where the freezing of the emission of carbon dioxide as early as feasible was proposed. Among numerous other international conferences, the Montreal Protocol together with the subsequent Helsinki Agreement, April 1989, where the abolishment of certain types of CFCs by the year 2000 was agreed on, seems to be the only one that will be effectively implemented, with substantial impact upon the depletion of stratospheric ozone and atmospheric warming. As for other greenhouse chemicals, the danger posed by the atmospheric concentrations is not as imminent and evident as CFCs, and the implementation of a program to curtail the emission levels to certain predetermined levels on a national basis seems to be contradictory to the decentralized, entrepreneurial framework.

Such a centralized plan may be feasible in some countries in the Pacific Rim, where the government exerts rather far-reaching, and occasionally decisive, influence over various aspects of economic, social, and cultural life. I am afraid that Japan may well fit into this category, and international agreements in which quantity curtailments on the national basis are stipulated can be effectively implemented in the case of Japan. However, in Japan, the government has consistently adopted policy measures to serve industrial interests, at the occasional expense of the general public or the national interest. The propensity of the Japanese government to serve industrial interests has been particularly salient with respect to environmental policies, as exemplified by numerous cases where the Japanese Environmental Protection Agency has taken steps to violate its mandate and side with those corporations that have been responsible for environmental disruption and pollution, with serious damage done to a large number of citizens. I am afraid that any attempt to centrally implement quantity constraints by the government might result not only in destabilizing the environmental equilibrium but also in accelerating the current trend toward political despotism in Japan.

Some of the developing countries seem to be in circumstances similar to Japan's, though to a lesser extent. However, the imposition of the carbon-tax system, even with the modification we have adopted in this chapter, tends to exert an unfavorable influence upon the process of economic development. In order to offset the adverse effect such a system may have upon the developing countries, it seems to be necessary to supplement it with a transfer scheme from the developed countries to the developing countries in the Pacific Rim. As tables 8.5 and 8.6 show, the developed countries will have substantial amounts of "surpluses" with respect to the greenhouse gas accounts and the forestry accounts. These surpluses are supposed to be disposed of in each country so as to offset the adverse effect the carbon-tax system will have upon the smooth operations of economic activities, but a certain fraction of each country's surpluses has to be allocated to developing countries in the region to help them overcome the financial and other burdens imposed by the carbon-tax system. Technical details for such a transfer scheme may be found in Uzawa (1990).

Note

I should like to gratefully acknowledge the expert advice of Morio Kuninori, Japan Development Bank. Comments by Professors William Cline, Peter Diamond, and Norman Rosenberg are also greatly appreciated. Technical details of the analysis developed in this chapter are discussed in a formal appendix, prepared as Uzawa (1990) and available from the editors or the author upon request.

References

Cass, D. 1965. Optimum economic growth in an aggregative model of capital accumulation. *Review of Economic Studies* 32:233–240.

Cicerone, R. J., and Oremland, R. S. 1988. Biogeochemical aspects of atmospheric methane. *Global Biogeochemical Cycles.*

Conway, T. J., et al. 1988. Atmospheric carbon dioxide measurements in the remote global trosphere. *Tellus* 40:81–115.

Crutzen, P. J., Aselmann, I., and Seiler, W. 1986. Methane production by domestic animals, wild ruminants, other herbivorous fauna, and humans. *Tellus* 38B:271–284.

Detweiler, R. P., and Hall, C. A. 1988. Tropical forests and the global carbon cycle. *Science* 239:4247.

Dickinson, R. E. 1986. The climate system and modeling of future climate. In *The Greenhouse Effect, Climatic Change, and Ecosystems,* ed. B. Bolin et al., 207–270. New York: John Wiley.

Dyson, F., and Marland, G. 1979. Technical fixes for the climatic effects of CO_2. In *Workshop on the Global Effects of Carbon Dioxide from Fossil Fuels,* 111–118. Washington, DC: U.S. Department of Energy.

Food and Agriculture Organization, Forest Resources Division. 1988. An interim report on the state of the forest resources in the developing countries. FAO, Rome.

Fraser, P.J., et al. 1986. Atmospheric CO_2 record from direct chemical measurements during the 19th century. In *The Changing Carbon Cycle: A Global Analysis,* ed. J. R. Trabalka and D. E. Reichle, 66–88. New York: Springer.

From, E., and Keeling, C. D. 1986. Reassessment of late 19th century atmospheric carbon dioxide variations in the air of Western Europe and the British Isles based on an unpublished analysis of contemporary air masses by G. S. Calendar. *Tellus* 38B:87–105.

Gornitz, V., Lebedeff, S., and Hansen, J. 1982. Global sea level trend in the past century. *Science* 215:1611–1614.

Hampicke, U. 1979. Man's impact on the earth's vegetation cover and its effects on carbon cycle and climate. In *Man's Impact on Climate*, ed. by W. Bach, J. Pankrath, and W. Kellog, 139–159. Amsterdam: Elsevier.

Hansen, J., and Lebedeff, S. 1987. Global trends of measured surface air temperature. *Journal of Geophysical Research* 92:13345–13372.

Hansen, J., and Lebedeff, S. 1988. Global surface air temperature: Update through 1987. *Geophysical Research Letters* 15:323–326.

Hansen, J., Lebedeff, S., et al. 1981. Climate impact of increasing atmospheric carbon dioxide. *Science* 213:957–966.

Houghton, R. A., et al. 1987. The flux of carbon from terrestrial ecosystems to the atmosphere in 1980 due to changes in land use: geographic distribution of the global flux. *Tellus* 39B:122–139.

Jacobs, J. 1961. *The Death and Life of the Great American Cities*. New York: Alfred A. Knopf.

Keeling, C. D. 1968. Carbon dioxide in surface ocean waters, 4: Global distribution. *Journal of Geophysical Research* 73:4543–4553.

Keeling, C. D. 1983. The global carbon cycle: What we know from atmospheric, biospheric, and oceanic observations. In *Proceedings of Carbon Dioxide Research Conference: Carbon Dioxide, Science, and Consensus*, U.S. Department of Energy, II.3–II.62.

Keeling, C.D., et al. 1976. Atmospheric carbon dioxide variations at Mauna Loa Observatory, Hawaii. *Tellus* 28:538–551.

Khalil, M.A.K., and Rasmussen, R. A. 1983. Sources, sinks, and seasonal cycles of atmospheric methane. *Journal of Geophysical Research* 88:5131–5144.

Komhyr, W. D., et al. 1985. Global atmospheric CO_2 distribution and variations from 1968–1982 NOAA/GMCC CO_2 flask sample data. *Journal of Geophysical Research* 90:5567–5596.

Koopmans, T. C. 1965. On the concept of optimum economic growth. *Semaine d'Étude sur le Rôle de l'Analyse Économétrique dans la Formulation de Plans de Development*, 225–287.

Lerner, J., Matthews, E., and Fung, I. 1988. Methane emissions from animals: A global high-resolution data base. *Global Biogeochemical Cycles* 2:139–156.

Mähler, K.-G. 1974. *Environmental Economics: A Theoretical Inquiry*. Baltimore and London: Johns Hopkins University Press.

Marland, G. 1988. The prospect of solving the CO_2 problem through global reforestation. U.S. Department of Energy, Office of Energy Research, Washington, DC, 66 pp.

McNeely, J. 1988. *Economic and Biological Diversity: Developing and Using Economic Incentives to Conserve Biological Resources*. Gland, Switzerland: International Union for Conservation of Nature and Natural Resources.

Menger, G. W., and Wien, Wilhelm Braunmüller. 1871. *Grundsätze der Volks-wirtschaftslehre*. Vienna. Translated by J. Dingwell and B. Hoselitz, *Principles of Economics*. Illinois: Free Press, 1950.

Myers, N. 1988. Tropical forests and climate. Unpublished paper, referred to in U.S. Environmental Protection Agency, *Policy Options for Stabilizing Global Climate*, ed. D. A. Lashof and D. A. Tirpak. Washington, DC.

Neftel, A., et al. 1985. Evidence from polar ice cores for the increase in atmospheric CO_2 in the past two centuries. *Nature* 315:45–47.

Nordhaus, W. 1980. Thinking about carbon dioxide: Theoretical and empirical aspects of optimal control strategies. New Haven, CT: Cowles Foundation Discussion Paper No. 565.

Nordhaus, W. 1982. How fast should we graze the global commons? *American Economic Review* 72:242–246.

Pearman, G. I., and Hyson, P. 1986. Global transport and inter-reservoir exchange of carbon dioxide with particular reference to stable isotopic distributions. *Journal of Atmospheric Chemistry* 4:181–224.

Ramanathan, V., et al. 1985. Trace gas trends and their potential role in climate change. *Journal of Geophysical Research* 90:5547–5566.

Rotty, R. M. 1987. Estimates of seasonal variations in fossil fuel CO_2 emissions. *Tellus* 39B:184–202.

Takahashi, T., et al. 1980. Carbonate chemistry of the surface waters of the world oceans. In E. Goldberg, Y. Horibe, and K. Saruhashi (eds.), *Isotope Marine Chemistry*, 291–326. Tokyo: Uchida Rokakuho.

Uzawa, H. 1974a. *Social Costs of the Automobile* (in Japanese). Tokyo, Iwanami.

Uzawa, H. 1974b. Sur la théorie économique du capital collectif social. *Cahiers du Séminaire d'Économétrie*, 103–122. Translated in *Preference, Production, and Capital: Selected Papers of Hirofumi Uzawa*, 340–362. New York: Cambridge University Press, 1988.

Uzawa, H. 1990. Imputed prices of atmospheric carbon dioxide and land forests. Unpublished notes.

Woodwell, G. M., and Houghton, R. A. 1977. Biotic influences on the world carbon budget. In *Global Chemical Cycles and Their Alternation by Man*, ed. by W. Stumn, 61–72. Berlin: Dahlem Konferenzen.

World Resources Institute. 1990. *World Resources, 1990–1991*. New York and Oxford: Oxford University Press.

Comments

Peter Diamond

Hiro Uzawa has given us a very interesting chapter, with a variety of dimensions, both descriptive and normative. I want to pick out two elements in his chapter to develop further. The first of these is the presence of policies that are desirable independent of global warming and can contribute to easing that problem. The second is income-related taxes (shadow prices).

In his discussion of specific policy proposals, Uzawa mentions changes in forestry practices, recycling newspapers, decreasing use of disposable wood products, decreasing reliance on automobiles (by taxing them and improving transportation alternatives), and restructuring cities. The character of these examples is the inadequate pricing that currently exists and so the inappropriate level of use at present, as well as inadequate development of public alternatives and public regulations of use. I would like to add to his list one element that has a large impact on global warming—population policy. Fewer people also will result in lower levels of externalities in general and contributions to global warming in particular.

On seeing a list of old policy proposals being brought out in the face of a new problem, one can react by thinking that the list is just what one would expect and presumably not the appropriate framework for approaching a new problem. I think this would be a wrong response to this list. In theoretical analyses of policy, it is common to assume a single problem in the world, and thus to isolate and analyze the policies that can improve the situation. But the world is a much more complex place in two ways. One is that there are many problems; the second is that many welfare-improving changes are not made. There is the possibility that the presence of a new problem may change the political environment sufficiently to get a satisfactory policy passed that would not otherwise have passed. This improvement may be large compared with the direct impacts available for the problem at hand. There is also the possibility that the presence of a group already favoring a particular policy proposal for other reasons makes this the proposal with the highest expected return, factoring in both the likelihood of adoption and the impact on the problem at hand. (Although the continuing failure of passage of these policies might just point in the opposite direction.)

But there is also an argument for focusing on areas in need of policy that is economic rather than political. This involves the costs associated with the side effects of any policy. Suppose that one wants to decrease the level of some activity in order to slow global warming. The gain from slowing global warming can be partially offset by the decrease in the activity if the activity yields net consumer surplus—gains from use in excess of the costs. But if there were some distortion in the determination of the level of this activity, coming from market power, externalities, or inappropriate government regulations, then the reduction in the level of activity could be associated with a smaller cost, or even a gain. That is, the identification of distortions is a way of identifying the lowest-cost ways of attacking the problem at hand.

Following his discussion of the current situation in the Pacific Rim and of concrete policy proposals, Uzawa gives us a wonderful presentation of the problem of determining shadow prices for an inherently dynamic problem. I have nothing to add to that presentation,[1] although I want to underline the importance of a dynamic approach. For example, assume that a 4° C rise in average global temperature would be no problem, but a 10° C rise would be a problem. Then one needs to consider the speed with which one wants to adjust levels of activity to allow a moderate rise but prevent a large one. Uzawa follows his presentation of the one-country dynamic optimization by proposing the following procedure. First, solve for the optimal resource use assuming no political constraints on resource redistributions across countries. The shadow prices on greenhouse gases and reforestation that come from this optimization can be related to many numeraires. Relate them to income per capita (which is equalized by the optimal allocation). Now adapt global warming shadow prices to the reality of limited income redistribution by using the optimal ratios of shadow prices to incomes per capita and actual incomes per capita.

The additional complexity in dealing with externalities that comes from limits on income redistribution is substantial. This is compounded by the fact that there are many ways in which one might describe the effective limitations. Without formal modeling of alternatives, it is hard to know how satisfactory an approximation is generated by Uzawa's proposal. Therefore, I have considered a simple static model (in the Appendix) to bring out some issues inherent in the interaction between limitations on income redistribution and slowing global warming. A fuller analysis will have to wait for someone to extend Uzawa's analysis to formally include income-distribution issues.

To get some flavor of the interactions, consider a single period. Countries decide how much output to produce. For simplicity, assume a fixed technological relationship between output produced and greenhouse gases produced. There is no international trade and no international movement of factors of production. In the absence of coordination, each country will set its greenhouse gas policy based on its self-interest. Each country will be interested in having each other country reduce its level of production and so its level of greenhouse gas emission. There is obviously room for mutually advantageous bargaining among countries. Any agreement that involves a small decrease in everyone's emission of greenhouse gases will be a gain for every country. But we are also interested in knowing how far countries should go. Assuming that countries agree on a formula for greenhouse gas reductions, country by country, but do not consider side payments, there is a condition that must be satisfied if the agreement is to be efficient. Of course there are many efficient agreements, with different countries shouldering different fractions of the burden. Having reached an agreement, a country could implement its part of the agreement by taxing emission of gases by producers in its country.

There are two alternative ways of describing such agreements. One way is to state the agreement in terms of quantities of emissions. For example, it might be decided to reduce all emissions by the same proportion. (This method is not necessarily efficient, but that factor is not important for the issues being presented here.) Alternatively, it might be decided to select a tax on emissions for each country and accept the reductions in emissions that are brought about by the different taxes. An example of such an agreement would be Uzawa's proposal that taxes be set proportionally to output per capita. Interestingly, this formula is precisely the solution if the marginal value of income across countries implicit in the bargaining outcome is proportional to the inverse of output. This would be the case with a logarithmic utility of income.

While this solution is efficient in a world where side payments between countries cannot occur, it is not generally efficient if side payments can occur. Then, having the same tax on emissions worldwide is a necessary condition for global efficiency, however one wants to weight the income needs of different countries. From the perspective of a one-period model, this seems like a sensible solution. However, it ignores some important issues that only arise in dynamic contexts. In particular, if country A pays country B not to emit gases year after year (by reducing production), then over time, the ability of country B to emit gases will go down as its capital stock depreciates and it adjusts to being subsidized. But there is no totally reliable way for country A to commit itself to go on paying country B for the rest of time. Thus the nature of repeated bargaining over time may make the no-side-payment solution seem more appropriate. A full analysis would have to consider dynamic bargaining as well as dynamic production of both output and greenhouse gases. Moreover, a richer description of the policy environment would recognize different types of payments (e.g., subsidizing more energy-efficient capital) and different types of greenhouse gas emission reductions.

Hiro Uzawa has given us a very thought-provoking chapter. It is a good foundation for further analysis of the design of emission taxes and forest subsidies that recognizes the complexities coming from many sovereign states.

Appendix

Let x_i represent the emission of greenhouse gases by country i, and let y_i be the production of transferable output in country i (equals consumption in the absence of side payments). Then

$$y_i = f_i(x_i)$$

(concentrating on the level of production, not the efficiency of production). Also, let z be equal to the aggregate emission of greenhouse gases:

$$z = \sum [x_i].$$

The expression $u^i(x_i, y_i, z)$ represents the utility of country i, assumed to be separable in (x_i, y_i) and z.

Nash Equilibrium in the Absence of Coordination
(but with Self-interested Concern about the Greenhouse Effect)

$$u_x^i + u_y^i f_{i'} + u_z^i = 0.$$

This can be supported as a decentralized equilibrium within each country if a tax is levied on the emission of greenhouse gases. Let p_i be the shadow price of greenhouse gas in country i. Then

$$p_i = -u_z^i / u_y^i.$$

Thus private decisions result in the equilibrium condition

$$u_x^i / u_y^i + f_{i'} = p_i.$$

Coordination Equilibrium without Side Payments

If the countries come together and decide to cut back on production of green-house gases, there are many combinations of cutbacks that raise the utility of every country. For small (derivative) cutbacks, any change that decreases z is an improvement for all countries. If the initial equilibrium ignores the own effect of the greenhouse gas, any derivative change that reduces z and reduces all the x_i is an improvement for all countries.

Efficiency in cutting back is equivalent to maximizing a weighted average of country utilities, for some positive weights:

$$\max \sum [w_i u^i].$$

The first-order conditions are

$$u_x^i / u_y^i + f_{i'} = \sum [w_j u_z^j] / (w_i u_y^i) = p_i^*.$$

Since there are many allocations that satisfy such a condition for different vectors w_i, there are many bargaining outcomes. While not necessarily efficient, bargains reducing all the x_i in proportion are obviously candidates. Similarly, bargaining could take the form of selecting a set of values p_i^*. The Uzawa proposal has a common ratio p_i^* / y_i. If utility is additive and logarithmic in income, that is the solution to this problem with equal weights ($w_i = 1$, $u_y^i = 1/y_i$).

Coordination Equilibrium with Side Payments

Allowing side payments introduces another vector of control variables, income transfers t_i that satisfy $\Sigma[t_j] = 0$. The first-order condition for optimal side payments to maximize a weighted sum of country utilities implies the constancy of $(w_i u_y^i)$ across countries. This naturally implies the equality of greenhouse shadow prices.

Note

1. I do have one small question about the details of the model formulation, although it has little effect on the basic presentation. Reforestation is assumed to use resources. Deforestation is a necessary input into some activities (e.g., wood-using activities). I do not see how the formulation allows land not in forests to be a constraint on economic activities. In many places it is not a

constraint in that the marginal nonforest land has no other uses. In some places, this might be a relevant constraint. If the current description of constraints cannot be reinterpreted to cover this issue, this inability would represent a small change in the model, which would not affect the basic interpretation of the determination of shadow prices.

Comments

Norman J. Rosenberg

Although not an economist, I can, nonetheless, recognize the importance of Uzawa's attempt to quantify the costs of greenhouse gas emissions and the role of forests in exacerbating the problem (deforestation) or mitigating it (afforestation).

I must admit, however, that as a natural scientist, I differ on a number of important points with Uzawa on the certainty he attributes to our knowledge of how greenhouse warming will affect global climate and what the impacts of changes in climate, if any, will be.

At this point I am more convinced than not that if emissions of radiatively active trace gases continue at present or even reduced levels, there will be some greenhouse warming in our future. Nonetheless, there may be surprises awaiting us in the behavior of the oceans, the feedback effects (positive or negative) of changes in cloudiness, or the behavior of the biosphere. More on the last of these later.

I am also less certain than Uzawa that atmospheric temperature has actually "risen continuously in the past 200 years." The applicable weather records are reliable for only the past 100 years, approximately. These records show a global warming from about 1880 to 1940 followed by cooling until about 1970. Since then, the mean global temperature has risen. Overall from 1880 to date the warming amounts to about 0.5° C. These records also show that the southern hemisphere has warmed more than general-circulation models (GCMs) predict it should have, and the northern hemisphere has warmed less in response to the increasing atmospheric burden of greenhouse gases. In addition, the forty-eight contiguous United States show no sign of having warmed (Hanson, Maul, and Karl 1989) or of precipitation having changed, one way or another, during the past century. The United States has had the most dense and continuously operating network of climate stations during these past 100 years, and so the significance of these findings must be given serious attention despite the fact that the area represented constitutes less than 2.0 percent of the earth's total surface.

The GCMs take enough of a beating from skeptics without my adding unnecessary blows. It is important to recognize, however, that not even the creators of the GCMs claim that they can yet be used to predict the regional distribution of climate changes that may follow from greenhouse warming. Thus we really have very little to go on when we attempt to define the economic and policy consequences of climate change for any particular region of the world. How much more difficult it is when we deal with the Pacific Rim, the nations of which now experience so vast a range of climates.

An exception to the last statement can be made with regard to sea-level rise (SLR). If the sea rises it will rise everywhere, but because of meteorological and tectonic factors the rise will not be identical on all the world's coastlines. In the course of the last decade estimates of SLR in response to an equivalent doubling of atmospheric CO_2 have ranged from many meters (collapse of the Antarctic ice shelf) to as little as 25 cm.

A rise of half a meter or so could increase the frequency of flooding in many low-lying agricultural lands, would disrupt mangrove forests, increase beach erosion, and alter aquatic habitats. But one wonders, as in an old American folksong, "Why do they put the shore so near the ocean?" We have always adapted to sea level because we have always had to. The Dutch have overcome their extreme vulnerability and, since the 1950s, have improved their traditional fortifications against North Sea storm surges onto their sub-sea-level lands. They have done so in the course of thirty years and for less than $10 billion. Cannot the threatened developing countries, with or without the help of the developed countries, cope with SLR of the modest proportions that our best current scientific information indicates is likely?

Another set of important scientific questions is raised in Uzawa's paper, relating to the amount of carbon that is actually being added to the atmosphere as a result of global—but especially tropical— deforestation. The numbers change constantly, but those I find most convincing put the impact of deforestation at between 0.2 and 1.2 GtC annually and the net contribution of the terrestrial biosphere

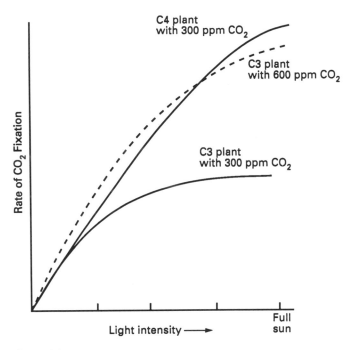

Figure 8.3
The CO_2 fertilization effect

near zero, and perhaps even negative. If negative, it can only be the result of natural and deliberate reforestation in the temperate zones or a stimulation of biomass production occurring in response to increasing atmospheric CO_2 content.

The evidence for the latter is of two kinds. Figure 8.3 illustrates what we call the CO_2 fertilization effect. It has been well established by means of laboratory and greenhouse studies that plants grow differently when the concentration of CO_2 in the ambient air is raised. In air with CO_2 of 300 ppm the rate of photosynthesis in C_4 plants (tropical grasses such as corn, sorghum, and sugarcane) at full sunlight is nearly double that of C_3 plants (small grains, legumes, root crops, and most trees). But when the CO_2 concentration is doubled (600 ppm) the C_3 plants are as productive as the C_4. In a review of some hundreds of studies Kimball (1983) concluded that a doubling of the ambient CO_2 concentration will increase the yield of most C_4 plants by about 15 percent and C_3 plants by about 35 percent (see also Rosenberg et al. 1990).

Carbon dioxide enrichment has another interesting effect on plants. The stomates (pores in plant leaves through which water vapor escapes into the air and CO_2 enters the plant) tend to close as the concentration of CO_2 rises. This response increases the resistance to the escape of water vapor into the air (transpiration) and actually reduces the amount of water used by plants. Photosynthesis is impeded slightly by stomatal closure, but to a much smaller degree than transpiration.

Because photosynthesis is increased and transpiration (water use) is decreased by CO_2 enrichment, water use efficiency (photosynthesis or yield per unit of water consumed) is improved. This effect makes more water available to permit extended plant growth, leaves more water in the soil for the next crop, or allows the irrigator to water larger areas with the savings. Such an increase in water-use efficiency can moderate the effects of a climate warming or reduction in precipitation. The CO_2 fertilization effect on photosynthesis is probably helping to absorb some of the CO_2 emissions now entering the atmosphere as a result of deforestation.

We know that about 5.2 GtC are emitted into the atmosphere yearly as the result of fossil-fuel combustion. An additional amount, say 0.8 GtC, is emitted as the result of tropical deforestation. But only about 55 percent remains in the atmosphere. The "missing" CO_2 is believed to be absorbed by the oceans and the terrestrial biosphere. Until recently it was thought that the oceans accounted for most of the CO_2 absorbed. However, it now appears that the oceanic capacity to absorb CO_2 is considerably less than previously thought (Tans, Fung, and Takahashi 1990). Either that capacity is declining, or it was seriously overestimated to begin with. What this statement means for our argument is that the terrestrial biosphere must be the major sink for the missing CO_2 and that, at least for now, it is helping to control the rate of CO_2 accumulation in the atmosphere and, hence, the emergence of greenhouse warming and attendant climate change.

Additional evidence for the importance of the terrestrial biosphere in controlling CO_2 increase in the atmosphere is to be found in the very record that has proven to us that the concentration is indeed increasing. The annual wave of CO_2 concentration measured at Mauna Loa Observatory in Hawaii since 1958 shows an increasing amplitude with time (Kohlmaier et al. 1987). The annual wave occurs because in the northern hemisphere spring and summer photosynthesis exceeds respiration, and the mean hemispheric CO_2 concentration falls. In the fall and winter, respiration exceeds photosynthesis and the concentration rises. That the amplitude of this wave is increasing is probably due in part to an increasing terrestrial biomass.

This does not mean that deforestation is not occurring in the tropics. It is! But, since photosynthesis and respiration do not vary much throughout the year in the tropics, that zone is not represented in the annual CO_2 wave at Mauna Loa. Probably reforestation in the temperate zones compensates or overcomes the CO_2 signal of deforestation in the tropics. There are other factors that may contribute to this amplitude change, but a growing terrestrial biomass provides at least one quite robust explanation.

These comments are intended to help my economist friends recognize that "greenhouse science" is still very shaky in a number of important areas. The responses of the biosphere to changing climate, and especially to changing CO_2 concentration, are not yet fully understood and it will be some time before they are. The nature of the climate changes that may follow greenhouse warming is also far from clear. It may take three or four decades, for example, before the regional distribution of precipitation change can be reliably predicted (Schneider and Rosenberg 1989). Economists must make room in their analyses for these kinds of scientific uncertainty and remember them when drawing out the policy implications from these analyses.

References

Hanson, K., Maul, G. A., and Karl, T. R. 1989. Are atmospheric "greenhouse" effects apparent in the climatic record of the contiguous U.S. (1895–1987)? *Geophysical Research Letters* 16:49–52.

Kimball, B. A. 1983. Carbon dioxide and agricultural yield: An assemblage and analysis of 430 prior observations. *Agron. Journal* 75:779–788.

Kohlmaier, G. H., Brohl, H., Sire, E. O., Plochl, M., and Revelle, R. 1987. Modeling stimulation of plants and ecosystem response to present levels of excess atmospheric CO_2. *Tellus* 39B:155–170.

Rosenberg, N. J., Kimball, B. A., Martin, P., and Cooper, C. F. 1990. From climate and CO_2 enrichment to evapotranspiration. Chap. 7 in P. E. Waggoner (ed.), *Climate Change and U.S. Water Resources*, 151–175. New York: John Wiley.

Schneider, S. H., and Rosenberg, N. J. 1989. The greenhouse effect: Its causes, possible impacts and associated uncertainties. Chap. 2 in N. J. Rosenberg, W. E. Easterling III, P. R. Crosson and J. Darmstadter (eds.), *Greenhouse Warming: Abatement and Adaptation*. Washington, DC: Resources for the Future.

Tans, P. P., Fung, I. Y., and Takahashi, T. 1990. Observational constraints on the global atmospheric CO_2 budget. *Science* 247:1431–1438.

9

Options for Slowing Amazon Jungle Clearing

Eustáquio J. Reis
and Sérgio Margulis

This chapter discusses the contribution of Amazon jungle clearing to the greenhouse problem and makes an assessment of long-run prospects. The introductory sections pose the problem from both international and Brazilian perspectives. The next section describes major features of the Amazonia ecosystems and presents methods and evidence on deforestation and on its impact on carbon dioxide emissions. Based upon cross-section information for a sample of municipalities in the Brazilian Amazon, the following section estimates elasticities of deforestation in relation to major economic factors—government policies included—and uses them to make projections for the future pace of deforestation. The last section discusses policy alternatives to slow down forest conversion.

Summing up major evidence on deforestation in the Brazilian Amazon: In 1989 deforested area was nearly 400,000 square kilometers (sq km) or 8 percent of the geographic area. Rates of deforestation were approximately 21,000 sq km per year. Estimates of carbon dioxide (CO_2) emissions caused by Brazilian Amazon deforestation are in the range of 0.29 to 0.41 gigaton (Gt) per year—that is, approximately, 4.7 to 6.6 percent of global emissions to the atmosphere. For the year 2000, projections show that deforested area will be nearly 700,000 sq km, and carbon dioxide emissions, according to estimates, will be in the range 0.9 to 1.3 Gt per year.

The Amazon as an International Problem

Global warming is now a priority on the agenda of international politics, for both public concern and official attention. Thus the most important Brazilian environmental problem by far is the devastation of tropical rain forests in the Amazon. Public concern is revealed by the extensive international press coverage of deforestation as well as the destruction of biological diversity and of Indian cultures.

The international alarm is based upon the belief that carbon dioxide emissions caused by Amazon deforestation make a large contribution to the greenhouse effect and, therefore, pose a real threat to the future growth of the world economy.

Despite a great deal of uncertainty, "scientific" common knowledge today holds that, at current rates, carbon dioxide concentration levels in the atmosphere will increase by 50 percent over the next fifty years. The predicted effects upon global average temperatures would be an increase in the range of 1.5° to 4.5° C. Historically, this would be an unmatched rate of climatic change with catastrophic consequences on the sea level, as well as on agricultural productivity and vegetation (see Chapters 1 and 2, by Solow and by Nordhaus, in this volume).

The greenhouse problem can be seen as a market failure resulting from the use of the atmosphere as a "global common" where carbon dioxide and other trace gases are disposed. From a policy perspective, the fundamental problem is in treating "critical" resources—the ozone layer, the carbon cycle, Amazonia—"as free goods when in reality they serve the most basic economic function: that of enabling people to survive" (*The Economist* 1989).

The first-rank status of Amazon deforestation as an international policy issue was evident in the Houston Economic Summit of July 1990 when, by initiative of the West German government, it was considered a top environmental priority and as such was explicitly mentioned in the final communiqué. World Bank loans and German government grants were immediately made available to help Brazilian environmental policies. Similar initiatives were also undertaken by the British and Italian governments.

The U.S. government position on the greenhouse effect is much more cautious and defensive, and to that extent, its concern with Amazon deforestation could be seen as a way of distracting attention from its own glass roof. Nevertheless, in October 1989, when President George Bush expressed to Premier Noboru Takeshita his concern about the devastation of Amazon forest to be caused by the Trans-Pacific road project, which the Japanese government planned to finance, "It was the first time that a U.S. President considered an ecological issue important enough to justify a tense moment in relations with the world's other economic superpower" ("A New Item on the Agenda," *Time*, October 30, 1989, pp. 24, 28).

Solutions of the Amazon deforestation problems will require deep changes in the attitude of the Brazilian government in relation to environmental issues. Because of its pressing social and economic problems, Brazil understandably takes a free-rider position at the international level in regard to issues like the ozone layer and global warming (see Chapter 6, by Schelling, for more elaborate arguments).

The incentive problem reproduces itself at the domestic level: The geographical vastness and demographic emptiness of the Brazilian Amazon make it an open-access resource that is overutilized from both global and local perspectives. Attempts at government regulation have thus far been doomed to failure by the institutional weakness in the region.

In addition to the inadequate institutional framework, misguided government policies have further stimulated unsustainable rates of natural resource depletion. Naturally, these policies will have to be drastically reoriented in order to reconcile economic growth and environmental protection. The new institutional and policy framework, however, cannot neglect the role of the Amazon as a resource frontier for the Brazilian economy.

The Amazon from the Brazilian Perspective

The picture of Eldorado, a golden frontier where immense riches are hidden, has always been the mythical image of the Amazon from the Brazilian perspective. When confronted with the harsh realities of the wilderness, paradise gives place to green hell. The recent failures and frustrations in developing the Amazonian frontier are just another chapter in this continually repeating history.

The Amazon tropical rain forest covers an area of 5.5 million sq km. Sixty percent of it—that is, 3.3 million sq km—is located in Brazil. Amounting to nearly 40 percent of the national territory, it almost coincides with the North region of the country which includes seven states: Rondônia, Acre, Amazonas, Roraima, Pará, Amapá, and Tocantins (see figures 9.1 and 9.2).

Up to the present, the North region remains very sparsely populated and settled. Thus, in 1985, the share of the North region in Brazilian population was only 5.7 percent and its contribution to GDP only 3.1 percent. Population density was 1.51 inhabitants per sq km—less than a tenth of the Brazilian average.

A disproportionate share of regional economic activity, government investment, and regional incentives take place along the west-

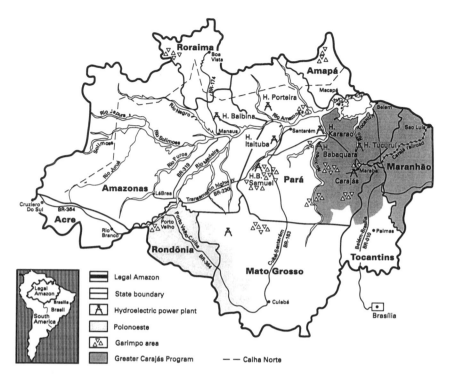

Figure 9.1
Legal Amazonia: Roads, mining areas, and major government projects
SOURCE: World Bank.

ern and southern borders of the tropical forest, located in the states of Tocantins, Maranhão, and Mato Grosso. Naturally, these are also the most deforested areas.

Starting in the late 1960s a genuine boom occurred in the Amazon frontier, as regional income per capita more than tripled and population grew at the astonishing rate of 5 percent per annum. More than 40 percent of that growth came from internal migration.

During the 1970s the region absorbed more than 20 percent of Brazil's interstate migratory flows. The origin of these flows was rural areas from the Northeast region and from the states of Minas Gerais and Paraná. Major push factors were the high rates of population growth, the low social mobility resulting from concentrated land ownership, and dislocation resulting from crop substitution and mechanization (Martine et al. 1989; Porto 1987).

The availability of land for agricultural and livestock development is, by far, the most important pull factor. Though only 7 percent of

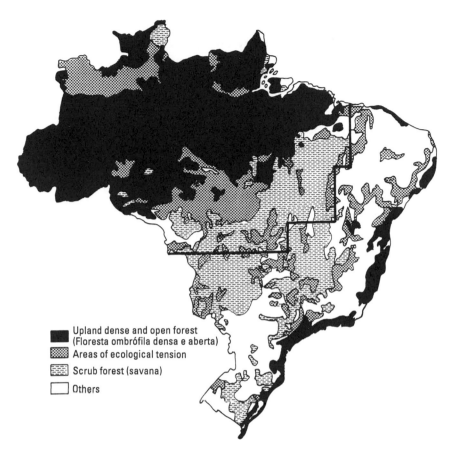

Figure 9.2
Major Brazilian ecosystems

SOURCE: IBGE.

the soils in the North region are considered adequate for agricultural activities (Schubart 1989a, 64), this region adds 250,000 sq km to the agricultural lands of Brazil.

The discovery and development of mineral and energy resources were also important factors in the economic boom experienced by the North region. As a mineral resource frontier, the region is particularly important. Estimated reserves in 1987 included 2.9 billion tons of bauxite, 1.2 billion tons of copper, and 17.7 billion tons of iron ore, accounting, respectively, for 88 percent, 75 percent, and 35 percent of Brazil's total reserves for these minerals. In addition, some 100,000 megawatts of hydroelectric potential, representing 45 percent of Brazil's total, is located in the region. At present, only four projects with less than 4,500 MW of capacity are in operation (Benchimol 1989), but expansion plans exist for thirteen new projects before the year 2000.

Finally, mention should also be made of the forestry resources, even though logging has played only a minor role up to now (Mahar 1989, 7). The available stock of broad-leaved timber in Amazonia is estimated to be 48 to 78 billion cubic meters with a market value of as much as US$1.7 trillion at 1984 prices (Repetto 1988b, 74).

The prime mover behind the explosive pace of frontier settlement was government policies, as expansion into the Amazon became an explicit objective of Brazilian development strategies. A key step in this process was the massive road-building program started in the mid-1960s. This provided, for the first time in history, overland connections between the Amazon and the rest of the country, thus permitting economic settlement away from rivers. Subsequent major policy initiatives included tax exemptions, fiscal and credit subsidies for investment projects, and the creation of the Free Export Processing Zone of Manaus (SUFRAMA).

Regional policies have moved in phases, emphasizing in turn industry, agricultural colonization, large-scale cattle ranching, mining, and hydroelectric projects. In the favorable economic context of the 1970s, the region responded to government incentives with impressive GDP growth rates—18 percent annually from 1970 to 1980. National recession slowed this trend in the early 1980s, although the Northern economy still sustained an average annual growth of 7.7 percent.

Recently, the boom has diminished notably. Hyperinflation and the fiscal crisis of the Brazilian state, together with foreign concern over the ecological disaster of deforestation, have curtailed frontier expansion. National security objectives led the government to maintain some regional development and road-building projects, such as the Calha Norte. By 1988, however, even government policy debates were directly addressing the deforestation issue, as in the Programa Nossa Natureza.

Prospects

Tables 9.1 and 9.2 present some projections for population growth and economic activity in North region. From 1985 to 2000, the population is expected to grow 3.2 percent annually, with net migration

Table 9.1
North Region (excluding Tocantins): Income per capita, population, share
of area in farms, and growth of cattle stock, 1970–1980, with projections
for 2000

Year	Income per capita (1985 U.S. dollars)[a]	Population (1,000)	Migration (percent per year)	Area in farms (percent)	Cattle growth (percent)
1970	273	3,603	0.06	6.5	3.3
1980	906	5,880	2.15	11.6	8.8
1985[b]	1,123[b]	6,849[b]	2.15	12.6	6.1
2000[c]	1,773[c]	10,940[c]	2.15	—	—

SOURCES: IBGE (1990), Martine (1989, 143).
a. 1985 exchange rate was Cz$6.127 per U.S. dollar.
b. Estimated.
c. Projected.

accounting for 40 percent of this increase. This projection was obtained by extrapolating recent trends (Martine et al. 1989). In particular, it assumed that the trends of declining fertility and mortality
would continue, and that the high pace of migration in the 1970s will
also continue. Regional economic activity is expected to grow by 6.2
percent annually, somewhat slower than the estimated pace during
1980–1985, but also more balanced. These projections derive from
a regional input-output model (Castro 1989, 303) assuming (1) that
national GDP will decrease by 3 percent in 1990 and increase 5 percent annually thereafter and (2) that the relationship between regional and national growth in the 1970s continued between 1985 and
1990.

Finally, in assessing future prospects for the Amazon, it should
be recalled that there is now a sizable contingent of landless and
unemployed people already within Amazonia, waiting for the next
economic frontier. Even if migration is substantially reduced, natural
increase will sustain high rates of population growth and frontier
expansion. The dynamics of frontier expansion are thus becoming
more endogenous.

The Contribution of Deforestation in the Brazilian Amazon
to the Greenhouse Effect

This section briefly describes the Amazon ecosystem, presents evidence regarding deforestation, and estimates the contribution of Amazon deforestation to the greenhouse effect.

Table 9.2
North Region: GDP growth and composition, 1960–1985, with projections for 2000

Period	GDP growth (percent per year)	Agriculture and cattle		Industry		Other	
		Growth	Percentage of GDP	Growth	Percentage of GDP	Growth	Percentage of GDP
1960–1970	6.5	6.1	23.6	5.3	15.1	6.9	61.3
1970–1975	15.4	13.6	21.8	22.1	20.0	14.2	58.2
1975–1980	21.4	14.3	16.1	37.4	37.2	16.2	46.7
1980–1985[a]	7.7	9.2	17.3	2.9	29.7	10.5	53.0
1985–2000[b]	6.3	6.0	16.5	6.3	29.4	6.5	54.1

SOURCES: IBGE (1987, 123), Castro (1989, 302).

a. Estimated.
b. Projected.

The Amazon rain forest, with 5.5 million sq km, represents between 45 percent and 68 percent of all tropical forests in the world. Like all tropical forests, it is an incalculably rich reservoir of biotic resources. Despite considerable lack of knowledge regarding the number of existing biological species, the Amazon forest is estimated to hold between 800,000 and 5 million species, representing 15 to 30 percent of all the species in the biosphere (Schubart 1989a). Its astonishing biodiversity is illustrated by the fact that 505 species of trees higher than 2.5 meter were found in 0.2 hectare of *terra-firme* (nonflooded land) near Manaus, while only fifty species may be found in all of France (Prance et al. 1976, quoted by Salati et al., n.d.).

The variety of existing plant and animal species is partially explained by the low nutritional content of soils. In contrast, the forest cover presents good nutritional conditions with a net annual primary productivity of 20 tons per hectare and a biomass content between 200 and 300 t/ha of dry organic substance (Schubart 1989b, 13; estimates from Martinelli et al. 1988, quoted by Salati 1989, are 400 t/ha). The contrast of the exuberant and diversified vegetation with the poor soil quality is explained by the fact that

most of the nutrient capital is held in the biomass rather than in the soils. Nutrients recycle very quickly into the shallow root structures of trees owing to the rapid degradation of falling detritus in the high humidity. When the forest is removed, most of the nutrients are lost. When the cover is not replaced by other protective vegetation, the soils, exposed to the elements, leach and erode. (World Bank 1980, 37)

Although the vast majority of the geographical area of Brazilian Amazonia is covered by tropical rain forests, a considerable part is covered by other kinds of vegetation, as shown in figure 9.2. For Legal Amazonia as a whole, at least 75 percent of the territory is covered by tropical forests, 22 percent by savanna or similar type of vegetation (*cerrados* and *campos*), and the remaining 3 percent by the so-called pioneer ecological formations (*campos inundáveis, mangues,* and *pantanais*). The data also show that nearly 12 percent of the moist forest cover is located in flooded lands (*igapós* and *várzeas*). These areas are exceptionally fertile when compared with the rest of Amazonian soils and therefore tend to show the relatively dense population usually associated with the cultivation of subsistence crops (rice, beans, and manioc/cassava) and vegetables, as well as cattle ranching. Due to this diversity in ecosystems, changes in vegetation cover in different parts of the Amazon do not necessarily imply the same impact upon the environment. This is an important factor to recall in assessing the contribution of deforestation to the greenhouse problem.

Tropical Deforestation and Carbon Dioxide Emissions

Although carbon dioxide is by far the single most important greenhouse gas, other trace gases together may contribute as much as 50 percent of the greenhouse problem. Among the most important are water vapor (H_2O), methane (CH_4), nitrous oxide (N_2O), tropospheric ozone (O_3), and the chlorofluorcarbons (CFC-11 and CFC-12). On a per-molecule basis, these gases absorb far more radiant heat than carbon dioxide. Therefore, despite their relatively low levels of concentration in the atmosphere, they can contribute as much as carbon dioxide to heat trapping (Mintzer 1987; Houghton and Woodwell 1989; Arrhenius and Waltz 1990; Grubb 1989). Table 9.3 summarizes information on greenhouse gases.

There is a great deal of uncertainty concerning the relative contribution of main sources—anthropogenic versus biotic—to carbon dioxide emissions, as well as on the timing and the magnitude of the effects upon global warming.

Compared to biotic sources, anthropogenic emissions of carbon dioxide are one order of magnitude lower. Biotic sources, however, are also responsible for most of the absorption taking place in the carbon cycle; hence, their net contribution is likely to be approximately balanced (Odum 1971; Houghton and Woodwell 1989). Thus, although statistical fluctuation or errors in biotic emissions could outweigh anthropogenic emission, the cumulative nature of the phenomena implies a significant contribution of the latter to the increase of carbon dioxide concentrations in the atmosphere.

Anthropogenic emission of carbon dioxide into the atmosphere is estimated in the range of 4 to 8 Gt per year. Fossil-fuel combustion by industrial plants is, by far, the most important single source. As such, it is the major factor responsible for the 25 percent increase in concentration observed since about 1860 (Houghton and Woodwell 1989; Mintzer 1987). Deforestation accounts for some 15 percent to 30 percent of anthropogenic emissions, that is, 0.4 to 2.5 Gt of carbon dioxide emissions per year (estimates by Houghton and Woodwell 1989).

Table 9.3
Estimates of the net enhancement of the greenhouse effect by major gases

Component	Atmospheric concentration (ppmv)	Atmospheric life span (years)	Annual increase (percent)	Relative efficiency ($CO_2 = 1$)	Past cumulative contribution (percent)	Current marginal contribution (percent)
CO_2	346–351	2–5	0.4–0.5	1	50	46–57
CFCs	0.2–0.6[a]	75–111	5.0–7.0	10,000–15,000	12–17	24–25
CH_4	1.7	0–11	1.0–1.1	11–32	17–25	12–18
O_3	0.02	0.1–0.3	0.5–2.0	2,000	8	7
N_2O	0.3	150	0.2–0.3	150	4–6	5–6

SOURCES: Arrhenius and Waltz (1990); WRI/IIED (1988); Houghton and Woodwell (1989); Mintzer (1987); Flavin (1990); Bouwman (1990); Bowman (1990); Grubb (1989).

a. In parts per billion by volume (ppbv).

On balance, carbon dioxide concentrations in the atmosphere are growing at an average annual rate of approximately 0.5 percent. Consequently, by 2030, concentration levels are expected to be twice the values observed in the preindustrial era, and that is considered "a benchmark level to indicate significant change in global warming" (Mintzer 1987).

The relatively small contribution of deforestation to carbon dioxide emissions, coupled with the fact that this gas represents only half of the greenhouse problem, leads to the conclusion that "the preponderance of greenhouse gases is produced by the highly industrialized sectors of the global economy. Accordingly, the practical potential for deforestation or reforestation to modify the greenhouse effect is ultimately limited, and should be kept in proper perspective" (Arrhenius and Waltz 1990, 37).

It should be noted that the Amazon may be responsible for 10 percent of global emissions of methane, but the effects of deforestation in terms of these emissions are not precisely known (Molion 1988).

Evidence on Deforestation in the Brazilian Amazon

The present extent of world deforestation is not precisely known. The 1987 World Resources Report estimates that Brazil accounted for 19.3 percent of the global deforestation in closed forests that took place in the 1981–1985 period. Indonesia, Zaire, Peru, and India were responsible for 16.3 percent in the same period. These countries have the largest areas of tropical closed forests after Brazil, and when combined their forest areas are approximately equal to that of Brazil.

Today, estimates of deforestation in Brazilian Amazon are usually based on satellite images. The region was first radar photographed in the early 1970s. Later, NOAA-AVHRR infrared images were used, but, since they overestimated the extent of deforestation, in more recent times LANDSAT images are preferably used by the Institute for Space Research (INPE) and by the National State Secretariat of Environment (IBAMA). Table 9.4 summarizes the results on a state level; figure 9.3 maps the results for the 1989 satellite images (the latest available) on deforestation in Brazilian Amazonia.

Data show that, until 1989, deforestation occurred mainly in the peripheral areas of Amazonia. Compared with the earlier estimates that presented rates in the range of 50,000 to 80,000 sq km per year

Table 9.4
Amazonia: Estimates of the deforested area, 1975–1989

State	Total area	Deforested area (million sq km)			Share, 1989 (percent)	Growth (percent per year)	
		1975	1980	1989		1989	1975–1989
Acre	153.7	1.17	4.63	8.83	5.7	22.7	15.6
Amapá	142.4	0.15	0.22[a]	0.87	0.6	50.3	13.2
Amazonas	1,568.0	0.78	2.93[a]	19.46	1.2	18.0	25.8
Pará[b]	1,246.8	40.48	65.74	140.37	11.3	9.5	9.3
Rondônia	238.4	1.22	7.58	31.40	13.2	7.1	26.1
Roraima	225.0	0.06	0.58[a]	3.51	1.6	35.7	34.6
Mato Grosso[c]	802.4	9.23	48.53	79.56	9.9	11.7	16.6
Maranhão[c]	260.2	63.67	71.70	88.47	34.0	7.5	2.4
Tocantins[c]	269.9	3.51	11.46	22.32	8.3	6.5	14.1
Legal Amazonia	4,906.9	120.25	213.36	394.77	8.0	10.0	8.9

Sources: INPE (1989); INPE (personal communication) 1989. For 1975 and 1978, original sources were INPE-1649-RPE/103; for 1980, IBDF (1983a).

a. Interpolated.
b. Includes the "old deforested" areas of the Bragantina Zone: 31,822 sq km in Pará and 60,724 sq km in Maranhão.
c. Area of the state that belongs to legal Amazonia.

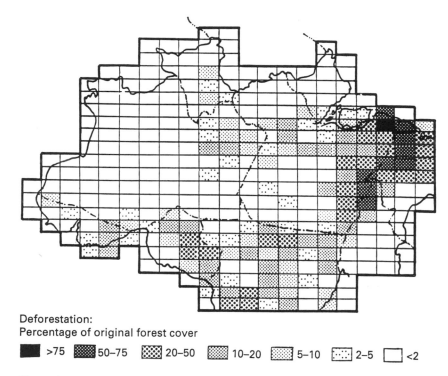

Deforestation:
Percentage of original forest cover

■ >75   ▨ 50–75   ▨ 20–50   ▨ 10–20   ▨ 5–10   ⬚ 2–5   ☐ <2

Figure 9.3
Satellite images of deforestation in Amazonia, 1989
SOURCE: INPE.

and a total area of 600,000 sq km (Myers 1989; WRI 1989; Mahar 1989), as well as with projections based on past trends (Salatti et al. n.d.; Fearnside 1988), the 1989 figures from INPE show that both the rate of deforestation and the size of deforested areas in the Brazilian Amazon were significantly overestimated. Thus the latest INPE estimate for the annual deforestation rate is 21,300 sq km (within a 10 percent band).

The Contribution to Carbon Dioxide Emissions

In the early 1980s the Amazon accounted for approximately 20.2 percent of the total contribution to carbon dioxide emissions from deforestation (Flavin 1990). Since deforestation accounted for nearly 36 percent of the gas generated by fossil fuel, deforestation in Amazonia contributed about 5.4 percent of global carbon dioxide emissions. Carbon dioxide emission in its turn was responsible for roughly 50 percent of the global greenhouse effect. Therefore, the impact of deforestation in the Amazon was almost 2.7 percent of the greenhouse effect in 1980. (WRI 1989 estimates are 4.7 percent of the global carbon dioxide emissions.)

During the 1980s the Amazon contribution seems to have increased. The estimate for carbon dioxide emission caused by fossil-fuel burning today is approximately 5.6 Gt per year (Myers 1989; Houghton and Woodwell 1989; Flavin 1990).

Estimates of the contribution of Amazon deforestation depend on the rate of deforestation (in hectares per year) and the rate of carbon dioxide emission (in tons of CO_2 per hectare). Estimates of the rate of deforestation range from 23,000 to 50,000 sq km per year (INPE 1989; Myers 1989). As for the rates of emission, estimates range from 90.8 to 223 tons of CO_2/ha (Myers 1989; Fearnside 1987; see also Goldemberg and Freitas 1989; Fearnside 1985; Salati et al. n.d.). This wide range is explained by disagreements on the amount of biomass per hectare, the share of biomass assumed to be burned, the rates of regeneration, and the carbon content of biomass in the average or typical hectare of Amazon forest.

These figures lead to estimates for the contribution of Amazonia to global carbon dioxide emissions that range from 0.2 to 1.1 Gt per year, or 4.7 to 16.6 percent of global carbon dioxide emissions. An upper bound is, perhaps, 9.2 percent—obtained by combining the average value of 160 tons of carbon dioxide per hectare with a deforestation rate of 36,000 hectares per year. Compared to the early 1980s, this figure implies that the relative contribution of Amazonian deforestation to global carbon dioxide emissions could have doubled.

If one makes the additional assumption that Amazonian deforestation was entirely concentrated in the last twenty years, total cumulative emissions from deforestation in Amazonia would have amounted to 6.4 Gt of carbon dioxide. During the same period emissions from fossil-fuel burning were roughly 132 Gt (WRI 1989). Conservatively assuming that deforestation in other countries accounted for only twice as much as the emissions from Amazonia, estimates of the cumulative contribution of Amazonia to global concentration of carbon dioxide would be 4.2 percent, or 2.1 percent of the total greenhouse effect.

Fearnside (1985) notes that converting the entire Amazon to pasture would cause carbon dioxide emissions on the order of 49.74 Gt. Emissions from fossil-fuel combustion are, therefore, equivalent to burning and converting to pasture one entire Brazilian Amazonia per decade.

When we look at the problem on a country basis, Brazil appears as the fourth-largest single contributor to carbon dioxide emissions, with a share of nearly 6.0 percent. Ahead of Brazil we find the United States, with 16.9 percent, the U.S.S.R. with 14.1 percent, and China with 7.7 percent. Naturally, on per-capita terms, Brazil would follow all the Western European countries and thus would not even be included among the fifteen largest (data from Goldemberg 1989).

Economic Aspects of Brazilian Amazon Deforestation

The rapid expansion of the agricultural frontier is the most important economic factor behind the recent deforestation of the Brazilian Amazon. Squatters who practice shifting cultivation are the leading agents in the conversion of forest lands to annual cropping. Conversion to pastures usually occurs in a second stage. Logging in Amazonia has generally been a by-product of clearing land for agricultural purposes. Mining and hydroelectric development, by contrast, played minor and indirect roles (Mahar 1989, 7).

The expansion of the agricultural frontier, however, has been decisively conditioned by the government's construction of roads, since the existence of a road network was a prerequisite for economic and demographic settlement of the so-called *terra-firmes* (nonflooded lands). The distribution of government subsidies through fiscal and credit mechanisms was also decisive for the profitability of certain agricultural activities, particularly cattle raising, that are considered economically unfeasible in the soil conditions prevailing in most areas of Amazonia (Yokomizo 1989; Mahar 1989; Hecht 1985; Hecht and Norgaard 1988). In these ways, the government came to play the leading role in settlement of the region.

The Road Network

Occupation and economic settlement of Amazonia have long been major objectives of the Brazilian government. The perceived threats to national security and territorial integrity posed by the region's extremely long international frontiers along with its vastness, emptiness, and rich resource endowments all compelled attention.

Until 1960 the size of the road network in the region was negligible:

280 km of paved roads and 6,000 km of unpaved local roads. A major expansion occurred in the 1960–1975 period when 22,000 km were built. The federal government was directly responsible for 36 percent of all road construction. Abundant external financing coupled with the priorities set by the military regime are major factors behind this expansion. Geographically, road construction was concentrated in the state of Pará, where at least 50 percent of this road construction occurred.

The development of the road network in Amazonia was based on the major axial roads shown in figure 9.1: the Belém-Brasília, with 1,800 km in the north-south direction, completed in 1964; the Transamazon, in the east-west direction, partially (2,300 km) completed in 1974; and the Cuiabá–Pôrto Velho, with 1,500 km in the northwest-southeast direction, completed in 1968. Two other important primary roads, both running parallel to the Belém-Brasília but further to the west, are the Pôrto Velho–Manaus and the Cuiabá-Santarém (1,800 km), completed in 1976.

From 1975 to 1985 the rate of expansion slowed, though more than 14,000 km was built. The process also became less centralized and geographically more dispersed, with states and municipalities taking more active roles.

The pace of road construction recovered during 1985–1988, when nearly 14,000 km was built in only three years. This process was led by states and municipalities. It should be recalled that federal financing of road construction places limits on the decisions of states and municipalities. However, once major primary roads are built by the federal government, political pressures that arise locally cannot be eliminated.

According to IBGE (1990) the expansion of federal and state roads planned after 1988 will bring an increase of nearly 25,000 km, or 100 percent, when completed. Furthermore, this expansion exceeds 300 percent for areas that are still relatively preserved, like the states of Acre and Amapá.

The effects of the enlarged road network on forest conversion are presumed to be significant. Transportation costs may be the major determinant of the expansion of the agricultural frontier. Road density is therefore expected to be highly correlated with population density, land settlement, economic activity, and consequently, deforestation.

Road construction has been estimated to account for 26 percent of tropical deforestation in Brazil (Davis 1977, quoted by Hall 1989, 154). It is not clear, however, whether this figure refers exclusively to direct effects of road building or whether it also includes the indirect effects of the road network. The figure is too large for direct effects alone, and "indirect" effects are extremely difficult to disentangle from other factors.

Colonization Programs

The completion of the Belém-Brasília highway in 1964 is estimated to have attracted approximately 350,000 migrants to the north of Goiás and south of Maranhão and Pará. Though a few official attempts were made at organizing rural occupation of these areas, the process of settlement was essentially "spontaneous" (Mahar 1989, 13; Hebbete and Marin 1979; Carvalho et al. 1978, 214).

Colonization programs became an important part of regional policies under the military regime that took power in 1964. The military ideology of development cum national security not only paid more attention to both the economic value of the region and international threats to it, but also recognized the potential of the Amazon to serve as a safety valve for pressing problems of rural poverty and urbanization in the rest of the country, most especially the Northeast (Cardoso and Muller 1977; Rattner and Udry 1987, 19). These projects also aimed to control the process of settlement in Amazonia, where the military government assumed leftist guerrilla involvement behind pervasive land conflicts.

The government implemented three major colonization projects. The first one in 1971 along the Transamazon highway had been designed with the specific purpose of linking the labor-abundant Northeast to the land-abundant North. Original projections were to settle 100,000 families in agricultural plots along the road from 1971 to 1974.

The Transamazon colonization project was a complete failure. By 1980 at most 13,000 families were settled at a cost of US$39,000 per family (Bunker 1985, quoted by Repetto 1988b, 80). Migratory flows from the Northeast were relatively small and negligible relative to out-migration and rural poverty problems of that region (Tolipan 1990, 15). Environmental effects, however, were not negligible. The figure for forest conversion to agriculture (probably overestimated) is 6,400 sq km, or almost 15 percent of deforested areas in the state of Pará and 4.3 percent in Legal Amazonia in 1983 (Repetto 1988b, 80; Hall 1989, 150).

The second experiment in colonization—the Executive Group for the Araguaia-Tocantins region (GETAT)—was established in 1980 to resolve the emerging land conflicts between early settlers brought by the Belém-Brasília highway and the new waves of migrants. Although figures are impressive—60,000 land titles granted covering 70,000 sq km—the program is considered a failure, especially in terms of its equity objectives (Hall 1989, 111). The major problems on environmental grounds were the bias toward cattle ranching and the small capacity to settle peasants on the land. The turnover rate among farmers reached an estimated 90 percent (Hall 1989, 114).

Finally, the third important colonization project is the Polonoroeste created in 1981. Though important measures aimed at protecting the environment were included in the program, the Polonoroeste's effects upon the forest are nothing short of disastrous. By 1983, 9,900 sq km of tropical forests were converted to farmland, representing 71 percent of total deforestation in Rondônia and 6.1 percent of Legal Amazonia at that time (Repetto 1988b, 81). To a large extent, it was responsible for the catastrophic increase in the deforested area of the state of Rondônia.

Fiscal and Credit Incentives

In addition to government investments, regional policies in Amazonia were based on a plethora of fiscal and credit incentives to the private sector. The size of the fiscal and credit incentives and the criteria used in allocating them were major determinants of the patterns of agricultural and industrial development in Amazonia. Their consequences, particularly for deforestation, were definitely negative (see, for instance, Hecht et al. 1988 and the references cited therein).

Four major kinds of fiscal incentives were administered by SUDAM. First, Brazilian corporations were allowed to deduct up to 50 percent of their income tax liabilities if savings were used for investment in Amazonia. The administration of these funds was assigned to Investment Funds for Amazonia (FINAM) which was also financed by personal income tax deductions (up to 6% of liabilities in this case). Second, at the discretion of SUDAM, business enterprises operating in Amazonia were eligible for tax holidays of up to ten years. Third, these enterprises could also be exempted from import and value-added taxes. Finally, firms could use 40 percent of their income tax liabilities for new equity subscription.

Subsidies granted by SUDAM made cattle ranching and land speculation privately profitable and, thus, had significant impact on deforestation. Thus SUDAM projects were responsible for 14,200 sq km
of deforestation in Mato Grosso and 6,700 sq km in Pará, or 18 and
4.8 percent, respectively, of the total deforested in each of these states
(Yokomizo 1989).

Deforestation and Major Economic Activities

This section discusses the relationship between major economic activities and deforestation and presents evidence based on a sample of
municipalities in the Brazilian Amazon.

Population Density
Table 9.5 shows a strong relationship between population density
and deforestation on a municipal level. The rate of deforestation increases monotonically with population density, leveling off with relatively high levels of population density.

Naturally, causal relationships cannot be inferred from the table.
The low levels of population density prevailing in Brazil immediately
dismiss any kind of neo-Malthusian explanation for the Amazonian
deforestation problem. In 1985 population density was only 16.8 persons per sq km in Brazil and 1.55 persons per sq km in the North
region. Hecht (1985, 679) rightly argues that "it is ludicrous to describe the environmental degradation in this situation as only a function of demographics." Factors like income and landownership
concentration, as well as misguided and compromised government
policies (Southgate 1988, 2), are more likely to be the culprits for the
explosive rates of deforestation observed in the recent past.

However, the correlation between population density and deforestation in table 9.5 is disturbing. Unless population settlement takes
place at much slower rates than those experienced in the recent past,
extrapolations of the pace of deforestation are far from reassuring.
Population settlement in the region will therefore have to be severely
restrained, a difficult task given the continental size of the region.

Squatters
Squatting and shifting cultivation are considered to be, after cattle
ranching, the most predatory processes in Amazonian deforestation.
These two phenomena are closely related, with common bases in the

Table 9.5
Amazonia: Population density and deforestation by municipalities

Inhabitants per sq km	Share of municipalities (percent)	Total area (percent)	Deforested area (percent)	Rate of deforestation (percent)
0–1	30.0	68.8	18.4	1.4
1–2	12.6	12.6	12.1	5.0
2–4	13.7	9.3	25.3	14.1
4–8	15.3	5.2	18.4	18.5
8–16	7.4	2.3	12.5	28.4
16 +	21.1	1.8	13.4	39.3
Total values	190[a]	3,846,876[b]	200,059[b]	5.2

SOURCES: IBGE and IBAMA.
a. Number of municipalities.
b. Total values in sq km.

flow of destitute peasants into Amazonia. Thus Myers (1988a, 35) refers to the "shifted" cultivator as

an agent far more destructive than the shifting cultivator of the traditional sort. The shifted cultivator is the man who finds himself landless in established farming areas of his country and who senses no survival option but to head for the forests with his machete and matchbox.

For the landless peasants, migration is basically motivated by the possibility of accumulating wealth (and, with luck, becoming a landowner) through the clearing of lands in a frontier area where property rights are still undefined.

Land clearing is usually accomplished through slash-and-burn techniques, and the amount of land cleared vastly exceeds land requirements for productive purposes. The explanation is that squatting is the most effective way to acquire claims on land in Amazonia.

From an individual perspective, slash-and-burn and shifting cultivation are undoubtedly rational decisions. Even from social and ecological perspectives, shifting cultivation might not be necessarily irrational. At the low population densities prevailing in Amazonia, it could even be considered "ecologically sound." The flaw of the argument is in the small regenerative capacity of Amazonian soils, especially if one considers the time horizon, the discount rates, and the fallow periods adopted particularly by the newly arrived economic agents in the Amazonian frontier. Thus "the essential mobility and high rotation required by this traditional system has broken down in many areas of Amazonia with the migration of large numbers of poor farmers accustomed to different practices" (Hall 1989, 151; see also Hecht 1985, 679).

Data on squatting by municipalities presented in table 9.6 do not display a strong relationship between deforestation and squatters. Higher percentages of squatters undoubtedly lead to higher deforestation rates, but the relationship is not monotonic, and it is apparently much weaker than the relationship observed for population density.

The lack of a clear relationship between squatting and deforestation could be partially explained by an underreporting bias. In this way, one could perhaps raise the hypothesis that population density is, in fact, a better proxy for squatter activity than the data on squatting itself. In addition, it could be argued that the dynamics of frontier settlement make the current extent of deforestation dependent not on the density of squatting today, but on the density of squatting in the past.

Cattle Ranching

Cattle ranching is considered the villain in Amazonian deforestation (Mahar 1989; Hecht 1985; Hecht et al. 1988; Binswanger 1989; Goodland 1985; Browden 1988). In the first place, pasture areas are the single largest use of agricultural land measured. In 1980 (the most recent official estimates available), pastures represented 7.8 percent of the geographic area of Legal Amazonia, while the share of crops was only 1 percent. In terms of farm areas, the figures were 36 percent and 4.7 percent, respectively.

Second, cattle ranching is considered to be "the worst of all conceivable alternatives" for Amazonia, on the basis of its high potential for soil degradation (Goodland 1980, quoted by Mahar 1989, 18). Evidence presented by Hecht (1985, 675) shows that the phosphoric content of soil—considered the most crucial element for pasture production in Amazonia—increases dramatically when forest is converted to pasture. Starting in the fifth year, however, it tends to decline continuously to one-tenth of what is considered the minimum acceptable level. Weed invasion and compaction are other factors responsible for the loss of soil nutrients. The consequences include drastically declining carrying capacities of ranches (as evinced by Hecht et al. 1988), overgrazing, limited pasture sustainability, and instability of livestock production (Yokomizo 1989, 23 et passim). For the environment it means impaired regenerative capacity.

Table 9.6
Amazonia: Squatter area and deforestation by municipalities

Squatter area (percent)	Share of municipalities (percent)	Total area (percent)	Deforested area (percent)	Rate of deforestation (percent)
0–1	34.6	59.8	31.1	2.7
1–2	15.2	14.4	16.0	5.8
2–4	18.8	10.4	13.9	7.0
4–8	14.7	6.9	20.6	15.6
8–16	9.9	5.7	11.3	10.4
16–32	4.2	1.9	4.7	13.2
32 +	2.6	0.9	2.4	14.0
Total values	191[a]	3,847,961[b]	200,844[b]	5.2

SOURCES: IBGE and IBAMA.
a. Number of municipalities.
b. Total values in sq km.

The dependence of livestock production on government subsidies is the third reason for its universal condemnation. The amount of subsidies and the mechanisms used in their distribution generated many kinds of distortions. Subsidies were largely based on the size of deforested areas; therefore, substantial amounts of land were cleared with the sole purpose of increasing subsidy income. Other consequences included an increase in land speculation and the exacerbation of land conflicts in frontier regions. In this context, extensive cattle raising had the dual function of allowing institutional rent extraction in the form of subsidies and avoiding squatter settlements.

Evidence of the relation between cattle ranching and deforestation is presented in table 9.7. Figures clearly suggest the importance of cattle ranching as a factor explaining the rate of deforestation.

Cropping

Forest conversion to crop areas could be called the silent partner in Amazonian deforestation. The main reason for this systematic omission is the small share of crop areas. In 1985, for instance, crop areas represented less than 5 percent of farm areas, and only 1.2 percent of the geographic area in Legal Amazonia. In most states crop areas were far below 1 percent of the geographic area. Although rarely mentioned, crop areas seem to be clearly associated with deforestation. Table 9.8 displays convincing evidence. Rates of deforestation increase pari passu with crop shares in the geographic area of munici-

Table 9.7
Amazonia: Herd density and deforestation by municipalities

Cattle density (animal units per sq km)	Share of municipalities (percent)	Total area (percent)	Deforested area (percent)	Rate of deforestation (percent)
0–1	40.3	71.6	19.3	1.4
1–2	8.9	7.3	9.2	6.5
2–4	9.9	7.0	12.5	9.3
4–8	14.7	6.6	23.9	18.8
8–16	14.4	5.7	23.8	21.7
16+	12.0	1.7	11.3	34.2
Total values	191[a]	3,847,961[b]	200,844[b]	5.2

SOURCES: IBGE and IBAMA.
a. Number of municipalities.
b. Total values in sq km.

palities. Saturation of the deforestation rate occurs only at very high levels.

Logging
The relationship between logging and deforestation in Amazonia is very difficult to specify. First, commercial logging in Amazonia is a subsidiary activity, occurring when land is cleared for agricultural purposes. Second, underreporting is very likely, since logging is usually a footloose activity, sometimes illegal and not directly undertaken by farmers. Finally, logging is expected to be more intense exactly in those areas which are less intensely cleared.

The scant evidence available, however, suggests that logging is not a major factor of tropical deforestation in the Brazilian case. The small scale of logging in the Brazilian Amazon is explained by the lower density of commercially valuable stands, compared with Southeast Asia. Thus, according to estimates of the IBDF (quoted by Hall 1989, 155), logging accounts for only 4 percent of the deforestation.

However, the stock of Brazilian Amazon broad-leaved timber is estimated to be nearly one-third of the world's total stock (Repetto 1988b, 74). As Asian reserves dwindle, logging for export will certainly increase its share as a factor in deforestation. Another major reason to anticipate increased logging is the supply of charcoal to the numerous pig-iron plants connected with the Carajas mining project (see Uhl and Vieira 1988 for evidence and catastrophic projections).

Data on logging by municipalities are presented in table 9.9. Unlike

Table 9.8
Amazonia: Crop area and deforestation by municipalities

Area of crops (percent)	Share of municipalities (percent)	Total area (percent)	Deforested area (percent)	Rate of deforestation (percent)
0–0.25	28.3	62.2	10.5	0.9
0.25–0.50	8.4	8.5	5.5	3.4
0.50–1.00	11.5	10.5	11.3	5.6
1–2	13.6	7.9	21.9	14.4
2–4	13.6	6.9	27.3	20.7
4–8	15.7	3.1	17.3	29.0
8–16	7.9	0.8	6.2	40.6
16+	1.0	0	0.2	98.1
Total values	191[a]	3,847,961[b]	200,844[b]	5.2

SOURCES: IBGE and IBAMA.
a. Number of municipalities.
b. Total values in sq km.

all the other variables, logging is a flow concept. For consistency, therefore, figures refer to cumulative logging in the 1982–1985 period.

Prospects for Deforestation in Amazonia

This section presents projections of future deforestation in the Brazilian Amazon based on a simple model of the deforestation process. Despite its simplicity, the model grasps the essential features of the dynamic of deforestation in Amazonia by relating it to the patterns of population growth and frontier expansion.

The Model

The model's basic equation describes the relation between the spatial density of major economic activities and the share of deforested areas. The previous discussion showed that densities of population, cattle units, crop areas, logging, and roads could all be considered major factors in the deforestation process. Consequently, they were selected as the independent variables of the equation.

Since deforestation is a process that tends to saturation, given the fixed geographic area, a logistic functional form was utilized. Thus it is assumed that major economic activities convert forest at increasing rates during early stages of the deforestation process, and at decreasing rates when forest becomes scarce.

The equation was estimated for a cross section of 165 municipalities

Table 9.9
Amazonia: Cumulative logging density and deforestation by
municipalities, 1982–1985

Logging density (m^3/km^2)	Share of municipalities (percent)	Total area (percent)	Deforested area (percent)	Rate of deforestation (percent)
0–0.1	14.3	16.8	4.9	1.5
0.1–1.0	25.9	42.1	15.2	1.9
1.0–10	27.5	25.5	40.2	8.2
10–100	19.6	11.2	20.9	9.7
100+	12.7	4.3	18.9	23.0
Total values	189[a]	3,833,841[b]	200,824[b]	5.2

SOURCES: See IBGE and IBAMA.
a. Number of municipalities.
b. Total values in sq km.

of the Brazilian Amazon for which data on deforestation and the
other variables were available. We also introduced two additional
variables: the distance to the state capital (to take account of pull
factors) and dummy variables for the state to which the municipality
belongs (to control for the differences in the time deforestation was
measured). The results of the estimation are as follows:

$$\begin{aligned}
\text{DEFOR} = {} & 0.30\,\text{POP} + 0.40\,\text{CROP} + 0.11\,\text{HERD} + 0.04\,\text{WOOD} \\
& (0.11^*) \qquad (0.11^*) \qquad\quad (0.06) \qquad\qquad (0.04) \\
& + 0.28\,\text{ROAD} - 0.02\,\text{DIST} - 2.42 + 0.17\,\text{D1} + 0.37\,\text{D2} \\
& \ \ (0.06^*) \qquad\quad (0.07) \qquad\quad (0.47^*)\ (0.37) \qquad (0.40) \\
& + 0.24\,\text{D3} - 0.69\,\text{D4} + 1.19\,\text{D5} - 2.89\,\text{D6} \\
& \ \ (0.36) \qquad (0.51) \qquad (0.31^*) \qquad (0.60^*) \\
& \text{Crsq} = 0.84 \quad \text{Rmse} = 1.02 \quad N = 165
\end{aligned}$$
(1)

where

DEFOR = $\log[S/(1-S)]$ and S is the percent share of deforested areas, circa 1985/1987,

POP = population per sq km in 1985,

CROP = percent share of crop areas in 1985,

HERD = cattle units per sq km in 1985,

WOOD = cubic meters per sq km of logging from 1982 to
1985,

ROAD = roads per sq km in 1985,

DIST = distance from the state capital,

D1, D2, etc. = dummies for states.

Furthermore, Crsq is the correlation coefficient corrected for degrees of freedom; Rmse is the root mean square error; N is the sample size; and the figures in parentheses are standard errors of estimates— which are statistically significant at the 1 percent level when followed by asterisks. Except for the dummies, all the other variables are in logarithms.

The equation fits the data sample extremely well. Coefficients for the major variables are also reasonably precise, despite the presence of multicollinearity problems. This is the case for population, crop areas, and roads and, to a lesser extent, for cattle (significant only at the 7% level); in contrast, the coefficient on logging is not significantly different from zero.

The highest value for the elasticity of deforestation is 0.40 in relation to crop areas. The elasticities of deforestation in relation to population and road density are also relatively high. But the estimate for the elasticity of deforestation in relation to cattle is approximately one-third the value found for crop area. This result is, perhaps, surprising when confronted with the statement often found in the literature on Brazilian Amazonia that "cattle ranching has been the foremost cause of forest conversion" (Repetto 1988b, 74).

Of course, the relative contribution of each economic activity to deforestation depends not only on the value of its elasticity, but also on its average rates of growth. It especially depends upon the spatial distribution of expansion of each activity—that is, to what extent higher growth rates are taking place on more highly deforested areas.

Data for the 1975–1985 period, however, show that in comparison to cattle, crop areas grew faster on average, and especially on less deforested areas. Moreover, simulating equation 1 for the historical values of the 1980–1985 period leads to estimated percent contributions to the growth of deforested areas of 49 percent for population, 20 percent for crop areas, 10 percent for cattle, 13 percent for logging, and finally 8 percent for roads. The role of cattle ranching, therefore, seems to be grossly overestimated.

By an alternative reading, however, one could argue that it is exactly the higher growth of cattle raising that caused some areas to be highly deforested today. Or alternatively, that it was cattle raising coming after cropping that made forest conversion irreversible. Unfortunately, the available data base is inadequate to deal with these dynamic issues.

To make predictions about the spatial patterns of growth for each major activity in the future, we estimated cross-section equations relating the growth between 1980 and 1985 to the density in 1980. This was done for population, cattle, crop areas, and logging (the period is 1982–1985 in the last case). The results are as follows:

$$G_{POP} = 0.19 - 0.02\,POP_{80} \qquad\qquad\qquad\qquad \text{period 1980–1985}$$
$$(0.01)\ (0.006) \qquad Crsq = 0.04 \quad Rmse = 0.20 \quad N = 335 \quad (2)$$
$$G_{HERD} = 0.37 - 0.09\,HERD_{80} \qquad\qquad\qquad \text{period 1980–1985}$$
$$(0.03)\ (0.01) \qquad Crsq = 0.12 \quad Rmse = 0.54 \quad N = 335 \quad (3)$$
$$G_{CROP} = 0.12 - 0.10\,CROP_{80} \qquad\qquad\qquad \text{period 1980–1985}$$
$$(0.03)\ (0.01) \qquad Crsq = 0.11 \quad Rmse = 0.45 \quad N = 335 \quad (4)$$
$$G_{WOOD} = 0.04 - 0.08\,WOOD_{80} \qquad\qquad\qquad \text{period 1982–1985}$$
$$(0.05)\ (0.02) \qquad Crsq = 0.03 \quad Rmse = 0.92 \quad N = 284 \quad (5)$$

where

$G_X = X_{85} - X_{80}$;

X_t = log of the density of X in year t;

X = POP, CROP, HERD, WOOD.

Naturally, equations 2–5 are too simple to be able to explain a large part of the variance of growth; thus Crsq values are extremely low. However, the slope coefficients for the density variables are precisely estimated in all cases.

A clear pattern of spatial growth in the 1980–1985 period emerges from the estimates. All the variables showed a tendency toward spatial dispersion: growth is smaller in areas with high densities. Dispersion is a natural result for agricultural activities in a frontier region. Cattle, crop areas, and logging display a similar pattern of spatial dispersion as shown by values of estimated coefficients that are approximately equal. Rates of dispersion for population are much smaller, perhaps suggesting that centripetal force due to frontier expansion are countervailed by urbanization and other agglomeration phenomena.

Projecting Deforestation and Carbon Dioxide Emissions
To project the future trend of deforestation in the Brazilian Amazon, the basic assumption was made that spatial growth patterns of 1980–1985 will be maintained through the 1985–2000 period. Equations 2–5, then, are used to predict the spatial distribution of the density of population, cattle, crop areas, and logging.

Growth rates for major activities and population growth are based on the figures presented in tables 9.1 and 9.2. Accordingly, average annual rates of growth expected for 1985–2000 are 3.1 percent for population, 8 percent for cattle, 6 percent for crop areas, and 7.5 percent for logging. Projections for roads were based on the planned expansion disaggregated by state (IBGE 1990). Thus it is assumed that planned roads will be effectively built in the 1985–2000 period. The results for the projections aggregated by state are presented in table 9.10.

Projected growth rates are impressive, especially for states and areas that are still relatively preserved like Amapá, Roraima, Acre, and Amazonas. For the Brazilian Amazon as a whole, it is projected that deforestation will grow by 5.2 percent per year and that 13.6 percent of Amazon forest areas will have been cleared by the year 2000.

According to our estimates, the area deforested in Brazilian Amazonia during 1989 was approximately $0.052 \times 394,772 = 20,528$ sq km. These numbers come quite close to the 21,318 sq km estimated to be (within a 10% range) the average deforestation rate during the eighties by INPE.

To make projections for 1990–2030 we assumed slower growth trajectories for major economic activities as follows: annual growth rates are 2 percent for population, 7 percent for cattle, 5 percent for crop areas, 6.5 percent for logging activity, and 2.1 percent for roads. As secular trends, these rates are still on the high side. The geometric growth rate projected for deforestation is 3.7 percent per year. Deforested areas in 2030 are projected to be 1,785,000 sq km, or 35.7 percent of the geographic area of Brazilian Amazonia.

For projecting CO_2 emissions we assumed, in accordance with Salati et al. (n.d.), that (1) the biomass available for burning in Brazilian Amazonia is in the range of 280–400 tons per hectare; (2) the biomass will always be completely burned; and (3) the biomass contains 50 percent of carbon dioxide. Thus the effects of deforestation upon carbon dioxide emissions would be 140–200 t/ha.

Based on these parameters, projections of the impact of deforestation in Brazilian Amazonia on carbon dioxide emissions into the atmosphere are presented in table 9.11.

According to WRI (1989; Flavin 1990), global CO_2 emissions to the atmosphere in 1989 are estimated at 6.19 billion tons (estimates for 1988 are 7.32 billion tons). Thus, for 1989, the potential marginal contribution of Amazonian deforestation to carbon dioxide emissions

Table 9.10
Brazilian Amazonia: Deforested area projected for 2000 by state

	Deforested area (sq km)		Growth		Deforested area (percent)	
	1989	2000	Total (sq km)	Annual (percent)	1989	2000
Rondônia	31,375	54,766	23,391	5.2	13.1	22.9
Acre	8,831	18,971	10,140	7.2	5.7	12.3
Amazonas	19,460	48,379	28,919	8.6	1.2	3.1
Roraima	3,560	9,451	5,891	9.4	1.6	4.2
Pará	140,366	239,423	99,057	4.9	11.3	19.3
Amapá	866	2,405	1,539	9.7	0.6	1.7
Tocantins and Goias	22,321	32,613	10,292	3.5	7.3	10.8
Mato Grosso	88,466	136,268	47,802	4.4	9.0	14.5
Brazilian Amazon	394,772	686,986	292,214	5.2	7.8	13.6

SOURCE: Authors' estimate.

Deforestation in Maranhão is presumed to grow at the average rate of the Brazilian Amazon.

Table 9.11
Projections for the range of potential carbon dioxide emissions to the
atmosphere due to Brazilian Amazon deforestation

Year	Deforested area (sq km)	Emissions per year (10^{15}g carbon)	Cumulative contribution (10^{15}g carbon)
1989	394,772	0.29–0.41	5.5– 7.9
2000	686,986	0.48–0.69	9.6–14.0
2030	1,774,785	0.92–1.31	24.8–35.5

SOURCE: Salati et al. (n.d.) and authors' estimate.
See text for assumptions.

into the atmosphere would be in the range of 4.7 to 6.6 percent, or
2.4 to 3.3 percent to the greenhouse effect.

For the future, WRI (1989) estimates that the concentration of CO_2
in the atmosphere will increase 1.01 percent per year between 1989
and 2030. If deforested areas increase at 3.7 percent annually, the
marginal contribution of Amazonian deforestation to carbon dioxide
emission to the atmosphere will be in the range of 14 to 18 percent
in 2030.

Policy Alternatives

This section discusses policy alternatives to retard the pace of forest
conversion in the Brazilian Amazon. In a skeptical mood, the discussion begins by identifying structural obstacles to the adoption of sustainable solutions. Next, it indicates the problems posed by the open
access to Amazonian forestry resources coupled with the legal and
institutional weakness. In a more positive stance, we appraise some
recent Brazilian policy initiatives in each instance. The section concludes with a discussion of the role for international agencies.

Major Policy Changes Required

The fundamental challenge in relation to Brazilian Amazonia is how
to reconcile the living-resource frontier with the survival of the
tropical-forest ecological system. With this in mind, the design and
evaluation of policy alternatives ought to start by recognizing some
essential dimensions of Brazilian Amazonia.

The continental size of the region and its overwhelming importance to Brazil as an underdeveloped resource frontier in agriculture, energy, mining, and forestry constitute one such dimension. Though quite obvious, this feature is sometimes overlooked in policy recommendations made from either a broad international perspective or else from strictly sectoral, regional, or ecological perspectives (see Repetto 1988b, 32–34; Fearnside 1988, 296).

History is another essential dimension. Despite all the misguided Brazilian regional policies of the last decades, the rapid pace of forest conversion in Amazonia is deeply rooted in the socio-historical patterns of Brazilian development. Agricultural frontiers have always played the role of safety valves for the explosive combination of high population growth and acute inequality in both income and landownership. In this way, the recent policy mistakes simply exacerbated secular compromise solutions.

This history is unfortunate, since it implies that the fundamentals for a sustainable solution to the deforestation problem depend upon government initiatives that would be much broader (and slower) than those specifically related to forestry resources or the Amazon taken by itself. In at least three major policy areas, the government will have to undertake structural reforms if the rates of inward migration and frontier expansion in Amazonia are to be reduced.

The first area involves regional policies, where the patronage system will have to be phased out. Large steps were recently taken in this direction, with the abolition of regional fiscal incentives. Some of these incentives, however, are granted by the Federal Constitution and still remain in effect, especially those related to the Free Export Processing Zone of Manaus (SUFRAMA).

Another important step is to rechannel incentives to the *cerrado* (savanna) areas in the Center-West, where there is plenty of land and, moreover, plenty of cumulative research and technical knowledge on production technologies.

Most important, however, the planned expansion of the road network in the region will have to be curtailed and made more selective so as to minimize overland access to uncleared areas with low agricultural potential (Mahar 1989, 47). A complementary measure to exhaust rents in frontier areas is to phase out the subsidies implicit in countrywide price standardization for diesel and other energy inputs to transportation activities (Fearnside 1988, 296).

The second policy area deserving drastic changes includes credit and fiscal taxation, especially in those aspects related to land and agricultural activities, which ought to become more progressive. Subsidized credit and tax exemptions for agriculture are capitalized in land prices, making access to landownership prohibitive for the vast majority of the rural population. As a consequence, better-off landless rural workers have no other option for upward mobility except to migrate to frontier areas (Binswanger 1989; Repetto 1988b, 27).

Finally, the third policy area requires reforms in the agrarian structure in the previously settled regions to increase access to landownership for rural workers, to create more rural employment, and to provide for social improvements in the countryside.

In conclusion, one cannot neglect the political constraints on these proposed reforms. To the extent that economic agents in the frontier areas are virtually free riders, political coalitions inside the region are strongly arrayed against any policy initiatives that seek to constrain frontier expansion. Agrarian and tax reforms also tend to mobilize strong political opposition from powerful and vocal interests all over the country. Therefore, they are more likely to be successful in a gradualistic fashion.

Resource Depletion, Open Access, and Market and Institutional Failures

In addition to slowing down inward migration, a sustainable pattern of development for Brazilian Amazonia will require that economic decisions inside the region lead to an efficient long run use of forestry resources.

The inefficient use of forestry resources in the Brazilian Amazon derives from two major sources. The first is the market failure caused by undefined property rights. The abundance of land, forests, and mineral grounds in the region make them open-access resources (i.e., resources that anyone can use). Consequently, from a social perspective, they tend to be overutilized (Gordon 1954; Southgate 1988, 7). The second source of inefficiency derives from institutional failures. The government's attempt to regulate property rights on open access resources is usually ineffective and sometimes even perverse—leading to further deforestation (Repetto 1988b, 37).

Institutional failures make the enforcement of decrees prohibiting deforestation—such as Law 7511 of July 7, 1986—virtually impossible to implement. Other examples of institutional failures are given by two major government regulations related to property rights. The first, for assigning property rights on land, accepts forest conversion as evidence of land improvement and therefore induces deforestation, since as much as three times the area of converted forests can be claimed by squatters in this way (Binswanger 1989, 9).

The other regulation, dating back to 1965, requires that at least 50 percent of farmland be kept as forest. High enforcement costs in Amazonia make this regulation ineffective (Mahar 1989, 37).

The fundamental problem lies in the lack of government institutions inside the region—which is exhibited in the weakness of administrative and juridical structures for dealing with the problems of forest conversion and the misuse of forestry resources. The relative emptiness and dispersion of economic activities inside the region create prohibitive political and economic costs for regulation, enforcement, and surveillance at the local level. The problem repeats itself in agriculture, cattle raising, logging, and mining.

The absence of political motivation at both the state and municipal levels is also partly responsible for the problem. Lack of capacity or motivation make these organs incapable of working in an integrated fashion with federal agencies. Thus, even when legislation is good, as it frequently is, it is simply not applied. The basic solution to these problems is to strengthen the institutional framework in the region, that is, to increase the technical and administrative capabilities of research, regulation, monitoring, and law enforcement at the local and national levels.

Some institutional strengthening has occurred at the national level in recent years (Seroa da Motta 1990). Thus, since 1981, when the National Environmental System (SINASMA) and the National Environmental Policy were first established by law, there has been substantial expansion in the demarcation of areas for all kinds of preservation purposes, as shown by table 9.12.

Other important steps were the government program Nossa Natureza and the legislation coming out of the 1988 Brazilian Constitution that defined Amazonia, as well as four other Brazilian ecosystems, as national patrimony deserving special regulations for the exploitation and preservation of natural resources. Finally, in March 1990, the new administration gave independent status to the Secretary of the Environment (SEMAM) allowing the executive agency for the environment (IBAMA) to become more effective in the surveillance of environmental problems in Amazonia.

For the immediate future, the task is to strengthen coordination of activities, to define ecological zones, and to set standards for regula-

Table 9.12
Amazonia: Preservation according to purpose and year of
establishment, 1990

Type	Total (sq km)	Established after 1980 (percent)
National parks	97,062	37
Biological reserves	29,830	66
Ecological stations	26,926	100
Ecological reserves	11,302	100
Protection areas	14,566	100
National forests	122,497	93
Extractive reserves	21,630	100
Indian areas	837,684	—

SOURCE: IBAMA.

tion and monitoring. It is also crucially necessary to devise more
cost-effective approaches to enforcement. These include not only the
use of more updated technologies, but also improving the system
of incentives for all kinds of monitoring—whether involving federal
treasury agents or local forest guards (Binswanger 1989, 19).

The Role of International Agencies

Tropical deforestation is naturally a matter of deep concern to the
international community. Estimated figures suggest that the costs of
Amazonian deforestation to the world at large could be dispropor-
tionately large when compared to the benefits it could bring to Brazil.
Clearly, some kind of international arrangement is necessary to reduce the pace of deforestation.

However, major economic issues are yet to be settled. Managing
the natural resources of Amazonia according to global objectives and
constraints will certainly impose costs on the region's development as
well as on the development of the country. Despite all the past ecological mistakes (see, for example, *The Economist* 1989), it is undeni-
able that "egoistic" Brazilian or regional development objectives
could be achieved faster or at lower cost if natural resources in the
Amazonian frontier were freely used—clearly presupposing greater
rationality than in the past.

On equity grounds, the country ought to be compensated for the
costs imposed by a restrained growth strategy. Compensation is

required, at a minimum, because developing countries like Brazil would be sacrificing growth to solve problems that are, to a large extent, the consequences of "unbridled" patterns of growth of rich industrialized nations. Nevertheless, Brazil would certainly not be exempted from its international responsibilities, and deforestation would still impose additional specific costs on Brazil. Of course, "the fact that national restraint would also be in the long-term interest of the developing country itself should not detract from compensation as a matter of right" (Handl 1990).

Even if compensation of opportunity costs is accepted, implementation is not an easy task. Three major questions would have to be addressed. First, what is the value placed on Amazonian deforestation from the Brazilian perspective? Second, who will pay for the costs of restraining deforestation? Finally, how can mechanisms be designed to make compensation effective?

There is no simple answer to these questions. In theory, market mechanisms could offer a nice joint solution to all of them through the renting or even the outright sale of autonomy of decisions in relation to the development use of tropical forests to international organizations and foreign countries. In terms of sovereignty, however, the market solution is unacceptable, as illustrated by the nationalistic reactions to the recent Bolivian debt-for-nature swaps (Bramble et al., n.d.). In short, we may conclude that, although targets are clear, there is plenty of space for disagreement and, consequently, for intermediation. In such a context, international institutions have a major role to play.

The debt-nature connection seems to be fertile ground for action. Since Brazil, like many other countries with large tropical forests, is a major third world debtor, the idea of a debt-for-nature policy package easily suggests itself as a solution to the questions posed by the need for compensation. Second thoughts, however, show that the contribution that can be expected from debt-for-nature swaps is negligible when confronted with both the size of the Brazilian debt and of the Amazon deforestation problem. To be of any significance the amount of such swaps would certainly harm domestic financial stability. Thus the greatest benefits that could be expected would be to provide financial backing for Brazilian nongovernmental organizations— which by itself is a worthy objective.

Most importantly, however, the debt-nature mix can be a most unfortunate direction for policies. "Green conditionality" can easily exacerbate confrontational attitudes based on sovereignty and nationalism. To that extent, international agreements would become unstable and environmental objectives undermined (Piddington 1989). In conclusion, external debt and environmental problems should be set apart. If tropical deforestation and carbon dioxide are considered a real threat to the world economy, additional resources should be raised to this purpose.

As conflict mediators, international agencies will have to convince all parties involved that restrained growth should and will be fairly compensated. Such compensation requires a comprehensive assessment of the major efficiency and equity issues related to global warming and the greenhouse effect. For the Brazilian case, it means a comprehensive evaluation of the costs and benefits of constrained growth strategies in Amazonia.

For the time being, the urgent priority is preemptive action to slow the current pace of forest conversion in Amazonia. International efforts should be directed toward strengthening Brazilian public and private institutions concerned with tropical deforestation, especially IBAMA. Technical and financial support to these institutions is required to enhance their capabilities for research, regulation, monitoring, and surveillance, and most importantly, for marketing ecological objectives.

Note

This chapter was presented at the conference Economic Policy Responses to Global Warming, Rome, October 5–7, 1990. Financial support from the Istituto Bancario San Paolo di Torino is gratefully acknowledged. We are especially grateful for the computational support provided by Marcia Pimentel and data handling by Claudia C. O. Souza. We also thank Elias Reis, Ricardo Paes de Barros, Ronaldo Seroa da Mota, Armando Castellar, Rudiger Dornbusch, and William Cline for their comments.

References

Arrhenius, Erik, and Waltz, Thomas W. 1990. The greenhouse effect: Implications for economic development. World Bank Discussion Paper 78. Washington, DC: World Bank, April.

Benchimol, S. 1989. *Amazonia: Planetarização e Moratória Ecológica.* Manaus: ISEA.

Binswanger, H. P. 1989. Government policies that encourage deforestation in the Amazon. Environment Department Working Paper 16. Washington, DC: World Bank, April.

Bouwman, A. F. 1990. Land use related sources of greenhouse gases; Present emissions and possible future trends. *Land Use Policy*, April, pp. 154–164.

Bowman, John. 1990. The greenhouse effect. *Land Use Policy*, Aprii, pp. 101–108.

Bramble, Barbara, et al. No date. A brief summary of debt-for-nature swaps. Unpublished report prepared for the Debt-for-Nature Ad Hoc Working Group.

Browden, John O. 1988. The social costs of rain forest destruction: A critique and economic analysis of the Hamburguer Date. *Interciencia* 13, no. 3 (May–June): 115–120.

Bunker, S. 1985. *Underdeveloping the Amazon: Extraction, Unequal Exchange and the Failure of the Modern State.* Urbana and Chicago: University of Illinois Press.

Cardoso, F. H., and Muller, G. 1977. *Amazônia: Expansão do Capitalismo.* São Paulo: Brasiliense.

Carvalho, José Alberto M., et al. 1978. Migrações internas na Amazônia. In Costa, José M. M. *Amazônia: Desenvolvimento e Ocupação.* IPEA, Série Monográfica, n. 29, pp. 193–243.

Castro, Newton R. 1989, Perspectivas do desenvolvimento regional. In *Perspectivas da Economia Brasileira—1989.* INPES/IPEA, Rio de Janeiro, cap. 8, pp. 287–318.

Davis, S. 1977, *Victims of the Miracle.* Cambridge: Cambridge University Press.

The Economist. 1989. Costing the earth; A survey of the environment. *The Economist* (London) 312, no. 7618 (September 2).

Fearnside, P. M. 1985. Brazil's Amazon forest and the global carbon problem. *Interciencia* (Caracas) 10, no. 4 (July/August): 179–183.

Fearnside, P. M. 1987. Summary of progress in quantifying the potential contribution of Amazonian deforestation to the global carbon problem. In D. Athie, T. E. Lovejoy, and M. Oyens, (eds.), *Proceedings of the Workshop on Biogeochemistry of Tropical Rain Forests: Problems for Research,* 75–82. Piracicaba: Univ. de São Paulo, Centro de Energia Nuclear Para a Agricultura (CENA).

Fearnside, P. M. 1988. Desmatamento e desenvolvimento agricola na Amazonia Brasileira. In *Amazonia: A Fronteira Agricola 20 Anos Depois,* Belém, December 5–7.

Flavin, Christopher. 1990. Slowing global warming: A worldwide strategy. Worldwatch Paper 91. Washington, DC: Worldwatch Institute.

Goldemberg, José. 1989. Amazonia and the greenhouse effect. In *Amazonia: Facts, Problems, and Solutions Meeting,* São Paulo, August, vol. 1, pp. 48–52. São José dos Campos: USP/INPE.

Goldemberg, José, and Freitas, M.L.D. 1989. Energy strategies for Latin America. Mimeo. Rotterdam.

Goodland, R. 1980. Environmental ranking of Amazonian development projects in Brazil. *Environmental Conservation* 18, no. 1 (Spring): 9–26.

Goodland, R. 1985. Brazil's environmental progress in Amazonian development. In Hemming, J. (ed.), *Man's Impact on Forests and Rivers.* Manchester University Press.

Gordon, H. 1954. The economic theory of a common property resource: The fishery. *Journal of Political Economy* 62, no. 2: 124–142.

Grubb, Michael. 1989. *The Greenhouse Effect: Negotiating Targets.* London: Royal Institute of International Affairs.

Hall, Anthony L. 1989. *Developing Amazônia: Deforestation and Social Conflict in Brazil's Carajás Programme.* Manchester University Press.

Handl, Gunther. 1990. Law and protection of the atmosphere. *Economic Impact* 71: 39.

Hebbete, Jean, and Marin, Rosa E. A. 1979. Colonização: Articulações no nivel economico e no nivel politico. In *Anais do VI Encontro Anual da ANPEC.* EMMA, Porto Alegre, vol. I, pp. 131–188.

Hecht, S. B. 1985. Environment, development and politics: Capital accumulation and the livestock sector in eastern amazonia. *World Development* 13, no. 6: 663–684.

Hecht, S. B., Norgaard, R. B., and Possio, G. 1988. The economics of cattle ranching in eastern Amazonia. *Interciencia* (Caracas) 13, no. 5 (September/October): 233–240.

Houghton, Richard A., and Woodwell, George M. 1989. Global climatic change. *Scientific American* 260, no. 4 (April): 36–44.

IBDF. 1983a. *Alteração da Cobertura Vegetal Natural do Território de Roraima: Programa de Monitoramento da Cobertura Florestal Brasileira: Relatório Técnico.* Brasília.

IBGE. 1987. *Estatísticas Históricas do Brasil.* Rio de Janeiro.

IBGE. 1990. *Anuário Estatístico do Brasil—1989.* Rio de Janeiro.

Instituto de Pesquisas Espaciais (INPE). 1989. *Avaliação da Alteração da Cobertura Florestal na Amazônia Legal Utilizando Sensoriamento Remoto,* 2nd ed. São José dos Campos.

Mahar, D. 1989. Government policies and deforestation in Brazil's Amazon region. In *Agriculture, Forestry and Global Climate Change: A Reader.* Washington, DC: Library of Congress.

Martine, George. 1989. Internal migration in Brazil. IPEA/IPLAN, Texto para Discussão n. 13 (June).

Martine, G., et al. 1989. A urbanização no Brasil: Retrospectiva, componentes e perspectiva. In IPEA/IPLAN, *Para a Década de 90—Prioridades e Perspectivas de Política Pública*, vol. 3: *População, Emprego, Desenvolvimento Urbano e Regional*, 99–159. Brasília.

Martinelli, Luiz Antonio, et al. 1988. Implantação de parcelas para monitoramento da dinamica florestal na Area de Proteção Ambiental, UHE Samuel, Rondonia. Relatorio preliminar, Centro de Energia Nuclear na Agricultura, Piracicaba.

Mintzer, I. M. 1987. *A Matter of Degrees: The Potential for Controlling the Greenhouse Effect*. Research Report 5. Washington, DC: World Resources Institute.

Molion, Luiz Carlos B. 1988. A Amazônia e o Clima do Globo Terrestre. *Pará Desenvolvimento*, no. 23 (January/June): 53–59.

Myers, Norman. 1988a. *Natural Resources Systems and Human Exploitation Systems: Physiobiotic and Ecological Linkages*. Environment Department Working Paper 12. Washington, DC: World Bank. November.

Myers, Norman. 1988b. Threatened biotas: "Hot spots" in tropical forests. *The Environmentalist* 8, no. 3: 187–208.

Myers, Norman. 1989. *Deforestation Rates in Tropical Forests and Their Climatic Implications*. London: Friends of the Earth.

Odum, E. P. 1971. *Fundamentos de Ecologia*, 3rd ed., Lisbon: Fundação Calouste Goulbenkian.

Piddington, Kenneth W. 1989. Sovereignty and the environment, *Environment* 31, no. 7 (September): 18–39.

Porto, C. N., et al. 1987. *Movimentos Migratórios no Brasil e seus Condicionantes Economicos (1872–1900)*. São Paulo: Convênio FINEP/FIPE.

Rattner, Henrique, and Udry, Olivier. 1987. *Colonizaçao na Fronteira Amazônica: Expansão e Conflito*. Instituto de Pesquisas Econômicas, FEA/USP, São Paulo.

Repetto, Robert. 1988a. *Economic Policy Reform for Natural Resource Conservation*. Environmental Department Working Paper 4. Washington, DC: World Bank, May.

Repetto, Robert. 1988b. *The Forest for the Trees? Government Policies and the Misuse of Forest Resources*. Washington, DC: World Resources Institute.

Salati, Eneas, et al. No date. Deforestation and its role in possible changes in the Brazilian Amazon. Mimeo. Department of Physics and Meteorology, ESALQ, Piracicaba. /s.n.t./24 p.

Schubart, Herbert O. R. 1989a. Ecologia da Amazônia. Apostilas do curso "Impactos ambientais de investimentos na Amazônia: problemática e elementos metodológicos de avaliaçao." Acordo SUDAM/PNUD, doc. n. 18-A. Manaus, 1989.

Schubart, Herbert O. R. 1989b. Diagnosis of the Natural Resources of Amazonia. In: *Amazônia: Facts, Problems and Solutions Meeting*. São Paulo, August 1989. Anais. São José dos Campos: USP/INPE, vol. 1. pp. 55–67.

Seroa da Motta, R. Recent evolution of environmental management in the Brazilian public sector: Issues and recommendations. Paper presented at the OECD Development Center Conference on Environmental Management in Developing Countries, Paris, October 3–5, 1990.

Southgate, Douglas. 1988. *The Economics of Land Degradation in the Third World.* Environmental Department Working Paper 2. Washington, DC: World Bank, May.

Tolipan, Sergio. 1990. A ocupação demografica da Amazônia e a Construção da rodovia Transamazônica. In Costa, Manoel (coord.), *Populacão, Meio Ambiente e Qualidade de Vida.* Rio de Janeiro: CEPPD—O Segundo Brasil, pp. 15–26.

Uhl, C., and Vieira, I.C.G. 1988. Extraçao seletiva de madeiras: Impactos ecológicos em Paragominas. *Pará Desenvolvimento*, no. 23 (January/June): 46–51.

World Bank. 1980. The integrated development of Brazil's northwest frontier, Report no. 3042a–BR, Washington, DC.

WRI/IIED. 1989. *World Resources 1988–89.* New York: Basic Books.

Yokomizo, Clando. 1989. *Incentivos Financeiros e Fiscais na Pecuarização da Amazônia.* Texto para Discussão 22. Brasília: IPEA/IPLAN, October.

Comments

William R. Cline

Reis and Margulis have provided an impressive examination of the issue of deforestation of the Amazon and its contribution to the global warming problem. Their review shows that deforestation has arisen primarily from migration on the agricultural frontier, spurred by highways built for reasons of national security. They report that the pace of this process was accelerated by an array of tax incentives and subsidies. They place the size of Amazon deforestation into perspective by providing a new estimate of its annual contribution to global carbon dioxide emissions, one that is lower than some international estimates. At the same time their projections of future deforestation indicate that the problem is likely to escalate to a larger share unless action is taken.

A first key issue is the amount of annual deforestation. The authors reject a World Resource Institute estimate of 80,000 sq km as too high.

They argue that the satellite observations in the NOAH-AVHRR data are excessively sensitive to heat and portray areas with small fires as being under general burning and clearing. They add that the 1988 base year was atypical because of the rush to clear land for fear of expropriation of unused land under the new constitution. They consider the LANDSAT images of the Brazilian Space Research Institute more reliable. Appropriately annualized, these images show a rate of 24,000 sq km for clearing in the 1988–1989 period. Under their central estimate of 162 tons of carbon emission per hectare cleared, their estimates indicate annual emissions of 389 million tons of carbon from deforestation.

The IPCC estimates global carbon emissions from deforestation at 1.6 billion tons of carbon (GtC) annually, plus or minus a wide range of 1 billion; it sets fossil-fuel emissions at 5.4 GtC. The Reis-Margulis estimate thus indicates that the Amazon accounts for 24 percent of world emissions from deforestation (with a wide possible range), and 5.6 percent of all man-made emissions. As the authors note, this 6 percent range ranks the Amazon somewhat below China and far below the United States and the U.S.S.R. as a source of carbon dioxide emissions.

There is ambiguity in the paper with respect to the role of cattle ranching in deforestation. The past literature has stressed the role of the sector, and this emphasis is logical. Grazing is far more extensive in its use of land than is crop production (that is, much lower value added per hectare). Slash-and-burn for purposes of cattle raising would thus seem particularly inefficient. However, in the author's statistical model, the coefficient on cattle is relatively low. Moreover, simulations of the model for 1980 to 1985 indicate that expansion of the cattle sector contributed only 10 percent of deforestation.

This result raises the question of whether the coefficients of the individual variables in the model are appropriately estimated. One suspects that the cattle coefficient is underestimated. Collinearity among the various variables would seem likely to be a problem. A possible alternative would be to calibrate the model by ex ante considerations (for example, expected area required per head of cattle) and then carry out the simulations, including sensitivity analysis.

Despite possible difficulties, the model probably provides a better basis for projection of deforestation than simple geometric extrapolation. The authors' simulations indicate annual growth of Amazon deforestation at 5.2 percent through 2000 and 4.4 percent through

2030. By 2000, the Amazon would contribute a central estimate of 580 million tons of carbon to annual emissions, and by 2030, 1.1 gigatons—three times the present rate.

This bleak prospect underscores the need for policy action. At the international level, it is informative to compare the economic costs that might be involved from limiting carbon emissions from Amazon deforestation against those associated with other international action. The stylized parameter from the Manne-Richels model is that the carbon tax based on backstop technology would have to reach $250 per ton of carbon to achieve a 20 percent cutback of carbon emissions by the year 2000 and stabilization thereafter (for the United States). Consider the corresponding costs in the case of the Amazon. The chapter reports that agriculture accounts for 17 percent of GDP in the Amazon, and the Amazon accounts for 3 percent of Brazilian GDP. The latter amounts to about $300 billion, so the entire agricultural output of the Amazon is only $1.5 billion annually. If agricultural production in the region were completely suspended, the result would be to eliminate 389 million tons of carbon annually at a cost of $1.5 billion in lost production—for a cost of only $4 per ton of carbon, a tiny fraction of the international carbon tax cost. If the Scandinavian countries find it more cost-effective to subsidize environmental cleanup in Poland than in their own countries because of cross-border spillover and severe environmental problems in Poland, it is likely that the OECD countries would find it even more profitable to compensate Brazil for reduced Amazon agricultural production than to achieve carbon reduction in their domestic energy sectors.

These considerations suggest that it would be well worth perhaps at least $500 million annually in an international program of grant aid in support of measures to halt Brazilian deforestation. A good example of concrete measures to fund would be assistance with the public administration required to issue land titles and monitor use of land—problem areas highlighted by the chapter.

For Brazil, an obvious implication of the paper is that subsidies and tax incentives to Amazon development should be terminated. Perhaps the mosty egregious aspect of past subsidies is that they were calculated in accordance with the number of areas slashed and burned—the tangible evidence that a farmer worked the land. A far better criterion would have been persistent farming of a given area over a sustained period such as three years. Fortunately, the government has stopped granting new subsidies and suspended most tax incentives, as part of the economic stabilization program of the administration of President Fernando Collor de Mello.

There are also implications for tax policy. Brasília could impose a special deforestation tax for the Amazon region. If the disproportionate role of cattle is confirmed, a special tax on cattle raised in the region might even be considered. It would be desirable if the authors could formulate their simulation model to calculate the prospective impact on deforestation of the termination of subsidies and tax incentives.

An important feature of taxation is that the Brazilian economy has suffered acutely in recent years from its weak fiscal capacity. Large fiscal deficits have been responsible for hyperinflation and severe recession. A deforestation tax would have the major side benefit of raising revenue for a resource-starved government.

Some activities ought not to be taxed. Logging, ironically, is one such. Despite its negative environmental image, logging does not contribute to the greenhouse effect. Lumber products wind up sequestering the carbon from the trees involved in furniture, buildings, and so forth. Similarly, some of the other dominant myths about Amazon forestry warrant dismissal. Inundation of forest area for hydroelectric dams does not cause a greenhouse problem, because the wood in question is sequestered under the water. Similarly, a common notion is that because trees scrub the atmosphere of carbon dioxide, a larger forest is better than a smaller one. Instead, contributions to the increase or decrease of atmospheric carbon come only from *reductions* or *increases* in forest size. The reason is that in a steady-state forest, the contribution of carbon to the atmosphere from decay of dead trees offsets extraction of carbon from the atmosphere by new, growing trees.

The worst myth of all is that Amazon deforestation destroys the "lungs of the world" and could leave the earth's population without enough oxygen to breathe. Oxygen supplied by forests as a by-product of photosynthesis is a tiny fraction of that available in the earth's atmosphere. There is enough concern about tropical forest destruction on legitimate grounds of carbon emission and species destruction without adding to outrage on the basis of such myths.

The authors rightly stress that Brazilian policy on agrarian structure ought to be changed to provide for meaningful land reform. Much of the impetus to migration into the Amazon has come from the lack of employment opportunities in the impoverished Northeast region.

Land redistribution would considerably increase labor intensity and land use (Cline 1970). Instead, government policy consciously pursued frontier colonization as a politically more expedient alternative than land reform.

From Brazil's standpoint, the question remains whether tax and other measures to slow Amazon deforestation will curb economic growth. Reis and Margulis cite remarkably high figures for GDP growth in the Amazon. Brazilian growth is a weighted average of growth in the region and that in other regions—which has been considerably lower. In part, high growth rates in the Amazon are a classic example of overstatement of welfare because of the failure to deduct environmental depradation from national accounts measures. In part, high Amazon growth has been artificial because of fiscal incentives. But some component remains of sacrifice in "real" growth if a high-growth area is curbed. International compensation is the logical implication.

Reis and Margulis doubt that debt-for-nature swaps are the answer to the need for some such international bargain. They recommend that the debt problem and the deforestation problem each be solved separately. I largely agree with their diagnosis. Advocates of debt-for-nature often fail to recognize that banks hold claims that are still worth 20 or 30 cents on the dollar, if not the original 100 cents. They are not in business for charity and cannot be expected to donate these claims to establish national parks. The authors rightly note that it is the nongovernmental organizations (NGOs) such as conservation groups that must purchase the debt from the banks at a discount and then donate it to the government in exchange for forest preservation. As NGOs are inherently limited in size, the scope for such operations is likely to be modest.

Nonetheless, there may be more potential for debt-nature swaps than the authors suggest. Export credit and other official agencies of industrial countries could forgive a portion of their bilateral claims in exchange for demarcation of preserved forest. The Bush administration's Enterprise for the Americas initiative moves modestly in this direction, although its potential is circumscribed by its limitations (25% of Export-Import Bank direct loans, excluding guarantees) and its formulation (private NGOs must buy the EXIM claims at a discount, rather than direct EXIM conversion with the Brazilian government). Truly serious concern by OECD governments about Brazilian deforestation could involve much larger programs. Even then, it would be necessary to deal with two other issues: first, the break with tradition that would be involved in forgiving bilateral debt for a middle-income country; and second, the potential inflationary effects of debt conversion into cruzeiros for land purchases.

Finally, it is possible that Brazilian domestic politics may be moving in a helpful direction. Although to a considerable extent the growing environmental movement in Brazil may remain limited to the cocktail liberals, and the key political forces are those of business groups in the Amazon, change is nonetheless occurring. Collor has shut down further development of the Indian reservation areas. As noted, his program eliminates fiscal incentives to development of the region, a 90° swing from policy for the last two decades. Perhaps the changing Brazilian political climate, sweetened with foreign cooperation, will eventually permit the swing to reach 180° through fiscal penalties for deforestation.

Reference

Cline, William R. 1970. *Economic Consequences of a Land Reform in Brazil*. Amsterdam: North Holland.

Name Index

Subject Index